PROMISED LAND

PROMISED LAND

Thirteen Books That Changed America

Jay Parini

DOUBLEDAY

New York London Toronto Sydney Auckland

DD

DOUBLEDAY

Published in the United States by Doubleday, an imprint of The Doubleday Publishing Group,
a division of Random House, Inc., New York. www.doubleday.com

DOUBLEDAY is a registered trademark and the DD colophon is a
trademark of Random House, Inc.

Page 386 constitutes an extension of this copyright page.

Book design by Casey Hampton

LIBRARY OF CONGRESS CATALOGING-IN-PUBLICATION DATA

Parini, Jay.
Promised land / by Jay Parini. — 1st ed.
p. cm.
Thirteen books that changed America.
1. American literature—History and criticism. 2. National characteristics, American, in
literature. 3. Literature and moral—United States—History 4. Literature and society—United
States—History. 5. United States—In literature. 6. United States—Historiography.
7. Books—United States—Reviews. 8. Books and reading—United States. I. Title.
PS169.N35P37 2008
810.9'35873—dc22
2008009990

ISBN 978-0-385-52276-2

PRINTED IN THE UNITED STATES OF AMERICA

1 3 5 7 9 10 8 6 4 2

FIRST EDITION

FOR DEVON
a promise kept

And Moses went up from the plains of Moab to Mount Nebo, to the top of Pisgah, which is opposite Jericho. And the Lord showed him all the land, Gilead as far as Dan, all Naphtali, the land of Ephraim and Manasseh, all the land of Judah as far as the Western Sea, the Negeb, and the Plain, that is, the valley of Jericho the city of palm trees, as far as Zoar. And the Lord said to him, "This is the land of which I swore to Abraham, to Isaac, and to Jacob, 'I will give it to your descendants.' I have let you see it with your eyes, but you shall not go over there."

— DEUTERONOMY 34:1–4

CONTENTS

ACKNOWLEDGMENTS

I am grateful to so many people who have helped me write and edit this book and who have shaped my thinking on these various books. Let me mention only the most obvious ones. Thanks to my editor, Gerald Howard, first of all. His encouragement and advice, as well as his firm editorial guidance, have been invaluable. I'm grateful to Geri Thoma, my agent, for her endless patience, cheerleading, and editorial advice. A few friends were especially helpful in reading over parts or, in some cases, the whole of this book, making countless suggestions for revisions. Among these were Charles Baker, David Bain, John Elder, Murray Dry, and James Ralph. I can't thank them enough. Finally, I must thank my wife, Devon Jersild, whose intellectual and moral standards keep me on my toes as reader and writer.

PROMISED LAND

INTRODUCTION

O N   A   B A L M Y   N I G H T in north London a few summers ago, I attended a lecture by Lord Melvyn Bragg, the well-known British
journalist. It was called "Twelve Books That Changed the World,"
based on a recent book of his. He chose twelve *English* books, of course,
including Newton's *Principia Mathematica* (1687), Adam Smith's *Wealth
of Nations* (1776), and Darwin's *On the Origin of Species* (1859). Provoked
by the lecture, I began to think about what twelve books had changed
America in important ways, jotting down titles in the margins of my
program. The list expanded wildly as I decided to write a study along
similar lines, based on major American texts. I found myself obsessing
over my choices and lay awake for weeks, adding and subtracting
works.

This was never meant to be a list of the "greatest" American books:
not *The Scarlet Letter, The Great Gatsby,* or *The Education of Henry
Adams.* Although I love poetry, I knew that not even Walt Whitman and
Robert Frost, let alone Wallace Stevens or Elizabeth Bishop, had noticeably "changed" America in any significant way (except among that
tiny group who actually *read* poetry). I was looking for books that
played a role in shaping the nation's idea of itself or that consolidated
and defined a major trend. Ideally, I wanted books that shifted con-

sciousness in some public fashion, however subtly, or opened fresh possibilities for the ways Americans lived their lives. Well over a hundred books came to mind. (See my appendix, where I list and comment briefly on one hundred more books that changed America.) The list could easily have expanded, if one allowed for important works of history and biography, or works that affected a particular academic field in important ways. (In the sciences, one more often hears of papers that changed the field, rather than books per se.)

In the end, I settled on *Of Plymouth Plantation, The Federalist Papers, The Autobiography of Benjamin Franklin, The Journals of Lewis and Clark, Walden, Uncle Tom's Cabin, Adventures of Huckleberry Finn, The Souls of Black Folk, The Promised Land, How to Win Friends and Influence People, The Common Sense Book of Baby and Child Care, On the Road,* and *The Feminine Mystique.* Of these, only *Walden, Huckleberry Finn,* and *On the Road* could be considered "great" books as such. But each of them changed America in some visible and profound way.

By books that "changed America," I mean works that helped to create the intellectual and emotional contours of this country. Each played a pivotal role in developing a complex value system that flourishes to this day. I expanded my list of works under discussion in *Promised Land* from twelve to thirteen, preferring the odd number, a baker's dozen, as it reflects the irregular nature of my project and distantly echoes the number of original colonies. I might easily have discussed fifteen or twenty books, but one has to stop somewhere, and I wanted to reflect certain major strains in American thought or culture without seeming encyclopedic.

Soon I realized that each of the books under view was not a single work but a whole climate of opinion (to adapt a phrase from W. H. Auden), a watershed of sorts. Dozens of ancillary books circled the one under observation, some anticipating it, others commenting on, refuting, or reacting to the work. The book itself often represented a strong reaction to trends already in place, or offered ways of circumventing or countermanding a tradition. Originality is always rare, and usually mistaken for something else, such as eccentricity or confusion. Often it simply marks a fresh approach to ideas or themes previously in motion. In choosing a single work to discuss, I understood I was taking on a field of inquiry, a tradition, a vein of significant thought. This was intimidating—but exhilarating, too. I would have to dig around the work under examination, sift the soil it grew in, pull out its roots and examine them carefully. I would have to scan the field to see where the seeds had blown, taken hold, and blossomed.

In discussing these thirteen books, I frequently refer to the works and ideas that swirl around them. *Walden,* for example, is a book that both creates and participates in the broad traditions of nature writing and memoir. It was dependent on Emerson's *Nature* (1836), for example, as a prior work in a more abstract mode, one that underlies *Walden* in fascinating ways, forming a kind of intellectual template. In discussing *Walden,* I also talk about the roots of transcendentalism in European (especially German) Romanticism. I look at American nature writing in general, too, identifying Thoreau's part in this tradition, looking forward as well as backward. And so Annie Dillard's wonderful *Pilgrim at Tinker Creek* (1974) represents a distant, further ripple of the stone tossed into Walden Pond.

A key aspect of *Promised Land*—as the title itself suggests—lies in its exploration of national myths. *Of Plymouth Plantation,* for instance, was a mythmaking book. Part history and part memoir, it was written by William Bradford, of the Plymouth Colony. He and his fellow Pilgrims arrived on the *Mayflower* in 1620, surviving a difficult first year with help from the local Indians. The Pokanoket tribe, led by a sympathetic chief called Massasoit, provided crucial survival skills as well as much-needed supplies to the white settlers. Massasoit and Bradford (who became governor of the colony) forged a truce that lasted for half a century—until chaos broke out with King Philip's War. If it were not for this major work by Bradford, the full story of the *Mayflower* crossing, the establishment of a colonial beachhead, and the beneficent role played by the Indians would have been lost. The manuscript disappeared for over two centuries and was rediscovered by an American tourist in London. Published in 1856, it became a national sensation. Americans found themselves staring, through the prism of this text, into their own complex and beautiful origins. Abraham Lincoln seized on the story, deciding—in 1863, in the depths of the Civil War—that Thanksgiving should become a national holiday, with its myth of survival through cooperation and mutual respect for those with different cultural and racial origins.

To one degree or another, each of the thirteen books discussed in these pages participates in the act of national mythmaking, creating stories to live by, reflecting our profoundest wishes for ourselves, helping us to see our lives against the backdrop of time and against the American landscape itself. Often there is a revealing backstory to the book as well, as with Bradford's memoir.

I separate my discussion of each book into four parts. First I talk about the book briefly, giving some sense of its importance to American culture, suggesting ways it "changed" the country or helped to forge its identity. In these preambles, I gesture in directions pursued more fully in the following sections. In the second part, I refer to the writer of the book, providing a biographical and historical context for the work under discussion and giving some account of its publication history or backstory. In one or two cases, I talk about my own relationship to the book (as with Dale Carnegie's *How to Win Friends and Influence People,* which had a marked effect on my own development—as it did on that of millions of other readers). I proceed to the main body of the text in the third part, where I describe the book in considerable detail. "Description is revelation," Wallace Stevens once wrote. Not surprisingly, it's difficult to describe a book in ways that reveal its inner contours, its ambience, its tonal complexity. The core of *Promised Land* lies in these parts. In the fourth and final part of each chapter, I deal with the legacy of the work, often mentioning books that followed in its wake and attempting to suggest the qualitative impact of the book on Americans.

Overall, *Promised Land* offers a reading of the American psyche through some of its most influential books, allowing us to reflect on what our past means for who we are now. Many of the dominant themes of American life emerge in these landmark texts: immigration and assimilation, religious concerns, our dream of independence from Old World constraints and values, our capacities for self-invention, the Enlightenment heritage that shaped our laws and concept of secular government, the wish to "light out for the Territory," as Huck Finn put it so well, and westward expansion itself (the movement that Robert Frost once described as "the land vaguely realizing westward"), the vision of nature, the problems of racial integration, and the conflicts that occurred when ideals (and cultures) collided, often violently. It's a book about continuous revolution and the American search for fulfillment through self-transformation. It's also a book about our deeply ingrained drive to occupy that promised land, only glimpsed in the distance—akin to what Moses and his wandering people sought in the Land of Canaan.

These thirteen books must be seen as representative, not definitive, works. They are nodal points, places where vast areas of thought and feeling gathered and dispersed, creating a nation as various and vibrant as the United States, which must be considered one of the most successful nation-states in modern history, and a republic built firmly on ideas, which are contained in its major texts. Where we have been must, of course, determine where we are going. My hope is that this book helps to show us where we have been and engenders a lively conversation about our destination, which seems perpetually in dispute.

HISTORY

OF

PLYMOUTH PLANTATION.

BY

WILLIAM BRADFORD,

THE SECOND GOVERNOR OF THE COLONY.

REPRINTED FROM THE MASSACHUSETTS HISTORICAL COLLECTIONS.

EDITED, WITH NOTES,

BY

CHARLES DEANE,

MEMBER OF THE MASSACHUSETTS HISTORICAL SOCIETY.

BOSTON:
PRIVATELY PRINTED.
M.DCCC.LVI.

ONE

Of Plymouth Plantation

I.

EVERY NATION HAS A FOUNDING MYTH, or myths: stories that talk of bright but challenging beginnings, portraying the drama of self-definition and establishment. The United States, with its complex origins and mixed identities, has many such myths, but among them is a primary text in the story of American colonial life: William Bradford's *Of Plymouth Plantation,* a journal written between 1620 and 1647. It tells the story of the original Pilgrims, who came to Plymouth in Massachusetts from northern England, via the Netherlands, on the *Mayflower* in 1620. The historical importance of this journal cannot be exaggerated. Apart from being a vivid account of what happened, it has immense credibility, having been written by a man who was an active agent (as governor) in the story itself.

The adventures and misadventures of the Pilgrims form the core of Bradford's journal, which recounts a thoroughly absorbing story about a people who managed against the odds to pull together for the sake of their community, to get control over their own rebels and malcontents, and to make peace among themselves and with the native population, the Wampanoag, with whom (after a difficult year of illness and privation, which reduced their numbers almost by half) they shared what has

become known as the first Thanksgiving: a celebration of mutual interests. Although the exact nature of this event, a harvest festival that occurred in the fall of 1621, has relatively little in common with the mythic
tale most Americans hear about in elementary school, it has become a
legend, one of those primal stories that have shaped our sense of who
we are.

II.

AMERICA WAS SORELY IN NEED of some mythic tale about itself
when, in 1855, the manuscript of Bradford's journal was discovered in the library of Fulham Palace, on the Thames, a summer retreat
for London bishops. A traveler called John Wingate Thornton from
Boston found it by chance. He was a man described by one acquaintance
as "an accomplished antiquary and a delightful gentleman."[1] He recognized passages by Bradford quoted in another book, which contained a
note about the full manuscript and its whereabouts. His discovery must
be considered one of the great literary finds.

Although missing for such a long time, the journal was not unknown. Passages from Bradford had been widely circulated for two
centuries, with extracts in the records at Plymouth. Early historians,
such as Thomas Prince and William Hubbard, apparently had the manuscript in hand when they wrote their classic accounts of the Plymouth
Colony. But the complete work—a handwritten journal—had disappeared, having been carried to England at some point, where it lay in
dusty obscurity until Thornton unearthed it. He laboriously copied the
work in full, then published it in the United States in 1856, attracting
huge attention in the disunited states of that era, when the Civil War
loomed offstage, but only just. Anyone could see that serious conflict lay
ahead, though a savage and relentless war could hardly be imagined. It
would take the outright slaughter of Antietam and Gettysburg for that
reality to dawn in full.

In the 1850s, there was also a good deal of anxiety in the air about
westward expansion. Lewis and Clark made their journey to the Pacific
coast and back to St. Louis at the beginning of the century, and excitement over the West grew as Americans learned more about the abun-

dant regions that lay on the other side of the Mississippi. The region beckoned to young men and women, who dreamed of wealth and adventure. Parents, as ever, worried about losing touch with their children—this was well before electronic communications shrank the distances that now commonly separate families. The snugness of colonial New England or Virginia was gone forever, and it seemed difficult to imagine a nation that could embrace large tracts of land as well as a restive population of Native American tribes, including the Apache, Blackfoot, Cherokee, and Cheyenne nations. Certainly it was hard to believe that numerous Mexicans could be absorbed in Texas and California, which had only just acquired statehood.

Bradford's account of the early Pilgrim adventures offered an alternative reality, a world in which fiercely united and determined men and women put their faith firmly in the will of God. They reveled in their independence from the Church of England and its hierarchies, which had forced them into exile in Holland. Unlike other Puritans who settled in New England (mostly in Massachusetts), these were the hard core, known as Separatists. They did not believe in trying to reform the Anglican church from within, as did most Puritans. They might well have remained in Leyden, where most of them were concentrated, had poverty as well as the prospect of Holland being overrun by Spanish Catholics not prompted them to set off for the New World.

We would have known relatively little about the Pilgrims of Plymouth had William Bradford (1590–1657) never kept a journal. He was present at every phase of the project, from the initial separation from England and removal to Leyden through the great journey on the *Mayflower* across the Atlantic, the establishment of the Plymouth settlement, its trials and triumphs, and its eventual decline as children of the original settlers lost faith in the overall project—much to Bradford's dismay.

As he was only human, Bradford skewed his account in favor of his own interests and friends. Of course he had the incomparable advantage, as historian, of being a player in the events described, with enviable access to everything that happened. He ran the inner council at Plymouth, so he knew what people said, even why they said it. As chronicler, he tended to dwell on things that interested him or showed him in a particularly good light—it's his journal, after all; he could (as he chose) suppress whatever displeased him. Historians have noted that he passes over many things in silence or, on rare occasions, alters the sequence of events. Bradford did not like opposition and dealt fiercely with those who displeased or countered him. Nevertheless, his account is noticeably balanced and scrupulous. In general, his account of the Plymouth Colony is without rival as a precious early document on this important subject.

III.

FROM THE OUTSET, Bradford assumes a reserved, ironic tone, quite in contrast to one notable outburst scribbled in the margins of the document after it was finished, where he registers a wail of disapproval for the younger generation:

O sacred bond, whilst inviolably preserved! How sweet and precious were the fruits that flowed from the same! But when this fidelity decayed, then their ruin approached. O that these ancient members had not died or been dissipated (if it had been the will of God) or else that this holy care and constant faithfulness had still lived, and remained with those that survived, and were in times afterwards added unto them. But (alas) that subtle serpent hath slyly wound in himself under fair pretences of necessity and the like, to untwist these sacred bonds and ties, and as it were insensibly by degrees to dissolve, or in a great measure to weaken the same. I have been happy, in my first times, to see, and with much comfort to enjoy, the blessed fruits of this sweet communion, but it is now a part of my misery in old age, to find and feel the decay and want thereof (in a great measure) and with grief and sorrow of heart to lament and bewail the same. And for others' warning and admonition, and my own humiliation, do I here note the same.[2] (xvi)

As this note amply suggests, Bradford felt a visceral disappointment with the younger colonists, who seemed willfully ignorant of their history and failed to realize the sacrifice of their parents and grandparents, who risked their lives for a cause of conscience, a dream of community.

But this marginal outburst stands in contrast to the journal itself, where the author writes with coolheaded grace, relying on what happened to inform his prose, a tale that required no embellishment.

Indeed, in the first paragraph he says he plans to write "in a plain style, with singular regard unto the simple truth in all things" or "at least as near as my slender judgment can attain the same" (1). He succeeds well at this, beginning in the reflective mode, with a chapter on Separatism. The basic idea, as he frames it, was to convince English churches to "revert to their ancient purity and recover their primitive order, liberty and beauty" (2). The Separatists formed a minority sect among the Puritans, itself a fringe of the Protestant Reformation, which had convulsed Europe in the sixteenth century. The church at Scrooby, in the English county of Nottinghamshire, was among the most radical of Puritan churches.

It was there that William Brewster, a friend and mentor to William Bradford, spread his Separatist views as minister to a younger generation. Brewster had gone to Cambridge University, where he came under the influence of Robert Browne, a founding theologian of the Puritan movement. Browne published two seminal books in 1582: *A Treatise of Reformation Without Tarying for Anie* and *A Booke Which Sheweth the Life and Manners of All True Christians.* In these stringent, influential works, Browne argued that one could not afford to wait for the state to take action—as John Calvin, a leading Puritan figure on the Continent, had suggested. Browne believed it was the duty of the individual to act according to what he or she felt was right, whatever the state thought. He was fond of quoting Saint Paul on this point: "Come out from among them, and be ye separate, said the Lord, and touch not the unclean thing" (2 Corinthians 6:17). This single verse provided the biblical foundation for Separatism.

There was, as one might guess, fierce resistance to the Puritan movement in England, and many of its leading lights were imprisoned or executed, driving the hard core of believers abroad for safety. By 1607, the political waters for religious rebels had reached a boiling point, and many from the Scrooby congregation found themselves under warrant for arrest. Not surprisingly, Bradford begins *Of Plymouth Plantation* here, with a tale of dispossession. His narrative is very much written like an Old Testament story, where God's people are driven off their land, suffer exile among heathens, and go off in search of their own promised land in the New World. The whole mode of the unfolding story, its flavor and texture, will be familiar to anyone who has skimmed the five books of Moses.

Led by Richard Clyfton, the Scrooby pilgrims set off on foot in the autumn of 1607 for the town of Boston, a journey of sixty or so miles. In secrecy, they boarded a ship for the Continent, only to find themselves turned away by the captain, who hoped for greater compensation. They returned to Scrooby, where several of them were arrested. But no trial was forthcoming, and these quiet Christians were soon freed, as their jailers could hardly believe they posed much of a threat to the community. A few months later, they tried to get away again and succeeded, taking a ship from a port near Hull. This was not an easy journey, with all sorts of dangers looming, including the threat of discovery: it was illegal to travel abroad without formal documents. The ship made its way into the North Sea, where dark waters nearly overturned the vessel. Yet they arrived in Holland in one piece, and others from Scrooby followed, finding illegal passage on other ships. Now they had to contend with a land where English was not spoken and where living conditions were harsh.

Bradford puts the journey of the Scrooby congregation in context, recalling earlier migrations to the Continent in search of religious freedom, quoting from the famous *Book of Martyrs* of John Foxe (1517–87). Under Queen Mary, a Roman Catholic who burned many Protestants at the stake, Foxe and others like him took up residence in a range of European cities, including Frankfurt, Geneva, and Basel, where Foxe originally published his book in Latin. Bradford glosses over nothing, recalling the bickering that took place among his fellow exiles over matters of dogma. He also puts this bickering in context. "And this contention died not with Queen Mary," he says, "nor was left beyond the seas" (5).

One goal of Bradford's generation of exiles was to ensure "the right worship of God and discipline of Christ established in the church, according to the simplicity of the gospel, without the mixture of men's inventions" (4). Bradford hoped to get back to basics, as preached by his mentor Richard Clyfton, "a grave and reverend preacher," as well as by John Robinson and William Brewster. What the latest band of pilgrims found in Holland, however, was hardly the promised land of Canaan, although Bradford skips rapidly over what happened on arrival in Amsterdam, where the English Separatists joined Puritan exiles from different places.

As often happens among isolated groups of exiles, conflicts arose. The various sects were in disarray, with any number of accusations flying about. There was, for example, a group called the Ancient Brethren, who battled each other with shocking displays of bad temper. One figure of note was Thomas White, a minister from the west of England who had arrived with a dozen followers. White's flock briefly worshipped with the Brethren, but were soon repulsed by their acrimony. They pulled away from the Brethren, whom White himself viewed as "rash, heady, and contentious."[3] He actually called the Brethren "a brokerage of whores," alluding to accusations of incest and adultery in a diatribe that was widely circulated. Bradford skips rather briskly over these conflicts. After a year, he and his group migrated to Leyden, "a fair and beautiful city." There he picks up the story with renewed energy.

Leyden was the home of a major university, a place where religious debates flourished, and the English Separatists spent a dozen years there. Yet they felt isolated from the local population and could not make a decent living despite their talents for handicrafts and trades. Poverty and poor living conditions were perhaps the main reasons for putting everything at stake by traveling to the New World, although Bradford prefers a political explanation—the Netherlands had forged a truce with Roman Catholic Spain that was about to end, in 1621. "The Spaniard might prove as cruel as the savages of America," Bradford writes, "and the famine and pestilence as sore here as there, and their liberty less to look out for remedy" (28).

North America was not the ideal destination for every Separatist, as Bradford recalls. The Amazon and other tropical regions attracted some, who imagined them as places "rich, fruitful, and blessed with a perpetual spring and a flourishing greenness" (29). But the Spaniards had been on the march in those areas as well. Furthermore, who could say what local dangers lay in store in hot regions, including the threat of disease? Virginia, on the other hand, was a familiar climate, and the Pilgrims hoped they would not be persecuted as Separatists there as they had been in England. To reassure themselves, they petitioned the Virginia Company in advance of their departure and were kindly answered, though they eventually settled on the "more northerly parts of that country, derived out of the Virginia patent and wholly secluded from their Government, and to be called by another name, viz., New England." This latter name, which stuck, was first used by Captain John Smith in his *Description of New England* (1616), an account of his travels to that part of the New World in 1614.

Elaborate negotiations occurred with certain London businessmen—mainly Thomas Weston, a wily fellow who headed a group of financial "adventurers" or venture capitalists. Bradford gives a thorough (if somewhat boring) account of these financial arrangements, which certainly plagued the Pilgrims for years to come, as the journey to New England was never a sound business proposition. In July 1620, the group of about 120 men, women, and children left Leyden, "that goodly and pleasant city which had been their resting place near twelve years," as Bradford says in his most biblical tones, "but they knew they were pilgrims."

They set off in two ships, the larger being the famous *Mayflower.* The smaller ship was the *Speedwell,* which proved hopelessly leaky and was quickly forced to return to England. It was necessary to winnow the group, and twenty or so were left behind, the rest crowding onto the *Mayflower,* which eventually departed on September 6. It was indeed a marvelous ship: broad beamed, with two decks, and "castles" fore and aft. Weighing 180 tons, it had been hauling wine in the Mediterranean for the past four years, making it what was called a "sweet ship." It could manage, with some discomfort, the 102 passengers who crammed aboard.

What is interesting is that so many of the original Pilgrims were not what we usually think of as Separatists in the vein of Bradford and his group. Only a few of them actually fit the description. No more than a third of the passengers were from Leyden and might genuinely be called Separatists, while only Bradford and William and Mary Brewster had anything to do with the original contingent from Scrooby. Many on the ship were "strangers," as Bradford calls them. Their reason for risking their lives in the New World was largely financial; like so many immigrants over the centuries to follow, they set off for the Americas to make their fortune. Among those on the *Mayflower,* a fair number belonged to the Puritan wing of the Church of England; but they did not believe in separation from the Anglican Communion. We know several of these "strangers" by name: Myles Standish and John Alden, for example, remain among the best known—even though Standish, a military man, seems never to have joined the congregation at Plymouth, as his name does not appear in their records. (Standish, in particular, would rise to fame in "The Courtship of Miles Standish," the popular narrative poem by Henry Wadsworth Longfellow, published in 1858.)

Being a gifted storyteller, Bradford fixes on exactly the right details as he describes the *Mayflower* and its Atlantic crossing, which took sixty-five days. In the early seventeenth century such journeys were never without incident. For a start, the ship was nearly overwhelmed at points by storm-driven seas. Moreover, sanitary conditions were such that infections and diseases spread rapidly, and a number of passengers succumbed, their bodies tossed overboard. Bradford begins chapter 9, which mainly concerns the crossing, with an eye-catching anecdote about a young seaman, "of a lusty, able body," who cursed the passengers who got seasick. He said he "hoped to help to cast half of them overboard before they came to their journey's end." But he himself soon came down with an inexplicable illness, dying "in a desperate manner" in matter of days, and was himself "the first that was thrown overboard" (66). Bradford considered this "the just hand of God." You don't mock His people without taking it in the neck yourself.

This no-nonsense tone lends a bracing air to the book, which might well be described as America's first immigration narrative. These are God's chosen people, after all, not unlike the tribes of Israel in the Old Testament. God keeps an eye on them, and they wear a kind of protective shield as long as they behave according to His will. Indeed, Bradford ends this chapter with a number of direct quotations from Deuteronomy and the Psalms, lending an aura of historical necessity to his narrative. God is with His people, Bradford is saying. Let those who come later understand that the Pilgrims "cried unto the Lord, and He heard their voice and looked on their adversity" (71).

The shipload of hopeful if anxious Pilgrims bumped along the coast, finally landing in a safe harbor in what is now Cape Cod. Ashore, they found a recently abandoned camp, where they discovered to their delight "Indian baskets filled with corn" (74). This offered a kind of instruction to them, as they were unfamiliar with Indian corn, and "got seed to plant them corn the next year, or else they might have starved" (75). So this first, indirect encounter between the Pilgrims and the native people was positive. Unfortunately, the first genuine meeting was marked by violence, with a shower of arrows and discharge of muskets. Bradford offers an almost comic description of the skirmish, which left nobody hurt.

The ship continued on, landing near Plymouth Rock shortly thereafter, a place marked by "divers cornfields and little running brooks" (79). Bradford ends the first part of his journal with the arrival, then begins "The Second Book"—starting with a recollection of the famous Mayflower Compact. The original document is lost, but we have two more or less identical versions, one here and one in *Mourt's Relation* (1622), the other major account of the Plymouth Colony, written by several hands, anonymously, although Edward Winslow—another of the original Pilgrims—is considered its main author. This compact was essentially a signed agreement to band together for the mutual safety and well-being of the group, creating a "Civil Body Politic." In this brief document, lost in time and filtered through these two reports, we see the shadowy beginnings of the American experiment in democracy. John Carver was chosen as the first governor. "In these hard and difficult beginnings they found some discontents and murmuring," but these were overcome soon enough (84).

The main problems that confronted the pilgrims were disease and starvation, which killed nearly half the colony within three months. By the end of February, barely fifty remained, with many ill or weak. Most of the women and children had died, and less than half of the original twenty-six men who headed families survived. Meanwhile, Indians lurked at the fringes, watching the invaders, wondering what to do about them. They would "sometimes show themselves" in the distance, but when approached by the colonists, "they would run away" (87). This cat-and-mouse game continued for some time, until suddenly an "Indian came boldly amongst them and spoke to them in broken English, which they could well understand but marveled at it" (87). This was Squanto—the sole survivor of the Patuxet tribe, which had been wiped out by disease. He had previously come into contact with English fishing expeditions—and was for a while a captive. With a notable gift for languages, he developed friendly (if self-serving) relations with the English, as described by Bradford, and would play a major role in negotiations with the Indians in the perilous times that lay ahead for the Plymouth colonists.

In 1621, William Bradford took over from John Carver as governor, due to Carver's death. In his account of the first year at Plymouth, we are introduced to various Pilgrim figures, including Isaac Allerton, one of the most energetic, complex, and selfish of the group. His various moneymaking schemes and political shenanigans occupy a good bit of Bradford's attention over the years to come. But the main thread of this narrative has to do with the Indians, with whom the Pilgrims maintained reasonably good relations for half a century, largely owing to the careful diplomacy of Bradford himself, a tolerant, generous, and restrained man who put forward a model of decent governance.

A brief account of what is now referred to as the first Thanksgiving occurs in chapter 12, a third of the way through Bradford's journal. Much of this crucial chapter is focused on encounters with the Indians. It begins with a story about a colonist who got himself lost in the woods and wandered about for five days, living on wild berries, before the Indians captured him. He was, in fact, safely returned; but there is tension in the narrative, which moves forward swiftly—the kind of abrupt storytelling technique one associates with the Old Testament. We are introduced to further characters of note, including Hobomok, a "proper lusty man" who belonged to the Wampanoag tribe, which was led by Massasoit, the legendary chief who forged a delicate alliance with Bradford and the Plymouth Colony. (Hobomok was the subject of a well-known novel called, simply, *Hobomok,* written by Lydia Maria Child and published in 1824.)

In their dealings with the Indians, the colonists showed considerable patience. They worked hard to behave in a just and rarely vengeful manner, and they established a pattern that would keep the peace for over half a century, before the terrible conflict called King Philip's War (1675–76) broke out. (It was named after Massasoit's son.) That war was devastating—killing large numbers of colonists and virtually destroying the Wampanoag. In many ways, this war sketched in the dark tones that would color relations between American settlers and Native Americans for generations to come.

However much he caught the attention of later readers with the incident, Bradford makes relatively little of the first Thanksgiving. It was actually Edward Winslow (quoting his own letter of December 11, 1621, in *Mourt's Relation*) who remembers this occasion as something special. It was a traditional harvest festival attended by Massasoit and ninety of his men. According to Winslow, the party lasted three days. The "great store of wild turkeys" eaten by the revelers is mentioned by Bradford, and is perhaps the basis for our current habit in the United States of eating turkeys on Thanksgiving.

Soon other ships arrived from England, such as the *Fortune,* and the body of Pilgrims rose in numbers. As Calvin Coolidge would later say, "The business of America is business," and this was certainly true of the original Pilgrims, who began to trade in beaver and otter skins, among other commodities. It seemed obvious enough to Bradford that Thomas Weston and his "adventurers" in London had no real chance of recouping their investment, at least not for many years. Nevertheless, they loaded the *Fortune* in December 1621 with furs and sassafras and oak boards—a cargo valued at roughly £500. This would have gone a long way toward satisfying their debts; but the *Fortune* was badly named. Seized by the French en route to Southampton, the cargo never made it to England. The Pilgrim community sank deeper into debt.

Yet Bradford and his colony had more on their minds than simple finances. No sooner had the *Fortune* departed than another of the local tribes, "that great people of the Narragansetts," as Bradford describes them, laid down the gauntlet in the form of a snakeskin tied around a bundle of arrows: a symbolic threat. This tribe didn't like the alliances that the Plymouth group had made with other tribes, especially the Pokanokets. Bradford responded firmly, returning the snakeskin filled with gunpowder and bullets.

Myles Standish, the military brains of Plymouth, took control of the situation, and the Pilgrims protected themselves with a makeshift fortress. All kinds of tricky political maneuvering followed, with intrigues involving the Indians Squanto and Hobomok, rivals who provided crucial links between settlers and the various native tribes. As Bradford ruefully notes: "Squanto sought his own ends and played his own game" (109). He was a malicious gossip who played one tribe off another, hoping to become a kind of chief or sachem in his own right.

Massasoit soon wanted his head, but Bradford—almost by accident more than design—didn't hand him over to the Indians. This caused Squanto "to stick close to the English" for the time being.

Bradford writes: "Sundry other things I pass over, being tedious and impertinent" (112). One wishes that he had given us the details of this impertinence, although he was probably right in thinking that we should be spared the tedious bits. Being a Pilgrim was, from the point of view of a natural storyteller, a fairly dull business. This was a hard life, a routine of survival farming and hunting, with lots of time spent in prayer or cloistered in religious meetings of one kind or another.

Bradford's journal is often occupied by the conflict between the Pilgrims and Weston as well as other "adventurers," some of whom bought out Weston in the vain hope of realizing a profit. He also writes about continuing strife with the native population. There was never an easy truce, and despite the generally peaceful nature of Massasoit he was hardly the only sachem in the region, and the threat of violence remained constant. The Pilgrims had no doubt heard about what had happened in Jamestown, Virginia, where hundreds of settlers had been massacred; they must have lived in constant fear of a similar attack. Some of the later chapters in Bradford's book focus on the continuing effort to get a decent minister from England. Several came and went, and none were satisfactory. (The Pilgrims—as worshippers—were notably hard to please.)

Under the strict eye of Bradford, and supported by church leaders of strong character, the Plymouth Colony prospered. (The same could not be said for other colonies in the area.) The group succeeded, in part, because they took their social compact seriously. Bradford writes interestingly about their systematic experiments in communal living, noting how they parceled out the land in a way that would have stirred the heart of Karl Marx, with each family getting a plot commensurate with its size. The land was given "only for present use" but without a provision for inheritance (133). The system worked well, for a while, among these "godly and sober men." Yet Bradford had an uneasy feeling about this venture. He owned a copy of Jean Bodin's *De republica* (1586), in whose pages the author makes fun of Plato's idealization of communal living, saying that the Greek philosopher "understood not that by making all things thus common, a Commonweal must needs perish."[4]

Bradford explains that the younger generation of Pilgrims, among whom he counts the most "able and fit for labour and service," disliked working for the benefit of other men's wives and children and without any profit for themselves. They considered this work "a kind of slavery" and resisted it. The author himself appears to side with the younger set, and felt that the system itself alienated men from each other, seeming to "diminish and take off the mutual respects that should be preserved amongst them" (134). In this anxiety about communal activity, Bradford anticipates a concern that ripples through American society at every turn, as its citizens ponder the degree to which they should band together for the common good, or not. During the Cold War (which plagued the United States for much of the latter half of the twentieth century), this fear became feverish, with diatribes against "socialized medicine" and all forms of collective thinking.

Americans still resist sharing the wealth, except in the form of voluntary charities. There is a deep-seated feeling that one should work only for one's self-interest, without regard for the larger group. Yet this must be seen as only one strain in our national discourse. A consistent push from the communal side appears throughout our history, especially with the various well-known experiments in utopian living that became prominent in the nineteenth century, including the Harmonists, the Shakers, and the Perfectionists of the Oneida colony. In a sense, this experimentation was reborn in countless hippie communes of the late 1960s and '70s. It's certainly fascinating to read Bradford in the light of later developments, and to realize how early the conversation on this subject had begun on these shores.

Bradford's continuing saga often recounts the arrival of newcomers. Some of them come to bilk the Pilgrims, others are simply in search of a decent living. One also hears about nearby settlements, few of them as coherent as the Plymouth group. The Massachusetts Bay Colony, of course, would eventually become the dominant settlement in New England, with Boston its center, and attract such important figures as John Winthrop (1588–1649). Indeed, there was a company in the area of what is now Boston as early as 1623, called the Dorchester Company, dedicated to fishing off the coast of Cape Ann.

Among the most absorbing characters whom Bradford writes about is Captain Robert Gorges, who arrives in Massachusetts Bay "with sundry passengers and families," intending to begin a plantation. He eventually supplants Thomas Weston as the chief antagonist of the Plymouth group, although Weston seems to persist and causes trouble for the Gorges colony as well. Bradford also takes great pains to answer charges made against the Pilgrims by travelers who visited the colony and found it wanting. Among the complaints brought against it were intolerance and a lack of religious diversity. In response, Bradford simply asserts there was "never any controversy or opposition" among the Plymouth settlers. Harking back to the controversy about communal work versus private labor, there was the accusation that some members of the colony refused to "work for the General" (158). Bradford writes that this is "not wholly true, for though some [work] not willingly, and others not honestly, yet all do it; and he that doth worst gets his own food and something besides" (158).

Perhaps the liveliest moment in the journal centers on the colorful figure of Thomas Morton and his revels at Merry Mount, which have become the stuff of legend, especially as reimagined by Nathaniel Hawthorne in "The May-Pole of Merry Mount" (1836), a classic tale based on the incident described by Bradford. Morton (1576–1647) was a Cavalier in every sense of that word, a liberal-minded, humane, irreverent fellow who first sailed to the New World in 1622, although he returned a year later, castigating the fierce Pilgrims, whom he regarded as intolerant. He came back to New England in 1624, as part of a commercial venture that clearly threatened the Bradford group, which had come to depend on the fur trade. Morton and his men got on well with the local tribe, the Algonquins, whom he later described as being more civilized than their European counterparts at Plymouth.

Morton squabbled with his business partner, and the latter took off for Virginia, leaving Morton and his merry band to enjoy themselves. And apparently they did. According to Bradford, "They fell to great licentiousness and led a dissolute life, pouring out themselves into all profaneness" (227). He dubs Morton the "Lord of Misrule" and recalls that the Englishman and his followers "set up a maypole, drinking and dancing about it many days together, inviting the Indian women for their consorts, dancing and frisking together like so many fairies, or furies, rather; and worse practices." Indeed, Morton had traded alcohol (these early settlers drank brandy and aqua vitae) and guns for furs, and so it was perhaps economic competition as much as anything else that spurred the Plymouth settlers into action. As Hawthorne later wrote with a certain wryness: "Unfortunately, there were men in the new world of a sterner faith than these Maypole worshippers." He refers, of course, to the Pilgrims.

The Plymouth settlers wrote to Morton to warn him about his unseemly and dangerous behavior. Selling guns to the native tribes was certainly no good thing for anyone. Soon they sent Captain Standish and his men to raid the Morton compound, and they did so, although not a man was killed or injured. Morton and his band were too drunk to resist, being "so steeled with drink as their pieces [guns] were too heavy for them." Morton was hauled before Bradford, who didn't dare execute a man so well connected among Royalists back home. Instead, he was exiled to a small island off the coast of New Hampshire, where he was picked up by a merchant ship and taken back to England.

Morton had many friends in high places in London, including Sir Ferdinando Gorges—father of Robert Gorges—who had been one of his original backers. With help from these associates, he waged a publicity campaign against the Pilgrims, publishing a vivid account of life in the New World, with his version of the events that unfolded, in *New English Canaan* (1637). This splendid book celebrates the bounty and beauty of the New England landscape and its native people and often mocks the Puritan settlers. Morton's pen was, indeed, mightier than many swords, and he did great damage to the image of the Plymouth plantation among the British upper classes. Defiantly, he returned to New England and was tossed into prison for a terrible winter. He eventually died among English settlers in Maine, as far away as he could get from Bradford and Plymouth, in 1647.

Of Plymouth Plantation is, as journals must be, episodic. One hears about various scandals, many of them associated with Bradford's former assistant governor, Isaac Allerton, who represented the Plymouth settlers in dealings with investors back in England. As Bradford suggests, Allerton had business interests of his own, and these often conflicted with those of his fellow settlers. Under his management, the Plymouth Colony fell into deeper debt, although Bradford himself was no businessman and the colony had persistent problems long after Allerton stopped being their representative. As Bradford notes, between 1631 and 1636, the colony shipped back to England pelts of beaver and otter worth £10,000 (over $2 million today). Nevertheless, their debt of £6,000 seemed never to dwindle. It was not until 1648, with the sale of a considerable tract of land, that they finally settled their debts with English investors or "adventurers."

Disease and hunger were constants in their lives, as in the lives of the Indians. Bradford describes a truly horrendous epidemic of smallpox. For "want of bedding and linen" the Indians fell into a lamentable condition as they lay on their hard mats, "the pox breaking and mattering and running one into another, their skin cleaving by reason thereof to the mats they lie on. When they turn them, a whole side will flay off at once as it were." This terrible suffering was "most fearful to behold" (302). The Pilgrims "had compassion of them, and daily fetched them wood and water and made them fires, got them victuals whilst they lived; and buried them when they died. For very few of them escaped, notwithstanding they did what they could for them to hazard of themselves. The chief sachem himself now died and almost all his friends and kindred. But by the marvelous goodness and providence of God, not one of the English was so much as sick or in the least measure tainted with this disease, though they daily did these offices for them for many weeks together" (303). In this compassion, we see the key to the good relations that prevailed between the Indians and the Pilgrims over more than half a century.

Things gradually fell apart, however. The original core of faithful had been small from the outset, and even with the begetting of children, and the conversation of many of the "strangers," the Separatists could not keep up with the rapidly shifting political and religious complexion of New England. Doctrinal differences were always a problem, as with Roger Williams, who lived among them before going off to found Rhode Island. Bradford's group never really got along well with other Puritans, such as those in the Massachusetts Bay Colony or those in Connecticut and elsewhere. In addition, Bradford records a breakdown in morals after 1642, with "sundry notorious sins" (351). Some were, indeed, rather bizarre.

Among the worst sinners, he says, was Thomas Granger, who admitted to committing buggery with a mare, a cow, two goats, five sheep, two calves, and a turkey. This eclectic taste went down very badly among the Pilgrim fathers, and he was tried and, as might be expected, executed according to the law (as in Leviticus 20:15). Indeed, even the poor animals who suffered his curious attentions were executed and thrown into a pit. It so happens that Mr. Granger picked up his bad habits from others, and Bradford rather solemnly wonders how so many bad eggs could have found a home among them. He comforts himself a little by recalling that "where the Lord begins to sow good seed, there the envious man will endeavour to sow tares" (357).

Near the end of his journal, Bradford meditates on the longevity of the original Pilgrims, observing that despite "many changes and hardships" and confrontations with "the many enemies they had," a number of them lived to a ripe old age. Among these were Brewster and Winslow, two pillars of the Plymouth group. Indeed, Bradford ends his long narrative with the final departure of Winslow to England, where he was sent to defend the Plymouth Colony against charges of scandalous behavior brought against them in the courts. Oliver Cromwell—the great Puritan leader—was now in control of England, having deposed and beheaded King Charles I, and Cromwell apparently liked Winslow. He sent him in partial command of an expeditionary force that captured Jamaica in 1655, although Winslow died on the return voyage to England—a terrible personal loss for Bradford.

The journal ends sadly, a tale of success followed by disintegration, fragmentation, and a loss of ideals. The younger generation was not as ideologically coherent as their fathers and mothers. Nor did they share the vision embodied in the original compact. Bradford was disheartened by all of this, recording with some distaste that the increase in the price of corn and cattle led to the ultimate downfall of Plymouth, as personal greed overwhelmed the sense of community.

IV.

COTTON MATHER (1663–1728), a Puritan theologian and central figure in the story of colonial America, famously referred to Bradford as "our Moses," but he was not so grand as this suggests and never made large claims for himself. As one sees in his journal, he was a modest man, if humorless and strict. He wrote beautifully in *Of Plymouth Plantation,* with economy of style and concreteness, understanding the historical significance of the Pilgrim story, as well as its power as myth. He made the most of its mythical resonance, in fact, comparing the colonists to the Israelites in their journey to the promised land (although often alluding to his own group for a point of contrast, not as a way of suggesting that he and his brethren were just like the wandering tribes).[5] While the story of the first Thanksgiving stays in the mind, and has played a formative role in shaping America's sense of itself and its relations with the indigenous tribes, there is a larger story here.

It's the story of a people who chose to live apart, to make their own way in the world, however difficult, and who largely succeeded, at least for nearly half a century, in translating their vision of a just and Christian society into reality. They were, in their idiosyncratic way, a democratic group, and their impulse to pull together for the benefit of the community is admirable, if complicated. The ultimate unraveling of the Plymouth settlement seems part of the American story, too: one cannot sustain any vision, however beautiful, forever. Greed and self-interest inevitably corrode the body politic, as individuals seek their own fortunes at the expense of the community at large. This is, perhaps, the overarching tale that Bradford tells.

It's worth noting that Bradford's journal is fundamentally a religious document, a personal testimony, suffused with the author's sense of God's acting in the lives of the faithful. The English settlers in the New World were generally devout Christians, having been granted charters in Virginia by King James I in order to evangelize among those "as yet live in ignorance of the true knowledge and worship of God."[6] Yet nothing that happened in Virginia comes close to the religious fervor demonstrated by the various strands of Puritanism in New England. John Winthrop, leader of the Massachusetts Bay Colony, famously declared in a sermon on the deck of the *Arabella* in 1630: "We must consider that we shall be as a city upon a hill." He talked repeatedly about having entered a covenant with God. But it was Bradford who embodied the religious vision of the Puritans in its purest form, aiming for "the resurrection of primitive Christianity," as Perry Miller observes.[7]

Bradford's journal ranks high among the many accounts of early settlements in the New World, but one should ideally read it against *Mourt's Relation,* mentioned above, which appeared only two years after the initial landing at Plymouth and radiates a freshness of observation. Its full title was *A Relation or Journal of the English Plantation Settled at Plymouth,* and it consists of ten "chapters," only five of which are signed. Little is actually known about the man called Mourt, whose name figures in the title. He apparently wrote only a brief section, although (according to one theory) the name is possibly a misprint for George Morton, who had been a member of the original Leyden group. (Morton joined the Plymouth Colony quite early, although he was not on the *Mayflower.*) None of the five major sections has an author's name attached, but it has always been assumed that Edward Winslow did much of the writing and that William Bradford was himself another contributor.

Thomas Morton's *New English Canaan* should also be read alongside Bradford, as it has a great deal to recommend it. Morton's tale of wild living among the Indians spread far and wide and did not go down well in Puritan circles. Indeed the tug-of-war between the secular libertine and the chaste puritan has been a constant of our history, and seems to have begun with Morton and Bradford. Yet Morton was neither crazy nor depraved, although he pushed the boundaries of acceptable behavior. He was a spirited figure who braved censure in mad pursuit of sensual pleasure, drunk on the heady freedom offered (at least in theory) by the New World. When kicked out of New England, he returned to London, where he wrote *New English Canaan* to justify himself and his followers and to promote a different view of New England, its natural and human landscape.

It is wicked in its satire, and playful on many levels, if always contemptuous of the Puritans. Published in three "books," Morton's account offered a fresh take on the native people of North America, who were commonly regarded as no more than savages in need of conversion. Jack Dempsey, a recent editor of *New English Canaan,* defends Morton in able fashion and notes that the practice of cohabitation between European settlers and tribal people was hardly extraordinary during the first century of European contact with the New World. Nor were maypole celebrations atypical. Dempsey also points out that the "trade of dangerous and/or 'forbidden' goods, including guns and liquors," was commonplace as well in the century after Columbus.[8] In other words, what Morton and his merry band were doing at Merry Mount was not as unusual as it appeared to Bradford and the Plymouth settlers. It was business as usual, however distasteful to the Puritan conscience.

I have focused on William Bradford's journal mainly because of its mythic aura. The Plymouth settlement has acquired a unique resonance in the memory of most Americans. And yet Plymouth Colony was not the first major settlement by Europeans in the New World. The English arrived in Virginia, at Jamestown, in 1607, although that settlement was far from successful, soon degenerating into savagery and chaos, as described by the prolific John Smith in several works, including *The General History of Virginia* (1624). Relations between these settlers and the local population, the Powhatan Indians, were notoriously fractious. Edmund S. Morgan, a distinguished historian from Yale, says that Jamestown was a pathetic failure, and claims that the work habits of the settlers were hardly exemplary; indeed, "they were idle much of the time."[9] On the other hand, recent archaeological excavations in Jamestown suggest that Smith and others may have exaggerated the problems at Jamestown in self-serving ways. Even Jamestown, however, must cede priority to St. Augustine, a thriving Spanish settlement in Florida that dates from 1565. By 1608, the Spanish had also settled in Santa Fe, thus opening the southwestern region of North America to Europeans.

Establishing a beachhead for Puritans in New England, the Plymouth Colony certainly outshone Jamestown for orderliness and cohesion. It has acquired legendary status mainly because of the first Thanksgiving, as described by Bradford and, later, translated into a national myth holiday that celebrates reconciliation and survival. The more visible, and powerful, Massachusetts Bay Company had its many historians, as did Jamestown. But Plymouth was lucky in many respects to have William Bradford. *Of Plymouth Plantation* holds a unique place among records of this period. It is, in itself, a brilliant literary text, written with luminous clarity and concreteness: a humane, many-faceted story of survival against the odds. The fact that Bradford and his brethren managed relations with frequently hostile native people was remarkable in itself, a tribute to patient diplomacy and restraint—and a model that would not always be followed by succeeding generations. Indeed, the devastation of King Philip's War was a consequence of ignoring the model established by Governor Bradford and his fellow Pilgrims.

THE

FEDERALIST,

ON THE NEW CONSTITUTION.

BY PUBLIUS.

WRITTEN IN 1788.

TO WHICH IS ADDED,

PACIFICUS,

ON THE PROCLAMATION OF NEUTRALITY.

WRITTEN IN 1793.

LIKEWISE,

The Federal Constitution,

WITH ALL THE AMENDMENTS.

———

REVISED AND CORRECTED.

——✳——

IN TWO VOLUMES.

....

VOL. I.

——✳——

COPY-RIGHT SECURED.

————————

New-York:

PRINTED AND SOLD BY GEORGE F. HOPKINS,

At Washington's Head.

....

1802.

TWO

The Federalist Papers

I.

THE FEDERALIST PAPERS must rank high on any list of essential American publications, as influential as any before or since in putting forward a vision of representative government as it would be practiced on this continent for more than two centuries. It consists of eighty-five essays in defense of the proposed U.S. Constitution, which had recently been drafted in Philadelphia. The essays originally appeared in New York newspapers, in 1787 and 1788, but were soon gathered in book format. The writing was blatantly rhetorical (with rhetoric defined as "the art of persuasion") and designed to persuade New Yorkers—and people in the rest of the states as well—to look favorably on this controversial document, which had many eloquent detractors.

It was signed Publius, in honor of an early Roman consul, Publius Valerius Publicola, whose name meant "friend of the people." It's worth thinking about this choice of a pseudonym carefully. Apart from the fact that essayists in the eighteenth century often hid behind a Roman name, it seems relevant that Publius was a founder and defender of the Roman republic—a form of government that served as an explicit model for framers of the Constitution. The Roman republic devolved (eventually) into tyranny, but it lasted for centuries. The early founders of the American republic (like the French revolutionaries) did everything they could to foster comparisons with early Rome. Indeed, Thomas Jefferson went so far as to suggest that George Washington pose for Jean-Antoine Houdon, the famous sculptor, in a toga. (Wisely, the general did not take to this notion.)

The Federalist (as it was actually called, though it soon acquired the more popular title) was written by three hands. Alexander Hamilton (1755–1804) composed fifty-two of the essays, while James Madison (1751–1836) wrote twenty-eight. John Jay (1745–1829) was responsible for only five. It is possible that a few of the papers were passed back and forth, making them a joint effort, and all three would have read the published essays of their co-authors and followed on from what had already been argued, so to an extent Publius is the "real" author: a name representing a blended effort by writers who, to a degree, suppressed their individuality, even their doubts and hesitations, to support this impressively durable document that lies at the very core of American governance. The framers, of course, knew that what had emerged from their convention in Philadelphia was only a proposal, needing at least nine states for ratification to happen.

It is no exaggeration to say that *The Federalist Papers* profoundly affected how Americans thought about themselves as a body politic, and lent a particular tone to the Republic. These sinewy, well-shaped, argumentative essays form the bedrock of American government, and they continue to shed light on how we the people imagine the political and legal contours, and destiny, of our country.

II.

THE THREE AUTHORS of these "papers" were men of the Enlightenment, steeped in the writings of Montesquieu, John Locke, and David Hume, among others—all figures who believed in the establishment of a rational and balanced government that served the needs of its people. The allusions to these writers in *The Federalist Papers* place Publius firmly in this tradition of secular thought, and informed Europeans understood this perfectly well. Lord Acton, for example (a major figure in British public life), when being installed as the Regius Professor of

History at Cambridge University, called these papers "paramount in the literature of politics." On native soil, Jefferson—author of the Declaration of Independence and one of the crucial framers of the Constitution—called these papers "the best commentary on the principles of government" that was ever written.[1]

The authors of *The Federalist Papers* seem worldly, superbly educated, and rational to the bone. They possess an easy knowledge of Greek and Roman history and have read the philosophers of the French Enlightenment—especially Montesquieu, author of *The Spirit of the Laws* (1748), and Voltaire, the witty humanitarian and author of *Candide* (1759). Their work also reveals an intimate and sympathetic acquaintance with British political theory (as well as practice) and with the so-called Scottish Enlightenment, which had David Hume as its central thinker but included Francis Hutcheson, the philosopher who believed that virtue was a primary impulse in good government, and Adam Smith, who wrote *The Wealth of Nations* (1776). Taken together, this was a rich and compelling intellectual heritage for the men who became Publius to have absorbed, and it remains foundational for the United States. This, indeed, is where we came from, who we are.

The authors of *The Federalist Papers* were also practical men who set out to imagine how the Constitution might play out in the years ahead, envisioning a system of government that would promote the well-being of the American people and create a balance between liberty and stability (or "safety")—always a delicate combination, as we have learned in the years after 9/11. As two of these writers (Hamilton and Madison) were present in Philadelphia when the document under discussion was framed, they enjoyed a subtle and privileged understanding of what was meant by the original framers.

Judges and legal commentators over the centuries have often returned to *The Federalist Papers* to try to uncover what the framers "really" meant, as the language of the Constitution itself is sometimes ambiguous, open to interpretation. From the outset, Publius was considered a reliable source. In 1825, Jefferson recommended these essays as the best guide to what was in the minds of the framers, perhaps even better than the actual document itself! Far too few Americans have actually *read* the Constitution, although a general impression of what this document says survives in the American memory. It was perhaps Publius himself who supplied this memory. (Madison took detailed notes during the convention at Philadelphia, and these were enormously useful to him in writing these papers.)

Madison drafted the Bill of Rights in 1789, drawing on his notes from the convention but mostly using the various state bills of rights—especially the amendments proposed by the legislature in Massachusetts, where the lack of a Bill of Rights had been a serious roadblock for ratification. This series of ten amendments to the Constitution was originally prompted by the Anti-Federalists, who thought it worth enumerating certain "natural" or individual rights, such as freedom of speech, freedom of the press, and the right to assembly—although Madison did not include some of the key Anti-Federalist amendments, such as those that would have limited the federal government's powers of taxation or its ability to raise an army.

As might be expected, there exists a long tradition of commentary on *The Federalist Papers*. Garry Wills does a splendid job of summarizing this tradition in *Explaining America* (1981), his bracing reappraisal of Publius. Wills regards Hamilton and Madison primarily as disciples of Hume—an argument that derives, as he notes, from Douglass Adair, an influential mid-twentieth-century historian. Wills has little patience with the famous reinterpretation of Publius put forward by Charles Beard in *An Economic Interpretation of the Constitution of the United States* (1913), a pivotal work that regards Madison (in particular) as an economic determinist who wished, above all, to protect the interests of the wealthy minority, as in the famous No. 10, which modern historians have regarded as the fulcrum of *The Federalist Papers*.

No. 10 has attracted a great deal of attention over the years, but there is much more to *The Federalist Papers* than what Madison offers in this brief essay, which has been read (by Beard and others) as reassuring the wealthy few that the landless mob would not overwhelm the country. In fact, Publius generally offers a version of American republicanism that is quite comfortable with putting the majority in control. The idea of a representative democracy energized the men who framed the Constitution, and Publius reflects this excitement. There is at times almost a giddy boldness in the prose. Hamilton in particular writes with a verve rarely encountered in political essays of this kind, rightly sensing the unique historical moment he occupied. He was, after all, present at the birth of a republic, the first modern government to attempt to put into action the principles of Enlightenment thought. A guarded optimism could be felt on the streets, in the minds of the original framers of the Constitution, and in seats of government across the thirteen states (eleven states already had impressive constitutions of their own: only Rhode Island and Connecticut still operated from their old, colonial charters). Superstition and privilege—the twin pillars of the Old World—would now be swept away. Public virtue would reign, and the people would check themselves, accepting a delicate system of mixed government, with its carefully framed separation of powers, including its checks and balances, as put forward in Philadelphia.

But can people really "read" *The Federalist Papers* nowadays? Should they? The answer to both questions is a resounding yes. Although written at great speed (Hamilton must have written a thousand or so words a day), they are models of classical English prose: clear and crisp, yet highly nuanced, with extraordinary flexibility and a mature sense of subordination—a far cry from the monosyllabic, flat style (with a fear of subordinate clauses) so popular today, post-Hemingway. The major purpose of this book is put forward in the first paragraph by Hamilton, who argues that "it seems to have been reserved to the people of this country, by their conduct and example, to decide the important question, whether societies of men are really capable or not of establishing good government from reflection and choice, or whether they are forever destined to depend for their political constitutions on accident and force" (27). It doesn't get more serious than that.

By chance of history, a small group of highly educated and enlightened men (it is almost as if women did not exist at this time) were given the opportunity to shape a system of government for the ages, to create a working model of representative democracy. They succeeded brilliantly, coming up with a form of government that would put into practice the will of the majority while protecting the interests of the minority. Its elaborate checks would, in theory, militate against the possibility of tyranny—always a problem in the past, as history up to the late eighteenth century was hardly more than a series of tyrants and despots who waged war on each other and crushed the people under their boots. The very notion of a secular government elected by the people and for the people was something amazing to behold in 1787, when

Hamilton, Madison, and Jay began to explain to a wary audience the merits of the proposed Constitution.

The writers of *The Federalist Papers* had no easy task before them, as there was passionately intelligent opposition to ratification. Immensely gifted writers argued against the Constitution under pseudonyms such as Brutus and Federal Farmer. Patrick Henry and George Mason thundered against it, too—both of them impressive orators and writers. Mason, who had been present in Philadelphia, refused to sign the final document: indeed, he made 136 speeches against it from the convention floor. His main belief was that the House of Representatives should have the lion's share of power and that the executive should be reined in; he also felt that giving a president the power to go to war and run it by himself was dangerous, and would lead to major conflicts over which the people themselves would have little control. In a similar vein, he thought that the House, not the president, should appoint federal judges and justices on the Supreme Court, as a president might be more tempted (and have a greater ability) to create partisan courts. It so happens that a fair number of Mason's worries have proved well-founded.

Even so wise and moderate a man as Benjamin Franklin, whose symbolic presence at the convention in Philadelphia had been crucial to its success, understood the problems inherent in the document as framed. He was eighty-one at the time and too feeble to speak often from the floor of the convention. Franklin delegated James Wilson, a good friend, to read his concluding remarks to his fellow framers, and they make for chilling reading: "I agree to this Constitution with all its faults, if they are such: because I think a General Government necessary for us, and there is no Form of Government but what may be a Blessing to the People if well-administered; and I believe farther that this is likely to be well administered for a Course of Years and can only end in Despotism as other Forms have done before it, when the People shall become so corrupted as to need Despotic Government, being incapable of any other." To this dire prophecy, he added a conciliatory note: "I doubt too whether any Convention we can obtain may be able to make a better Constitution."[2]

Hamilton and Madison had their own reservations about this now-sacred document. (Madison, like Thomas Jefferson, did not favor the idea of a strong executive and preferred a three-person executive. He was also against the idea of multiple terms.) Yet they also understood that this was a unique chance to set something in motion that might work for the benefit of the people at large. They regarded the American republic as a grand experiment, and one that must be attempted, as the Articles of Confederation (established after the Revolutionary War as a means of uniting the thirteen former colonies in some formal way) had failed on so many counts to provide a secure governmental structure, as George Washington observed on May 18, 1786, when he wrote to John Jay: "That it is necessary to revise and amend the Articles of Confederation, I entertain no doubt; but what may be the consequences of such an attempt is doubtful yet something must be done, or the fabric must fall, for surely it is tottering."[3]

It is important to recall that monarchy was still the dominant form of government in the world, and that many Americans would not have objected had George Washington—after his magnificent role in the Revolutionary War—simply declared himself King George I. Had he done so, we might still have a hereditary monarchy in place (some will argue that we do, in fact, tend to rotate the White House among a few chosen families). Quite boldly, in this context, Publius emerges as defender of this document that had been sweated out, argued over, and put anxiously before the various states for ratification. Hamilton, Madison, and Jay understood how difficult it might be to convince a majority of Americans that this Constitution functioned in their best interests.

III.

HAMILTON LAYS out the general idea of *The Federalist Papers* in one crucial paragraph, and—by and large—he and his co-authors stick pretty closely to this outline: "I propose, in a series of papers, to discuss the following interesting particulars:—*The utility of the UNION to your political prosperity—The insufficiency of the present Confederation to preserve that Union—The necessity of a government at least equally energetic with the one proposed, to the attainment of this object—The conformity of the proposed Constitution to the true principles of republican government—Its analogy to your own State constitution*—and lastly, *The additional security which its adoption will afford to the preservation of that species of government, to liberty, and to property"* (30).

In the first paper, a masterful piece of rhetoric, Hamilton puts forward one face of a many-sided argument, alluding darkly to the Anti-Federalist cadre, which had many strong minds working overtime to persuade the states *not* to ratify the proposed Constitution. One of the most vigorous of these was Federal Farmer (the author of these essays has never been identified), whose command of rhetoric matched Hamilton's. In his first paper (October 8, 1787), he noted derisively that the convention in Philadelphia had been called to regulate trade and no more. He maintained that "one government and general legislation alone" could never "extend equal benefits to all parts of the United States."[4] In his view, the states were too various for such domination by a single government. He saw a diminishment in liberty everywhere and worried about an "unreasonable mixture of power in the same hands." Hamilton, barely containing his irritation and mistrust of those (like Federal Farmer) who felt suspicious of a strong federal system, argued that "the vigor of government is essential to the security of liberty" (29). He warned his fellow citizens to be "upon your guard against all attempts, from whatever quarter, to influence your decision" on ratification, as if he were not attempting the same thing himself!

John Jay then got to work, writing four essays on foreign policy. He was a well-known lawyer—later our first chief justice of the Supreme Court—who had drafted the New York Constitution (1777). With Benjamin Franklin and John Adams, he had forged the Treaty of 1783, which formally brought the Revolutionary War to an end. Though brief, his contribution to Publius remains significant, as it lays the foundation for American foreign policy based on the support of the people— a foundation that has been painfully ignored in recent history, when executives (Lyndon B. Johnson and George W. Bush, in particular) with an expansive sense of their own power took it upon themselves to engage in wars (Vietnam, Iraq) not easy to regard as being in the interests of the American people, or anyone else.

Jay begins in No. 3 by asking "whether so many *just* causes of war are likely to be given by *united America* as by *disunited* America" (36–37). He rightly (in my view) takes the stance that wars in general threaten the welfare of the American people, their peace and prosperity, and should be avoided when possible. As Garry Wills notes, most people today would assume that union was good because a united people could more easily defeat warlike neighbors than a disunited people. Jay doesn't go there, however. This was Enlightenment America, and so war becomes a test of one's own virtue. Jay suggests that it is more important to worry about the warlike tendencies of the American people than about possible aggressors from the outside. He worries in particular about the Indian population, which he sees as vulnerable and liable to be attacked and destroyed.

With astonishing foresight, Jay observes in No. 4 that there are *"pretended* as well as just causes of war." He points out that tyrants "will often make war when their nations are to get nothing by it, but for purposes and objects merely personal, such as a thirst for military glory, revenge for personal affronts, ambition, or private compacts to aggrandize or support their particular families or partisans" (40). He refers, of course, to tyrannical monarchs here, not future presidents of the United States. Presidents (he believes) should behave more virtuously, and sensibly, avoiding conflicts that will almost certainly lead to instability and cost the taxpayers a good deal of hard-earned cash.

"An entire and perfect union will be the solid foundation of lasting peace," Jay writes, quoting (verbatim) Queen Anne's letter of July 1, 1706, to the Scottish parliament. In this, as in so much that was already in the minds of the Founding Fathers, the British model of government was hugely influential. (The British, of course, had no written constitution, a point that motivated the framers in Philadelphia. It seemed necessary to have these important matters in writing.) The American version of republican government is mainly based on the British model, with its bicameral legislature and independent judiciary. Yet the American model would revise the British parliament in fairly radical ways, adding an elected senate in place of the hereditary House of Lords— although some in the deliberations in Philadelphia had actually argued for a senate based on wealth. The idea of a limited role of the executive branch would move far from the idea of monarchy, though allowing for "mission creep" on the part of power-hungry presidents. (Madison had argued in Philadelphia that a president should not, himself, have veto power; it should be shared with a number of judges, thus further limiting executive powers and making them, in effect, a council of revision, as in the constitution of the state of New York.)

As the only writer of the three who had considerable experience with foreign policy and international treaties, Jay was a good choice to lead off. In Nos. 2–5, he argued for union on the grounds that a unified entity was less likely to be attacked by foreign states than a loose confederation. A union was also less likely to wish to attack others; indeed, a republic of virtue would be established, wherein common sense and genuine decency would override selfish and belligerent factions. Jay stepped aside after No. 5, but was brought back to elaborate on treaty-making powers of the Union in No. 64. Here he maintains that the president himself cannot, and must not, have the power to make war or create treaties. Two-thirds of the Senate must agree with the president on these crucial matters. Importantly, Jay emphasizes that both the president and the senators should be mature men (over thirty-five if president, over thirty if senator) distinguished by their disinterested virtue. He warns fiercely against being "deceived" by those who exhibit "genius and patriotism," traits that "like transient meteors, sometimes mislead as well as dazzle" (389).

The first thirty-six papers make the argument for union in the context of the Anti-Federalists, who had many big guns on their side (although not on a par with the galaxy of nationally known leaders who supported ratification). These guns boomed in the daily press. While some states (Delaware, Pennsylvania, and New Jersey) ratified the new Constitution quickly and with obvious enthusiasm, a few major states dragged their heels, including New York, Virginia, and Massachusetts. In the latter, for example, there was hot debate about the lack of a Bill of Rights, which was created as a result of the ratification debate. The Anti-Federalists preferred the idea of a loose confederation of states, with power centered on state capitals. Hamilton believed in a strong central government, and Madison (to a degree) concurred, as did Jay. George Washington and Benjamin Franklin (among many others) threw their considerable weight behind the proposed Constitution, swaying the vote in its favor.

A point of worry among the original framers, often expressed at the Philadelphia convention, was that too much power would accrue to the majority, thus stifling the voice of those who owned property, large tracts of land, banks, and businesses. It was this fear that Madison addressed cogently in No. 10. The new Constitution, he maintained, would shift authority from the states to a central government, where the passions of the majority could be made "safe" by the forces of pluralism and fragmentation. It is worth looking closely at No. 10, which follows on from Hamilton's beautifully marshaled argument for union on the grounds that it offers a safeguard against domestic "faction" and insurrection in No. 9.

Hamilton famously writes in No. 9: "It is impossible to read the history of the petty republics of Greece and Italy without feeling sensations of horror and disgust at the distractions with which they were continually agitated, and at the rapid succession of revolutions by which they were kept in a state of perpetual vibration between the extremes of tyranny and anarchy" (66). One can feel the shudder in Hamilton, who did not want to live in some "petty republic" that might easily be overthrown. He falls back upon the authority of Montesquieu here, as elsewhere, being fully aware that the Anti-Federalist camp had invoked the French philosopher as well. Montesquieu had been a leading proponent of the separation of powers, and—as such—Hamilton believed he stood firmly under his shield. He quotes *The Spirit of the Laws* to great effect, citing the Frenchman's belief in "a confederate republic." Hamilton's definition of this republic is framed in these terms: "It is a kind of assemblage of societies that constitute a new one, capable of increasing, by means of new associations, till they arrive to such a degree of power as to be able to provide for the security of the united body" (69).

Madison seized and refined this idea in No. 10, which should be read in the double context of following upon Hamilton's argument for a strong state (the notion of "the enlargement of the orbit" being central to Nos. 9 and 10) and the Anti-Federalist uncertainty about majority rule. Madison writes: "The instability, injustice, and confusion introduced into the public councils have, in truth, been the mortal diseases under which popular governments have everywhere perished" (72). He plays to the Anti-Federalists here, raising the specter of "an interested and overbearing majority" who use their "superior force" to squash minorities of one kind or another But he does so in a way that, in effect, neutralizes them, as he generally supports the proposed Constitution and urges ratification: if Madison, with his genuine fear of this "overbearing majority," believes that all will be well, there cannot be too much to worry about on that count.

Madison says that factions will always arise, thus diluting majorities, "as long as the reason of man continues fallible" (73). He sees people breaking into factions for many reasons, including the "zeal for different opinions" on matters such as religion and political ideology. He also faces directly into a major point of conflict, which he characterizes as an "unequal distribution of property" (74). People with property and people without property fall on either side of a great divide; but even on the side of the "haves," there is a division into landed gentry, merchants, and "many different interests" as well as "classes." So the "regulation of these various and interfering interests forms the principal task of modern legislation." This is true to this day, when "unequal distribution of property" creates tensions and instability.

Interestingly, Madison does not believe that "enlightened statesmen" will necessarily be capable of regulating these varied interests, nor does he think that such men will "always be at the helm" (75). Therefore the system has to be arranged in such a way that the brute will of the majority finds a counterbalance in minorities with some leverage. As he makes clear, republics are not pure democracies, as raw political power is delegated to a few, the representatives of the people. Madison seems to believe that simply by having a large number of representatives, one guards against "the cabals of a few" (77). On this latter point he insists that a large electorate will prefer virtuous representation, and "unworthy candidates" will not have an easy time of it when they attempt to practice their "vicious arts." (This seems a very dubious proposition to me, but there it is.)

The argument from "extent of territory" follows, as an elaboration of the above. Indeed, one of the major innovations of the Constitution was the idea that a large republic would function better than a small one. Until this point in time, the general belief was that republics must be small to operate well. And so Madison argues that "the greater number of citizens and extent of territory which may be brought within the compass of republican than of democratic government" will be useful in squashing those who wish to "invade the rights" of others. In effect, he addresses the minority here, those wealthy landowners and merchants who were, indeed, the visible leaders of this nascent society. He reassures this prominent group that minority interests will not be overridden by an unruly mob. But, as the constitutional scholar W. B. Allen has recently noted, Madison also argues that republican government creates a system that actually favors the production of a virtuous majority.[5] Madison believes implicitly that the three branches of government both refine and harmonize various factions, and that one branch will consistently check the possible excesses of another.

No. 10 is, to a degree, coy and ambiguous. It has been subjected to fierce analysis (by Robert Dahl especially[6]) and found wanting, but it argues mainly for a strong national government. This is true of these essays generally. As one recent historian has said, "Above all, Publius is a nationalist."[7] This is certainly true of Madison in this pivotal paper, where he puts forward "a republican remedy for the diseases most incident to republican government." And this remedy rests on "the extent and proper structure of the Union." That is, it is large enough to contain (quite literally) various opinions and is set up (with checks and balances) in such a way that it will be difficult for any faction to cancel or diminish another. For the most part, this essay was reassuring to many who might have still harbored doubts about the proposed Constitution, and it helped in subtle ways to aid the campaign for ratification.

Overall, the first thirty-six papers argue against the current system of confederation, which had failed to produce a coherent or sustainable model of government. "We may indeed with propriety be said to have reached almost the last stage of national humiliation," Hamilton writes in No. 15. "There is scarcely anything that can wound the pride or degrade the character of an independent nation which we do not experience" (101). This is, of course, an exaggeration of the situation, meant to frighten readers and to persuade them to support ratification. The tactic lends a note of extravagance and urgency to these early papers.

Hamilton begins his parade of arguments with a surprisingly sustained metaphor, one that offers a key to his method, which is distinctly literary: "If the road over which you will still have to pass should in some places appear to you tedious or irksome, you will recollect that you are in quest of information on a subject the most momentous which can engage the attention of a free people, that the field through which you have to travel is in itself spacious, and that the difficulties of the journey have been unnecessarily increased by the mazes with which sophistry has beset the way. It will be my aim to remove the obstacles to your progress in as compendious a manner as it can be done, without sacrificing utility to dispatch" (100).

This elaborate conceit reveals the subtlety of Hamilton's approach. The metaphor of the "road" persists from first to last, embodying the idea of the "journey," which has a beginning (in a state of peril and demoralization) and a conclusion (which is safety and pride). All worthwhile journeys were probably "irksome," especially in the eighteenth century, when bandits lay beside the road, ready to overcome a coach and its hapless passengers. Hamilton cleverly flatters his audience, calling them "a free people." He widens the metaphorical range a bit, calling it a "field" as well as a road. Then, in the context of Anti-Federalist propaganda, he adds a further wrinkle: the mazes of sophistry to which his reader has doubtless been subjected. He swears to "remove the obstacles" to this reader's progress as well as he can, in the "compendious" manner indicated, by which he means thorough and exhaustive. This is brilliant rhetoric, laying out a strategy, engaging the reader's sympathy for a long journey. The style of the writing is superbly concrete, even muscular. And it does indeed prepare readers for the road to come, with its many twists.

Hamilton's grasp of world history is a constant recourse and lends a note of authority to his papers. In No. 18, for example, he offers a confident survey of Greek history, referring to the ancient republics that gathered, uneasily, under the Amphictyonic council. He observes that this council "bore a very instructive analogy to the present Confederation of the American States" (118). Had the Greeks been as wise as they were courageous, he writes, they would have seen the need for "closer union." But Athens and Sparta soon fell upon each other, becoming "first rivals and then enemies." (One has to wonder how Hamilton might have felt if he could have looked into a crystal ball at the Civil War.) He recalls that in Greece "mutual jealousies, fears, hatreds, and injuries ended in the celebrated Peloponnesian war, which itself ended in the ruin and slavery of the Athenians who had begun it" (121).

The historical sweep continues, alluding to unsatisfactory confederations in Saxony and elsewhere, building on Hamilton's primary concerns, discussed in No. 22. These are mainly the lack of power to regulate commerce and raise armies in a consistent and fair manner. In

No. 23, he offers a summary of his position: "The principal purposes to be answered by union are these—the common defense of the members; the preservation of the public peace, as well against internal convulsions as external attacks; the regulation of commerce with other nations and between the States; the superintendence of our intercourse, political and commercial, with foreign countries" (149). The casual reader in the twenty-first century will find much of this repetitive; but it must be kept in mind that these papers were published individually, and none of the writers could assume that readers had already encountered everything that had gone before, or could recall the arguments in perfect detail; so repetition became part and parcel of the method—and one of its major stylistic defects for modern readers. The papers were also written in a hurry, so the authors could never pause to think about the fact that future scholars of the Constitution would subject them to intense scrutiny, looking for clues to what the original framers meant in their essays (which were, after all, pieces of journalism, not legal briefs).

Hamilton concludes his trashing of the current system of confederation in No. 36, then passes the baton to Madison, his unlikely colleague. I say "unlikely" because they became, in due course, bitter political enemies, representing broadly different temperaments and constituencies. The New Yorker Hamilton was urban and commercial in his interests and affections. The Virginian Madison allied naturally with the farmer, the landowner, the rural and agricultural elements. Yet Garry Wills has done a good job of marrying the two, referring to the "Hamiltonian" Madison and the "Madisonian" Hamilton. He thinks Publius was not as schizophrenic as many readers have assumed, suggesting that "people who bring the stereotypical view of Hamilton and Madison to *The Federalist* could be fairly easily confounded if given isolated passages and asked to identify the author."[8] He observes, by way of example, that Hamilton, not Madison (as might be expected), writes in a cautionary way in No. 35 about the dangers of tariffs, which "tend to render other classes of the community tributary in an improper degree to the manufacturing classes, to whom they give a premature monopoly of the markets" (208).

The fact is both Hamilton and Madison repressed their individual views (as expressed in other places, outside of *The Federalist Papers*) to argue on behalf of the proposed U.S. Constitution, taking the larger

view of those who framed the document. They were themselves prominent among the original framers, which is why subsequent historians, as
well as sitting judges and legal scholars, have long resorted to these papers in a reverential way, assuming (rightly or wrongly) that as Hamilton and Madison were there, at the deliberations in Philadelphia, they
knew what was meant.

This has led to some odd moments in judicial history, as Wills observes, noting that the Constitution itself never actually mentions the
theory of the separation of powers, even though Justice Louis D. Brandeis wrote (in *Myers v. United States,* 1926) that "the doctrine of the separation of powers was adopted by the Convention of 1787." Chief Justice
Earl Warren repeated this notion in 1965 (*United States v. Brown*). The
Constitution creates separate powers, of course, and supports them implicitly, but does not seek to justify this separation on theoretical
grounds of any kind; the work of creating a "doctrine of the separation
of powers" was taken up by Hamilton and Madison, who developed the
theory of checks and balances as one of the great benefits of "mixed government," as Montesquieu referred to this kind of system.

As noted above, the mix of branches was explicitly based on the
British model, with its legislature set up to check the power of the
monarch and with an independent judiciary. Both Voltaire and Montesquieu revered the British model, the latter basing his theory of the
separation of powers on this example. Hamilton is explicit about this
and says in No. 65 that the impeachment process imitates the British system; in No. 75 he argues that the power of the president is firmly held
in check by the Congress, which has the power of the purse—another
British influence. As Hamilton points out, the proposed legislature can,
if it chooses, not fund any wild plans that the president may decide to
pursue, much as the House of Commons in Britain "reduced the pre-
rogatives of the crown and the privileges of the nobility" (433).

A complex defense of the proposed Union occupies Publius in succeeding papers, beginning with No. 37, where Madison states that "the
ultimate object of these papers is to determine clearly and fully the merits of this Constitution, and the expediency of adopting it" (220). He pro-
poses a "thorough survey of the work of the convention." And so follows
in Nos. 37–40 a close look at the "general form" of the new Union, with
further elaboration of republican principles and of the very idea of fed-

eralism itself. In Nos. 41–46, Publius locks horns with the Anti-Federalists, who frequently asserted that it was dangerous to give so much power to a new government and that the rights of states would be severely diminished if the Union went into effect. Not so, Publius argues, as the system was set up to assure that states maintained a degree of control over their own affairs.

Publius tells us repeatedly that checks and balances were established to ensure that no particular branch of government acquired too much power. And so the theory of the separation of powers occupies much of the ground through Nos. 47–51. Nos. 52–83 offer a portrait of these proposed branches and their duties, with three papers (Nos. 59–61) on the regulation of elections. In No. 84, various objections to the new Constitution, including the lack of a Bill of Rights, are taken up. No. 85 both summarizes and recapitulates earlier points, defending the republican model on the basis of its similarity to what the states have already achieved in their state constitutions. Finally, Publius notes the "additional securities" offered by Union, with its ability to defend liberty and property in a more efficient manner than the Articles of Confederation—a return to arguments laid out in the earlier papers. In general, as Bernard Bailyn has shrewdly remarked of these papers: "Their aim was simply to convince people whose minds and experiences were shaped by the Revolutionary ideology that the principles they revered, especially the preservation of private rights, would still apply under the powers of the new federal government."[9] In his view, the considerable achievement of Publius was that Hamilton, Madison, and Jay "sought to embrace the Revolutionary heritage, and then to update it in ways that would make it consistent with the inescapable necessity of creating an effective national power."[10]

Hamilton quotes directly from David Hume in his final thrust, admitting the massive difficulty of agreeing upon any system at all, especially a rational one. "To balance a large state or society," writes Hume, "whether monarchical or republican, on general laws, is a work of so great difficulty that no human genius, however comprehensive, is able, by the mere dint of reason and reflection, to effect it. The judgments of many must unite in the work" (526). It is the collective judgments of the framers, sitting in Philadelphia, that Publius celebrates, pitting himself against "powerful individuals" who are "enemies to a general national government in every possible shape" (527). These are, indeed, the last words of Publius—a warning about the Anti-Federalists, who with equal eloquence tried their best to squash the new Constitution before it was even tried.

In many ways, *The Federalist Papers* remains a curious, if eloquent, document, full of omissions (there is not a word about slavery) and contradictions and thoroughly grounded in the language of eighteenth-century philosophy and psychology, as Morton White has shown in *Philosophy, "The Federalist," and the Constitution.*[11] An idealistic note will be heard throughout, as Hamilton (in particular) puts a huge emphasis on public virtue as the underlying force that promises to hold the new republic together, to make it work. Publius was—like David Hume—suspicious of factions (although Madison could see their value), and so political parties were seen as divisive. Hamilton genuinely (if naively) believed that parties would become irrelevant in American society and that unruly passion in politics was a very bad thing. "The republican principle demands," he writes in No. 71, "that the deliberate sense of the community should govern the conduct of those to whom they intrust the management of their affairs" (430). It was, in fact, the passion of the House that worried him most of all—this volatile and largest branch of government, which controlled the purse strings. It could, if it so chose, control operations from the ground level, therefore having excessive influence on public policies.

Hamilton believed that down the road, difficulties with the American system would arise from the House holding sway over the Senate, the president, and the Supreme Court as well. To him, there was a danger that the president and the Supreme Court might bow down in "absolute devotion" to the House (431). As history has shown, Hamilton had nothing to worry about, as the presidency has (insidiously perhaps) managed to acquire more and more authority. The power of veto, which Publius thought quite ineffective, has proved otherwise. And Publius could hardly have known about the bully pulpit, which presidents would use to great effect to go around the legislature. Nor did Publius imagine that the Supreme Court might itself become so partisan, with judges affiliating openly with one party or another or with a distinct ideology—although this might have been averted or moderated, had the legislature rather than the president been responsible for choosing judges at the federal level.

Publius certainly understood that many intelligent citizens in the thirteen states felt deeply suspicious of this proposed Constitution, despite its elaborate system of mixed government, with checks and balances strategically planted to ensure that, if worst came to worst, deadlock would occur—not always a bad thing. Madison, at least in No. 10, seems quietly on the side of deadlock, which in his view would serve the interests of the wealthy minority, who might need to put a brake on populist measures for legitimate reasons. It seems doubtful, however, that Madison's view was as important as later historians, such as Charles Beard, believed. (Morton White shows, convincingly, that Madison understood there were "other causes of factions besides this economic cause," which Beard had focused on to the exclusion of other possibilities.[12])

When one thinks about *The Federalist Papers* retrospectively, knowing full well what unfolded from the Constitution, it's amusing to look at Hamilton's No. 72, which puts forward all manner of arguments for *not* limiting the presidency to any specific number of terms. His view was shared widely by many of the original framers, who imagined that bad things might come of limiting the president's ability to be reelected again and again, if the people wished to have him. Mainly, he argued that restricting the president to a set number of terms (as we now do) would militate against the exercise of virtue or "good behavior" by the man in office (435). "There are few men who would not feel much less zeal in the discharge of a duty when they were conscious that the advantage of the station with which it was connected must be relinquished at a determinate period" (435). Even worse, if a greedy or corrupt man became president, he would be tempted to steal and do as much harm as he could before having to give up office, feeling the pressure of time. Hamilton terrifies his readers by asking them to imagine what it would be like to have former presidents—all furious because they were deprived of their former glory—"wandering among the people like discontented ghosts and sighing for a place which they were destined never more to possess" (437).

In this, Hamilton seems to have been misguided. Most of our former

presidents have behaved well in retirement, often serving in the role of
elder statesmen, lending a voice on matters of public concern, traveling
as ambassadors-at-large to distant parts. But it was impossible for Publius to see into the future. Not surprisingly, a lot of his guesswork about
what might happen proved wrong, and his fears unfounded.

Nevertheless, Publius attempted to envisage all manner of developments, proper and improper, and his efforts were mighty and visionary.
It is often suggested that Hamilton in particular was an elitist, nervous
about democracy in a form too raw for checking firmly. Yet Hamilton,
not once but three times, makes the point emphatically that the American republic as put forward in the Constitution should be *overthrown* if
it should prove tyrannical or unworkable. In No. 33, he writes: "If the
federal government should overpass the just bounds of its authority and
make a tyrannical use of its powers, the people, whose creature it is,
must appeal to the standard they have formed, and take such measures
to redress the injury done to the Constitution as the exigency may suggest and prudence justify" (199). Garry Wills suggests that he means
revolution here, and I would agree. This word—hardly alien to an
eighteenth-century ear—is used explicitly in No. 60, and a justification
for revolution lies at the center of No. 78, where Hamilton worries
about "dangerous innovations in the government" and "serious oppressions of the minor party in the community." He says explicitly that
"friends of the proposed Constitution will never concur with its enemies
in questioning that fundamental principle of republican government
which admits the right of the people to alter or abolish the established
Constitution *whenever they find it inconsistent with their happiness*" (468).
The italics are mine, meant to highlight this astonishing and often overlooked phrase. This was, after all, the Age of Revolution, and Hamilton
himself had recently been a revolutionary. He understood that any constitution, including the ingenious document that he and his co-authors
supported in *The Federalist Papers,* was nevertheless a human one, fallible, subject to modification and—if necessary—overturning.

Certainly the Supreme Court, in Hamilton's view, had a limited role
in the overall system of government. He notes in No. 78 that "the judiciary is beyond comparison the weakest of the three departments of
power," citing Montesquieu as an authority here: "Of the three powers
above mentioned, the JUDICIARY is next to nothing." In writing this,

however, he had in mind the Anti-Federalists, such as Patrick Henry and George Mason, who thought that altogether too much power lay in the hands of justices and judges put forward by the executive branch, and predicted that such a system would end in tyranny under "one consolidated government."[13] Hamilton chooses (not so convincingly) to emphasize that the judiciary is clearly *not* superior to the legislature, writing: "It can be of no weight to say that the courts, on the pretense of a repugnancy, may substitute their own pleasure to the constitutional intentions of the legislature" (467). This still rings a bit hollow, and the arguments about which branch of government had more weight were often tedious and (intentionally, I suspect) confusing.

It must have been difficult for Publius to write constantly about hypothetical situations, guessing at what might happen, but this was indeed his task, and he performed it well, ranging in many directions, attempting to foresee circumstances that might be far from plausible in the real world. He often falls back, for comfort, on the fact that the U.S. Constitution relies heavily on "copying from the models of those constitutions" which have proved successful over time. In particular, Hamilton cites the "experience of Great Britain," which the U.S. model reflects in so many ways. If it had worked so well in the British Isles, it would probably work on these shores, too.

IV.

WHAT INFLUENCE DID *The Federalist Papers* actually have? How did it help to shape the American mind, if such an extrapolation exists? These papers certainly proved persuasive, as ratification in due course occurred—although not without furious debate. As the final paper said explicitly, in a gesture toward opponents, the Constitution was hardly "perfect," being full of obscurities and compromises. "I never expect to see a perfect work from imperfect man," writes Hamilton. The document drafted in Philadelphia in 1787 remains a product of "errors and prejudices" as well as "good sense and wisdom" (523). The key to making such a document work for the benefit and freedom of the people was *responsibility*—a willingness to answer (as in the root sense of the word, *respondio*) to the people and to promise (*spon-*

deo) to act in a virtuous manner, putting one's own interests aside for the benefit of the community at large.

As for the shaping of the American mind, there can be no doubt that the manner of argument—rigorous, tolerant of competing viewpoints, radically innovative, rational—had an effect on future thinkers, whose writing on political matters would always (implicitly) be judged against the rhetorical finesse and easy erudition of Hamilton, Madison, and Jay. The Enlightenment mode, with its emphasis on secular government, has been deeply influential: to this day, Americans widely assume that the government is not affiliated with a particular creed (although some continue to resist the separation of church and state, and dream of theocracy). *The Federalist Papers* put forward an ideal system, of course; its realization could hardly meet that ideal, as times change and each generation confronts a different set of circumstances.

It remains difficult to imagine our politicians in the terms that Publius, a child of the Enlightenment, envisaged. We have seen endless corruptions and scandals over the years, shocking abuses of power, and threats to liberty from within as well as from without. But there is a residual force at work in the considerable intellect and collective wisdom embodied in the U.S. Constitution, for all its faults and compromises. It has proved remarkably durable, as modified by various amendments and as put into practice by fallible men and women over the centuries. Publius understood the value of this document, even its drawbacks. Any citizen will benefit from dipping into *The Federalist Papers* periodically, as it calls us to what Lincoln famously in his first inaugural (1861) referred to as "the better angels of our nature." These angels are real, and flutter above us, and beckon.

THE

LIFE

OF

Dr. BENJAMIN FRANKLIN.

WRITTEN BY HIMSELF.

SECOND AMERICAN EDITION,

PHILADELPHIA:

Printed For BENJAMIN JOHNSON,
No. 147, High-Street.
M, DCC, XCIV.

THREE

The Autobiography
of Benjamin Franklin

I.

AMONG THE MANY THINGS that Benjamin Franklin invented was autobiography itself. There had, of course, been memoirs before. But they were limited in scope, consisting of the recollections of triumphs by great men: soldiers and statesmen, merchant princes, and so forth. There was a limited tradition of the spiritual or intellectual autobiography, too, going back to the *Confessions of Saint Augustine* from late in the fourth century or the *Confessions of Jean-Jacques Rousseau* (1782). But until the posthumous *Autobiography of Benjamin Franklin* appeared in 1793, the world had no obvious model for this kind of memoir, one that tracks the creation of an individual self. It remains a foundational book for Americans, in that it offers a template for self-invention and a good deal of inspiration as well.

In America, the myth of self-creation and pulling oneself up by the bootstraps is pervasive, although its reality is too easily assumed in a world where class, race, and gender still pose formidable barriers. Nonetheless, the American dream of class mobility is sacred, as expressed by Franklin in this memoir, published in truncated form after his death and later amplified by additional material. The story itself concerns a boy who—without the benefits of family connections, a formal education, or inherited wealth—rises through the ranks of colonial society to a position of wealth and influence. This rise is self-effected, the product of hard work and ingenuity. Franklin became—within his own lifetime—an American icon, as impregnable as Fort Knox, and deeply familiar to a broad population.

The entire story of Franklin's vast, almost unfathomable career moves well beyond the boundaries of *The Autobiography of Benjamin Franklin*. Yet it's the place to start, and it traces an archetypal story that, on so many levels, offered Americans a template of sorts, a way of proceeding in the world. Franklin both contributed to the American character and created it. The influence of this book can hardly be calculated, in fact. While few Americans will actually have read it, few will not feel strangely familiar with its contents, which have entered the public domain as a founding myth, making Franklin the Founding Fathers' founding father, the paterfamilias of an entire nation.

II.

E VERYONE KNOWS BENJAMIN FRANKLIN (1706–90), as his agreeable face adorns so many public surfaces. Stores, schools, and banks bear his name, as do foundations and financial trusts. Peering at us from the $100 bill, he is the mold from which we were all cut, or like to imagine ourselves cut. Among the Founding Fathers, he presents the most accessible figure by far. George Washington and Thomas Jefferson seem titans by comparison, all but unapproachable. We have all met Franklin a thousand times, in the shops or offices along Main Street: the young man on the make, sweetly affable, eager to please, a bit wily perhaps, but always ready to pitch in. All Rotarians can trace their origins to this man, the public-spirited individual who loves company. Indeed, as a successful printer in Philadelphia, young Ben eagerly organized his fellow shopkeepers and merchants into groups to discuss interesting topics and promote the public good.

He had an uncanny capacity to create entities that would promote the welfare of his fellow citizens, founding the first subscription library on American soil. He established a volunteer fire department and started a hospital as well as the academy that evolved into the University of Pennsylvania. He served as postmaster of Philadelphia and was a magnificent fund-raiser who devised the capital-raising vehicle of matching funds. He thought up the idea of fire insurance. And we all know about his varied inventions, some of which bear his name, such as the Franklin stove: a clean-burning device that improved the lives of householders in colonial America. He was a scientist, too: the man who figured out that lightning was a form of electricity (he famously flew a kite to experiment with the theory and—luckily—didn't fry himself in the process). Following on from this discovery, he invented the lightning rod. He crafted the first bifocal glasses: one of his most enduring and useful inventions. He produced the first urinary catheter, designed streetlamps, created (and named) the storage battery, and fashioned a plumbing system that used hot water to heat a building. A printer by profession, he tinkered endlessly with the mechanics of his craft, making improvements in copperplate design. His scientific experiments ranged broadly, too, from the pioneering work in electricity and meteorology to refrigeration and hull design for ships. He was interested in magnetism and optics and seems always to have been fascinated by medicine, where he made numerous innovations and suggestions that have shown him astonishingly prescient.

For all of this, he was also a statesman of unusual skills. His role in the creation of the American republic was nothing less than central. He was present at the beginning and worked ceaselessly to further the cause of American independence. He served as a key ambassador abroad, persuading the French to lend crucial support to the Revolution. He served important diplomatic roles in London before the outbreak of the war, and in Paris thereafter. Without his careful, ingenious diplomacy, the American Revolution may not have succeeded. His success in helping to craft a peaceful settlement with Britain after the Revolutionary War surprised many of his detractors. Last but hardly least, he was an essential figure in the composition of three major documents: the Declaration of Independence, the treaty of alliance with France, and the final treaty of peace with Britain. As he famously said: "There never was a good war or a bad peace."

Which brings us to what Ben Franklin said. His sayings (as printed over the years in the famous *Almanack* that he published under the pseudonym of Poor Richard) helped to shape the American character and

remain part of our mental fabric. They include: "Haste makes waste,"
"Make haste slowly," "Little strokes fell great oaks," "Fish and visitors
stink in three days," "A penny saved is Twopence clear," and "The
sleeping fox catches no poultry." He also said, "The sting of a reproach
is the truth of it" and "No gains without pains." His attitudes toward
money seem implicit in his words, as when he wrote: "Necessity never
made a good bargain." Betraying his Puritan roots, he also quipped:
"God helps them that help themselves." As Franklin was the first to acknowledge, many of these sayings existed in earlier forms. In his autobiography, he confesses that "not a tenth part of the wisdom" that
appears in these sayings was his own; indeed, most of these well-known
aphorisms were adapted from older sayings. One will find, for example,
versions of "Early to bed and early to rise / Makes a man healthy,
wealthy, and wise" in standard anthologies of English proverbs. He
lifted, almost verbatim, from Daniel Defoe one of his most famous
quips: "In this world, nothing can be said to be certain except death and
taxes." What Franklin did was burnish the old sayings, make them
memorable, give them a local accent—all in keeping with the tradition
of aphorisms, which are just clever sayings that go around . . . and
around.

Franklin was so witty, talkative, and convincing that Americans
tend to think he said things that more or less sound like him. (In this
sense, he reminds one of Yogi Berra.) He did not, for example, say
"Honesty is the best policy." That was Cervantes. Yet people also tend to
reshape his actual sayings in their own heads, as when they mutter to
themselves in the gym: "No pain, no gain." Indeed, the public memory
is constantly revising Franklin, much as he revised the public memory.

Franklin had few pretensions and wished to be remembered mainly
as a printer. In keeping with this, he often signed himself as "B.
Franklin, printer." This was perhaps more than just a sign of modesty:
Franklin understood that his public image mattered, and he liked having this association with a trade. Long after he no longer had to fetch paper personally, he would wheel a barrow full of rolls down Market
Street to his shop, advertising his own hard work and his professional
role. He also preached order and diligence (although he could also be
sloppy and lazy himself).

This laziness annoyed some. For instance, when John Adams ar-

rived in Paris in 1778, joining Franklin in his diplomatic efforts on behalf of the rebellious colonies, he was scandalized by the "dissipation" of
the famous American sage, whom the French revered and placed on a
pedestal beside Voltaire himself. Adams recorded his impressions of
Franklin in his journals:

> I found out that the business of our commission would never be
> done unless I did it . . . The life of Dr. Franklin was a scene of con-
> tinual dissipation . . . It was late when he breakfasted, and as soon as
> breakfast was over, a crowd of carriages came to his levee . . . some
> philosophers, academicians, and economists; some of his small tribe
> of humble friends in the literary way whom he employed to trans-
> late some of his ancient compositions . . .
>
> He was invited to dine every day and never declined unless we
> had invited company to dine with us. I was always invited with him,
> till I found it necessary to send apologies, that I might have some
> time to study the French language and do the business of the mis-
> sion.[1]

It was Franklin's habit, at least while in France, to sleep late, work
whenever he felt like it, and dine through the evening with his friends,
many of whom were society ladies, with whom he flirted shamelessly.
Yet it might be argued that this behavior was shrewdly calculated to
achieve certain ends and effects. Franklin understood that the French
admired men who took pleasure in life. On the other hand, he really *did*
take pleasure in life and had, after all, earned the right to behave like
this, having spent many hours in the printing shop as a young man and
racked up a sizable show of accomplishments. Even as a high-living
diplomat in Paris, he got his work done and never ceased to think in creative ways.

As an elderly man, he continued to function in a public role. Indeed,
his iconic presence at the Constitutional Convention in Philadelphia in
1787—at the age of eighty-one—was considered crucial to its successful
outcome. And Franklin, despite his reservations (expressed so boldly at
the convention itself), stood firmly behind the proposed U.S. Constitution. His doubts remain perceptive: he objected to an excessively strong
executive branch, with a single person serving as president with insuffi-

cient checks on his authority. He thought it possible that the proposed system would end in tyranny after a certain period (as I have noted in the previous chapter, quoting Franklin's speech to the convention).

Franklin was attached to his status as printer for good reasons. He had managed to turn this trade to account, acquiring his own shop (with a little help from his friends) in his mid-twenties. He applied himself to the task at hand with an aggressive self-discipline, rising early and working late. More important, he used his formidable social skills to create an ever-expanding network of acquaintances and business associates. Still in his twenties, he bought a newspaper from a former employer who had fallen on hard times, and transformed this into a popular organ, the *Pennsylvania Gazette*. He became a major publisher of books as well, often supplying copy himself. His *Almanack* became a bestseller throughout the colonies, establishing Franklin as a national voice. In relatively short order, he became an influential man of business, with any number of enterprises and franchises. He was, indeed, one of the first media barons on American soil.

For our purposes here, Franklin also became a significant writer, one of the most influential of his era. His work ranged widely over science, politics, and philosophy—his collected papers fill a long shelf in every major library. But of all the writings he left behind, *The Autobiography of Benjamin Franklin* remains the centerpiece of his achievement, a fundamental work of literature that helped to mold the American character in countless ways.

It was, unfortunately, unfinished at the time of his death and published posthumously (in a truncated form) in 1793. The history of the manuscript and its fate would fill a small volume by itself. Some of the problems lay with William Temple Franklin, the author's eldest grandson and former secretary in Paris, who was left in charge of Franklin's papers. It would take many years before his official edition of the papers began to appear, in 1817. Later in the nineteenth century, earlier and variant manuscripts of the *Autobiography* became available, and scholars began to correct the "corrections" made by Temple, who had systematically bowdlerized his grandfather's work, taking out what he considered "rude" phrases, making them more polite and general and abstract. So when Franklin describes his printing colleagues in London as "great Guzzlers of Beer," they become, in Temple's rephrasing, "great drinkers

of beer." In every case, Franklin's own phrasing outshines the replacement.

III.

THE *AUTOBIOGRAPHY* FALLS INTO FOUR PARTS, written at different times. The first, most memorable section took the form of a
letter to the author's son, William (from whom he was later estranged
because William had sided with the British during the Revolution). It
was begun in August 1771, at the elegant country house of his friend
Jonathan Shipley, the bishop of St. Asaph. (Under the influence of
Franklin, Shipley had become a fierce advocate of American independence in the House of Lords.) According to legend, Franklin worked on
this project for several hours a day, often writing in the garden. He
would read the results to the Shipley family after dinner, around a fire
in the sitting room. Part 1 was completed rapidly, perhaps within two
weeks, then put aside as other tasks absorbed Franklin.

As he set about his work, Franklin had few models for this kind of
writing, although Lord Herbert of Cherbury had published a well-
known memoir a few years earlier. Yet Franklin was hardly a noble-
man. He was no ordinary man, of course—his achievements in business,
science, government, and public service lit the path before him where he
traveled—but he had neither family connections nor inherited wealth,
so it was a bold act, almost revolutionary in itself, to put forward his recollections. The sheer confidence of the voice, its easy self-acceptance,
continues to give this book a particular glow.

Franklin had a very special subject, the story of a young man who
put himself bravely forward in the world with shrewd calculation. By
thrift and diligence, and by constant application to the work of self-
perfection, he achieved amazing things. This pattern became, in due
course, a model of self-invention, and one that would shape a nation's
sense of itself as a place where anything was possible if you tried hard
enough. This was, at its most elementary level, the American dream.

Franklin seems not to have taken the role of autobiographer too seriously, as his book sat on the back burner for nineteen years, receiving his
full attention for discrete, rather brief intervals. Indeed, he never both-

ered to pull the work together, although Part 1 is neatly shaped. It covers
his first twenty-five years, in Boston and Philadelphia, beginning with
his origins in "poverty and obscurity." We learn that although he lacked
a formal education, he had an intense desire to learn about the world.
With a fondness for his own ingenuity and guile, he recalls his appren-
ticeship as a printer and his steady march through the world, a progress
that led ultimately to the establishment of his own printing business and
his rise to fame in the worlds of publishing and public service.

By the time Franklin set about writing these memoirs, he was sixty-
five and probably the most widely known American of his day. In
Part 1, he sizes up the person he had been so many decades before. The
tone he adopts is genial, even whimsical, as when he says: "I shall indulge the Inclination so natural in old Men, to be talking of themselves
and their own past Actions, and I shall indulge it, without being trou-
blesome to others who thro' respect to Age might think themselves
oblig'd to give me a Hearing, since this may be read or not as any one
pleases" (44).[2] He remained highly self-conscious about the work of recollection, which meant living his life over again. (The fact that he never
completed the book may suggest a fear of ending his own life, as if clo-
sure were a form of suicide.)

As a printer, quite naturally he fell into metaphors associated with
his craft. And so errors in his life became (somewhat clinically)
"errata"—printer's errors. Because he was never a man of notable spiritual depth, *sins* were not something he much worried about. But errors
one could obviously correct. He says he would have liked to live his life
all over again, "only asking the Advantage Authors have in a second
Edition to correct some Faults of the first" (43).

Autobiography is a kind of fiction, perhaps even less "true" than
most novels. It depends on the fragile work of memory, which shapes
events to suit the needs of the present. Like most autobiographers,
Franklin consistently improved his story in retrospect, rarely seeing
himself as someone in the wrong, often changing the order of events to
enhance the narrative impact. Forgetfulness is, of course, one of the
great blessings of age, and *The Autobiography of Benjamin Franklin* is a
book of absences and evasions. (For example, the true nature of
Franklin's marriage, such as it was, does not concern him, and he barely
mentions his children. Even his relationship with his parents remains

obscure, although one can read between the lines and realize that problems existed.)

Franklin's schooling ended early, he tells us; the family could simply not afford to educate him formally, despite his obvious intelligence. Young Ben was taken into his father's business, which was that of a "Tallow Chandler and Sope-Boiler" (53). He recalls quite simply: "I dislik'd the Trade and had a strong Inclination for the Sea." He "learnt early to swim well" and spent a lot of time in the water, often teaching others to swim. His father realized that a discontented child might choose to run away to sea (one son, Josiah, had already done so); he therefore took the trouble to introduce his son to a variety of trades, hoping to find one that might interest him. Franklin notes that ever since that time he enjoyed seeing men work at their various trades and liked tinkering with things. "It has been useful to me, having learnt so much by it, as to be able to do little Jobs my self in my House, when a Workman could not readily be got; and to construct little Machines for my Experiments while the Intention of making the Experiment was fresh and warm in my Mind" (57).

From an early age, Franklin read widely, and "all the little Money that came into my Hands was ever laid out in Books" (57). He particularly admired John Bunyan's *Pilgrim's Progress* (1678) and consumed works of history, such as Plutarch's *Lives*—perhaps the first important work of biography—in which the Greek writer recounts the lives of forty-six figures, Greek and Roman, often putting their life stories side by side for comparison. He also read Daniel Defoe, the English novelist, with whom he had much in common as a writer: a frank, clear style and a rather commonsensical approach to life. In many ways, Franklin was a version of Robinson Crusoe, the practical man who pieced his world together from whatever lay at hand.

This bookish quality in young Ben determined his father to put his son to work as a printer, and he apprenticed him to James, his older brother, who had made some headway in that profession. James was nine years Ben's senior, a figure of authority, and a good deal of friction developed between the brothers—again, one must read between the lines to get at such truths. Yet Ben took to the trade, as it had many advantages for a boy of his disposition. The work put him into contact with many booksellers, for example, and this provided access to books;

his taste in reading widened. He soon became close friends with another young man who liked reading, one John Collins, and they happily traded books and opinions. Franklin writes about this and calls attention to his early belief that women should be educated—a point on which Collins strongly disagreed with him. Throughout his life, Franklin strongly supported the rights of women—not an especially popular cause in the eighteenth century. (The rights of his wife were apparently another matter.)

It was during his apprentice years that Franklin encountered the *Spectator*: a popular journal written in London by Joseph Addison and Richard Steele. James Franklin owned a bound set of these papers, and Ben studied them closely. The lucid, familiar style, with its easy elegance and sharp focus, appealed to the young man, who began to model his own prose on these essays. Franklin says, "I thought the Writing excellent, and wish'd if possible to imitate it" (62). He set himself the exercise of imitation and learned to write well in the process. He also took to poetry, although he had no special talent for this genre; the mere attempt to put ideas into verse nevertheless disciplined his mind and enhanced his style, which is known for its economy and precision.

Franklin got up early to read and write, devoting Sundays to these activities, "evading as much as I could the common Attendance on publick Worship" (63). Throughout his life, he avoided churchgoing most of the time and subscribed to no particular creed. This pattern reminds us that he came of age during the Enlightenment, when religious fervor dwindled in intellectual circles. In this, Franklin reminds us (as he did the French) of Voltaire, the towering French skeptic, who considered himself a Deist, embracing a remote, impersonal God who set the universe in motion and stepped back to watch it move. A personal God held no appeal to Franklin. He considered Jesus the finest example of human behavior, a model for people to follow; but nowhere in his voluminous writing did Franklin ever mention the divinity of Jesus. He went through a brief phase of renewed interest in religion in middle age, yet backed away toward the end of his life, opting for a vague Deism. On the other hand, he had nothing against public worship for other people, arguing it was good for society as a whole, as it encouraged moral behavior.

Franklin talks openly about his skeptical nature and his Deism, explaining that as a young man, he studied the works of Shaftesbury and Collins. The Earl of Shaftesbury (1671–1713) was a fierce moralist and religious skeptic, whereas Anthony Collins (1676–1729) was a Deist. Franklin became "a real Doubter in many Points of our Religious Doctrine," he confesses (64). Of course, Franklin fell into step here with many of the other Founding Fathers, who were often Deists and skeptics—a point that seems lost in the twenty-first century, when religious fundamentalists appear determined to blur the line between church and state. This was a line those who founded this nation were determined to hold. Franklin and his fellow Deists would have found many of the politicians of today quite primitive in their literalism, and their theocratic tendencies would have alarmed them.

Franklin's gaze turned firmly toward the world at his feet, and he rarely looked up—except when flying a kite. He was Mr. Fix-It, always trying to improve the gadget in his hands or working to promote the public good. He was practical in the extreme, even when it came to sexual relations. And he was sharply independent as a thinker, with a deep-seated hatred of authority, disdaining those who pulled rank they had failed to earn. His brother's manner of lording it over him, for instance, was more than just an irritant. "I fancy his harsh and tyrannical Treatment of me," writes Franklin, "might be a means of impressing me with that Aversion to arbitrary Power that has stuck to me thro' my whole Life" (69).

Ben ran away from home at seventeen, evading his brother's tyranny. He took off for Philadelphia, where he arrived in a fairly dreadful state of disarray: "I was dirty from my Journey; my Pockets were stuff'd out with Shirts and Stockings; I knew no Soul, nor where to look for Lodging. I was fatigu'd with Travelling, Rowing and Want of Rest. I was very hungry, and my whole Stock of Cash consisted of a Dutch Dollar and about a Shilling in Copper" (75). He ambled up Market Street and glimpsed, in the doorway of one house, the young woman who would later become his common-law wife: Deborah Read. The sight of young Ben with three bread rolls under his arm is one of the most indelible images in American history. In what is an equally unforgettable moment, Franklin gives two of his three rolls away to a woman and her child. This generosity and thoughtfulness was characteristic of the man, who also wanted to be *seen* as generous and thoughtful.

The tale unfolding in this autobiography is the essential American story about a young fellow who comes to town with nothing; by hard work and steadiness of vision he rises in the world, becoming a man of parts. In keeping with this mythic tale, Franklin set about getting a job in a printer's shop, and found one with Samuel Keimer—a well-known figure in the profession in Philadelphia. Ben soon became the most valuable person in this shop and fortified his position by every means available, making himself indispensable. He lodged with John Read, his future father-in-law. "And my Chest and Clothes being come by this time, I made rather a more respectable Appearance in the Eyes of Miss Read, than I had done when she first happen'd to see me eating my Roll in the Street" (79).

A key sentence follows: "I began now to have some Acquaintance among the young People of the Town, that were Lovers of Reading with whom I spent my Evenings very pleasantly and gaining Money by my Industry and Frugality, I lived very agreeably, forgetting Boston as much as I could, and not desiring that any there should know where I resided, except my Friend Collins who was in my Secret, and kept it when I wrote to him" (79). Apart from the run-on thinking, which shifts blithely from topic to topic (mimicking, perhaps, an adolescent turn of mind), the passage contains clues to the author's character. Young Ben had a gregarious nature and attracted interest from others. Soon he found a circle of like-minded friends. They were all "Lovers of Reading," he tells us; in other words, he didn't associate with just anyone, preferring young men on the make, men not unlike himself. This group read books to better themselves, and they formed an inner circle of associates who would help Ben further his career; indeed, the topic quickly shifts to "gaining Money." Franklin wants us to know that he acquired his wealth by "Industry and Frugality." These twin virtues are the cornerstones of his self-edifice.

Franklin worked hard for his success, so he tells us repeatedly—in case we somehow might forget. He came to the shop early and left late. If he accidentally dropped and scattered the letters in his press, he picked them up and started over again, refusing to abandon the shop until a job of work was accomplished. He wasted nothing. And he relied on his cluster of good friends (such as Collins) to keep his secrets and to assist him as needed. Throughout his life he could depend on his circle of friends, which grew impressively wider as the decades passed.

There was often a major patron: someone of considerable wealth or position who spotted the talents of this aggressive young man and pushed him forward in the world. His first crucial patron was Sir William Keith, governor of the province. Keith happened to be shown a letter that Franklin scribbled in his own defense to his brother-in-law, to whom he explained why he had left Boston in such haste, without proper words of goodbye. Keith soon became a sponsor, appearing at Keimer's printing shop to seek out the bright young man who wrote such a good letter. Needless to say, Keimer was jealous of this contact and stared at Franklin "like a Pig poison'd." He could hardly believe the governor had asked young Ben instead of himself to retire to a tavern. Relations with Keimer, as might be expected, declined and continued downhill from that moment. In due course, Franklin abandoned Keimer entirely to establish his own rival firm.

As the tale proceeds, we learn a good deal about Franklin's daily habits and flexible morality. He was mainly a vegetarian at this time, for example, although he could often find a good reason to eat meat or fish if he felt like it. "So convenient a thing it is to be a *reasonable Creature,*" he writes with impish glee, "since it enables one to find or make a Reason for every thing one has a mind to do" (88). This was, after all, the Age of Reason. (One should not for a second doubt that Franklin was thoroughly in command of his image and was more than willing to give the intelligent reader many clues to what lay behind the public image. Indeed, he seems to want us to know him truly, and to love him all the more for whatever we discover.)

"I had made some Courtship during this time to Miss Read," Franklin tells us offhandedly. This was the same woman who first glimpsed young Ben upon his entrance in Philadelphia, bread rolls under his arm. He was attracted to her, and she to him. They would, in due course, marry—after a fashion, in a common-law arrangement. Franklin writes firmly: "I took her to Wife Sept. 1, 1730" (129). This is not literally true, as it suggests a formal ceremony. Instead, they simply moved in together, which at this time was tantamount to declaring themselves married (Deborah was already married, but her husband had disappeared to Barbados and was presumed dead). It was an odd relationship, as Deborah did not like to travel and would never accompany her husband to Europe on his lengthy visits, if indeed he ever invited her along. She spent the last years of her life alone, with Franklin abroad on official business. Their correspondence during this period was matter-of-fact, and Franklin often seems to have willfully ignored her emotional needs. This was perhaps his great, if unacknowledged, erratum.

The relationship with Governor Keith meant everything to Franklin during his first year in Philadelphia, as the governor promised to set him up in business. Keith grandly proposed to send Franklin to London, with letters of credit, to buy fonts and a press for himself. And so, in 1724, the young man boarded a ship for London, although he quickly learned that his patron was fickle, if not utterly unreliable. The governor had not only failed to supply the promised letters of credit; he had no credit to extend. This was an important lesson for the impressionable young man. He could not trust everyone and must always check out the source when offered assistance.

Franklin did not cancel his voyage and soon met another would-be patron aboard ship, a wealthy merchant called Thomas Denham. They became good friends and would stay in touch. Franklin had a travel companion in James Ralph, a dreamy young poet with whom he would soon quarrel over a woman. But this friendship helped him get over the initial transition in England: "Ralph and I were inseparable Companions" (95). While Ralph wasted his time in London, Franklin made his way as a printer with alacrity, working for two well-known printing houses in succession. He also befriended a seller of secondhand books and found opportunities galore for deepening his education. This was, of course, the London of Pope, Swift, Defoe, and Richardson. Huge cultural resources lay at hand, and Ben took advantage of them, attending the theater often, reading widely, engaging in serious conversation with intelligent and well-educated people. The world opened before him in ways that could never have happened in Philadelphia.

But Franklin did miss home. "I was grown tired of London," he writes, contradicting Samuel Johnson, who claimed: "When a man is tired of London he is tired of life." Franklin "remember'd with Pleasure the happy Months" he had spent in Philadelphia and longed to return to that cozy world (105). He was doing well in London, but Denham promised to set him up on his own in Philadelphia, after he had learned the mercantile trade. This was, for such an ambitious young man, an irresistible offer, even if it made little sense for Franklin to change professions at this point in his career.

The relationship with Deborah Read had never been a factor in drawing him back across the Atlantic. In all his time in London he never wrote to her "more than one Letter, and that was to let her know I was not likely soon to return" (96). This was another "erratum," he says, falling back once more upon a printing metaphor. He never "sinned," per se, and would have shrunk from a sermon along the lines of Jonathan Edwards's "Sinners in the Hands of an Angry God." The Deist Franklin could not imagine an angry or vengeful God. His sins were his own problem, reduced to printer's errors. They could be "corrected," as one might correct a typo. And for Franklin, there was always a new edition forthcoming.

In midsummer of 1726, he sailed for the colonies, arriving in early October to find Keith no longer governor; indeed, he passed him in the streets, and his former patron looked aside, in embarrassment. Franklin was now under the spell of Thomas Denham, his new patron, yet the mercantile business faded as a possible occupation, as Franklin must have realized that changing professions entailed a waste of effort. He went back to work for Keimer, whose printing shop he found in disarray. By his own testament, Franklin labored mightily to "put his Printing House in Order" (108). He had a gift for organization and could make order out of chaos if that was required. As before, Keimer proved a difficult boss and tried to force his old apprentice to accept lower wages. He was critical of Ben in a number of ways, which irritated the young man, who considered himself beyond petty criticism. "I went on nevertheless with a good deal of Patience," Franklin informs us (110). Patience was a virtue that he possessed in abundance, and one that served him well. He kept an eye out for his next big chance.

It was not long in coming. One of his friends in the shop, Hugh Meredith, had a moderately wealthy father, and Mr. Meredith liked young Ben, whom he considered a good influence on Hugh. He was willing to set his son up with Franklin in the printing business. A press was expensive, of course, as it had to be imported with an array of type from London, so this was no small offer. Franklin and Meredith worked secretly, behind Keimer's back, to put their plans into action. In the spring of 1728, they were ready to roll, setting up on their own in a shop on Market Street.

Meredith drank heavily, however, and soon abandoned the newly founded press, with Franklin buying out his stake. Through diligence and his network of friends, Franklin established himself as one of the most formidable of printers in the colonies, successful as both printer and publisher, eventually driving Keimer out of business and buying his fledgling newspaper, the *Pennsylvania Gazette*. But in his autobiography, Franklin talks less about his business skills than about his moral development. One can only see his acumen, even his ruthlessness, between the lines.

Part 1 ends abruptly with Franklin setting up the first subscription library on American soil, a major bragging point for him: "This was the Mother of all the American Subscription Libraries now so numerous" (130). It was a secular library, so very different from most libraries in the colonies, which were largely devoted to sermons and theological discourses. Thus Franklin the public servant begins his long and splendid career.

Part 2 was begun thirteen years later—a vast gap. It starts off with a preamble that consists of letters urging Franklin to continue with his memoirs. The reader is thus given to understand that Franklin is doing us a favor by telling his story. Never for a second does he appear to entertain doubts about the legitimacy of his project. His life and ideas about life absorb him fully, as they tend to absorb the reader.

Now he recalls his so-called junto, the circle of like-minded young men who gathered on a regular basis to discuss books and ideas. Franklin occupied the center of this circle. And his business life prospered, to the degree that he soon became the most successful printer in the city. "My Circumstances," he tells us blithely, "grew daily easier." He puts this down to the fact that his "original Habits of Frugality" continued (144). He cites Proverbs 22:29 here: "Seest thou a Man diligent in his Calling, he shall stand before Kings." There is a literal truth here: Franklin, having become a man of considerable importance in the world, would stand before kings in Europe, his head unbowed. This self-confidence, bordering on arrogance, would also become a part of the American character.

Franklin wants us to know exactly how he set about to perfect himself, as a moral creature, and how he did so without recourse to revealed religion. Once again, he explains that he has abandoned traditional forms of worship, preferring a self-devised plan of earthly salvation. "I had been religiously educated as a Presbyterian," he recalls. But "some of the Dogmas of that Persuasion, such as the Eternal Decrees of God, Election, Reprobation, &c. appear'd to me unintelligible, others doubtful, and I early absented myself from the Public Assemblies of the Sect, Sunday being my Studying-Day" (145–46). If Franklin did not have much time for revealed religion, he would nevertheless create a contemplative space for himself on Sundays. During this secular time, he would read and study, determined to improve himself as he saw fit. He drew up his famous list of thirteen virtues, each of which in turn he would attempt to cultivate (149–50).

The list follows:

1. TEMPERANCE. Eat not to Dulness. Drink not to Elevation.
2. SILENCE. Speak not but what may benefit others or yourself. Avoid trifling Conversation.
3. ORDER. Let all your Things have their Places. Let each Part of your Business have its Time.
4. RESOLUTION. Resolve to perform what you ought. Perform without fail what you resolve.
5. FRUGALITY. Make no Expence but to do good to others or yourself: i.e. Waste nothing.
6. INDUSTRY. Lose no Time. Be always employ'd in something useful. Cut off all unnecessary Actions.
7. SINCERITY. Use no hurtful Deceit. Think innocently and justly; and, if you speak, speak accordingly.
8. JUSTICE. Wrong none, by doing Injuries or omitting the Benefits that are your Duty.
9. MODERATION. Avoid Extremes. Forbear resenting Injuries so much as you think they deserve.

10. CLEANLINESS. Tolerate no Uncleanness in Body, Clothes or
    Habitation.
11. TRANQUILITY. Be not disturbed at Trifles, or at Accidents com-
    mon or unavoidable.
12. CHASTITY. Rarely use Venery but for Health or Offspring; Never
    to Dulness, Weakness, or the Injury of your own or another's Peace
    or Reputation.
13. HUMILITY. Imitate Jesus and Socrates.

Franklin planned "to give a Week's strict Attention to each of the
Virtues successively" (151). The idea was to master each virtue by concentrating on it exclusively for a week at a time, much as tennis players
might concentrate on footwork, stance, or a particular shot in perfecting
their game. There is something oddly secular about this list. The Puritan fathers would not have liked what they heard from young Ben. In
Salem, he might have been burned at the stake or at least put in the
stocks for a few days, to reconsider his priorities. Providence plays no
role in Franklin's vision of reality. Jesus and Socrates rub shoulders as
worldly philosophers who preach a form of humility, which Franklin
regards as a virtue mainly because it draws others toward you.

Looked at negatively, Franklin could be regarded as a mercenary,
self-absorbed, even wily figure—a man on the make. There is, to be
sure, a line (however crooked) that runs from Benjamin Franklin
through Horatio Alger (who wrote endless books about heroes who go
from rags to riches) and Dale Carnegie to the sad, pathetic salesman at
the center of Arthur Miller's *Death of a Salesman*. Yet Franklin's secular
approach to morality, conceived as a way of promoting his fortunes in
the world, does have a marvelous aspect, and his attitudes to life have
been palpably influential in America, where everybody wants to "get
ahead" and where self-invention is the rule of the day.

Moderation, silence, and tranquillity are useful traits to cultivate, as
Franklin suggests. One should not be wasteful. One should not overdo
it with alcohol or sex, for any number of good reasons, many of them
having to do with self-preservation. These points notwithstanding,
Franklin was a human being and frequently strayed from his thirteen
virtues. In later years, acquaintances (as noted above) condemned his
slothfulness, his attraction to petty gossip, and his vanity. Yet he consis-

tently set goals and achieved most of them. He was intensely creative, full of energy, self-delighting. If a measure of self-satisfaction creeps into his tone at times, one can easily forgive him. He was always himself, and many have benefited from his innovations and discoveries, and the success of the United States as a political entity owes much to his efforts.

There is a kind of honesty in the *Autobiography* that endears him to the reader, as when he writes: "In Truth I found myself incorrigible with respect to *Order;* and now I am grown old, and my Memory bad, I feel very sensibly the want of it" (156). The thirteenth virtue, humility, was appended later, he tells us, after a Quaker friend informed him that generally he was not regarded as a humble man. Says he, in later life: "I cannot boast of much Success in acquiring the *Reality* of this Virtue; but I had a good deal with regard to the *Appearance* of it" (159). Some disagreed with the latter part of this boast, but one can only enjoy Franklin's attempt to write honestly about himself, and admire his practicality. (Hypocrisy did not worry him in the least.)

Franklin developed his own understanding of what makes a moral man. To his credit, he never lost sight of this conception and often felt himself in "error." He also believed that his plan "might be serviceable to People in all Religions" (157). He was, after all, promoting a kind of secular religion, one with genuine (if dangling) Puritan roots, as in the belief that one should perpetually self-correct and in the core belief in hard work and self-discipline. We still refer to these virtues as "puritanical," often as a way of dismissing them. Yet there is nothing wrong with trying to establish, for oneself, a sense of what virtues are primary, then attempting to live by a system that promotes the cultivation of these virtues.

For the most part, Franklin remained frugal, industrious, temperate, clean, and considerate of others throughout his long life. One of the odd virtues he celebrates is "silence." One does not normally think of this as a virtuous trait. But Franklin rightly discerned that one should, in public meetings especially, avoid excessive talking. He enjoyed gossip among friends, to be sure; but he chose his words carefully when part of any committee, as during the last great triumph of his life, his role at the Constitutional Convention of 1787, where his cool head and considerable reputation mattered and his silences weighed heavily. Thomas Jefferson was present and noted that both Franklin and Washington—the two most illustrious men in attendance—were careful not to intrude. They spoke rarely and judiciously: "I never heard either of them speak ten minutes at a time, nor to any but the main point which was to decide a question. They laid their shoulders to the great points, knowing that the little ones would follow of themselves."[3]

Part 2 is brief, focused mainly on the author's plan for self-improvement. Having discovered some notes from 1731, Franklin took up his memoirs again in 1788. These notes dealt with his habits of reading, and some concerned his Deism. After careful deliberation, Franklin came around to the idea that the individual soul was eternal and that God should be worshipped. He believed strongly that "the most acceptable Service of God is doing Good to Man" (162). In this, he moves far from the Pauline idea of justification by faith, preferring the idea (put forward most famously in the Epistle of James) that good works are the way to salvation. Franklin (perhaps a little in jest) proposed getting young men to agree to his "religion" and put his list of thirteen virtues into practice. He writes: "I have always thought that one Man of tolerable Abilities may work great Changes, and accomplish great Affairs among Mankind, if he first forms a good Plan, and, cutting off all Amusements or other Employments that would divert his Attention, makes the Execution of that same Plan his sole Study and Business" (163).

Franklin now begins to recount his successes, which include the publication of *Poor Richard's Almanack* (1732, first issue). This series made him wealthy and famous, although he conceived of it as a means of educating the public in the virtues of hard work and frugality, moderation, and good sense. He also writes about the *Pennsylvania Gazette,* another instrument for educating the public in the Franklin religion. He writes: "In the Conduct of my Newspaper I carefully excluded all Libelling and Personal Abuse, which is of late Years become so disgraceful to our Country" (165). One can only imagine what Franklin would have thought of our current crop of press barons.

Franklin recalls his support for the education of women: a subject on which, for his time, he was advanced in his thinking. (It's worth remembering, perhaps, that many of our best colleges in the United States, such as Dartmouth, refused to admit women students until the early 1970s. Franklin would, I suspect, have been appalled to learn it would take so long for women to get a foothold in the academic village.)

As many have noticed, Franklin rarely talks about anything personal, topics that might have provoked strong emotions. One finds only a glancing allusion to the death of his son Francis in 1736—a shattering event for him. The boy died from smallpox, and Franklin "regretted bitterly" his own failure to inoculate the child against this horrendous disease. After this, he was a leading proponent of inoculation and felt compelled to print a piece in his newspaper saying that his boy had died from smallpox itself, not from an inoculation—a false rumor that had spread through the community, much to Franklin's dismay.

Among the achievements Franklin mentions in Part 3 are his work toward establishing a City Watch (in effect, a police department) and "a Company for the more ready Extinguishing of Fires" (174). Observing the lack of a college for advanced studies, he "drew up a Proposal for establishing an Academy" (182). Apparently one of the most satisfying of his accomplishments was his work in helping to erect a public hospital in Philadelphia for the "Cure of poor sick Persons" (199). Franklin used his newspaper to solicit contributions. Among the many inventions he writes about here is the Franklin stove, which vastly improved on earlier technology (although the stove that bears his name is a much simplified version of the original design, which proved too elaborate to work as efficiently as its inventor had hoped). Interestingly, Franklin refused to take out a patent on this stove, although one was offered. It was so with many of his inventions. He felt "no Desire of profiting by Patents my self" (192). The public good came before his personal wealth. In this, he differs markedly from most entrepreneurs of today. Throughout his long life, Franklin worked to benefit his neighbors, and that was enough for him. He felt no need to increase his personal fortune beyond a certain point.

Uncharacteristically taken by modesty, Franklin says relatively little about his scientific experiments in the field of electricity, even though later scientists, such as J. J. Thomson (who discovered the electron), would argue that his experiments "can hardly be overestimated." As his biographer Walter Isaacson writes: "He was one of the foremost scien-

tists of his age, and he conceived and proved one of the most fundamental concepts about nature: that electricity is a single fluid."[4] Franklin
does, however, note that both Harvard and Yale gave him honorary degrees for his scientific work, referring to his experiments "on the Same-
ness of Lightning with Electricity" in passing, mainly to establish that
he was indeed taken seriously as a scientist in England and France (242).
One wishes Franklin had chosen to give readers a more detailed and
personal account of his famous encounter with lightning. As it stands,
most historians rely on the verbal account he gave to his friend Joseph
Priestley, the English inventor and experimental physicist, who
recorded these details in *The History and Present State of Electricity*
(1767).

Part 3 ends with a haphazard account of Franklin's journey to London on behalf of the Pennsylvania Assembly—a diplomatic mission that
lasted some five years. But the account quickly becomes absorbed in the
physics of hull construction, which began to fascinate the author on his
outbound transatlantic journey. "This is the Age of Experiments," he
writes boldly (257). He briefly describes various experiments he under-
took on the aerodynamics of sailing. Apparently nothing fell beyond his
curiosity, and he never worried about being an expert before attempting
an experiment or pursuing a line of inquiry. If anything, this is the underlying message of his memoir. Anything and everything absorbed
Benjamin Franklin, and he moved through the world with staggering
self-confidence, willing to take risks, even to make a fool of himself.

Part 4 is extremely brief, consisting of a limited account of Franklin's
activities in London on behalf of the assembly. After a few pages, it trails
off into an outline, as Franklin hoped one day to complete this account
of his life and work. It never happened, as he lost interest in the book,
and it lay about in different manuscripts. It was published posthumously—in a truncated form, in 1793, three years after Franklin's
death. The wayward journey of the manuscript toward publication—
in various editions—would fill a small volume by itself, as I suggest
above.

IV.

THE POSTHUMOUS CAREER of Benjamin Franklin was inextricably linked to this *Autobiography,* in which the canny author presents a version of himself for posterity to judge. This work remains foundational, in part because the American character itself—as self-delighting, self-inventing—can be traced to Franklin's portrait of himself. Needless to say, many readers would dislike the secular nature of this book and Franklin's blunt refusal to accept class norms. A revolutionary fervor courses through the book, which might be considered a primer of American democratic values.

Franklin was no aristocrat; indeed, he belonged to the leather apron set and remained a hardworking tradesman until middle age, never losing interest in the printing profession. He was a democrat to the bone, rejecting all forms of autocratic government, leaping over class barriers with impunity. As noted earlier, he played a key role at the Constitutional Convention and rejected the idea of a strong presidency, preferring an executive council. He greatly feared what might happen if the wrong man became president and used the considerable power at his disposal in ways contrary to the will of the people. He warned against tyranny, which he believed would almost certainly follow at some point, given what he regarded as flaws in the Constitution.

Franklin preferred a more direct democracy and generally opposed those elements in the Constitution that diluted this spirit. For instance, he opposed a bicameral legislature, believing that the Senate (as constituted by the convention) would have too much power in its hands and could subvert the more democratic House. But his suggestions fell mostly on deaf ears. He was treated with great respect, yet some regarded him as a bumbling old man by this time.

The American people certainly admired, even revered, Franklin. Even his critics, such as John Adams, wrote highly nuanced appreciations of the man after his death. Here was a true hero of the Enlightenment, the American equivalent of Voltaire. But with the coming of the Romantic period, in the early nineteenth century, harsher criticisms of Franklin appeared. John Keats, the English poet, decried his "thrifty maxims." In 1855, Herman Melville made fun of him in *Israel Potter,* a novel. Even Ralph Waldo Emerson, who owed a good deal to Franklin in his essay "Self-Reliance," expressed doubts, writing that "Franklin's man is a frugal, inoffensive, thrifty citizen." To a degree, this was all true; but such a description of Franklin hardly takes the full measure of the man.

Perhaps the most vicious assault on Franklin, as he portrayed himself in his autobiography, came from D. H. Lawrence, in his influential study of classic American literature, which appeared in 1923. Lawrence, a neo-Romantic, could hardly tolerate the figure of young Ben, with his list of thirteen virtues. "Benjamin had no concern, really, with the immortal soul," Lawrence complains. He puts forward his own idiosyncratic reason for hating Franklin: "I'm not going to be turned into a virtuous little automaton as Benjamin would have me . . . He tries to take away my wholeness and my dark forest, my freedom." This is rather mad, and perhaps beside the point; but Lawrence has an interesting take.

Franklin is certainly never dark, nor does he plumb the depths of human experience. Instead, he stays close to the surface of life, tinkering with gadgets, improving everything around him as well as he can. He avoids feelings and does not despair or fret over his sins, any of the little "errata" that crop up in the text of his life. One can easily see why such prophetic writers as Emerson and Lawrence turned away from him, and why the young Jay Gatz (who became Jay Gatsby in F. Scott Fitzgerald's shimmering novel) adopted him as a model of systematic self-invention.

Nevertheless, Franklin demands a good deal from those who follow in his splashy wake. I suspect we could all benefit from attention to his list of virtues and measure ourselves against his fierce concern for the welfare of those around him. We might ask if we really do believe in democracy as passionately as he did. In raising such issues, Franklin remains our contemporary, a man who asks us to do more than we can. He suggests that we try to improve the lot of our neighbors, whom we must treat as we would have ourselves be treated. In this, Franklin seems more of a Christian than most, and surely more than many who make huge claims for themselves in this regard.

Franklin's clear-eyed, humane, and positive tone—as adopted in his memoirs—is always a tonic, an inspiration to move forward boldly and deliberately in the world. Common sense and good cheer remain his touchstones. It did not surprise me when, some years ago, I heard that *The Autobiography of Benjamin Franklin* was among the few books that Davy Crockett kept beside him during the final siege at the Alamo. I, too, would want Ben beside me in such dire circumstances.

THE

JOURNAL

OF

LEWIS AND CLARKE,

TO THE MOUTH OF THE COLUMBIA RIVER
BEYOND THE ROCKY MOUNTAINS.

IN THE YEARS 1804—5, & 6.

GIVING A FAITHFUL DESCRIPTION OF THE RIVER MISSOURI
AND ITS SOURCE—OF THE VARIOUS TRIBES OF INDIANS
THROUGH WHICH THEY PASSED—MANNERS AND CUS-
TOMS—SOIL—CLIMATE—COMMERCE—GOLD AND
SILVER MINES—ANIMAL AND VEGETABLE
PRODUCTIONS, &c.

NEW EDITION, WITH NOTES.

REVISED, CORRECTED, AND ILLUSTRATED WITH NUMEROUS
WOOD CUTS.

TO WHICH IS ADDED

A COMPLETE DICTIONARY OF THE INDIAN TONGUE.

DAYTON, O.

PUBLISHED AND SOLD BY D. F. ELLS.

JOHN WILSON, PRINTER.

....

1840.

FOUR

The Journals of Lewis and Clark

I.

WHAT *THE JOURNALS OF LEWIS AND CLARK* has meant to the American people has shifted constantly since a copy of this voluminous work arrived on the desk of President Thomas Jefferson, who had shown a keen interest in exploring the West for many years. Jefferson had personally commissioned Captain Lewis, his private secretary, to form an expedition that would explore the vast territory recently added to the United States by the Louisiana Purchase, and to push westward to the Pacific—ostensibly in search of a trade route through the Northwest and to collect scientific (geographical and botanical) information about the region.

The *Journals*—a rich trove of descriptive material and narrative interest—found an audience of readers eager to learn about this newly acquired territory. Westward expansion, this "land vaguely realizing westward" that Robert Frost wrote about in "The Gift Outright," still lay ahead, but not far ahead. Expansion to the Pacific fired the imaginations of many within the seventeen states already part of the United States, and Lewis and Clark provided the raw data for a systematic occupation of the West. They proved beyond doubt that this wilderness was not only passable but wonderfully rich in natural resources. All manner of wildlife could be found there. It boasted teeming forests, where furs, pelts, and timber could be culled.

The *Journals* mirrors the journey itself, forming a kind of parallel excursion in language. It galvanized the attention of a nation eager for information about its newly acquired territories, offering a treasury of material that moves well beyond a mere record of the physical and social geography of the regions "discovered." Both Lewis and Clark keenly observed and described the plants and animals, the birds, the people— and their ecology. They sketched images of animals, plants, examples of Indian crafts and tribal costumes. Clark himself drew remarkable maps. In all, the *Journals* represents a thrilling and humanly complex adventure that never loses its fascination.

As the reach of American power in the twenty-first century continues to grow, benevolently or less so, there is every reason to reconsider Lewis and Clark, who provided excellent models in their modesty and shrewd application of intelligence to the world as they discovered it on their westward travels. Certainly the American character itself was affected by the heroic efforts of these adventurers, who inspired two centuries of explorers, including Neil Armstrong and Buzz Aldrin, the astronauts who landed their lunar module on the moon in 1969.

II.

MERIWETHER LEWIS (1774–1809) and William Clark (1770– 1838) took daily notes, which they later transferred into bound journals kept in tin boxes for preservation from the elements. Occasionally Lewis or Clark would write directly into the journals. In any case, the final results are fluent, vivid, detailed, and descriptive. They conduct the willing reader along the trail, over eight thousand miles, beginning in St. Louis in 1804, then moving along the Missouri River to a winter camp in what is now North Dakota, continuing on through spring over the Continental Divide with marvelous new guides and translators: Toussaint Charbonneau (a Canadian trapper) and his Shoshone bride, Sacagawea. This group of about forty men and one woman made their way by horseback and canoe down various rivers to the mouth of the Columbia on the Pacific coast. After wintering out in what is now Oregon, they returned as heroes to St. Louis, arriving in late September 1806.

The *Journals* found an audience greedy for information about this wilderness wonderland, with its exotic birds and animals, its thrilling landscapes, and its native people. The exploits of the Corps of Discovery helped to whip up enthusiasm for the acquisition of the Oregon Territory and settlement of the West. The eventual shape of the United States began to dawn on Americans who could suddenly imagine what it might mean for the country to own the entire continent, coast to coast. (The concept of Manifest Destiny would arise later in the century, following naturally from the tentative beginnings of westward expansion.) Lewis and Clark also provided a model for how to deal with the Native American population—through a show of strength that combined with it a genuine interest in their customs and concerns.

For the most part, the Corps enjoyed peaceful relations with the various tribes they encountered along the way and came to rely on them for help. They actually could never have completed their arduous trip without the Indians, who fed and sheltered them and provided horses and information about the route. A model of interdependence between invader and invaded was thus established (not dissimilar to that seen in the Plymouth Colony nearly two centuries before), although others would sadly destroy this model in the decades to come. The appalling violence that later marked our westward expansion continues to boil up and disfigure our emotional landscape.

Countless versions of the *Journals* were published in the nineteenth and twentieth centuries. Within a few years of the completion of the journey, excerpts were included in various accounts of the expedition. The *Journals,* as edited by Nicholas Biddle, came out in 1814, although this was a much abbreviated version, cutting out many of the botanical and zoological observations for which Lewis and Clark have become famous. Editions followed in London in 1815 and Dublin in 1817. Translations appeared as well, including a well-known Dutch version in 1816. Between 1904 and 1906, Reuben Gold Thwaites brought out a comprehensive edition of the *Journals,* and this was revised by Gary Moulton's landmark edition in thirteen volumes—the definitive version, still in print.

The shape of the *Journals* has shifted from generation to generation, often reflecting current interests and concerns. In 1953, for instance, Bernard De Voto published a popular selection. At this time, the *Journals* spoke clearly to a Cold War audience—a readership with concerns about American power in the wake of World War II. The journey of Lewis and Clark became a story of American power triumphant against the odds. (This edition remains the most accessible version in print today.) More recently, the *Journals* has spoken to an audience in search of early models for nature writing. And there is no doubt that Lewis and Clark rank high among our naturalists, standing beside Audubon or Thoreau as patient recorders of a varied and abundant landscape, with its profuse flora and fauna. To those interested in our Native American heritage, the *Journals* also provides invaluable information.

The original journals (housed at the American Philosophical Society, in Philadelphia) comprise eighteen small notebooks—typical of those used by surveyors in the early nineteenth century. Thirteen are bound in red morocco leather, while four are covered in marbled boards and one in brown leather. They remain a magnificent literary achievement. The style of the poetic, often moody Lewis blended well with the more level-headed and scientific approach of Clark. (Clark himself kept separate journals, now owned by the Missouri Historical Society.) Several companions of Lewis and Clark (including Patrick Gass, Joseph Whitehouse, John Ordway, and Charles Floyd) also kept diaries, the most famous being that by Gass, first published in 1807, and therefore the first impression of the journey itself to reach the eyes of readers.

In a letter of June 20, 1803, Thomas Jefferson wrote to his friend and former secretary Meriwether Lewis, who was about to lead an official expedition into the Louisiana Territory and beyond: "The object of your mission is to explore the Missouri River, & such principal streams of it as by its course and communication with the water of the Pacific ocean whether the Columbia, Oregon, Colorado or any other river may offer the most direct & practicable water communication across this continent for the purposes of commerce."

Commerce was in fact a primary reason for opening a route between the Atlantic and the Pacific. It had long been a dream of Jefferson's. As early as 1783, he had tried to persuade the explorer George Rogers Clark to visit the western territories. As secretary of state under George Washington, he had attempted to mount an expedition, although this failed for political reasons: the United States might well provoke an international incident by such an adventure. When he became president, in 1801, Jefferson's mind returned to the notion. A man of intense curiosity about the world, he wondered about the specifics of western geography. He would have realized that current maps were more fantasy than fact. But there were other reasons as well for hoping to pursue this project of exploration.

At the turn of the nineteenth century, the Spanish and the British had traders on the ground, and both would have liked access to the immense wealth that lay west of the Mississippi. The idea that this upstart, fledgling republic should control such a massive region was unthinkable, except by the Americans themselves, who understood that their power (and sense of security) would grow exponentially if they could extend their sovereignty westward. The Louisiana Purchase, of course, made this expedition all the more pressing and exciting.

Louisiana and its capacious territory had belonged to Spain during the American Revolution; as such, the territory offered a minimal threat to the new republic. Spain was, at best, a lethargic giant that had not aggressively explored or developed its possession (it had acquired the territory from France in 1762, in compensation for Spanish losses as France's ally in the Seven Years' War). The Treaty of San Ildefonso (1800), which brought Louisiana into French hands, again was all part of Napoleon's expansive vision: the emperor wished to restore the French Empire in North America, although this idea unnerved Americans, who could not happily entertain the notion of having a major empire on their western flank.

Fortunately for Jefferson, the French colonizers got bogged down in the Caribbean, where the army had been sent to Santo Domingo to recapture the island (now divided between Haiti and the Dominican Republic) from Toussaint-Louverture, the upstart black rebel. Yellow fever thinned the European invaders to a ragged, ineffectual force. With French power thus seriously compromised in the New World, Napoleon decided to focus on Europe. He agreed to sell the entire Louisiana region to the United States, in part to keep the British from marching in and controlling this territory. It was into this favorable situation that James Monroe stepped when he arrived in Paris (in theory) to negotiate trade rights on the Mississippi and, perhaps, to purchase New Orleans and its immediate environs. Monroe joined his colleague Robert R. Livingston (the American ambassador to France), whom he found already in conversation about acquiring the whole of Louisiana—a geographical territory larger than the thirteen former colonies combined.

One can hardly imagine the magnitude of the Louisiana Purchase. In a single stroke, the United States doubled its size, annexing a region of astonishing (if undetermined) value, as anyone could guess. Except in the minds of the British, who continued to hope for influence in North America, it now seemed obvious that the United States would eventually control the entire continent of North America—an assumption already in place in most diplomatic circles. Security was the primary issue for Americans. Now it would forever be guaranteed, and American power in the world would issue from this solid core. Our history and psychology as a nation would have been wildly different had we not rather miraculously, and peaceably, come into possession of this territory. And it took *The Journals of Lewis and Clark* to make its extent and interest clear to the American people.

Lewis and Clark kept a close eye on the lucrative trade in fur and pelts, which had thus far been cornered by the North West Company. This group had already explored the Canadian west, developing the beaver trade along the Saskatchewan and Athabaska rivers and extending its influence into the Arctic while pushing to the south as well. Among the explorers working for this company was Alexander Mackenzie, who had tried for some years to find a path to the Pacific along water routes. In 1793, he had managed to get to the Pacific along a sequence of waterways that had little commercial value because they involved long and difficult portages. But Mackenzie had carved a place for himself in history, being the first white man to make it to the Pacific (north of Mexico) since Cabeza de Vaca in 1536. Mackenzie still hoped to return to the West and to stake a claim to the Columbia River for Britain (although an American ship, *Columbia,* had previously found the river and named it in 1792, under Captain Robert Gray).

This complicated history lies behind the journey of Lewis and Clark, who had any number of reasons to propel them westward. They had one clear and luminous goal: to find the fabled Northwest Passage. Such a route would have inestimable commercial value, connecting the United States with the maritime trade on the Pacific. To the south, the Spanish and the French competed for this trade, while to the north the British Canadians did their best to exert influence. Pressure came from all sides, even from within, as Lewis and Clark could hardly deny the presence of major tribal nations, each of them with legitimate claims to the territory. In short, this was no innocent walk in the wilderness. The journey cut its way through a complex political wilderness as well.

One must keep in mind that geographical understanding was severely limited in 1804. For a very long time it had been assumed that the Missouri led to a western river and that only a brief portage was required to reach the Columbia. In 1765, Robert Rogers had proposed a journey from the headwaters of the Mississippi to the Oregon River. He assumed (based on no real information) that a portage of about 20 miles linked the two rivers. The fact that the Rocky Mountains got in the way did not factor into his calculations. Although Mackenzie had crossed the Rockies, a true knowledge of the difficulties they presented had yet to enter the popular imagination. As Clark would note in his journal entry for February 14, 1806, the 20 or so miles that everyone had predicted for a land traverse amounted to some 220 miles. And those were not easy miles.

Lewis was twenty-nine in 1803, and Clark thirty-three. They were old friends and former comrades. Both were professional soldiers, and Clark himself had some experience of the various Indian tribes. They knew the challenges and delights of the wilderness, and came to this expedition with excitement, prepared for its rigors and ready to grapple with them. That they shared leadership of the Corps equally is itself remarkable, although Lewis had a natural tendency to lead and Clark to follow, and this affected the nature of their command. Yet the two worked together well, and their example remains a singular one, unique in the annals of exploration.

Lewis was somewhat dreamy by nature, but he fully understood the diplomatic and commercial implications of this journey. Clark was more practical, the sort of man who took control of day-to-day operations, negotiating with his men as well as with the Indians encountered along the way. Lewis had a mind for the details of botany and zoology, and his talent as a naturalist informs the *Journals* at every stage. Clark had a better than adequate knowledge of geography and topography, and he was also a gifted outdoorsman. Both men were skilled with boats, although Clark outshone Lewis in this area. As a result, responsibility for the boats fell mainly on the shoulders of Clark. Lewis was, by temperament, subject to bouts of anger and depression; Clark was a steadier and more practical fellow who often had to calm his mercurial comrade. But the combination of their talents worked well.

The expedition proceeded with unusual calm and deliberation—a sign of competence and experience in wilderness travel. The Corps faced impossible terrain at times (jagged peaks, dense forests) as well as perilous waters, extremes of climate, and periods of near starvation (as in the Bitterroots). A few crises occurred, but only one member of the expedition, Charles Floyd, died along the way, probably from a ruptured appendix—something nobody in those days could do anything about. Over twenty-eight months of arduous travel, covering eight thousand miles, the expedition held together, physically and emotionally.

This expedition easily ranks as one of the most astonishing of journeys ever taken in North America, and this classic account (in any one of its various incarnations and selections) remains unparalleled as a report of its progress. The writing is clear, clean, and swift—like a brook that bristles in a field. Its abundant pages contain a few moments of introspective speculation (always by Lewis); for the most part, however, the journals offer a matter-of-fact record of the physical and human geography encountered along the way. *The Journals of Lewis and Clark* has long been a resource for Americans, who admire both leaders of this expedition for their practicality and professionalism. Their journey (and journal) of exploration becomes ours as well: a way into the wilderness, and a way home.

III.

THE CORPS OF DISCOVERY would vary in number, made up mostly of soldiers, including four sergeants (John Ordway, Nathaniel Pryor, and Charles Floyd, with Patrick Gass later elevated to this rank), a corporal, and twenty-nine privates. Pierre Cruzatte and Francois Labiche came along as expert boatmen, and George Drewyer was a professional hunter. York was a black servant who accompanied Clark.

(Whether or not York was a "slave" exactly seems open to interpretation, although he behaved like one.) A contingent of fifteen men accompanied the expedition only as far as the Mandan villages along the upper Missouri—a last point of civilization before the wilderness began in earnest; they had been hired to carry supplies and help to repel (potential) attacks from Indians. The party—led by Clark alone at first—set off from Camp Dubois in St. Louis in three boats on May 14, 1804. The lead boat was an impressive keelboat of fifty-five feet. It drew three feet of water and had a sail as well as oars and boasted a small cabin and forecastle. The other boats were smaller and could be rowed or sailed as well. Two horses followed the party along the banks. For the most part, the swift current and the sails moved the party along quite nicely. But rowing was often necessary. In the most difficult stretches, men on the shore dragged the boats forward: this unpleasant work was called "cordelling." The expedition would average anywhere from ten to fifteen miles per day.

"I Set out at 4 oClock P.M., in the presence of many of the neighbouring inhabitents, and proceeded on under a jentle brease up the Missouri to the upper Point of the 1st Island 4 Miles and camped on the Island which is Situated Close on the right (or Starboard) Side, and opposit the mouth of a Small Creek called Cold water," writes Captain Clark (3).[1] As with Lewis, he uses quaint and variable spelling (a typical habit before spelling had settled into conformity). Capital letters appear randomly, although occasionally for emphasis. The punctuation is erratic, with odd spacing between the letters at times—as would be natural in any journal. (I use normal spacing when quoting from the *Journals,* except where it seems obvious that the spacing is a kind of punctuation itself, useful for isolating clusters of words, much as a poet might do.)

The journey got under way properly when Lewis and his contingent joined up in St. Charles, a day later. The surging stream nearly overwhelmed the boats on May 21. The men camped "at the mouth of a Creek called River a Chouritte, above a Small french Village of 7 houses and as many families" (5). The spot mentioned is La Charrette, as we now spell it. It so happens that Daniel Boone, the famous pioneer, lived nearby, at the mouth of the Femme Osage River. He was now seventy and a legend among pioneers, although Lewis and Clark either were unaware of his presence or did not think it worth mentioning. Certainly no effort was made to contact him.

Here the Corps set about trading with the local Indians and hunting in the woods. George Drewyer proved his worth at once: he was fearless, astoundingly gifted as a hunter and woodsman, and the expedition came to rely on him for meat. He and a few others remained onshore, with the horses, and they would frequently go off by themselves for days in search of game. His adventures form almost a parallel journey to that of the Corps. Lewis and Clark frequently allude to his heroics, which seemed to amuse and fascinate them.

Early in the journey, Clark (who had practical command of the men) exerted his authority by singling out two of his company for drunkenness and disorderly conduct. They were subjected to lashings—a common form of punishment at this time. This demonstration of power worked its magic, and there was little in the way of insubordination on this expedition. As it were, Clark meticulously removed the sentences referring to these lashings from the journal at a later date, aware that many eyes would eventually read his words (although others on the journey kept journals, too). A few of the men would misbehave in minor ways, stealing whiskey and getting drunk on watch, but such incidents were rare, considering that these were young men under immense pressure.

The *Journals* ferries us along the Dubois River to the Platte. Clark's account takes the form of shorthand as he notes various problems along the way, such as snags and high winds. Clark alludes to the "Kansas Nation" of Indians, most of whom were "now out in the plains hunting Buffalow" (6). One gets the sense from these entries that the wilderness along the river teems with human life: French settlers, Canadian traders, Indians from different tribes. For the most part, the Indians remain out of sight, although Clark feels their presence when he writes about their paintings and carvings on limestone rocks. (Here I thought of *Heart of Darkness,* Joseph Conrad's novel about a journey along the Congo River into the bush, enclosed by a jungle where natives lurk ominously, glimpsed more than encountered from aboard the narrator's steamer. In Conrad, however, the native population terrifies the narrator, and the bush threatens—a place beyond rational comprehension. Clark does not seem especially frightened by the dense woodlands or his glimpses of Indian life; he is, if anything, curious about the native people along the river and their habits.)

A number of men in the Corps kept diaries, and they concur on one point: the Missouri was a startling and beautiful river. The landscape captivated them. They simply brushed off, quite literally, the endless mosquitoes and ticks, which Clark describes as "noumerous & bad." As one might expect on the Missouri in high summer, the weather offered a challenge, intermittently blazing and wet. The rains were almost tropical, switching on suddenly like a shower, driving hard, then clearing miraculously. Bouts of muggy heat overwhelmed the Corps at times, and cases of sunstroke and heatstroke had to be dealt with.

Clark remains the diarist through summer, offering a meticulous account of everything that breaks into view: "The River meandering the open and butifull Plains, interspursed with Groves of timber, and each point Covered with Tall timber, Such as Willow Cotton sum Mulberry, Elm, Sucamore Lynn [probably linden] & ash (The Groves contain Hickory, Walnut, coffee nut & Oake in addition)" (14). This is typical of Clark, the hard-core naturalist. He is specific and unemotional, though aware of the majesty of his surroundings. There are animals on view as well, such as the badger described as a "French Brarow," a creature who "Burrows in the Ground and feeds on Flesh, Prairie Dogs Bugs & Vigatables." This animal's unusual features are detailed: "His Shape & Size is like that of a Beaver, his head mouth etc is like a Dogs with Short Ears, his Tail and Hair like that of a Ground Hog, and longer; and lighter" (15). Clark's description continues at length.

The party met various Indians, including six who were chieftains. "Capt. Lewis & myself met those Indians & informed them we were glad to see them" (16). Speeches were made, gifts exchanged, and warm feelings arose. Even the air seemed congenial—an important point at a time when medical opinion held that diseases such as typhoid and malaria were airborne. "The air is pure and helthy so far as we can judge," writes Clark, after talking about the Indians for some time. In this case, the weather itself becomes a metaphor; the atmosphere was healthy, *as far as Lewis and Clark could judge.* The implication, not spelled out, was that trouble lay ahead. But they managed to hold their fear in abeyance, putting an example of courage before their men.

Problems abounded, but they were minor. In early August, there was a desertion. Private Moses Reed simply took off with one of the boat crew, abandoning the expedition. On August 19 the illness of Sergeant Floyd brought everything to a standstill: "all attention to him" (21). Mercifully, he died within a few days and was buried near the top of a hill overlooking the river, near what is now Sioux City, Iowa (a monument still marks the spot). As noted above, this was the single fatality along the way. In this respect, one must consider the members of the Corps amazingly lucky in their good health, especially as the threat of infection was considerable in this period, long before the advent of antibiotics. The smallest abrasion could rapidly turn lethal.

By the end of August, the Corps approached one of their goals: the Sioux nation. This tribe (which had various branches) had been driven west by the Chippewa, yet were quite strong and warlike. They controlled the Missouri on the approach to the Mandan settlement, where British fur traders had established a lucrative business. President Jefferson wanted very much for Lewis and Clark to make contact with the Sioux and to see if anything could be done about the interruption of trade on this valuable stretch of the river. They met up with the Sioux near the James River. The Yankton Sioux, as they were called, welcomed the Americans and seemed agreeably disposed to make peace. (The Teton Sioux were much less amenable to peacemaking, but they still lay ahead.)

The *Journals* becomes intensely anthropological at this point, as both Clark and Lewis report on the language and customs, the tribal outfits, weapons, eating habits, and religious beliefs of the Indians. To this day, these reports remain invaluable to historians and anthropologists. Whenever Lewis steps in as diarist, as on September 17, 1804, the writing becomes more fluent and digressive. Lewis reminds one of Hemingway at times, writing with clarity and force about the natural world. The long entry for this warm day at the end of summer begins: "Having for many days past confined myself to the boat, I determined to devote this day to amuse myself on shore with my gun and view the interior of the country lying between the river and the Corvus Creek" (28). The scenery was "rich pleasing and beautiful." This entry proceeds like a story, accumulating detail, building to the point where the hunter-narrator finds "the Antelope extremely shye and watchfull." He views a herd in the distance, amazed by their magical, almost ghostly presence: "I beheld the rapidity of their flight along the ridge before me." One gets a deep sense of Lewis, the hunter as writer, his eye trained on the object with peculiar intensity, a vision unfolding.

In late September the narrative quickens as the Corps meets up with the much fiercer Indians of the upper Missouri (a mix of Teton Sioux, Omaha, and Arikara), who had been plaguing French and Spanish traders for some time, often stealing their goods and roughing them up. Lewis and Clark understood what they would have to do in order to exert authority: present a bold front, and frighten them. Clark suffered many nights of bad sleep, as he notes on September 27. The tension builds, and a confrontation occurs. It seemed crucial for American sovereignty that the Corps should remain unperturbed and unmolested. Fortunately, the Indians refused to fight, despite their larger numbers; they preferred classic guerrilla tactics anyway, as their later encounters with the white settlers would suggest.

In mid-October, another member of the expedition was given seventy-five lashes for insubordination—the last time this would happen on the trip. An Indian chief witnessed this whipping, and he cried aloud at the sight of it. Clark notes with some astonishment that "his nation never whiped even their Children, from their burth" (51). Word may have spread among the Sioux that these American explorers did not mess about and that a violent streak ran through them. In any case, the Corps had no trouble along this stretch of the Missouri from the Indians, who remained cool but not unfriendly.

The company would pass the winter among the Mandan Indians, near what is currently Stanton, North Dakota. The Hidatsa tribe lived nearby, along the Knife River. These were sedentary tribes who built imposing structures from cottonwood logs, which they sank into the ground and covered with earthen roofs. Their population had dwindled in recent decades, afflicted by disease (usually smallpox) and the attrition of endless wars with the larger, more belligerent Sioux nation. Lewis and Clark imitated the Mandan lodges in building Fort Mandan, where they aggressively set about creating a store of food for the coming winter months. The construction work continued through much of November. Wisely, they began the wintering process early, as "Ice began to run in the river" on Tuesday morning of November 13. Three days later, at dawn, Clark saw "a verry white forest all the trees all covered with ice" (65).

The huts they built for themselves were "situated in a point of low ground" on the north side of the Missouri, "covered with tall and heavy cottonwood" (66). The Corps duly set about getting "fresh meat" and welcomed the Indians into their fort, feeding them, getting to know them. This was all part of the careful work of diplomacy that marks relations between the Corps and the various tribes they encountered. "We gave them assurances that we would protect them from all their enemies," Clark writes (67). In effect, he established an American presence along this part of the Missouri, saying: We will protect you if you accept our sovereignty. It was, for the Indians, a devil's bargain. The way of life they had followed for centuries was, for the first time, under threat.

Snows arrived in late November, over a foot deep. When Sioux warriors attacked the Mandans on November 30, the Corps—as promised—came to their aid. Clark writes: "The Indians not expecting to receive Such Strong aide in So Short a time was much supprised and a littled allarmed at the formadable appearence of my party" (70). He refers to the Mandans explicitly as "our dutifull Children." This paternalistic and patronizing tone was consistent with the general approach of Europeans to Native American people, whom they considered inferior and childlike, in need of a firm and fatherly hand.

In the *Journals,* Lewis and Clark make relatively little of the fact that their party now added to their ranks a mercurial French-Canadian trapper, Toussaint Charbonneau, and his intelligent sixteen-year-old wife, Sacagawea, a member of the Shoshone tribe. Sacagawea had been captured from her own tribe in the Rocky Mountains by Hidatsa warriors at the age of eleven and brought to a trading post on the Knife River, where she met Charbonneau. Charbonneau and Sacagawea in due course became major figures on the journey, and without them it seems probable that the expedition would not have succeeded as well as it did. On February 11, 1805, Sacagawea gave birth to an infant son, Jean Baptiste (later called Pomp). Lewis draws a brief but memorable description of this birth, including the fact that he offered "a small portion of the rattle of a rattlesnake" as medicine to hasten the birth. It apparently worked. That this infant actually traveled with the Corps seems almost unimaginable, although Lewis and Clark were unperturbed by his presence, which they simply took for granted. (Clark grew so attached to the child that he later paid for his education in St. Louis.)

The main task for winter, apart from survival itself in harsh and unfamiliar territory, was to gather information about tribal life in the upper Missouri. Lewis mainly attended to this work and kept separate notebooks, which he drew upon to make an independent report to the U.S. Congress on behalf of his friend and patron, Thomas Jefferson. This was anthropological work of a fairly high order, and the subsequent report remains useful for historians. On his own, Clark compiled notes on the geographical character of the region, observing the weather patterns as well as plant and animal life.

The camp broke up in April as the ice melted and buds popped out. On April 7, as Lewis records, the long keelboat was sent back to St. Louis with a small crew, reducing the number in the party to thirty-three. The keelboat carried a metal box containing botanical and zoological samples as well as reports and maps of the river. Apart from the obvious fact that the keelboat was not suited for wilderness travel and had to be abandoned at this point, this was a good way for Lewis and Clark to jettison members of the expedition who seemed less than companionable or competent.

The most adventurous part of the journey now began, taking the party through territories rarely if ever seen by white men before. Lewis and Clark kept their eyes on the long-imagined prize: a tributary that would enter the Missouri below the Canadian border and take travelers to the Columbia, from which they might enjoy an easy ride to the Pacific. It was commonly believed that such a route existed and would open trade with the West, even China. It was further thought that a single portage of only a day or so would be required. The Corps questioned traders and Indians regularly about this matter, although nobody had solid information. They apparently had great hopes for the fabled White Earth River, which (later) proved—to their huge disappointment—a mere trickle of a creek.

Imagine what it felt like to push along the Missouri, uncertain about the route itself. Many tributaries fed into the main trunk of the waterway, and it was difficult to decide on which fork was the "real" Missouri. And what about the legendary river that would take you westward to the Saskatchewan, the ultimate highway to the rich fur trade of the far north? On May 8, Lewis writes with some anxiety about the so-called Milk River, which suddenly appeared before them, branching off in a tantalizing way. Was this what the Indians referred to as the River That Scolds All the Others? Might this actually be the fabled waterway they sought?

Probably not, Lewis and Clark jointly decided, continuing up the main trunk of the Missouri. They moved through gorgeous country that teemed with bear and elk, buffalo and deer. Riveting accounts of hunting these creatures appear in the *Journals,* mostly in the hand of Lewis, who makes general observations such as this, on May 31: "The hills and river Clifts which we passed today exhibit a most romantic appearance. The bluffs of the river rise to the hight of from 2 to 300 feet and in most places nearly perpendicular; they are formed of remarkable white sandstone which is sufficiently soft to give way readily to the impression of water" (123). Clark, the least dramatic of men, would have left off the first sentence here and gone straight to the measurements.

The party sailed, rowed, and pulled their boats up the Missouri through what is now Montana, where they hunted grizzly bears, some of them so fierce that even repeated shots from Drewyer's trusty rifle did not slow them down. Lewis and Clark were thrilled by these great beasts. They also marked the presence of unusual breeds of antelope and deer and were fascinated by prairie dogs, which appeared in large numbers and created underground villages of their own. At one point the party viewed a shimmering, thunderous herd of ten thousand buffalo— an awesome sight indeed.

A crisis occurred in early June, when a major fork in the river presented itself. Lewis frets: "The whole of my party to a man except myself were fully persuaded that this river was the Missouri" (132). In democratic fashion, he and Clark consulted everyone in the group. Many of them were experienced woodsmen, and the general consensus was that the clearer branch was the correct one. Lewis and Clark averred, and the Corps followed their leaders, hoping that the big waterfall that Indians had mentioned would soon appear to confirm their choice of route. They called this stretch of the journey Maria's River.

A tense few days followed, as the expedition thought it might have taken the wrong fork, thus wasting precious time. An error here could have derailed the project, forcing an early retreat. Making matters worse, Sacagawea fell ill. The mysterious illness is described by Lewis as a "cold." She was given sulfur water from a spring to help her, although Lewis also records that he applied a poultice to her pelvic region (not the obvious remedy for a cold). Clark blamed Charbonneau for his wife's illness, and recent historians tend to think that Sacagawea was actually pregnant again and aborted the child.[2] This would certainly explain the poultices, as well as the blame attached to Charbonneau, who was regarded by Lewis and Clark as irresponsible. To get his wife pregnant again, so soon after the birth of Pomp and while traveling through the wilderness, was more than irresponsible. It was crazy, even dangerous. This particular crisis, however troubling, soon passed.

Lewis stayed calm, as ever, revealing almost nothing of his anxieties during this stretch of the *Journals;* instead, he focused on the natural beauty and robust animal life so abundant everywhere. These wonders left him breathless as they progressed, slowly and methodically. He and Clark plotted their course as best they could, noting latitudes, frequently consulting earlier maps, such as that by a celebrated English cartographer, Aaron Arrowsmith, who had worked from information gathered by Peter Fidler, a surveyor and explorer who had been in this region a decade before on behalf of the Hudson's Bay Company. Not surprisingly, Fidler was quite inaccurate in his calculations.

The party continued on, listening for the telltale misty din of a waterfall, which at last appeared in the middle distance: the Great Falls. It came as a relief to everyone that the expedition had not wasted its time. Lewis and Clark had guessed correctly, and this boosted the confidence of the entire Corps in the wisdom of their leaders (as journals by other members of the group suggest). Yet a portage of eighteen miles was required to get around this major obstacle, a series of five falls. In the tradition of can-do Americans, the Corps constructed rather crude but functional carts, cutting solid wheels from the trunks of trees. They abandoned their boats, carrying supplies along difficult terrain for many days. Dugout canoes would take them the rest of the way. (Lewis had brought along a kit for a metal boat, but it did not work when he tried to assemble it.)

As they moved beyond the Great Falls to what they called the Three Forks, Lewis experienced some understandable fear about what lay

ahead. Quite literally, this was uncharted territory. On top of this
uncertainty, Captain Clark was ill, suffering from muscle aches,
headaches, and intermittent fevers; nevertheless, Clark put misery to
one side, plodding on, eventually shaking off this illness. Lewis writes
that he and his party also "begin to feel considerable anxiety with rispect
to the Snake Indians. If we do not find them or some other nation who
have horses I fear the successful issue of our voyage will be very doubt-
full" (168).

The landscape was strangely devoid of human life in early summer.
Where were the Indians? Lewis knew they *must* find them. If no Indians appeared, it would mean these areas were not especially habitable
and that horses would not be obtainable. That would bring their adventure to a halt. In late July, however, they saw smoke signals in the
distance: always a sign of Indians. The river moved through fertile
plains, rather uneventfully. But one can easily forget, in reading the
Journals, just how terrifying this stretch of the journey must have been.
They traveled through wilderness country: savage and beautiful, utterly
unfamiliar. The Three Forks appeared in mid-August, and the party
turned up a branch of the Missouri they called the Jefferson. Soon
enough they reached its long-sought headwaters, a mere trickle that a
man could bridge with his own feet.

It must have been hugely disappointing when the fabled Columbia
River did not present itself. Instead, the Rocky Mountains spread in all
directions: a gorgeous, frightening prospect of high jagged peaks. As
Lewis and Clark understood at a glance, a substantial overland journey
lay ahead of them, and without horses it would prove impossible. Yet
they struggled on, trusting to their luck, until the hoped-for miracle occurred in the shape of a few Shoshone tribesmen, who appeared on
horseback. One of them was obviously a chief, and when Sacagawea
saw him, she broke into a dance of joy, then wept profusely. This was,
in fact, her brother. The reunion was bittersweet, however, as she
learned from him the sad news that most of her family were dead, except for two brothers and one nephew, the son of a deceased sister. The
presence of Sacagawea (however coincidental and unlikely) was crucial
here, as through her intercession the Indians supplied the necessary
horses as well as sound advice on crossing the Rockies.

Lewis took fascinating notes on life among the Shoshones. Their sexual practices entranced him, especially the fact that "the chastity of their women is not held in high estimation" (208). For a trifle, such as a colorful bead, husbands would sell their wives into prostitution for a night or two. Yet "some of their women appear to be held more sacred than in any nation we have seen." Lewis took some care to explain to his men that they should not sleep with Indian women without the consent of their husbands, as he did not want problems to arise. (It should not surprise anyone that a band of lusty young explorers should wish to have sexual contact with Indian women who crossed their path.)

Lewis and Clark enjoyed the company of Indians, and they made a huge diplomatic effort to promote good relations. The long entry for August 22, 1805, for instance, describes a meeting with various chieftains of the Shoshone tribe, and how the Corps fed them and explained to Sacagawea's brother that "it would not be many years before the whitemen would put it in the power of his nation to live in the country below the mountains where they might cultivate corn beans and squashes" (220). One has to wonder how the Shoshones took this news, which cannot have pleased them.

The journey proceeded, with the help of Shoshone horses, over the Continental Divide. Lewis writes on August 29: "I somewhat feared that the caprice of the Indians might suddenly induce them to withhold their horses from us without which my hopes of prosecuting my voyage to advantage was lost" (231). But these fears proved unjustified, and the expedition continued, sometimes along small streams and rivers, as when at the end of August they followed the Lemhi River to the Salmon River, which turned into Tower Creek and then into the steep canyon of the North Fork. The party moved into the Bitterroot valley, where they discovered a trail used by the Nez Percé tribe to cross the Rockies to get to the buffalo plains on the western side. On through September the party crossed overland, on horseback, to the Lolo Trail. Breathtaking views of the Rockies appeared, as Clark (usually unimpressed by dramatic scenery) notes on Sunday afternoon of September 15: "From this mountain I could observe high rugged mountains in every direction as far as I could see" (259).

The Lolo Trail nearly finished them off, as many in the Corps grew sick from "Lax and heaviness of the stomack," as Clark recalls. This was probably dysentery, which may have come from their odd diet, which included a few grouse, coyotes, even crows. The Nez Percé proved friendly and gave the ailing explorers dried salmon and flour made from the camas root; but neither of these cured their intestinal troubles. While nobody died, the digestive problems continued through much of autumn. The *Journals* suddenly becomes a catalog of illness, as on October 4, where Clark writes that "as our horse is eaten we have nothing to eate except dried fish & roots which disagree with us verry much." He adds: "Capt Lewis Still Sick but able to walk about a little" (242).

The Nez Percé had never seen white men before, yet they appear to have liked the encounter. They certainly helped the Corps a good deal, serving as guides and providing food. At last, the party reached the rivers they sought: the Clearwater, Snake, and Columbia. Relieved, they fashioned dugout canoes from ponderosa and yellow pine, leaving their horses behind (for the return journey) in the care of the Nez Percé, whom they obviously trusted.

Clark writes at length about the Nez Percé, whom he describes as "Stout likely men" who have "handsom women." The women are "verry dressey in their way" (246). The men cloak themselves in robes of white buffalo or elk skins, whereas the women "dress in a Shirt of Ibex or Goat Skins which reach quite down to their anckles with a girdle, their heads are not ornemented, their Shirts are ornemented with quilled Brass, Small peces of Brass Cut into different forms, Beeds, Shells, & curious bones" (248). Much of their time is spent gathering food, which usually means fishing for salmon or hunting deer. He says they are wonderfully robust and "make great use of swetting." That is, they would gather in sweat lodges: an Indian religious practice that also promoted good health.

The party moved swiftly in their fresh canoes, running with the stream. Various tribes of Indians met them, often serving as temporary guides; the friendliness of the Indians came as a welcome relief. Lewis carefully noted the condition of their health, their habits and clothing, their social practices, as far as he could judge them on brief acquaintance. On November 5, Clark writes: "This is the first night which we have been entirely clear of Indians since our arrival on the waters of the Columbia River" (277). A slight note of relief will be heard in that remark, suggesting that the party as a whole must have always felt a sense of threat, however ambiguous. They knew they would never have made it so far without strategic help from the indigenous population. Of course, the Indians were back the next day, hoping to trade with the white men.

On November 7, Clark records a landmark moment for the expedition: "Great joy in camp we are in *view* of the *Ocian,* this great Pacific." It was the stupendous view they had "been so long anxious to See" (279). Clark kept a separate notebook, in which he recorded bearings and courses. Here he allowed himself a little more expressiveness: *"Ocian in view! O! the joy."*

Having arrived on the Pacific coast at last, the Corps had to make a decision about where to pass the winter. It was a cold and wet autumn, suggesting a fierce season ahead; having lived through the previous winter in the mountains, the group had no interest in trying to rush home over the Rockies in deep snows. In a generous (and intelligent) move, Lewis put the decision to a vote. Even Sacagawea and York, a black man, were allowed to participate. Here, indeed, was a glimmer of the New World: the democratic impulse given full vent.

The group wisely decided to spend this winter on the south side of the Columbia, near what is now Astoria, Oregon. Aware of the potential hazards of the approaching season, they set about to construct Fort Clatsop, establishing daily routines with care. (To preserve whatever fish and meat they should find, a small contingent was delegated to make salt from the Pacific waters on the beach at Tillamook Head.) As the Corps settled in, the *Journals* reflects mostly the interests of Lewis, who made extensive notes on the local surroundings, the flora and fauna, and the social habits of the native population. Clark, always more reticent, devoted himself to geographical data and mapmaking.

Although not severe, the weather was uncomfortable and monotonous. Boredom became a problem, and some of the men consorted with the local Indians, a few acquiring venereal diseases. Severe colds ran through the Corps, too, as did various infections; but nobody suffered a life-threatening illness—something of a triumph in itself. One of the universal remedies for whatever ailed them was something described as "Scotts pills." This was probably a laxative of some kind, and it often seemed to alleviate an array of problems. The ancient practice of bleeding a man who fell ill was also used on occasion, as Lewis records on March 18, as the party had just begun the return journey (331).

Most of the Indians met in Oregon were sorry-looking, with bad teeth and various skin ailments. Inadequate supplies of food proved a major issue for these indigenous people, who survived on dried fish through much of the winter. While not as devoted to cleanliness as the Indians encountered earlier on the journey, they were peaceful by nature, although prone to petty thievery. The fickleness of the Indians annoyed Lewis, who writes on April 2: "I purchased a canoe from an Indian today for which I gave him six fathoms of wampum beads; he seemed satisfied with his bargain and departed in another canoe but shortly after returned and canceled the bargain, took his canoe and returned the beads. This is frequently the case in their method of traiding and is deemed fair by them" (338). As ever, Lewis remained levelheaded in these situations and accepted the habits of the Indians, however irritating, as a given.

Having settled in beside the Pacific, the Corps hoped to make contact with mercenary vessels; a few of the men might well have preferred to go home via Cape Horn rather than risk another wilderness journey. But no ships appeared, so all members of the group had to return to St. Louis as they had come. Needless to say, it was a grueling trip. At least they had experience on their side now, and the maps that Clark sketched on the westward journey would serve them well as they retraced their steps. As expected, they found the Nez Percé patiently tending their horses. They waited in the Indian villages for spring snows to melt, guessing (correctly) that passage over the Rockies would be difficult until June.

At last they set off, dropping back into the Missouri River basin, where they divided into two bands at the Lolo Pass: a move designed to increase their geographical knowledge. One route might be preferable to another for future travelers, and these intensely professional explorers wished to perform their task as thoroughly as possible. Lewis and his smaller group took a northern fork, while Clark passed with his larger contingent (including Sacagawea) to the south, along the Yellowstone River.

Lewis, it so happened, had much more trouble along the way, having to fight off a band of Blackfeet Indians who tried to steal their guns and horses. In another incident, Lewis himself was shot in the backside by one of his own men while hunting. The wound took weeks to heal properly, and it prevented Lewis from writing in his journal for a stretch, as sitting was painful. As planned, the groups joined forces again in what is now North Dakota, where the rivers merged. They returned without incident to the Mandan villages, where Charbonneau, Sacagawea, and their son—now a great favorite of the Corps—parted company with the expedition.

Lewis and Clark persuaded an Indian chief called Sheheke (or "Big White") to return with them to Washington, to meet President Jefferson. They also brought along Sheheke's wife and family. For the most part, the *Journals* remains matter-of-fact near the end, revealing little of the joy that must have rippled through the Corps, who must have wondered if they would ever return to civilization. On September 16, Clark writes: "The Day proved excessively worm and disagreeable" (474). A few days later he reports an eye irritation that has spread among the men: "Three of the party was unable to row from the State of their eyes" (476).

On September 23, he writes that the party "descended to the Mississippi and down that river to St. Louis at which place we arrived at 12 oClock. We Suffered the party to fire off their pieces as a Salute to the Town. We were met by all the village and received a hearty welcome from its inhabitants etc." The next-to-last entry notes without enthusiasm: "in the evening a dinner and Ball" (478). There was, in fact, considerable amazement in St. Louis, as many believed the Corps had surely perished in the wilderness. Excitement about the completion of the expedition spread quickly through the United States, and the journey became the stuff of myth almost at once. The *Journals,* in its various forms, only fed the legend.

IV.

WHAT DID THIS JOURNEY, and its subsequent embodiment in the *Journals,* mean to Americans? The obvious answer is that the expedition was a show of power, the beginning of American imperial exertion in the world. With the Louisiana Purchase accomplished, there was still a good deal of diplomacy required to alter conditions on the ground. It took a long time for French and Spanish traders in this territory to accept the fact of American sovereignty. The expedition, with the *Journals* as its testament, worked to bolster American claims to the region, and to enhance American interests (if not claims) in the Northwest itself. If anyone had any doubts about this now, the entire continent lay open to the United States. They would occupy the land as they saw fit.

The commercial angle was important, if not central, to the expedition. The fur trade, for example, had long been a point of great interest. Money was to be made on several fronts, and from this time on there would be continued exploration and development of various commercial interests in the West. On another level, Lewis and Clark stand at the beginning of a thirst for westward expansion that never abated. Americans in the nineteenth century watched the drama slowly unfolding: the gradual occupation of this vast region west of the Mississippi. The building of a transcontinental railroad played a role, too, in linking the coasts (the Union Pacific tracks joined those of the Central Pacific Railroad on May 10, 1869—a symbolic moment). Ultimately, the settlement of the entire continent seemed inevitable, part of our so-called Manifest Destiny (a term heard often after 1845, when it was coined by John L. O'Sullivan, a journalist and politician from New York).[3]

The peaceful relations with the Indians that Lewis and Clark modeled were not, unfortunately, the norm for future relations, as the many tribes were driven off their land into reservations or, in some cases, massacred. The *Journals* nevertheless had lifted an ideal before the eyes of the reading public. Lewis and Clark focused intensely on the customs of the Indians, and this had a genuine impact on many. Interest in Native American history has only increased in recent years, and Lewis and Clark stand out as pioneers in the field. Their anthropological notes on the habits of various tribes from the Mandan villagers to the Indians of the Rockies and the Pacific coast have been valuable beyond calculation.

The same could be said for the maps that Clark drew, which proved invaluable to later explorers. Overall, Lewis and Clark did yeoman work in charting the true course of the upper Missouri and its tributaries. While their measurements of latitude and longitude were often mistaken, their notes on the weather assisted later explorers in their preparations. Their pioneering trek across the Rockies and down the Lolo Pass established firmly that no easy river access could be had, thus shattering a dream of generations. But they disclosed a region of prolific beauty and abundant natural resources.

In the tradition of nature writing, Lewis and Clark rank high as practitioners. Their close observation of the western landscape, its vegetation and animal life, still inspires awe. They offered the first descriptions of numerous wild creatures, as in their depictions of grizzly bears, prairie dogs, antelope, and mountain goats—and, alas, mosquitoes. These moments in the *Journals* dazzled readers and established a mode of reporting about the natural world that persists in writers like Barry Lopez and Gretel Ehrlich.

As noted above, succeeding generations of Americans have used the *Journals* in different ways, often viewing the work through a particular lens. But the *Journals* offers a kind of bedrock experience for American readers: Here is the West opening before us, in all its richness and variety. Here is potential itself. "The world was all before them," Milton wrote at the end of *Paradise Lost,* as Adam and Eve stepped into the wilderness of their future. This was true of Lewis and Clark as well. Their journey, as embodied in their writing, remains a mythic journey, part of every American's imaginary landscape, endlessly shifting before us, at once a dream of the promised land and a story about what it means to confront the "other," those who lie beyond the reach of American power and custom and who may wish to resist our efforts of appropriation.

WALDEN.

By HENRY D. THOREAU,
AUTHOR OF "A WEEK ON THE CONCORD AND MERRIMACK RIVERS."

I do not propose to write an ode to dejection, but to brag as lustily as chanticleer in the
morning, standing on his roost, if only to wake my neighbors up. — Page 92.

BOSTON:
TICKNOR AND FIELDS.
M DCCC LXII.

FIVE

Walden

I.

HENRY DAVID THOREAU DEFINES American independence. He moved from the Concord village to the nearby woods at Walden Pond on July 4, 1845, declaring his own liberation from a world of material obsession, war, and slavery, as well as ordinary pettiness and spiritual lassitude. Nature entranced him. Indeed, he found in nature, as one visitor to Walden Pond (E. P. Whipple) noted, what other men found in religion. Like the Greeks, whom he admired, he searched among the pines and beside the water for a true and sane vision of the things of this world. As his biographer Robert D. Richardson has observed: "He was not interested in a religion that strove to redeem man from this world, or to raise him above it. He sought clarity of mind, not ecstatic transport; knowledge, not grace."[1]

Walden (1854) was his major work, and it has a unique place in American literature as a work of spirituality, autobiographical adventure, and natural description. An account of one man's attempt to live simply in the woods, it has inspired generations of young people to go off by themselves, to separate from the pack, listening instead of talking, reading, making notes, marching to the beat of a different drummer. They are often backpackers who trek into the wilds to "front only the essential facts of life," as Thoreau beautifully put it. He speaks for all seekers when he writes: "There is commonly sufficient space about us" (175).[2] It is only a matter of finding this space, which is both literal and figurative. "The thick wood is not just at our door, nor the pond, but somewhat is always clearing, familiar and worn by us, appropriated and fenced in some way, and reclaimed from Nature."

Thoreau was not so much a seeker as a finder, discovering this "little world all to myself." It was the world of nature, but also a world of words in touch with natural things, with a language that reflects nature, inhabits it, makes it visible. In finding this amazing place, Thoreau became a genuine prophet, summoning a vision of purity and grace. As he wrote in his first book, *A Week on the Concord and Merrimack Rivers* (1849), "The most glorious fact in my experience is not any thing that I have done or may hope to do, but a transient thought, or vision, or dream." But he follows this wish for vision with hesitation and modesty: "I would give all the wealth of the world, and all the deeds of all the heroes, for one true vision. But how can I communicate with the gods who am a pencil-maker on the earth, and not be insane?"[3]

Thoreau did somehow manage to communicate with the gods, but with readers as well. The record of this sublime conversation will be found in *Walden,* a perpetual fountain of linguistic youth, which never loses its freshness and which remains as important today as it was on its day of publication.

II.

THOREAU (1817–62) WAS INDEED A MAKER of pencils. This was his father's business, and one that sustained him through his life, although he worked only intermittently in the family firm, preferring to read and write and to walk in the woods. He was born and raised in Concord, now a suburb of Boston but in Thoreau's day a considerable journey from the city by coach or (later) train. He studied at Harvard, from which he graduated in 1837. He returned to Concord in the fall of 1837 (commencement occurred on the last day of August, as was typical in those days) and took up a position as village schoolmaster. He lived with his parents in a house called the Parkman house that faced Main

Street, on the site where the public library now stands. This was a time of crisis in the United States, as the country had fallen into a serious recession (it lasted into the 1840s), and so Thoreau must have felt lucky to have any job at all and fortunate that his father had prospered as a maker of pencils.

Thoreau failed quickly as a teacher, as he refused to give daily canings to those pupils who did poorly in their studies. One member of the school board in Concord called the young schoolmaster onto the carpet for this squeamishness, telling him that he must cane the children or quit. The young man obeyed. He stormed into his classroom, singled out six boys at random, and caned them hard. Then he resigned. Obviously shaken by the experience, he determined to avoid such humiliating situations in future years. In effect, he consigned himself to an independent life, throwing himself on the goodwill of friends and family, who never refused him food or lodging. He lived not so much by his pen as by his father's pencils.

He stayed for a couple of years with Ralph Waldo Emerson and his family, who were neighbors in Concord. Emerson had moved to Concord from Boston in 1834, when he was just thirty-one, and Thoreau just seventeen. A significant swath of life lay behind Emerson at this point: he had experienced the tragic death of his first wife, Ellen, and resigned from his pulpit in a Boston church to pursue a life of writing and lecturing. As America's first major philosopher and essayist, he became "the aid and abettor of those who would live in the spirit," as Matthew Arnold would say of him. By the time Emerson arrived in Concord, he had already made an impression on William Wordsworth and Carlyle, whom he met on a trip to Britain in 1833. In 1836, he published his seminal work, which is still one of the most influential works ever written in the United States: *Nature*. This lengthy essay—a foundational work for all who identified themselves with the so-called transcendentalists— became a bible of sorts for young Thoreau, influencing his philosophy of nature. Its language and thinking spread beneath the pages of *Walden* like a deep and sturdy foundation.

Walden is a major text for American nature writers, a book that defines their ways and means. It also marks a defining moment for American autobiography, a native genre invented by Benjamin Franklin. Thoreau knew Franklin's book well, and he offers a parody of this classic in places, beginning his own book with a chapter called "Economy," which is full of mock-scrupulous accounts of what it actually cost him to live in the wilderness. (Note that Emerson's *Nature* also includes an early chapter called "Commodity" and moves, like *Walden,* toward more elevated or spiritual topics.) As if teasing Franklin, Thoreau jokes about not having sufficient capital behind him for this enterprise at Walden and professes to adhere to strict business habits while at the pond. This lengthy initial chapter offers a subtle critique of Franklin, with his gospel of hard work, his pervasive need to establish himself in the world's eyes as a man of parts, his accountant's mentality. Where Franklin acquired things, Thoreau shed them, pitying those who cannot easily slip out from under their inherited yokes of property and position in society.

"I see young men," says Thoreau, "my townsmen, whose misfortune it is to have inherited farms, houses, barns, cattle, and farming tools; for these are more easily acquired than got rid of" (47). He reminds us that "men labor under a mistake," believing they will last forever, that life is not impermanent. "The better part of the man is soon ploughed into the soil for compost," Thoreau writes, with an economy of emotion that is breathtaking. Most men lead lives of "quite desperation," and the brutal fact is that "even in this comparatively free country," these unfortunate people, "through mere ignorance and mistake, are so occupied with the factitious cares and superfluously coarse labors of life that its finer fruits cannot be plucked by them" (48).

Liberation is the constant cry of *Walden.* In this, Thoreau's work finds a parallel in the slave memoirs that suddenly achieved popularity in these tense days before the Civil War, when abolition was a passionate obsession with Northern intellectuals, including Emerson and Horace Greeley, the latter an influential editor in New York who was among Thoreau's early friends and patrons. The very summer that Thoreau moved to Walden Pond, Frederick Douglass published the first edition of his popular autobiography, *Narrative of the Life of Frederick Douglass, an American Slave, Written by Himself.* This was a seminal work, perhaps the most important book published by an African American in the nineteenth century, and it riveted the North, telling a story of liberation: a black man, a slave, flees the South, becomes a free man. The implicit message in this compelling work is that a black man must in every way—intellectually, spiritually—be considered the equal of a white man. The idea of human equality itself undermined the argument for slavery, and Douglass dealt a devastating blow to those who wished to perpetuate this cruel institution. Thoreau was affected by his work, as one can see from a piece he wrote for a journal called the *Liberator,* where he calls Douglass "a fugitive slave in one more sense than we; who has proved himself the possessor of a *fair* intellect, and has won a colorless reputation in these parts; and who, we trust, will be as superior to degradation from the sympathies of Freedom, as from the antipathies of Slavery."

Implicit in these words is the idea that freedom itself—as white men and women experienced it in the North—did not necessarily guarantee liberation. The shackles of civilized life in the North were real, however invisible to most. Thoreau experienced the life of a middle-class white man in Massachusetts as a kind of enslavement to norms and expectations. He therefore saw himself, in going to Walden Pond, as a self-liberator. He sought autonomy and wanted to discover for himself what lay beyond the superficial accumulation of worldly goods and social status. It may seem crude to make a comparison between Thoreau's liberation and the sort that Douglass had achieved, as the life of a slave was infinitely more painful and confining in every way than that of a middle-class white man. Viewed in a certain light, Thoreau can seem like a spoiled child, someone given every opportunity in life who still complains about his situation. But in the larger sense he was right: One can be "enslaved" by values and social circumstances. One can fall out of touch with one's inner life and out of touch with the natural world, which is everywhere around us but unseen, an undiscovered country.

Thoreau was a fierce abolitionist and would write a full-throated defense of the infamous rebel against slavery John Brown, whose attack on Harpers Ferry in 1859 was a pivotal event in the months leading up to the Civil War. His support for Brown's violent effort to liberate slaves cuts against his own regard for civil disobedience, which he championed in his essay on this subject. "A foolish consistency is the hobgoblin of little minds," Emerson once said. Certainly Thoreau had no such consistency on the use of violence. His most influential essay, nevertheless, was "Civil Disobedience," which had small effect at the time of its publication and was largely ignored. It was later, however, taken up by the socialist English Fabians and progressive parliamentarians in London, then adopted by Mahatma Gandhi, who found in Thoreau's idea a way forward in South Africa and India, where nonviolent resistance proved immensely effective against British colonialists. Martin Luther King often referred to this essay during the heyday of the civil rights movement, and it became a central text for those who resisted the Vietnam War in the late 1960s and early '70s. Yet Thoreau is more than merely an early advocate of peaceful resistance to forms of unjust authority. In *Walden,* he offers his readers a program for self-liberation and a reading of nature as the symbol of spirit—as Emerson would have said.

Despite its merits, this major text was relatively unknown in its day, taking five years to sell out its modest print run of two thousand copies. Thoreau had published his first book, *A Week on the Concord and Merrimack Rivers,* two years after leaving the pond. It attracted few reviews or sales, and so Thoreau felt demoralized. He certainly did not rush into print with *Walden.* Having written the first draft while at the pond (from July 1845 until September 1847), he held on to the manuscript for several years, refining it, adding material from his abundant journals, shaping the work for maximum rhetorical effect. The natural cycle of a year, with its unfolding seasons, offered a pattern for the narrative, and so the fact that Thoreau lived at the pond for more than two years was largely elided, though Thoreau does mention the exact amount of time he spent at Walden at the outset. The author is the hero of this work, and his spiritual fluctuations follow the mood of the seasons. The book tracks the rhythm of the writer's awakening, his spiritual revival and refreshment. *Walden* opens for all readers the possibility of their own self-liberation. As such, it remains a revolutionary work.

Thoreau lived with Emerson and his family in 1841 and 1842, and he associated with Emerson as a close friend and mentor throughout his life (indeed, Emerson would speak eloquently at Thoreau's funeral). He became, with Emerson, a key figure in the transcendentalist movement. This term refers to a group of New England intellectuals who offered an American version of the idealist philosophy that had taken root in Germany in the eighteenth century and migrated to England in the early years of the nineteenth century. This loose association included, apart from Emerson and Thoreau, such writers as Frederic Henry Hedge, Bronson Alcott, George Ripley, Elizabeth Peabody, Orestes Brownson,

Margaret Fuller, Convers Francis, and Jones Very. In essence, the group believed in the spiritual realities of natural forms—the idea that nature embodies spirit. They were eclectic thinkers, drawing ideas from Plato and Immanuel Kant, from F. W. J. Schelling and a wide array of other philosophers and poets. One writer in the *Dial,* a journal closely associated with this movement, spoke of transcendentalism as "the recognition in man of the capacity of knowing truth intuitively." Most vividly, the group focused on the ethical implications of their philosophy, moving away from technical philosophical inquiry. In this, they prefigured William James and the American pragmatists, who dwelled on the practical and moral implications of their work.

Emerson founded what Harold Bloom has called "the American religion," and *Nature* is the primary text of this religion. It is a work of immense subtlety and influence. Certainly *Walden* could never have been written without it. Thoreau was no abstract philosopher, nor was he an original thinker. Instead, he sought what Emerson called "an original relation with the universe." Emerson had shown him how to do this—not in church, but in the church of the woods, alone. This was quite revolutionary in itself. One did not hover over sacred texts, but simply went off into the natural world to make contact with the divine spirit. (This was also the way of the ancient Stoics, who rejected the norms of society and the creeds of religion.)

In *Nature,* Emerson writes about acquiring a sense of what he calls "correspondence," having one's inner vision of nature "adjusted" to one's outer senses: "To speak truly, few adult persons can see nature. Most persons do not see the sun. At least they have a very superficial seeing. The sun illuminates only the eye of the man, but shines into the eye and the heart of the child. The lover of nature is he whose inward and outward sense are still truly adjusted to each other; who has retained the spirit of infancy even into the era of manhood. His intercourse with heaven and earth becomes part of his daily food."[4]

Importantly, Emerson taught that the human mind was the same at all times, in all places, despite local differences or cultural inflections. Homer and Shakespeare never lose their relevance, and one cannot say that the teachings of the Buddha have any less meaning than the teachings of Christ. Every age is equal. This, of course, elevates the individual in interesting ways, suggesting that one's own thoughts have value commensurate with those of Plato and Aristotle, Aquinas and Kant. One could look inside one's own heart for all the information one needed to form a true and valuable picture of the world. And one did not need the great libraries and universities of Europe to advance one's thinking, to stand on equal footing with the intellectual figures of history. The radical nature of this thought struck Thoreau, as it has struck generations of American readers, as liberating. (It is worth recalling that Emerson wrote "Self-Reliance," too: a major statement of American individualism.)

The section in *Nature* called "Language" has particular relevance for writers, and Thoreau in particular. Emerson puts forward a useful theory of language that rests on three principles:

Words are signs of natural facts.

Particular natural facts are symbols of particular spiritual facts.

Nature is the symbol of spirit.[5]

In the first precept, Emerson plays with the idea that words have buried within them an imagistic content and that language evolves in the direction of abstractness. In their root sense, as he observes, the words "right" and "wrong" mean "straight" and "crooked"; they are utterly devoid of moral implication. Nevertheless, these extremely concrete words evolved into our most elevated (and portentous) abstractions. Similarly, the word "transgression" means "crossing the line." The word "supercilious" means "raising of an eyebrow." And so on. Most words have both an abstract meaning and fresh, concrete, pictorial meanings that lie at their linguistic core. (Even the word "abstraction" itself contains a picture: "abs-" = away from; "traction" = to pull or draw. Hence, the abstraction pulls away from the original concrete picture. The "tractor" of time—in the evolution of the word—yanks the word loose from its original meaning as it suppresses the metaphor.)

Emerson's second and third precepts focus on the idea that nature and spirit operate in some occult relation. Emerson develops the idea of correspondence here—a theory taken from the seventeenth-century Swedish mystic Emanuel Swedenborg—that we live in two worlds at once. Spirit and nature move together, as the shapes of nature gesture toward spiritual truths. Thus, every bird or bush, tree or rock, becomes a sign of some spiritual reality, points on a map that can be followed. For those willing to take the journey into nature, this map can lead to spiritual revelations. One can even transcend reality by climbing "the ladder of creation"—a phrase often used by Platonists. But language is the vehicle in which this journey occurs, as the mind needs concrete embodiments for its intuitions. *Walden* (more so than Walden Pond itself) becomes, in this train of thought, a stand-in for nature. The concrete images that abound in this intensely poetic text gesture toward higher things; we move through language into a deeper spiritual reality.

As Richardson says: "From the beginning, Thoreau's writing was marked by an intense interest in the wonders, not of the invisible, but of the visible world."[6] And so, much like Emerson, Thoreau believed that the writer's function was to pierce through the abstract and "rotten" quality of language to "fasten words again to visible things." So Thoreau, in *Walden,* looks into the eye of the pond with a kind of steely ferocity, seeing things otherwise invisible, as near the end of his chapter called "The Ponds," where he writes about the clarity of the water itself: "This pond has rarely been profaned by a boat, for there is little in it to tempt a fisherman. Instead of the white lily, which requires mud, or the common sweet flag, the blue flag (*Iris versicolor*) grows thinly in the pure water, rising from the stony bottom all around the shore, where it is visited by humming birds in June, and the color both of its bluish blades and its flowers, and especially their reflections, are in singular harmony with the glaucous water" (246–47). The pond eventually becomes the lens through which Henry Thoreau sees the human soul.

III.

IN HIS OPENING CHAPTER, "Economy," Thoreau recalls his recent past: "I went on thus for a long time, I may say it without boasting, faithfully minding my business, till it became more and more evident that my townsmen would not after all admit me into the list of town officers, nor make my place a sinecure with a moderate allowance. My accounts, which I can swear to have kept faithfully, I have, indeed, never got audited, still less accepted, still less paid and settled. However, I have not set my heart on that" (61). Benjamin Franklin (a surprising influence on Thoreau) would have cringed to read such a passage, which vividly mocks the small-business man and his obsession with accounts and audits. Thoreau's sojourn in the wilderness was a "business" that he would enter "without the usual capital," he says (63).

Simplicity is the condition Thoreau sought. He reflects: "The very simplicity and nakedness of man's life in the primitive ages imply this advantage at least, that they left him still but a sojourner in nature" (80). To get back to nature remained his goal throughout his years in the woods. Unlike the hardworking Franklin, who boasted of long hours at the press, Thoreau explains: "My days in the woods were not very long ones" (85). He required plenty of time "off" for reading and writing, lazing about in the woods, by the pond, or just walking. "I made no haste in my work," he tells us, as if chiding Franklin directly.

Franklin put forward strict accounts, and so does Thoreau (however mockingly). He provides a detailed expense list, which includes $.14 for hinges and screws and, indeed, $.01 for a piece of chalk—the absurdity inherent in the tiny amounts. The transportation of materials from town to the pond itself cost him $1.40. "I carried a good part on my back," he informs us casually. He went to school in the woods, so to speak, and compares the total price of building his shelter at Walden (a little over $28) with that of renting a room at Harvard for a year. The expense of a college education troubles him. While a student is "reading Adam Smith, Ricardo, and Say"—the great economists—he also "runs his father in debt irretrievably" (95). By implication, "real" education is self-education and requires no dormitory room or college tuition. One needs only a book and a log to sit on, and perhaps a tree for shade.

Thoreau thought that most people wasted their time and money on lavish accommodations and styles of living that fit their status but exceeded their genuine needs as human beings. "I learned from my two years' experience," he tells us, "that it would cost incredibly little trouble to obtain one's necessary food, even in this latitude; that a man may use as simple a diet as the animals, and yet retain health and strength" (104). One might wish to say: Tell that to the starving in Africa. But Thoreau's point is worth taking seriously: in a country as abundant as the United States, there should be enough food for everyone. And one should perhaps rethink the nature of one's labor. What are we really working *for*? Status and wealth? Later in this initial chapter, he notes that he has generally found "that by working about six weeks in a year," he could meet "all the expenses of living" (112). If Benjamin Franklin is our Founding Yuppie, as David Brooks once quipped, then Thoreau is our Founding Hippie.

The chapter ends with a long quotation from a Middle Eastern sage, one Sadi of Shiraz. Thoreau, in his penultimate paragraph, writes: "Our manners have been corrupted by communication with the saints" (122). This is, indeed, a highly secular book in its way, one that looks away from any traditional creed or scripture. Instead, Thoreau studies the book of nature, reading its dappled pages, drawing from its resources what spiritual life he needs to sustain him. If he is critical of middle-class economics, he remains eager to examine what it takes to live in the woods as a fully realized human being. One did not need excess or abundance to live well; one only required the bare necessities. Enough was really enough. By heading to Walden, this "place of pines," Thoreau hoped to reset the calculus, putting himself forward as an example, a test case. "To be a philosopher," he muses, is not "to have subtle thoughts, nor even to found a school, but ... to live ... a life of simplicity, independence, magnanimity, and trust"—such as all men should live (57).

In the second chapter, "Where I Lived, and What I Lived For," we get the marrow of the book in a statement of purpose: "I went to the woods because I wished to live deliberately, to front only the essential facts of life, and see if I could not learn what it had to teach, and not, when I came to die, discover that I had not lived" (135). Notice the *active* quality of this writing, with its shocking directness. Instead of "confront," which would be more abstract, he pares the verb to "front," giving it a physicality missing in its fuller implementation. The paradoxical nature of the last clause, with its play on "lived" and "die," forces readers to sit up and face their own mortality. *Walden* presents a challenge on every page, as Thoreau lays down the gauntlet, saying: Look at me. Then look at yourself. Are you living up to your potential? Are you learning from life what it really has to teach? Have you ever fronted the essentials in your own fashion?

"We must learn to reawaken and keep ourselves awake," he writes, "not by mechanical aids, but by an infinite expectation of the dawn, which does not forsake us in our soundest sleep" (134). Here is the Thoreauvian faith, its fundamental creed. This is what Thoreau believes: that morning lies ahead of us, that dawn will break again, even after our "soundest sleep," which is death. The natural religion implicit in such a statement is intriguing. The author demonstrates a belief in the redemptive cycles of nature. This is Henry Thoreau's version of the Great Awakening: a fundamental belief in the perpetual renewal of spring and dawn. One can, in fact, track these symbols of renewal, which take many different shapes, throughout the book, moving toward a glorious finale in the "Conclusion," where he writes: "Only that day dawns to which we are awake. There is more day to dawn. The sun is but a morning star" (382).

"Reading," the third chapter, records the beginnings of daily life at Walden Pond. One should keep in mind that Thoreau is self-consciously creating a classic as he writes; he puts before the reader a text to live by. His words become deeds (the phrase belongs to Wendell Berry). In his view, one must take seriously the strenuous work of reading, which is hard work, as he reminds us: "To read well, that is, to read true books in a true spirit, is a noble exercise, and one that will task the reader more than any exercise which the customs of the day esteem. It requires a training such as the athletes underwent, the steady intention almost of the whole life to this object. Books must be read as deliberately and reservedly as they were written" (146).

Thoreau asks us to read him carefully. To a degree, he warns us that we can only misread him, as when he writes: "The works of the great poets have never yet been read by mankind, for only great poets can read them" (149). But he understands that a reading is often a misreading, that every writer reinvents his own literary predecessors and willfully misconstrues them. And one can only read fully whatever one can fully create, or re-create—in one's own mind and heart. So readers of *Walden* must commit unreservedly to the text, to the experience described, intuitively grasping whatever truth lies at its core; and some vital part of this truth must come from the reader. Notably, the author does not offer a program of reading; he drops the names of a few well-known writers, including Homer, Dante, and Shakespeare, but he understands that reading is a personal adventure, a journey that involves getting lost in the dark wood—the *selva oscura*—of Dante's pilgrim. It means leaving behind one's preconceptions, reservations, and prejudices. It involves self-liberation as one invites contact with another world, the one created in the revolutionary language of a major text.

The narrative proceeds to "Sounds," a brief meditation on the things that Thoreau could hear from his cabin at Walden Pond. Certainly the locomotive made a fierce impression on him, with its implications for a changing landscape. The city of Boston had suddenly become a neighbor. *Walden* is, as much as anything, a book that recognizes the advent of a new world, one in which the wilderness is no longer wild—or not as wild as it once was. There are deep regrets here, and a sense of loss is part of the heritage of every nature writer after Thoreau. Nothing is what it once was. In this age of global warming, for instance, when the destruction of nature itself seems at hand, *Walden* becomes a harbinger of disaster. The train, with its chuffing locomotive and rattling boxcars, destroys the author's peace, and he cries out defiantly: "I will not have my eyes put out and my ears spoiled by its smoke and steam and hissing" (168).

With more detachment, Thoreau says that "all sound heard at the greatest possible distance produces one and the same effect, a vibration of the universal lyre" (168). He refers to the wind harp or so-called aeolian lyre, a popular piece of household furniture in the eighteenth century. This instrument was played by the wind itself, which passed over its body and caused vibrations that turned into a natural music. Poets found this a marvelous analogue to human creativity, as Shelley says in his "Defence of Poetry" (1821): "Man is an instrument over which a series of external and internal impressions are driven, like the alternations of an ever-changing wind over an Aeolian lyre, which move it by their motion to ever-changing melody." It is worth reading *Walden* in the context of Romantic poetry and theory, which informed so much that Emerson wrote and which Thoreau understood and utilized in his own way. He was particularly conscious of Romantic metaphors and used them throughout his writing, assuming that his audience would recognize the echoes.

Thoreau elaborates upon the idea that nature is "the universal lyre" in "Solitude," one of the poetic heights of *Walden*. The opening lines of this chapter read like part of Walt Whitman's "Song of Myself," with its celebration of the soul made manifest in the world of nature. "This is a delicious evening," Thoreau writes, "when the whole body is one sense, and imbibes delight through every pore. I come and go with a strange liberty in Nature, a part of herself" (175). Such a sentiment would seem to echo William Blake, the visionary poet, who wrote in *The Marriage of Heaven and Hell* (1790–93): "Man has no Body distinct from his Soul; for that call'd Body is a portion of Soul discern'd by the five Senses, the chief inlets of Soul in this age."

The constant interpenetration of inner and outer worlds, with fluctuations of mood and weather, is part of Thoreau's technique, which is brought to a point of perfection in "Solitude," as when he writes: "Some of my pleasantest hours were during the long rain storms in the spring or fall, which confined me to the house for the afternoon as well as the forenoon, soothed by their ceaseless roar and pelting; when an early twilight ushered in a long evening in which many thoughts had time to take root and unfold themselves" (177). Note the sleight of figuration here, as thoughts "take root," thus transforming the abstraction of thinking into the physical and organic process of a rooting and unfolding—the metaphor of the plant underlying the phrase.

Thoreau often works by irony and paradox, as when he says: "I have a great deal of company in my house; especially in the morning, when nobody calls" (182). This is the same man who has traveled widely in Concord. He goes nowhere at high speed. The drollery of this writing is a source of constant pleasure to the attentive reader. In the above case, Thoreau elaborates on the "great deal of company" he has, saying that among his visitors is "an old settler and original proprietor" who has dug Walden Pond and stoned it and fringed it with pines. There was no such visitor, not in a literal sense. There was "an elderly dame" as well, another beloved visitor, one who "has a genius of unequalled fertility" and whose memory runs "back farther than mythology" (183). Are these the father-god and mother-goddess of nature itself? Whimsy is perhaps the point of such passages, and Thoreau delights in this tongue-in-cheek writing, adopting a sly tone that never loses its sweetness.

He refers to a range of visitors, real or imagined, to his cabin at the edge of a pond, some of them refugees from local madhouses. Of the insane, Thoreau says with droll wisdom: "With respect to wit, I learned that there was not much difference between the half and the whole"

(196). There is a constant disparagement of figures from the town who appear at the hermit's doorstep, these "restless committed men, whose time was all taken up in getting a living or keeping it" (198). Thoreau allows them a grudging respect, however. On the other hand, he derides the "ministers who spoke of God as if they enjoyed a monopoly of the subject, who could not bear all kinds of opinions." He also alludes to visits from "doctors, lawyers, uneasy housekeepers who pried into my cupboard and bed when I was out" (198). One has to wonder if these people really came to his door at Walden. A few did, no doubt. More important, Thoreau uses the notion of visitors to supply a catalog of people and types, commenting on their attitudes and styles of life. They provide a point of contrast for the reader, who measures Thoreau against his neighbors and visitors, real or imagined.

"The Bean-Field" follows, no less whimsical in tone. "I was determined to know beans," Thoreau says (206). Overall, he displays a large knowledge of gardening here and notes the variety of weeds: Roman wormwood, pigweed, sorrel, piper grass. After Thoreau, American nature writers would feel compelled to offer a similar specificity. This is part of his permanent legacy.

Husbandry becomes, for Thoreau, the acquisition of knowledge: "Those summer days which some of my contemporaries devoted to the fine arts in Boston or Rome, and others to contemplation in India, and others to trade in London or New York, I thus, with the other farmers of New England, devoted to husbandry" (207). A constant widening of the circle of attention becomes part of the writer's pastoral technique. And in the true pastoral tradition, he presents himself as a sophisticated man who talks about rural things for an urban audience, seeking a broad, international audience, one that runs down the ages. Allusions to Greek and Roman literature and history abound in these pages, and there is a lively sense of the author as someone who belongs in sophisticated and worldly company. Indeed, one of Thoreau's self-conscious models was Goethe, the august German writer whose posthumous book about his travels in Italy as a young man offered a constant source of inspiration.

As a gardener and husbandman, Thoreau preached the long view. "The true husbandman will cease from anxiety," he tells us, as the squirrels show no concern about whether the woods will bear chestnuts this year or not, "relinquishing all claim to the produce of his fields" (212). This attitude carries over into the professional life of the writer. Thoreau cannot guarantee anything: a readership, even a real book. His work is the work of knowing, which he accomplishes through the work of writing—or knowing-through-writing. He does this work cheerfully, giving himself fully to the task at hand. Readers can take what they want from him, he suggests. They can ignore him or forget him if they so choose. They can feed or not. Thoreau relinquishes all claims to the produce of his fields.

He did not hole up by himself for two years of isolation at Walden, he informs us in "The Village." He "strolled to the village to hear some of the gossip" every day or two and did not cut himself off from his family and friends (213). He spent *most* of his time alone at the pond, reading and writing or cultivating his bean field; but there was lively company in the town, and Thoreau partook of it, as needed. It's in this chapter that he recalls, casually (if not coyly), that he was "seized and put into jail" one afternoon near the end of his first summer at the pond. He had refused to pay his poll tax, not wishing to support a "state which buys and sells men, women, and children, like cattle at the door of its senate-house" (217). Perhaps not wishing to cloud or mix his motives, he doesn't mention his objection to the Mexican War—another good reason for refusing to pay his taxes. But slavery is what he chose to underscore: it had become a clamorous issue by mid-century, and Thoreau was (as noted above) a strong abolitionist, writing a book about freedom from slavery—the slavery of middle-class life. So it probably made sense to pare down this account of his own motives, to "fictionalize" his situation (from the Latin *fictio,* meaning "to shape"). Thoreau wanted freedom from a certain aspect of American life, but he acknowledges (bitterly) that "wherever a man goes, men will pursue and paw him with their dirty institutions, and, if they can, constrain him to belong to their desperate odd-fellow society" (218). Quite brilliantly, Thoreau turns the tables on society. *He* is not the odd person, *they* are.

Thoreau tacks in fresh directions in "The Ponds," moving away from civilization again, this time going "farther westward" (220). He often begins a paragraph with reference to the village, then proceeds to the pleasures of retreat and solitude, as in this example: "Sometimes, after staying in a village parlor till the family had all retired, I have returned to the woods, and, partly with a view to the next day's dinner, spent the hours of midnight fishing from a boat by moonlight, serenaded by owls and foxes, and hearing, from time to time, the creaking note of some unknown bird close at hand" (222). One has to wonder what kind of fish he sought, as he has told us earlier that the pond held no real interest for the angler; but perhaps that is being too literal. In this chapter, he peers into Walden and neighboring ponds for mental associations, contemplating the shifting colors, the effects of light on water. A pond becomes a symbol of the mind itself. The poet in Thoreau emerges as he creates images that become symbols; that is, they become metaphors in which the so-called tenor is severed from its vehicle. (If a poet writes, "My love is like a red, red rose," as Robert Burns does, the tenor is "my love," and the rose is the vehicle that carries the metaphor. If the poet writes, "O Rose, thou art sick," as William Blake does, tenor and vehicle are separated; the rose becomes a symbol, with endless referential possibilities, a luminous and free-floating object of its own.)

One example from this chapter illustrates the technique. Thoreau recalls a time when he accidentally dropped his ax into a hole in the ice when he was ice fishing on the pond:

> Out of curiosity, I lay down on the ice and looked through the hole, until I saw the axe a little on one side, standing on its head, with its helve erect and gently swaying to and fro with the pulse of the pond; and there it might have stood erect and swaying till in the course of time the handle rotted off, if I had not disturbed it. Making another hole directly over it with an ice chisel which I had, and cutting down the longest birch which I could find in the neighborhood with my knife, I made a slip-noose, which I attached to its end, and, letting it down carefully, passed it over the knob of the handle, and drew it by a line along the birch, and so pulled the axe out again. (225)

The anecdote becomes a little myth, or symbol cluster: a conceit. The writer dips into his own icy depths, using his ingenuity to fashion from the natural surroundings a necessary tool. The "pulse of the pond" signifies the life contained in those waters. Thoreau's writing itself is astoundingly clear, as limpid as the waters of the pond. His mind, too, is clear; he can gaze into its depths and locate objects on the bottom as they sway. He can get a noose around these objects and raise them to the light. This is a metaphor, perhaps, for writing itself.

It has often been observed that *Walden* is a book of seasons. In six major drafts, Thoreau worked hard to make the volume conform to seasonal shifts, although he often refers to other seasons within any given part. Many books had been structured this way, including one of Thoreau's favorites, *The Natural History of Selborne* (1789) by Gilbert White, an English writer who also liked to stay near home, walking in the southern and central counties of England. White wrote objectively in the vein of scientific writing. Thoreau, by contrast, adds an element of subjectivity to almost every observation, and the reader remains alert to his presence as manipulator of words and ideas. His language turns figurative almost reflexively, as when, in "The Ponds," he writes: "A lake is the landscape's most beautiful and expressive feature. It is earth's eye; looking into which the beholder measures the depth of his own nature" (233).

Many such passages were added in later drafts, as Thoreau shaped and expanded his original manuscript, dividing the work into discrete chapters, putting in material so that the cycle of the seasons became apparent as a governing principle of organization. In the section called "Higher Laws," Thoreau added material about "wildness." "Once or twice, however, while I lived at the pond," he writes, "I found myself ranging the woods, like a half-starved hound, with a strange abandonment, seeking some kind of venison which I might devour, and no morsel could have been too savage for me. The wildest scenes had become unaccountably familiar. I found in myself, and still find, an instinct toward a higher, or, as it is named, spiritual life, as do most men, and another toward a primitive rank and savage one, and I reverence them both" (257). A tug-of-war between the physical and the spiritual worlds occurs. It is worth noting that in a section titled "Higher Laws," Thoreau spends so much of his time on the savage or wild aspects of life. In this, he dismantles the distinctions between "high" and "low," making connections between the individual body and the body politic, for instance, as when he suggests that as civilization increases, the drift toward a vegetarian diet naturally follows: "I have no doubt that it is a part of the destiny of the human race, in its gradual improvement, to leave off eating animals, as surely as the savage tribes have left off eating each other when they came in contact with the more civilized" (263).

Despite this appreciation of vegetarianism, Thoreau informs us with a certain glee that he can "eat a fried rat with a good relish" (264). His dining habits, he says, have become coarse over time, and he does not politely ask a blessing at the table before launching into a hunk of meat. He has become increasingly "conscious of an animal" within him, a beast that awakens as the spiritual life slumbers. This chapter shifts bizarrely from topic to topic, often summarized by fierce aphorisms, such as: "All sensuality is one, though it take many form; all purity is one" (267). And yet the chapter moves toward a general recognition that mind and body interact in vital ways. "Every man is the builder of a temple, called his body," he says. "We are all sculptors and painters, and our material is our own flesh and blood and bones. Any nobleness begins at once to refine a man's features, any meanness or sensuality to imbrute them" (269).

It was in the fifth draft, in the summer of 1853, that he widened the social dimensions of *Walden*. Moving swiftly through the manuscript, he layered in portraits of visitors from first to last, including references to Indians and Eskimos as well as Jesuit missionaries and a few black residents of the Walden region, such as Cato Ingraham and Fenda Freeman. He mentions some good friends, too, such as William Ellery Channing, the poet who "came from farthest to my lodge," and Bronson Alcott, "one of the last of the philosophers." Oddly, even sadly, he offers only an oblique glance at his closest friend, Emerson. "There was one other with whom I had 'solid seasons,' long to be remembered, at his house in the village, and who looked in upon me from time to time," he recalls of the man who housed and fed him for such a long time. Emerson often stopped at Walden Pond, and his writings were the icy spring from which the lucid waters of *Walden* emerged. But Thoreau could not bring himself to acknowledge openly the man whose influence was perhaps a little overwhelming.

The book moves through winter now, the season introduced by a line in "House-Warming": "The north wind had already begun to cool the pond, though it took many weeks of steady blowing to accomplish it, it is so deep" (289). As winter settled in, the cabin became home to various creatures: "The moles nested in my cellar, nibbling every third potato, and making a snug bed even there of some hair left after plastering and of brown paper; for even the wildest animals love comfort and warmth as well as man, and they survive the winter only because they are so careful to secure them" (300). Thoreau took pains to secure himself against the harsh elements, and this work occupies the quiet center of several chapters here, including "Winter Animals" and "The Pond in Winter." The latter is exquisite, with its description of the frozen pond: "Like the marmots in the surrounding hills, it closes its eye-lids and becomes dormant for three months or more" (331). As ever, the pond reflects the writer's moods and internal seasons, a mirror of the mind. Thoreau offers a detailed survey of the pond's geography and meditates on the laws of nature, drawing parallels between outer and inner worlds: "If we knew all the laws of Nature, we should need only one fact, or the description of one actual phenomenon, to infer all the particular results at that point" (338).

Good writers have always used the figure of speech known as synecdoche, in which the part stands in for the whole. Emerson wrote intriguingly in "The Poet" about this form of thought, saying "there is no fact in nature which does not carry the whole sense of nature." "I believe in what the Greeks call synecdoche," said Robert Frost, in his Emersonian mode. He defined synecdoche as "the philosophy of the part for the whole" and referred to this way of thinking as "skirting the hem of the goddess," saying "all that an artist needs is samples."[7] Taken to an almost sublime level, this figure—or technique—amounts to a philosophy of knowledge. One can intuit the whole of creation by getting to know one little piece of it; the piece itself leads the knower into wider knowledge. In Thoreau's version of this figure, one examines a single fact of nature in order to intuit the whole of creation, including the natural and spiritual realms—if, indeed, one can allow this kind of dualistic separation. At heart, Thoreau could not; for him, "higher" laws seem part and parcel of the physical or "lower" world.

During the winter chapters of *Walden,* Thoreau digs into himself, questioning the universe, trying to discern his own natural faith. In "The Pond in Winter," a number of large metaphysical questions appear, as the writer wonders: "as what—how—when—where?" Nature answers these blunt questions, with its implicit message of renewal. The day itself, which cycles to dawn from the depths of night, traces a little season of its own; but the larger cycle moves toward spring, as the awakening of the pond mirrors the awakening of the mind. Rebirth, of course, lies at the center of the Christian message; but it is naturalized here, taken back to its most concrete form. Spring becomes, for Thoreau, a secular moment of renewal, as it coincides with Easter, part of the cycle of vegetable life. "Only that day dawns to which we are awake," writes Thoreau toward the end of his "Conclusion," and this becomes a central point of *Walden,* with its call to observation and attention (382).

"Spring" is the final major chapter before the postscript, "Conclusion." Thoreau writes: "One attraction in coming to the woods to live was that I should have leisure and opportunity to see the spring come in" (350). Spring is something most of us observe in a glancing way. But Thoreau, as he would, peered intensely into this season, noticing the details, such as how the ice on the pond began to turn into a honeycomb as it thawed. Fogs, rains, and warmer suns melted the snow, trickling into the soft and fragrant earth. The sounds of animals and birds overwhelmed the ear. "Walden is melting apace," he writes, with obvious joy (359). There is not one season called spring, as it were, and Thoreau describes countless gradations within the season, as the slow warming shifts earth and sky, provoking a "memorable crisis" (360). Toward the end of the chapter, he exclaims: "And so the seasons went rolling on into summer, as one rambles into higher and higher grass" (367).

On September 6, 1847, Thoreau put his life at the pond behind him, moving from the experience of Walden to the text of *Walden*. In his "Conclusion," he reflects on the meaning of this sojourn, writing what amounts to a beautifully shaped prose poem. The book opened not with a seasonal chapter but with a thoughtful meditation on the economy of life, so *Walden* ends not seasonally, with "Spring," but with a philosophical and poetic call to arms. Now Thoreau challenges the reader to live more directly, as he has done. In going to the woods, he did not put himself forward in some egotistical attempt to rise above the community; he was no hermit there, as he reminds us again and again. He did not preach submission to the natural cycles. Nature, as he suggests, invites us to look beyond—or through—its sumptuous displays and to discover within us a spiritual life that is *grounded,* quite literally, in the atmosphere of our awakening.

"I learned this," he writes, with an almost religious fervor, "at least, by my experiment; that if one advances confidently in the direction of his dreams, and endeavors to live the life which he has imagined, he will meet with a success unexpected in common hours. He will put some things behind, will pass an invisible boundary; new, universal, and more liberal laws will begin to establish themselves around and within him; or the old laws be expanded, and interpreted in his favor in a more liberal sense, and he will live with the license of a higher order of beings" (371).

"Why should we be in such desperate haste to succeed, and in such desperate enterprises?" (374) Thoreau wonders, putting the question bluntly before his readers. Why do we rush? What are we trying to accomplish? How much is enough? What do we really want? How can we simplify our lives? How can we learn to live in harmony with our natural surroundings, and really *see* them, and feel the uplift of spring, the shift of seasons as a necessary internal shift? "However mean your life is," Thoreau writes, "meet it and live it" (376).

One could hardly ask for better advice. *Walden* is, and will remain, a central American text, one that has permanently changed, and continues to change, the physical and spiritual life of all who wish to live deliberately, in sustained contact with the natural world, and in community with their neighbors.

IV.

DURING HIS RELATIVELY BRIEF LIFE (tuberculosis killed him at the age of forty-four), Thoreau published only two books, *A Week on the Concord and Merrimack Rivers* and *Walden*. These were largely ignored in the press, although each attracted a few thoughtful readers. He was nonetheless fortunate to live in Concord, at the center of the transcendentalist movement, and to have Emerson for a mentor. Who could find a better reader? As it were, his friends would see to it that he was not forgotten, and that the writing he left behind—a trove that included forty-seven volumes of his journal in bound manuscripts—would be edited and published.

This material was left in the hands of the author's sister, Sophia, who worked with Emerson, Franklin B. Sanborn, and William Ellery Channing to cull several volumes in the decade after Thoreau's death, including *The Maine Woods* and *Cape Cod*. By the turn of the century, Thoreau had found a small but devoted audience. In 1906, Houghton Mifflin brought out the twenty-volume "Walden edition" of his work, *The Writings of Henry David Thoreau*. This marked the canonization of Thoreau, who took his proper place on the shelf beside Emerson, Whitman, Dickinson, and others.

Six hundred copies of the Walden edition formed the Manuscript Edition, so called because the first volume of each set had tipped into its pages an actual manuscript page by Thoreau—a bizarre idea, and one that has driven scholars mad as they have tried to track down these scattered pages, many of which have been lost. These wonderfully printed books were based on earlier editions, and therefore incomplete. Not until the early 1970s did a more scholarly edition of Thoreau's work begin to appear in the form of *The Writings of Henry D. Thoreau*, published over many years by Princeton University Press and edited by different hands. (The work of editing Thoreau has never been completed, as he left behind such voluminous material in the form of essays, poems, letters, and miscellaneous notes.)

Scholars have written a good deal about the worldwide influence of Thoreau's "Civil Disobedience" on such figures as Tolstoy and Gandhi.[8] *Walden* has also had a profound effect on generations of readers, serving as an aid and inspiration for those who want to get closer to nature and to seek in solitude the kinds of spiritual rewards that Thoreau describes. Yet it remains difficult to gauge exactly what influence Thoreau has had on shaping the American imagination. As Lawrence Buell suggests in *The Environmental Imagination*, the story of Thoreau's place in American culture has been complex; his reputation has shifted wildly over generations.[9] In the nineteenth century, Thoreau was largely seen as a minor figure in the transcendental school, a "character" who went off by himself into the wilderness, a writer of natural observations. He was taken up in the early twentieth century by critics who wished to elevate him as they wished to demote other, more "genteel" writers, such as Whittier and Longfellow. In the 1930s, with the publication of a major biography of Thoreau by Henry S. Canby, he was seen as an American dissenter, a critic of materialism. It was not until F. O. Matthiessen analyzed *Walden* at length in his masterwork, *American Renaissance* (1941), that Thoreau took his place as an American classic. Soon critics (such as Joel Porte) began to draw distinctions between Emerson and Thoreau, with the former pictured as a philosophical "idealist," the latter an empiricist. Stanley Cavell, himself a philosopher, began to regard *Walden* as part of a post-Kantian effort to recover the "thing-in-itself," which (I will guess) means that he saw Thoreau as moving beyond the idealism of Kant and his followers, grappling with the "real" hard surfaces of life, fixing on items that could be touched and tasted, such as the water in Walden Pond. With dozens of major studies appearing in the 1960s and '70s, Thoreau became a complex figure of unquestioned literary status.

As Buell explains, Thoreau adored travel narratives and had read nearly two hundred books in this genre, his favorite being Darwin's *Voyage of the* Beagle (1839). Buell rightly positions Thoreau and Darwin on the same plane, as both contributed to an ecological vision that has, over the years, only grown in intensity. "Darwin's ideas and Thoreau's art have influenced not only the course of modern science and modern environmental writing, respectively, but also the rewriting of history, so that we now imagine nineteenth century thought as leading up to Darwin and early American environmental writing as an antediluvian phase 'before Thoreau.' "[10] In truth, one cannot imagine the world of American nature writing without Thoreau. He gave us a body of work that lovingly evokes the natural world and discovers endless "correspondences," in the Emersonian sense, with the spiritual world. He created a genre of writing that has been endlessly productive. Over time, *Walden* has gathered a trail of books in its wake, many of them sparkling.

Books in the Thoreauvian tradition range from *The Mountains of California* (1894) by John Muir to Edward Abbey's *Desert Solitaire* (1968) and beyond. Abbey's work is based on the writer's experience as a park ranger in southern Utah, a landscape more primitive and devoid of human traces than anything Thoreau experienced. Echoing Thoreau, Abbey claims that he went into the desert "to confront, immediately and directly if it's possible, the bare bones of existence." He adds: "I dream of a hard and brutal mysticism in which the naked self merges with a nonhuman world and yet somehow survives still intact, individual, separate."[11] Among more recent books that owe a great deal to *Walden* is

one of my favorites, *Pilgrim at Tinker Creek* (1974) by Annie Dillard—
a book about the author's experience of natural life in a valley of the
Blue Ridge Mountains. Like Thoreau, Dillard explores the possibilities
of seeing, finding all around her transcendent analogues of spiritual reality. One might also mention *Into the Wild* (1996) in this context, the
bestselling book by Jon Krakauer about a young adventurer and ascetic,
Christopher McCandless, who disappeared into the Alaskan wilderness
in 1992. McCandless was passionate about Thoreau and kept a journal
during the wilderness sojourn that led to his premature death. (Mc-
Candless represents the darker side of the Thoreauvian influence: the
freefall descent into solitude that becomes solipsistic, even destructive.)

What marks all writing in the vein of Thoreau is the self-reflective
turn. By putting himself at the center of his work, combining the native
genre of American autobiography with nature writing of a profound order, Thoreau created in *Walden* a book that continues to invite us to live
more deliberately, in closer touch with the natural world, questioning
the values that we hold and the broad assumptions of society at large.
This book presents a direct challenge to American materialism and
serves as a marvelous counterpoint to elements in this country that perpetually insist that enough is not enough, that we must aspire to more
and more *things,* such as houses and cars, clothes and gadgets. Thoreau
found a source of happiness in simple living, and he tells us over and
over that the good life lies around us, at hand.

In *Walden,* he asks: "How many a man has dated a new era in his life
from the reading of a book?" How many indeed? And how many of
those would count *Walden* as this book? A fair number of them, I would
guess. In "Going to *Walden,*" the poet Mary Oliver reflects on the complex "message" of Thoreau. In her poem, she responds to friends who
suggest that she drive to Walden Pond for a day trip, to get in touch
with the meaning of Thoreau's masterwork. She resists going on this
physical journey, suggesting that

> *Going to Walden is not so easy a thing*
> *As a green visit. It is the slow and difficult*
> *Trick of living, and finding it where you are.*

UNCLE TOM'S CABIN;

OR,

LIFE AMONG THE LOWLY.

BY

HARRIET BEECHER STOWE.

VOL. I.

BOSTON:
JOHN P. JEWETT & COMPANY.
CLEVELAND, OHIO:
JEWETT, PROCTOR & WORTHINGTON.
1852.

SIX

Uncle Tom's Cabin

I.

No less a reader than Henry James recalled, in his autobiography, that *Uncle Tom's Cabin* (1852) affected him fiercely as a young man, in the early 1850s. "We lived and moved at that time, with great intensity, in Mrs. Stowe's novel," he said, describing this popular novel as "much less a book than a state of vision." In truth, few books in any generation compare with *Uncle Tom's Cabin* for sheer impact. Not only was it a bestseller of gigantic proportions, breaking all records for the nineteenth century, but it changed the way people thought about race—perhaps the dominant issue in American culture over the past two centuries. It fueled the abolitionist movement in obvious ways, drawing attention to the horrors of slavery and putting African American characters before a mass (largely white) audience in vivid ways.

Welcoming its author, Harriet Beecher Stowe, to the White House in 1862, Abraham Lincoln was said to have exclaimed: "So you're the little woman who wrote the book that started this great war!"[1] Little woman, indeed. Her novel galvanized antislavery sentiment in the Northern states, and it has permanently affected our understanding of slavery. While its readership has ebbed and flowed, it has never been far from the center of American discussions on the subject of race, and it remains an American classic, a work of unprecedented power to change hearts and minds. Whether it can be called a "great" work depends, of course, on your aesthetic criteria; George Orwell called it "the supreme example of the 'good bad' book," but conceded that, however "ludicrous," it is "deeply moving and essentially true."[2]

This novel about a genial black man sold by his hapless owner to a sadistic fiend is compulsively readable and affecting, as readers from Charles Dickens to George Sand and Leo Tolstoy have observed, although the characters often strike contemporary readers as stereotyped and the plot melodramatic—not surprising for a book that created many of the stereotypes we associate with slavery in the South before the Civil War. Given its theme and historical value, the book has enjoyed a revival in recent years, and critics have reclaimed it on many fronts. It remains a work of unusual seductive power, as a work of art and as a social document. It certainly gripped Stowe's generation and continued to directly influence ideas of race in America for decades. (A popular play version of the novel was performed well into the 1930s.)

II.

HARRIET BEECHER STOWE (1811–96) wrote this novel (her first) in a rage against the infamous Fugitive Slave Act of 1850, a bill that had come about as a compromise fashioned by Henry Clay, Daniel Webster, and others who should have known better. The new law proclaimed that runaways could (and should) be recaptured and sent back into slavery. Those who aided their escape were in legal jeopardy, as partners in a crime. The bill denied captured slaves the right to a jury trial and expanded the number of federal officers involved in catching runaways. Today one can hardly comprehend this action by Congress, but this was a delicate moment in the United States, when the entire project of union seemed more fragile than ever, largely because of the issue of slavery.

Many questions hovered, unresolved. Would new territories being added to the Union, including California, become slave states? How could a humane and democratic country, one founded on the notion that all men are created equal, allow slavery and the slave trade to survive?

The English had abolished the practice in 1833, and the eyes of the world fixed upon the States. Intellectuals in the North, such as Emerson and Thoreau, had become passionate abolitionists, and newspapers focused on the abolition movement sprang up everywhere, including the *National Era,* edited by Gamaliel Bailey.

Stowe, a housewife and mother married to a low-key theology professor, wrote a persuasive nonfiction piece to protest the Fugitive Slave Act, which Bailey had admired and published. She had also written a handful of short stories, demonstrating talent for fiction. In 1851, she outlined her idea for the novel that became *Uncle Tom's Cabin* in a letter to Bailey, who wrote back with enthusiasm, urging her to proceed. Soon the tale began to appear in regular installments, proving a major coup for Bailey and his paper, and for the abolition movement in general. The mere fact that Stowe had chosen to write for the *National Era* instead of one of the popular magazines for women, such as *Godey's Lady's Book,* says a lot about Stowe. Although women did not have the right to vote, she bravely assumed her right to speak, as did many of the women who became leading abolitionists.

Stowe had been lucky in her education. Her older sister ran a secondary school for women in Connecticut, and Harriet was sent there by her parents. She soon proved a formidable intellect, writing essays and rising to prominence as a leader among the student body. As part of a family that included nine full siblings and four half siblings, she had already learned to fight for her right to speak.

Her father, Lyman Beecher, presided over this talkative brood. He was a well-known Congregationalist minister and theologian who became president of Lane Theological Seminary in Cincinnati in 1832. The move from Connecticut to Ohio proved a good one for young Harriet, who joined the Semi-Colon Club, a thriving literary society, where she found an active circle of conversation. As Ohio, a non-slave state, and Kentucky, a slave state, were separated by the Ohio River, the issue of slavery was dramatically at hand; the river itself became a symbol of freedom. Many of those around her in Cincinnati harbored runaway slaves, and the Underground Railroad—a subterranean system for getting fugitive slaves to Canada and freedom—was very much in evidence among her friends and associates.

At meetings of her club, she encountered a shy young widower who, like her father, was a professor of theology and a minister. She married Calvin E. Stowe in 1836 and seemed quite willing to settle down. But she felt an urge to write and in 1843 published a volume of stories about Pilgrim life in early Massachusetts that attracted a small but interested readership. The marriage was, as far as one can really tell from such distance, a good one, and the family income was hugely amplified by Stowe's writing, though making money was never her goal.

She was drawn to the abolitionist cause quite early, but didn't speak up until 1836, when she wrote a protest letter about the trashing of an abolitionist paper, the *Philanthropist,* which was edited by James G. Birney (a friend who had encouraged Harriet in her literary work). Her fiery letter appeared anonymously in the *Cincinnati Journal,* edited by one of her brothers, Henry Ward Beecher—a prominent clergyman, abolitionist, and public intellectual who became one of Mark Twain's close friends. Harriet's sister Catharine was already an outspoken abolitionist and in 1837 would publish an essay on slavery and the duty of American women to rise up against it. Two of Harriet's brothers were also strong abolitionists, and so a climate of acceptance for abolition surrounded her. Yet nobody could have predicted that she would write a book like *Uncle Tom's Cabin*—a novel that would appeal to millions of readers, on many levels.

Stowe's personal life remains something of a mystery, although various biographers have written about her at length. Her relationship with her husband remains puzzling. They had many passionate interests in common, including a devotion to the cause of abolition. Yet they struggled, as did many couples in this period, with the issue of contraception, spending a good deal of time apart—just to make sure Harriet was not always pregnant, as Joan D. Hedrick points out in her life of Stowe.[3] The letters exchanged between Harriet and Calvin reveal the depths of their intimacy, and also betray a strain of unacknowledged bisexuality in Calvin. As Hedrick tells us, Calvin had many close relationships with men, and when Harriet was abroad or visiting spas or relatives, he would sometimes sleep with a friend. "When I get desperate," he tells his wife, "& cannot stand it any longer, I get dear, good kind hearted Brother Stagg to come and sleep with me, and he puts his arms round me & hugs me to my hearts' content." (Stagg is well named.) Another friend, one "Mr. Farber," also enjoyed sleeping with Calvin, who confesses to Harriet that "he kisses and kisses upon my rough old face, as if I were a most beautiful young lady instead of a musty old man. The Lord sent him here to be my comfort." He adds: "He will have me sleep with him once in a while, and he says, *that is almost as good as being married*—the dear little innocent ignorant soul."[4]

One must keep in mind that during this period it was not uncommon for men to sleep together and that sexual intimacy was not *necessarily* involved. Nevertheless, one can hardly deny the homoerotic undercurrent of Calvin's letters to his wife, and must assume she did not think ill of her husband for his intimacies with Stagg and Farber, among others. She would have been less willing, perhaps, to have Calvin spend time in the sack with young women.

Major biographical questions can never be "solved," but one can often see where ideas have their murky origins. *Uncle Tom's Cabin* doubtless had many sources in the author's life. It's fascinating to note where Stowe herself located the beginnings of this tale. On December 16, 1852, she wrote to the abolitionist Eliza Cabot Follen:

> I have been the mother of seven children, the most beautiful and most loved of whom lies buried near my Cincinnati residence. It was at his dying bed and at his grave that I learned what a poor slave mother may feel when her child is torn away from her. In those depths of sorrow which seemed to me immeasurable, it was my only prayer to God that such anguish might not be suffered in vain. There were circumstances about his death of such peculiar bitterness, of what seemed almost cruel suffering that I felt I could never be consoled for it unless this crushing of my own heart might enable me to work out some great good to others.
>
> I allude to this here because I have often felt that much that is in that book had its root in the awful scenes and bitter sorrow of that summer. It has left now, I trust, no trace on my mind except a deep compassion for the sorrowful, especially for mothers who are separated from their children.[5]

In addition, Stowe had various external sources to inspire her. She had before her, for example, Frederick Douglass's popular autobiography and a book by a runaway slave called Josiah Henson, who had worked in Maryland on a tobacco farm before his flight to Canada in 1830. (After the success of *Uncle Tom's Cabin,* Henson's publishers reissued his book under the title *Uncle Tom's Story of His Life.*) There were other recollections by former slaves, many of them recounting incidents similar to the events described in Stowe's book. As Stowe explained in *A Key to "Uncle Tom's Cabin"* (1853), she drew on myriad sources, including interviews with escaped slaves and reports from one of her brothers, who evidently met a man very like the wicked slave owner Simon Legree. It is nearly impossible to guess what sources were most important to Stowe, who insisted to her readers that the incidents making up this story were "to a very great extent, authentic" (462).

Readers certainly discovered in *Uncle Tom's Cabin* a story of considerable relevance and appeal. Eight presses had to run night and day to keep up with the demand, which seemed inexhaustible. Three hundred thousand copies were sold in the first year alone, and this was just the beginning. The novel became not just an American but a world phenomenon, selling more copies than any book in the nineteenth century except for the Bible. Fresh editions appeared annually for over fifty years, and there were numerous adaptations for the stage and (later) screen. The book's commercial success became a news item in itself, not unlike the Harry Potter series in our time. But Stowe's book leaves the little boy with round glasses and a zigzag scar on his forehead in the dust. *Uncle Tom's Cabin* actually changed—or massively helped to change—the way countless readers in the United States thought about race and slavery, perhaps the central issues in American history.

III.

THE NOVEL OPENS WITH A CRISIS. The apparently benevolent slaveholder Arthur Shelby may lose his plantation in Kentucky because of financial incompetence. The scene is painful to read, as the self-indulgent Shelby meets with a coarse slave trader, Mr. Haley, who manages to purchase from Shelby a middle-aged and beloved slave, Uncle Tom, as well as a young boy, Harry, who is the son of Eliza, a servant to Mrs. Shelby. As Shelby says in his wishy-washy way: "I would rather not sell him [Harry]." His reasoning is thus: "I'm a humane man, and I hate to take the boy from his mother, sir" (9). But this is just what he does, however reluctantly.

Eliza overhears this conversation and is horrified by the betrayal. She reveals her worries to her mistress, who quickly assures her that her husband would never do such a terrible thing. Stowe writes: "Mrs. Shelby, being entirely ignorant of her husband's embarrassments, and knowing only the general kindliness of his temper, had been quite sincere in the entire incredulity with which she had met Eliza's suspicions" (15). Nonetheless, the truth emerges, and Eliza bravely decides to flee with her son, thus following her husband, George Harris, a fiercely competent fellow from a neighboring plantation who has recently fled northward himself after promising his wife that he will somehow manage to win freedom for her and their son.

It's a poignant setup for a novel that never fails to move swiftly from vivid scene to scene. Stowe's language is clear and fresh throughout, as readable today as it must have been when it appeared in serial form. Stowe often writes metaphorically, as when Haley and Shelby finish the initial conversation and Shelby mulls over his options: " 'Well,' said Haley, after they had both silently picked their nuts for a season, 'what do you say?' " (12). (They eat nuts, quite literally; but to pick one's nuts for a season was figurative as well as literal.) A momentous decision is taken, and "a season" was necessary to make it, in the form of a long pause for thinking. Similarly, when Haley first sees Eliza, he says: "There's an article, now!" (9). She is, as it were, an "item," with all the sexual associations we still attach to that term. But this handsome young woman is also reduced to something that can be "shopped." She is property. As we see, the language operates on many levels.

We meet Uncle Tom in chapter 4, "An Evening in Uncle Tom's Cabin." The cabin is a beautiful place, immaculate in every respect, in bold deviation from the racist line that black people could not keep a house or themselves clean. "In front it had a neat garden-patch, where, every summer, strawberries, raspberries, and a variety of fruits and vegetables flourished under careful tending," Stowe writes. "The whole front of it was covered by a large scarlet bignonia and a native multiflora rose, which, entwisting and interlacing, left scarce a vestige of the rough logs to be seen" (25). What should be noticed here, I think, is the particularity of the writing, its knowledgeable specificity, and the elegant unfolding of the information in an agreeably complex syntax. John Updike could not do better. The linguistic medium of *Uncle Tom's Cabin* is everywhere noteworthy and undermines the frequently voiced opinion that this novel is hopelessly second-rate and no work of art at all.

Objections to the novel usually turn on its "sentimentality," its excess of emotion, and its melodramatic plotlines. Certainly Stowe may be placed squarely in the tradition of sentimental fiction, a form that rose to its high-water mark in the nineteenth century. This kind of novel was meant to appeal to female readers in particular, and women's issues lie at the center of this book. The female characters are strong, and one gets the sense that Stowe believed slavery would only be ended by women. Sentimental novels fell out of favor with serious readers in the early twentieth century, however, and Stowe's reputation tumbled. As Hedrick notes, Stowe's "decline resulted from the removal of literature from the parlor to institutions to which women had limited access: men's clubs, high-culture journals, and prestigious universities."[6] Judged by the aesthetic standards of its day, her novel should in fact be regarded as a distinctive achievement, one that sits comfortably on the shelf with others by Sir Walter Scott and Charles Dickens, both favorites of Stowe's. (For a well-informed review of the sentimental tradition in which Stowe's novel lies, see "Sentimental Power: *Uncle Tom's Cabin* and the Politics of Literary History" by Jane P. Tompkins.[7])

Chloe is Uncle Tom's wife and the mother of his children. "A cook she certainly was," Stowe writes, "in the very bone and centre of her soul" (26). Despite the children, the marriage appears sexless; their bed is "covered neatly with a snowy spread" to suggest a kind of innocence, even virginity. But Tom himself is physically impressive: "He was a large, broad-chested, powerfully-made man, of a full glossy black, and a face whose truly African features were characterized by an expression of grave and steady good sense, united with much kindliness and benevolence" (27). That Uncle Tom is a caricature as well cannot be denied; his portrait remains one-sided, even lopsided. He seems too good for his own good. As such, the figure of an "Uncle Tom" became (especially during the militant phase of the civil rights era, in the late 1960s) a derisive way of talking about a black man who kowtowed to white men. But in Stowe's mind, Tom is the perfect Christian gentleman.

We also meet young George Shelby in this chapter. A boy of thirteen, he worships Uncle Tom, and Tom seems more attached to the boy than to his wife and children (with whom he appears to have little real contact). Whenever Tom is around his own family, he speaks in dialect. In the company of educated white men and women, he speaks like them. This implies a level of intelligence and linguistic flexibility denied most of Stowe's white characters. Although many readers admire her with good reason, Chloe is something of a stock figure, never quite fully realized. A flatness of characterization has generally led to the charge that Stowe deals in stereotypes. To me, this seems only partially true and does not detract from the novel so much as point to its context. Many novelists of this period, including Dickens, made no attempt to round out their characters. "Roundness" of character was not part of their aesthetic.

The novel surges, its plot cranking at high speed, designed (as in the serialized novels of Dickens) to snag readers' attention, to keep them turning the pages. Chapter 5 is titled with typical Stowe irony: "Showing the Feelings of Living Property on Changing Owners." Now Mrs. Shelby discovers the horrors about to take place and expresses her anguish; but she is naive about her husband's finances, even his character. She often speaks in quasi-biblical language, as do many characters in this novel. Stowe consistently reveals her biblical knowledge, as when Mrs. Shelby says in disgust to her husband: "I'll be in no sense accomplice or help in this cruel business. I'll go and see poor old Tom, God help him in his distress! They shall see, at any rate, that their mistress can feel for and with them. As to Eliza, I dare not think about it. The Lord forgive us! What have we done, that this cruel necessity should come on us?" (42). Stowe's readers would have heard echoes of various well-known verses, including Luke 23:34, where Jesus says, "Father, forgive them, for they know not what they do," and Numbers 22:28–30, in which an ass is beaten by its master, and an angel speaks for the ass, crying: "What have I done to you that you beat me three times?" This chapter ends with Eliza fleeing with her child, en route to Canada, where she hopes to reunite with her husband. It's a wrenching development for everyone concerned, including Uncle Tom and Chloe, who are aghast when they learn that Mr. Shelby has stooped so low as to sell Harry and Tom.

Eliza's flight is discovered in chapter 6, and soon the chase begins, with Haley setting off in pursuit of his newly purchased property. Chapter 7 begins: "It is impossible to conceive of a human creature more wholly desolate and forlorn than Eliza" (57). The writing here is especially taut, concrete, and striking. Eliza speeds her way toward the Ohio River, and allusions to crossing various rivers in the Bible, such as the Jordan, hover in the background. Stowe elevates the flight of Eliza and Harry to mythic status as the chapter moves toward a famous scene, with Eliza leaping from ice floe to ice floe across the semi-frozen river, the child in her arms:

> The huge green fragment of ice on which she alighted pitched and creaked as her weight came on it, but she staid there not a moment. With wild cries and desperate energy she leaped to another and still another cake;—stumbling—leaping—slipping—springing upwards again! Her shoes are gone—her stockings cut from her feet—while blood marked every step; but she saw nothing, felt nothing, till dimly, as in a dream, she saw the Ohio side, and a man helping her up the bank. (67–68)

This passage has been illustrated by many artists and persists as one of the central images of the novel. It includes action writing of a high order, not far behind Dickens, who had a particular gift for such scenes and was able to sustain the tension over many paragraphs.

Stowe carries the tension forward by calling her next chapter "Eliza's Escape." But she has already escaped, hasn't she? Not quite, it so happens. The Fugitive Slave Law has made it illegal for anyone to harbor or assist an escaping slave. Until Eliza and her child reach Canada, they remain threatened, and now the hideous Tom Loker gets on her trail. He is bad Tom, as opposed to Uncle Tom, or good Tom. Loker's assistant is called Marks, described as a "mousing man," as in a cat that toys with its prey before pouncing. Haley hires these men to catch his runaway slaves, and Stowe nicely captures the mode of conversation among these low types, offering this aside to her audience: "If any of our refined and Christian readers object to the society into which this scene introduces them, let us beg them to begin and conquer their prejudices in time. The catching business, we beg to remind them, is rising to the dignity of a lawful and patriotic profession" (79–80). This withering irony produces a strong rhetorical effect, pushing forward the polemics of the novel with a sly wit.

A new subplot involving Senator Bird of Ohio and his wife begins in chapter 9. Here Stowe offers a direct polemic against the Fugitive Slave Law. The kindly and well-meaning senator voted against the law, but he feels obliged to uphold it. His wife, however, is shocked by his attitude, arguing that a Christian has a duty to "feed the hungry, clothe the naked, and comfort the desolate" (88). The senator is torn between his roles as politician and husband, yet Stowe remains firmly on the side of Mrs. Bird, believing that a husband's first duty lies there, with his wife. Like George Harris, Senator Bird is a devoted husband, but he feels committed to upholding the law, at least on some theoretical level.

All of this theorizing stops when Eliza suddenly appears, a "young and slender woman, with garments torn and frozen, with one shoe gone." Mrs. Bird vows to protect this runaway slave and her son. "Nobody shall hurt you here, poor woman," she says, defying her husband (90). As he questions Eliza himself, Senator Bird discovers that she was about to have her child taken away from her. So the issue of losing a child rises to the fore, one that deeply affected Stowe, who had lost a child of her own. Mrs. Bird, it so happens, has lost a child as well. As readers, we sense that Eliza and her son are in safe hands at last.

The plot switches to Uncle Tom now, with a chapter called "The Property Is Carried Off." This is witty and pointed: Tom is "property." He can be carried like any inanimate object. The drama of his separation from his family is affecting, although it seems less vexing than the separation between George Shelby and Tom. This is highlighted when George ties his dollar on a string around Tom's neck, and Tom is seen "stroking the boy's fine curly head with his large, strong hand, but speaking in a voice as tender as a woman's" (110). It would be excessive to call this homoerotic, but that element occurs, however subliminally; the sexuality may fly under the radar of most readers, as it should. Stowe works (unconsciously or semi-consciously) by evasion, a "sentimental" writer in that she portrays many overt emotions; but they are the conventional ones. The real novel lives in the margins of the text, or between the lines.

Stowe never lets up on her portrayal of the horrors of slavery, and so when Tom goes downriver en route to his new owner, the trip is horrendous, as in chapter 12, where a slave woman commits suicide by jumping overboard because her child has been taken away from her. This scene foreshadows the portrait of Eva, or Evangeline, in chapter 14. The beautiful child catches the attention of Uncle Tom from his first glimpse of her. "Her form was the perfection of childish beauty, without its usual chubbiness and squareness of outline. There was about it an undulating and aerial grace, such as one might dream of for some mythic and allegorical being" (155). Eva is too good to be true perhaps— one in a long succession of child-heroines in nineteenth-century fiction, a first cousin of Little Nell in *The Old Curiosity Shop* (1841), which Charles Dickens himself noted when he suggested that Stowe was "a leetle unscrupulous in the appropriatin' way."[8]

Uncle Tom is overwhelmed by Eva, and their relationship—while hardly sexual—is nevertheless intimate. "Tom watched the little lady a great deal, before he ventured on any overtures towards acquaintanceship" (156). Again, the language is that of romance fiction; but the object of Tom's gaze is a mere child, and therefore beyond the realm of overt eroticism. Their relationship develops when Eva falls overboard and Tom rescues her: "He caught her in his arms, and, swimming with her to the boat-side, handed her up, all dripping, to the grasp of hundreds of hands, which, as if they had all belonged to one man, were stretched eagerly out to receive her" (158). In effect, Tom also rescues himself, as the girl's father buys him from Haley. Augustine St. Clare is "the son of a wealthy planter of Louisiana," although the family was originally from Canada—which may account for his lack of racism in Stowe's eyes. He provides an appropriate and comfortable home for Tom. As Eva says: "Papa is very good to everybody, only he always will laugh at them" (161). One cringes slightly in the presence of this perfect child and her innocent father; Stowe has cut them out of cardboard.

As the story progresses, she introduces a number of characters who represent different attitudes to both race and slavery. One is Marie St.

Clare: the spoiled, selfish mistress of the house—a common figure in abolitionist literature. She is no housekeeper, we are told. Nor was her mother before her. Both are called "indolent and childish, unsystematic and improvident" (216). By contrast, Miss Ophelia (Augustine's cousin from Vermont) is a wonder of domestic activity. She is "up at four o'clock" and busily turns everything upside down to clean the house: "The store-room, the linen-presses, the china-closet, the kitchen and cellar, that day, all went under an awful review. Hidden things of darkness were brought to light to an extant that alarmed all the principalities and powers of kitchen and chamber, and caused many wonderings and murmurings about 'dese yer northern ladies' from the domestic cabinet" (216). Here Stowe echoes the New Testament, as in Romans 8:38–39: "Neither death, nor life, nor angels, nor principalities, nor powers, nor things present, nor things to come, nor height, nor depth, nor any other creature, shall be able to separate us from the love of God, which is in Christ Jesus our Lord." These powers are, ironically, reduced to "kitchen and chamber."

St. Clare gets into heated arguments with Miss Ophelia, who believes that slavery is wrong but seems to distrust black people. Among the many black characters entering the narrative at midpoint in the novel is a young black girl called Topsy, a child of no known origin. "Never was born," she tells us, "never had no father nor mother, nor nothin'" (254). (The phrase "grew like Topsy" is a common one in the language now, referring to anything that grows wildly.) Stowe uses Topsy—a bright and original creature, and one of her finest inventions—as a way of arguing that black people are just as smart as their white counterparts. Only their situation in life has caused them to appear backward. "Topsy was smart and energetic," Stowe tells us. She learns with "surprising quickness. With a few lessons," says Stowe, "she had learned to do the proprieties of Miss Ophelia's chamber in a way with which even that particular lady could find no fault" (261). An unruly, fun-loving, clever, and charismatic figure, Topsy is one of the most interesting of Stowe's creations. In her, the author moves well beyond the usual stereotypes of sentimental fiction, although (inadvertently) she may have created another stereotype, as later writers often summoned versions of Topsy.

For two years, as we learn in chapter 22, Tom lingers in the bower of bliss with the St. Clare family. Little Eva often sits on his knee. They hold hands and walk together in the Edenic world of St. Clare's estate. The prose in this chapter glows, turning radiantly purple at times. But there is something amiss, as we soon learn: "The faithful old heart felt a sudden thrust; and Tom thought how often he had noticed, within six months, that Eva's little hands had grown thinner, and her skin more transparent, and her breath shorter; and how, when she ran or played in the garden, as she once could for hours, she became soon so tired and languid" (274). Eva, whose name means angel (as well as evangelist), seems already a ghost of herself, and she will soon die of consumption, a disease familiar to Stowe's readers.

Eva is a stock figure: the little child who, in her suffering, spreads goodness and light and the Christian message. "Dear papa," she says to her father as she lies on her deathbed, "how I wish we could go together!" Her father wonders where. "To our Saviour's home," she explains (292). The death scene occurs in chapter 26, and Eva embodies the role of evangelist here, as her name implies. She tells her father that she will soon see Christ face-to-face. "Eva, after this, declined rapidly," Stowe writes (307). The death itself is on a par with the death of Little Nell, and it wrenched the hearts of Stowe's readers. We are not used to such scenes in the twenty-first century, so the deathbed narrative may seem remote and "sentimental." For Stowe, of course, who had been through such an experience herself, the scene had an immensely realistic side. "Pray that this may be cut short!" St. Clare says, near the end. Soon the child cries: "O! love,—joy,—peace!" (312). The dialogue sounds highly unreal to a contemporary reader, yet the passage remains affecting to those willing to read the book without prejudging its emotional content, which owes much to the traditions of melodrama.

The effects of Eva's death on the family, and Tom, consume Stowe for a couple of chapters. St. Clare himself begins to topple in the direction of Christianity, which he has resisted thus far. Uncle Tom plays the role of spiritual director for him. Eva's mother, Marie, "felt the loss of Eva as deeply as she could feel anything"—a highly ambiguous line indeed. Then everything turns on a dime when St. Clare unexpectedly dies. He is sitting in a café, by himself, when two drunks begin to fight. In an effort to separate the men, "St. Clare received a fatal stab in the side with a bowie-knife, which he was attempting to wrest from one of them" (333). Marie, as might be expected, goes into "convulsions." Only Tom and Ophelia show any presence of mind in the midst of this chaos.

Tom is unprotected now, in a legal sense. He can and will be sold, the reader senses. And he is. In chapter 30, Stowe conjures a vision of hell as a warehouse full of slaves waiting to be auctioned on the block. "A slave-warehouse," she tells her reader, "is a house externally not much unlike many others, kept with neatness; and where every day you may see arranged, under a sort of shed along the outside, rows of men and women, who stand there as a sign of the property sold within" (343). The conversation among the slaves is chilling, as when a mother advises her daughter to hide her beautiful hair, fearing it might attract an owner who would turn her into a sex slave—a common situation. "Respectable families would be more apt to buy you, if they saw you looked plain and decent," she tells the girl (348). Alas, the child is separated from her mother and sold to the infamous Simon Legree, whose name has become a synonym for sadist.

Legree appears for the first time toward the end of this chapter, described as "a short, broad, muscular man, in a checked shirt considerably open at the bosom, and pantaloons much the worse for dirt and wear" (350). Later, he is called a "bullet-head," suggesting hardness, an inflexibility of mind, with a streak of violence in his character. That his shirt is "open at the bosom" suggests rakishness as well, and this makes him all the more threatening for the young girl. As for Tom's reaction: "From the moment that Tom saw him approaching, he felt an immediate and revolting horror at him" (351). The reader's worst fears are realized when Tom is sold to Legree. Needless to say, from this point on his fortunes crumble.

Chapter 31 opens with an indelible image of Tom in chains aboard a slave ship: "On the lower part of a small, mean boat, on the Red river, Tom sat,—chains on his wrists, chains on his feet, and a weight heavier than chains lay on his heart" (354). Tom's sweet Kentucky home, his wife and children, the benevolent St. Clare, and the golden-headed Eva all lay behind him, barely retrievable in memory: "All had faded from his sky,—moon and star." As she often does, Stowe works metonymically: "moon and star" symbolize the shimmering, distant loved ones in his private universe; these have sadly "faded."

Legree takes center stage at this point, pictured as a man compacted of sexual desire and hard, sadistic energy. His "greenish-gray eye" glares at his new possession, Uncle Tom. He sips whiskey—a great vice, in the eyes of Stowe and many of her readers. There is no subtlety about Legree, who boasts of his business acumen as a slave owner: "When one nigger's dead, I buy another" (358). One of the most common critiques of this novel centers on the portrayal of Legree, who appears one-dimensional. All cruelty and meanness of spirit harbor in him. Yet the portrait works well; he is Satan, and one can hardly imagine a well-rounded Satan who also likes children and animals. This novel works by contrasts, and the multidimensionality of Stowe's fictive world is achieved by combining the various parts, creating a balanced overall impression.

Stowe continues to give her chapters ironic titles, and one often has to read on to discover the exact nature and quality of her satire. "Dark Places" is the title of chapter 32, and it's a grim one. An epigraph from Psalms 74:20 signals the tone of the narrative: "The dark places of the earth are full of the habitations of cruelty." The story opens: "Trailing wearily behind a rude wagon, and over a ruder road, Tom and his associates faced onward" (360). As they are being driven toward Simon Legree's hellish plantation, there is no doubt about the multiple associations of "rude," which means crudely fashioned as well as inhuman, unformed, and noxious. In its Anglo-Saxon root sense (Stowe is always attentive to such) the word means a "cross to bear." These sad travelers pursue a "wild, forsaken road." And so one thinks of Christ on the cross, when he asks why God has forsaken him. These religious undertones become the dominant chord in the hymns that Tom begins to sing, as in: "Jerusalem, my happy home, / Name ever dear to me!" (Slaves often sang hymns and songs, as Frederick Douglass recalls in his 1845 *Narrative*: "I did not, when a slave, understand the deep meaning of those rude and apparently incoherent songs . . . Those songs still follow me, to deepen my hatred of slavery, and quicken my sympathies for my brethren in bonds."[9])

Legree's plantation had once belonged to "a gentleman of opulence," and he kept it nicely. Now it exudes a "ragged, forlorn appearance." Its new owner has used the property, "as he did everything else, merely as an implement for money-making" (362). Stowe underscores this idea: to squeeze every ounce of profit from one's possessions is to abuse them and to abuse one's role as caretaker or husbandman of resources. Naked capitalism offends her. One must always, as Stowe suggests, take into account the human costs of operation and behave in ways that enhance the spirit, not degrade it. In writing this, Stowe anticipates arguments that would naturally arise during the so-called Gilded Age, when raw capitalist urges were given full vent and the poor as well as the middle class suffered the consequences.

Simon Legree may be evil, but he shows considerable skill in managing his property to benefit himself. He notices that Tom is "a first-class hand," and so tries to maximize his talents. But he hates Tom as darkness hates the light. Stowe seems unable to grapple in a complex way with Legree's antipathy, which she calls the "native antipathy of bad to good" (369). In a modern novel, perhaps, one might have a much fuller sense of Legree's background, coming to understand what drives him to act as he does, why he dislikes Tom so much, and so forth. We get only the haziest glimpse of the diabolical inner workings of Legree's mind. In any case, he hopes to "break" Tom in whatever ways he can. When he tries to make him a slave driver, Tom refuses, saying: "I'm willin' to work, night and day, and work while there's life and breath in me; but this yer thing I can't feel it right to do;—and, Mas'r, I *never* shall do it,—*never!*" (374–75). Legree now has what he wants: a reason to whip Tom, and he does.

Tom is brutally beaten, and as chapter 34 opens he lies "groaning and bleeding alone, in an old forsaken room of the gin-house, among pieces of broken machinery, piles of damaged cotton, and other rubbish which had there accumulated" (377). Again, one admires the metonymic range of associations. The gin house refers to the cotton gin, invented by Eli Whitney in 1793. This product of the industrial revolution further dehumanized men and women, vastly increasing the profitability of slaveholders. The ruins of agribusiness lie about Uncle Tom, symbolized by the broken machinery and damaged cotton. Miss Cassy helps Tom now; she is a slave "whom long practice with the victims of brutality had made familiar with many healing arts" (378). Lovingly, she applies cooling applications to the wounds of the broken man. Soon one learns that she is a mother torn from her own children. Having lost faith herself, she challenges Tom on his religious beliefs. "You tell me," she says, "that there is a God,—a God that looks down and sees all these things" (386). Obviously she cannot accept this possibility. Tom's response to her is fairly hackneyed: "O, Missis, I wish you'd go to him that can give you living waters!" (387). But Cassy refuses to believe, seeing nothing in her life but "sin and long, long, long despair."

As it turns out, there are limits to Legree's influence, and one of the agents of pressure on him is Cassy herself, a wily creature who figures on many levels of Stowe's narrative (in a bizarre Dickensian twist, she actually turns out to be the mother of Eliza, with whom she is reunited in Canada). Acting deranged on purpose, she terrifies Legree, "who had that superstitious horror of insane persons which is common to coarse and uninstructed minds" (389). Stowe makes a halfhearted attempt to "explain" Legree in chapter 35, telling us about his pious mother and dreadful father. But her explanations fail. Perhaps a dreadful mother would have been difficult for Stowe to imagine: motherhood is itself sacred to her. "Boisterous, unruly, and tyrannical," Legree ignores his mother (391). She prays for him earnestly, and for a brief time his better angels seem to win out; but sin overwhelms him again as he falls back upon his own "rough nature."

In chapter 37, aptly called "Liberty," we return to Eliza and George in their flight to Canada, where a heady promise of freedom awaits them. Earlier in the novel, Tom Loker had been attacked by George, in self-defense; but Eliza had mercifully taken him to "a most immaculately clean Quaker bed," where Loker's moral and spiritual transformation occurred (402). The situation of *this* Tom forms a counterpoint to the story of Uncle Tom. As always, Stowe attends to the shape of her larger narrative and likes to balance images and supply countercurrents to narrative streams.

The novel flows toward its climactic phase as Cassy and Emmeline escape from Legree's plantation and Uncle Tom suffers his final humiliations. Tom will not submit fully to his earthly master, preferring his heavenly one. Annoyed beyond all measure, Legree loses control and (in the chapter sententiously called "The Martyr") brutalizes Tom as "the spirit of evil" invades him. Now "foaming with rage," Stowe writes, he "smote" his victim to the ground. The biblical "smote" adds to the some-

what overbearing nature of the description. Just before passing out entirely, Tom cries (in Christlike fashion): "I forgive ye, with all my soul!"
(434). This response has been hard for modern readers to swallow.

Young George Shelby, the benevolent master and old friend to Uncle
Tom, appears in the nick of time, so that Tom can expire in his loving
arms. As Tom dies, he cries (more to the audience of readers than to
George): "Who,—who,—who shall separate us from the love of Christ?"
(440). With that, "he fell asleep," as Stowe puts it, using a typical euphe-
mism for dying. Infuriated by Tom's fate, George determines to fight
slavery as best he can: "I will do *what one man can* to drive out this curse
of slavery from my land!" (442).

Stowe the plot maker sets to work vigorously, tying up the disparate
threads of the story into a neat bow before offering her "Concluding Remarks" in a final chapter. In this postscript she speaks directly to her
readers, explaining that her novel is based on real events: "The separate
incidents that compose the narrative are, to a very great extent, authentic, occurring, many of them, either under her own observation, or that
of her personal friends. She or her friends have observed characters the
counterpart of almost all that are here introduced; and many of the sayings are word for word as heard herself, or reported to her" (463). What
nonsense this is, a sop to skeptical readers, especially those in the South,
many of whom attacked the novel as antislavery propaganda as soon as
the first chapters began to appear. Of course incidents along the lines of
those imagined by Stowe could have really happened, and she had in
fact witnessed slavery firsthand on a visit to Kentucky in the 1830s. (She
had also interviewed numerous runaway slaves while living in Cincinnati.) Yet Stowe had nevertheless to imagine the truth of what she knew
and to shape a fiction that would reveal all the lines in the ugly face of
slavery.

Among the overlooked features of the novel—and one that may
have played some role in its attraction for readers—is its robust sexuality, as Henry Louis Gates has noted. The story opens with Eliza and
George, two handsome, young, and recently married slaves. Theirs is a
passionate marriage, and Stowe makes no bones about it. Uncle Tom
gives off sexual vibrations, too, as when he rescues Little Eva, who has
fallen into the water. He is described in the rescue scene as "broad-

chested, strong-armed." When Eva's father buys Tom, he falls happily into a kind of paradise in which he cultivates a platonic relationship with the sweet blond girl. They drift through a dreamlike world, holding hands. They even kiss.

Of course Stowe never meant, at least not consciously, to imply a sexual aspect to this friendship, and one should not overemphasize the quasi-sexual undercurrents of the novel. Nevertheless, an energy that might be called erotic courses through the writing, often disguised or subverted. As Gates says, "The language of Stowe's contemporary reviewers often echoed the submerged discourse of arousal: 'It is a live book, and it talks to its readers as if it were alive. It first awakens their attention, arrests their thoughts, touches their sympathies, rouses their curiosity, and creates such an interest in the story it is telling, that they cannot let it drop until the whole story is told.' "[10] Even today, readers will find the book's sensibility surprisingly physical, and this adds to its continuing appeal.

IV.

IN ITS TIME, Stowe's novel forcefully shaped the way Americans thought about slavery by giving it a palpable reality. In the Northern states, abolition had its enthusiasts; but there was never a general opposition to slavery. With her monstrously huge bestseller, Stowe almost single-handedly created a mass audience for the antislavery movement, helping to generate the kind of support needed (eventually) to prosecute a successful war against the South. "Poetry makes nothing happen," W. H. Auden once said; but fiction does, at least on rare occasions.

As might be expected, *Uncle Tom's Cabin* had its opponents as well as its supporters. In the South, any number of pro-slavery pamphlets and books appeared within a year or two. William Gilmore Simms, one of the most popular Southern authors of the day, roundly denounced Stowe's work in *The Sword and the Distaff,* and a number of anti-Tom books arose, including *Aunt Phillis's Cabin* by Mary Henderson Eastman and *The Planter's Northern Bride* by Caroline Lee Hentz. (Ironically, Hentz had once been a friend of Stowe's in Cincinnati.) Published in

1854, Hentz's book, telling the story of a Northern woman who marries a Southern plantation owner, found a sizable audience as well. Her heroine is the daughter of an abolitionist, but she comes to see the "good" side of slavery. Over two dozen books in this vein appeared in the decade after *Uncle Tom's Cabin,* but each has been swallowed by time. For her part, Stowe did not sit back idly and watch the attacks proceed. She published *A Key to "Uncle Tom's Cabin"* in 1853, talking about the "real life equivalents" of her major characters and marshaling even more arguments against slavery. This, too, became a bestselling book, much to the dismay of Southern readers, who wished Mrs. Stowe would simply go away.

Uncle Tom's Cabin translated well to the stage, and probably more people were introduced to the story through plays and musicals than in its original form. The copyright laws at that time being lax, it was possible for anyone to mount what was called a "Tom show," and they did. These skits, which retained their popularity through the early decades of the twentieth century, absorbed elements of melodrama and blackface comedy. But their fidelity to the original novel varied; indeed, some were actually pro-slavery in character, much to Stowe's dismay. The most popular of the "Tom shows" was written by George Aiken, and Stowe was persuaded by friends to see it. From all accounts, she was pleased by what she found. Stage adaptations gave way to any number of film versions, including one directed by Edwin S. Porter in 1903 (one of the earliest of silent films). Interestingly, the novel was considered too hot to handle by Hollywood after the last silent film version appeared in 1927. A 1947 production at MGM was killed in preproduction when the NAACP (National Association for the Advancement of Colored People) objected to the stereotyping of black people.

The novel created or amplified many stereotypes, but the character of Tom has been the most influential. His acquiescence in the face of suffering led to the notion of an Uncle Tom figure, the subservient black man who gives in easily to white demands, currying favor with the masters, willing to accept abuse. As the civil rights movement evolved into the Black Power movement in the late 1960s, Stowe's famous character became a hated symbol of African American passivity. Other stereotypes also caused annoyance, including the matriarchal figure of the

mammy (several of these appear in the novel, but there is most importantly the character of Mammy herself, a cook at the St. Clare plantation
house). Topsy embodied the figure of the pickaninny, a stereotype of
black children. The tragic, sexy mulatto (embodied in Eliza, Cassy, and
Emmeline) also struck some readers as caricatured. Not surprisingly,
Uncle Tom's Cabin troubled many African American readers.

James Baldwin skewered the novel in a 1949 essay called "Everybody's Protest Novel," which appeared in *Notes of a Native Son* (1955).[11]
He called it "a very bad novel" and noted its "self-righteous, virtuous
sentimentality." Yet Stowe's book continued to attract readers, if on a
much-reduced scale. In *Patriotic Gore* (1962), Edmund Wilson claims he
was quite overwhelmed by *Uncle Tom's Cabin* and found reading it "a
startling experience." More recently, feminist scholars such as Ann
Douglas, Elaine Showalter, and Jane P. Tompkins have revisited the
novel, finding much to admire in its rhetorical force, its powers of persuasion. As they argue, the work suffered from the changing aesthetics
of modernism, which made the sentimental novel seem unfashionable,
even silly. But this is to dismiss a novel of genuine cultural importance,
one that still breaks on the reader like a ferocious tidal wave. "*Uncle
Tom's Cabin* is a great book," writes Ann Douglas, "not because it is a
great novel, but because it is a great revival sermon, aimed directly at the
conversion of its hearers."[12]

Jane Smiley, the novelist and critic, went even further than Douglas
in an essay in *Harper's,* confessing that she preferred Stowe's novel to
Huckleberry Finn.[13] This blasphemy provoked quite a controversy
among readers of *Harper's,* as one might expect; but Smiley, in a later interview, stood by her assessment. "When I re-read *Uncle Tom's Cabin,* I
was 45," Smiley recalled, "and I thought I would have to hold my nose
to get through it. But by chapter two, I was gawking, it was so interesting and terrific. By the end I was in awe. It featured such a fascinating
galaxy of characters, both black and white. My point was not to deni-
grate *Huck Finn,* I was not saying that it is *not* the central American
novel and that *Uncle Tom* is, but simply that *Uncle Tom's Cabin* is a better book than people thought, and that people should read it."[14]

Whatever its status as a work of art, Stowe's novel remains a key
document in American culture and a staple of college courses in American studies. It has influenced a range of writers over the years, includ-

ing Toni Morrison—in *Beloved,* especially, she inhabits much of the same physical, even emotional, territory as Stowe, exploring the issues of race, slavery, and redemption. In short, Harriet Beecher Stowe opened a vein of discourse in *Uncle Tom's Cabin* that has never been exhausted, illustrating the ravages of slavery and the slave trade and recalling with extraordinary power the bleak history of race relations in this country.

ADVENTURES

OF

HUCKLEBERRY FINN

(TOM SAWYER'S COMRADE)

Scene : The Mississippi Valley
Time : Forty to Fifty Years Ago

BY

MARK TWAIN

(SAMUEL L. CLEMENS)

WITH 174 ILLUSTRATIONS

London

CHATTO & WINDUS, PICCADILLY

1884

[All rights reserved]

Frontispiece

HUCKLEBERRY FINN

SEVEN

Adventures of Huckleberry Finn

I.

CRITICS HAVE SEARCHED high and low under every woodpile for something called "the great American novel." As Ernest Hemingway once declaimed, it already exists: "All modern American literature comes from one book by Mark Twain called *Huckleberry Finn*."[1] One might of course question the whole notion of a single masterwork that begot all others: the Holy Grail might be easier to find. Yet Twain's *Adventures of Huckleberry Finn* (1885) easily ranks among the most influential American books. As with any classic, it has consistently attracted and influenced readers and writers across the spectrum, speaking to widely different audiences over time.

In writing this novel, Twain forged a fresh medium for the American language, creating a salty, amusing vernacular, a flexible medium that could range from the highest to the lowest levels of thought and feeling in colorful, even "coarse" diction. The book's authentic note is heard from the outset: "You don't know about me, without you have read a book by the name of 'The Adventures of Tom Sawyer,' but that ain't no matter. That book was made by Mr. Mark Twain, and he told the truth, mainly." Without fanfare, this feisty author opened a deep, rich vein in the language. He did so in the context of a picaresque road novel, one that gave birth to countless other novels about two characters on a journey to freedom, literal or imagined. Twain showed us how to talk and handed us one of our founding myths, which involves lighting out "for the Territory," heading off into unknown regions in search of the fabled promised land.

Although the novel appeared in 1885, the story takes place a quarter century before this, during the years when slavery was still in place, though fraying at the edges. In this, Twain treads some of the territory already occupied by *Uncle Tom's Cabin;* but he and Harriet Beecher Stowe attack slavery in very different terms. Twain's polemic is, perhaps, even more powerful than Stowe's, as it comes at the subject indirectly, simply by showing us the nobility of Jim. A black man, he is by far the least vain, petty, and morally flawed character in the novel, and his example matters in the life of young Huck. This unlikely couple floats down the Mississippi, in flight from captivity of one kind or another; in the course of this journey, they meet a cross section of American society in the Old South as they accidentally skip past Cairo, Illinois, into slave territory. And what an array of liars, thieves, murderers, pretenders, con men, and fools crosses their path! Twain holds up a mirror to this part of America, and the reflection is not a pretty one.

In the flowing course of the narrative, Twain addresses nearly every major theme in American literature and thought, including the subtle power of nature and the mysteries of religion. Family is another consistent topic, but—as ever—Twain looks at his subject in a fresh way, asking questions about parentage, family structure, and emotional ties that bind, or fail to bind. He interrogates race in a most delicate fashion, putting a black man up against white society and finding him at least equal to the best of them, doing so without a trace of the sentimentality that marks *Uncle Tom's Cabin.* Most centrally, Twain asks his readers to consider the value of civilization itself. As Huck says at the outset and conclusion, he does not want anyone to "sivilize" him. Beneath such a statement lie questions about what it really means to be civilized.

Huckleberry Finn is a book one reads in childhood for the adventure itself, the thrill of imagining a wild boy who runs away from home, lighting out for the territory. In young adulthood, the novel must be read again, for the questions it poses about the meaning of maturity, for the directions for living it offers. In middle age, the novel works its magic in other ways, by dislodging us from our comfortable lives, offering alternative visions, including the vision of nature as a resource for rehabilitation. The hypocrisies of "civilized" life strike us freshly and force us to rethink our assumptions about what matters. In later life, it must be read again, for what it says about the ultimate nature of reality. A novel of this complexity and imaginative strength cannot be digested in a single reading or at one stage of life. It requires a lifelong devotion to its fluttering pages, to the shifting images of Huck and Jim in their encounters with the world, in their experience of the big river and woods that sustain it, and with their own ample, contradictory natures. One rides the river with them, again and again, and the journey is never complete, as another bend in the river always appears. There is, indeed, that final lighting out for the territory, but this destination ultimately lies beyond human comprehension or confines, a glimmer on the horizon.

In these ways, and more, *Adventures of Huckleberry Finn* defines the American project, its strenuous search for liberty, equality, and the pursuit of happiness. It offers us a way to think about ourselves, and a way to put our feelings into words. It teaches us, miraculously, to sound our own depths (as the pseudonym Mark Twain suggests, referring to a term of measurement used by boatmen on the Mississippi).

II.

MARK TWAIN was Samuel Langhorne Clemens (1835–1910)—a figure who became a representative American. His fame spread far, and he was welcomed into the courts of kings and emperors as he tramped the globe, spouting witticisms, offering shrewd, irreverent critiques of the world that opened before him. He was a welcome visitor at the White House, where a succession of presidents sought his company, even though he was never polite about their imperialist policies. (An early opponent of the American empire, Twain denounced expansionist policies in his last years.) Although he came from an ordinary background, and had very little in the way of formal education, he seems to have met everybody who was anybody. Having named the Gilded Age, he lived on a grand scale himself, winning and losing several fortunes in his lifetime.

At one point or another, he had been a printer's assistant, a prospector for gold, a steamboat captain, a journalist and world correspondent, an adventurer, the owner and editor of a newspaper, a public speaker and popular entertainer, a business entrepreneur and financial speculator. He was certainly a devoted husband and father. Most important, he was a writer of hugely popular books, including *The Innocents Abroad* (1869), *Roughing It* (1872), *The Adventures of Tom Sawyer* (1876), *Life on the Mississippi* (1883), *Adventures of Huckleberry Finn* (1885), *A Connecticut Yankee in King Arthur's Court* (1889), and *Pudd'nhead Wilson* (1894). Many of his short stories, such as "The Celebrated Jumping Frog of Calaveras County" and "The Man That Corrupted Hadleyburg," count among the classic examples of this genre.

Twain was also our first media-savvy writer on a large scale and turned himself into an American institution. His face became nearly as familiar as those belonging to Franklin, Washington, or Lincoln, although Twain was in many ways the anti–Ben Franklin, saying things that all rakes, charmers, con men, and scoundrels still admire, as in:

Man is the only animal that blushes—or needs to.

Always do right. This will gratify some people and astonish the rest.

An Englishman is a person who does things because they have been done before. An American is a person who does things because they haven't been done before.

Fiction is obliged to stick to possibilities. Truth isn't.

Education: that which reveals to the wise, and conceals from the stupid, the vast limits of their knowledge.

I have never let my schooling interfere with my education.

Honesty is the best policy—when there is money in it.

I thoroughly disapprove of duels. If a man should challenge me, I would take him kindly and forgivingly by the hand and lead him to a quiet place and kill him.

One can only love a man who said things like that.

But what matters most about Mark Twain is that he wrote *Adventures of Huckleberry Finn*. It's not *The Adventures* (as in *The Adventures of Tom Sawyer*) but simply *Adventures*. The loss of the definite article signals a gain of mythic potential. These adventures are not located definitely in space and time, nor are they limited to those constructed on the page; they have always been with us, and always will be: shaping the American voice and character, refining morality at every bend in the river, which is still breaking before us—so long as we continue to live. For the devoted reader, *Huckleberry Finn* is life itself, a figurative life that repeatedly invades and transmogrifies its literal counterpart.

Twain originally thought he would simply expand *Tom Sawyer,* as that volume—a boy's book—had been so popular. His friend and editor, William Dean Howells, suggested continuing the adventures of Tom into adulthood. Quite rightly, Twain rejected this notion. Tom Sawyer was frozen in place and time, and there was no future in his story. In any case, Twain preferred Huck Finn, the outsider who had been the most interesting (if peripheral) character in the earlier book. Twain was himself a version of Huck, the wild but innocent boy who refused to be "sivilized." His anarchic streak appealed to the wily author, who enjoyed lighting a fuse, watching it burn, waiting for the boom with hands (almost) covering his ears.

Readers who loved *Tom Sawyer* wrote letters, begging for a sequel. Such was the demand that Twain made up a form letter:

I HAVE THE HONOR TO REPLY TO YOUR LETTER JUST RECEIVED, THAT IT IS MY PURPOSE TO WRITE A CONTINUATION OF TOM SAWYER'S HISTORY, BUT I AM NOT ABLE AT THIS TIME TO DETERMINE WHEN I SHALL BEGIN THE WORK.[2]

Twain worked on his sequel intermittently through the hot summer of 1876, often writing in a gazebo at Quarry Farm near Elmira, New York: a house that had been bought by his wealthy father-in-law some years before as a country retreat. He modeled the new novel on *The Adventures of Gil Blas,* by Le Sage—a popular eighteenth-century work in the tradition of picaresque fiction that reaches back to *Don Quixote.* Blas is the picaro here, a French country boy who tells his own story. He lives on the margins of society, like Huck, and talks about his adventures in an idiosyncratic (and obviously limited) voice. He's a bighearted fellow, also like Huck, and when he encounters a hypocritical society, he is upset and confused. The reader, of course, sees more than he does, thus allowing for a context of dramatic irony.

Twain's manuscript seemed to grow by itself, reaching some 446 pages by the end of August, when the author suddenly quit writing— almost in mid-sentence. (This version of the novel was lost for over a century, only to be rediscovered in 1991; since then, it has been closely analyzed by scholars, such as Victor A. Doyno, who notes that the early working title of the manuscript was *Huck Finn's Autobiography.*[3]) Puzzled by what he had written—almost in a dream—Twain simply put the manuscript in a drawer, turning to other work. He finished *A Tramp Abroad* (1880) and began to work on *The Prince and the Pauper* (1881). It was his habit to work on many projects at the same time, shifting among them as the spirit moved him.

He returned to Huck in the spring of 1880, writing another 216 pages in his highly regular hand, drawing on deep reservoirs of memory and feeling. The early manuscript left off with Huck separated from Jim, entering the strange world in which the Grangerford clan feuded obsessively with the Shepherdson clan—a feud that had gone on for so long that nobody recalled what had started it. Twain had actually abandoned the manuscript with Huck's baleful, potent question: "What is a feud?" What, indeed? And why would otherwise decent people attack each other so viciously, without a reason? Perhaps irrational violence preyed on his mind now, as he was writing during the years of Reconstruction, when the United States struggled mightily with the legacy of slavery. The wounds of that war had not yet healed, and bitterness often yielded to acts of cruelty. In effect, slavery was reborn, as African Americans found themselves unable to vote or to work freely, in hock to white society, which would not really grant their freedom (except on paper).

Twain began to see how this book could become something more than just another book for boys. Yet the second installment ground to a halt as abruptly as the first. Unable to continue, Twain turned to other projects, including a trip down the length of the Mississippi, recapitulating a journey he had made so many times in his early years as a steamboat captain. This was research for *Life on the Mississippi,* his sumptuous memoir of the river and its world, which he wrote at high speed and had typed by a pair of secretaries from Elmira, New York: perhaps among the earliest practitioners of this profession. With that memoir behind him, he returned to *Huckleberry Finn* in 1883, writing in a blaze of newly discovered inspiration. Now he saw at last that one of the grand themes of this unfolding novel was freedom itself: the freedom of Jim as well as the freedom of young Huck. Like *Walden,* it was written to celebrate American independence.

The novel is set during the period when Missouri was a slave-owning state, so Jim was mere property, hardly a human being at all—as far as the law was concerned. It was, of course, a serious breach of law to assist a runaway slave. Twain knew what he was writing about here, having been raised in the South, where he experienced slavery firsthand. His uncle John Quarles owned a 230-acre farm where he deployed a small number of slaves, "fifteen or twenty negroes," as Twain wrote in 1897. Among these was "Uncle Dan," who was given his freedom by Quarles in 1855. Dan was six feet tall, a man of considerable intelligence and poise who served as a model for Jim, as Twain suggested late in life when he wrote that Uncle Dan "has served me well these many, many years. I have not seen him for more than half a century and yet spiritually I have had his welcome company a good part of that time and have staged him in books under his own name and as 'Jim,' and carted him all around."[4]

Huckleberry Finn is covert autobiography, and many of the characters and scenes in the novel have origins in figures and incidents from the author's past. Not surprisingly, scholars have picked over this field. It has often been noted, for example, that Huck was based on Twain's boyhood friend named Tom Blankenship—a poor, unsupervised boy with a big heart. Tom's older brother had once smuggled food to a runaway slave on an island in the Mississippi, and Twain remembered that. One can draw parallels between John Quarles, the author's uncle, and the novel's sweet, absentminded slave owner, Uncle Silas Phelps. In

Twain's Missouri boyhood, there was a long-running feud between two clans that resembles the feud between the Grangerfords and the Shepherdsons. The point remains, however, that Twain managed to absorb these figures and incidents, to transform them into major fiction.

Twain was obviously writing in *Huckleberry Finn* about a world he knew well and recalled with hallucinogenic clarity. The geography, history, and politics of Missouri set the scene for him. It is worth recalling that the Missouri Territory had been a controversial region for some time, with many arguments about whether or not slaves would be allowed there. The Missouri Compromise of 1820 had stated that Missourians could hold on to their slaves, but that slavery was forbidden in any future state established over the line of 36°30′ (to the Mason-Dixon Line). Thus Missouri stuck out like a sore thumb, being above this demarcation, a state where slaves existed but surrounded by free states. (Hannibal itself—the town where Mark Twain grew up and which he mythologized in his fiction—lay only sixty-five miles south of Iowa, and Illinois was just across the river—both states that forbade slavery.) It was Henry Clay who had argued for the Missouri Compromise, and (not by chance) it is the speeches of Henry Clay that lie on the table in the Grangerfords' plantation house in Twain's novel: a subtle allusion to the troubled history of this region.

Having traveled the southern part of the river again for *Life on the Mississippi,* Twain found his thoughts returning to Huck and Jim and their life on the river. "I haven't had such booming working-days for many years," he wrote to his beloved mother, Jane Clemens, in Hannibal. "I am piling up manuscript in a really astonishing way . . . This summer it is no more trouble to me to write than it is to lie."[5] This burst of writing ended with a pile of nearly seven hundred handwritten pages, with Twain (as usual) revising constantly as he wrote, crossing out words and sentences, with emendations in the margins or wedged between lines. With this heap of pages, Twain left his gazebo in Elmira for Hartford, Connecticut, where he worked over a freshly typed manuscript for another six months. Although this typescript has been lost, one sees by comparing the earliest manuscript with the final printed version that many shrewd changes occurred.

One example will do to illustrate the sorts of revisions that Twain would make. Compare the rough draft with the final version of a brief passage from chapter 16:[6]

> They went off & I hopped aboard the raft, saying to myself, I've done wrong again, & was trying as hard as I could to do right, too; but when it come right down to telling them it was a nigger on the raft, & I opened my mouth a-purpose to do it, I couldn't. I am a mean, low coward, & it's the fault of them that brung me up. If I had been raised right, I wouldn't said anything about anybody being sick, but the more I try to do it right, the more I can't.

> ————

> They went off, and I got aboard the raft, feeling bad and low, because I knowed very well I had done wrong, and I see it warn't no use for me to try to learn to do right; a body that don't get *started* right when he's little, ain't got no show—when the pinch comes there ain't nothing to back him up and keep him to his work, and so he gets beat.

Twain compresses the first passage, finding more concrete and fully embodied ways to say what he means. There was, for example, no need for Huck to confess that he was a "mean, low coward" or to rely on the hackneyed self-justification that his defects were "the fault of them that brung me up." A transformation of this point occurs in the idea that "a body that don't get *started* right when he's little, ain't got no show." Only a writer with Twain's gifts could have achieved such concentrated effects in such a short space.

With the novel finished, Twain agreed to let a popular magazine, *Century,* publish three installments (the editor, Richard Watson Gilder, tried his best to get Twain to let him publish more of it, but Twain was a canny fellow, and thought that if too much of the book appeared in serial format, his sales would suffer). Interestingly, this same magazine was currently printing in serial form two other classic American novels—*The Rise of Silas Lapham* by William Dean Howells and *The Bostonians* by Henry James—so the editor had an eye for quality.

Adventures of Huckleberry Finn appeared in book form on February 18, 1885. It was, as expected, a commercial and critical success, although some critics (and not a few librarians) could not too easily swallow its "rude" language, or the unsettling originality of the whole. Even today, the novel unsettles readers. As T. S. Eliot, himself a child of the Mississippi River, says in *Four Quartets*: "Human kind cannot bear very much reality."

III.

THE NOVEL OPENS, as we have seen above, with Huck's deferral to Mark Twain, his creator. This self-referential note lends the book a metafictional undertone from the outset, as the author shows his hand, even waves it boldly: I'm here, underneath this voice of Huck, and I know what I'm doing, he tells us. You can trust me, as I tell the truth, "mainly." Then again, "I never seen anybody but lied," Huck admits. He has Twain's number there. Writers lie and deceive, which is why Plato wanted to kick them out of his ideal republic. But their lying allows truth to show its face in ways it otherwise might never dare.

Twain launches the novel by explaining that Huck and Tom had gotten rich from money that robbers had hidden in a cave. "We got six thousand dollars apiece—all gold" (17). That was a heap of money, and there was no doubt that trouble would follow. Trouble always follows the money.

We soon encounter the Widow Douglas, who has been attempting to "sivilize" Huck, a poor motherless boy. His father, known as Pap, has split the scene. But that's a good thing, as Pap is a violent drunkard and scoundrel. The tone from the outset is wonderfully charming, full of dramatic irony: that is, the audience often knows more than the speaker. Of course the speaker is a mere boy; more than that, he's a rough, uneducated boy. And so we see through what Huck says, discovering (as he only partially does) a world full of hypocrisy. Miss Watson, the widow's sister, lives in the house as well, and she tries to improve Huck's spelling and behavior. She even suggests that if he persists in his ways he will wind up in hell, although she never mentions hell literally. Huck puts it like this: "Then she told me all about the bad place, and I said I wished I was there. She got mad, then, but I didn't mean no harm. All I wanted was to go somewheres; all I wanted was a change, I warn't particular" (19). Huck maintains his naive quality here, with his creator behind him; we hear Twain, almost see him winking at us, as Huck speaks. And so we get this double voice at all times, a naive voice and its knowing after-echo.

Through its first few chapters, *Huckleberry Finn* reads like a standard boy's adventure story, a sequel to *Tom Sawyer*. Indeed, Tom plays a significant role at first, with his impish ways. It is, after all, Tom who wishes to play a trick on "Miss Watson's big nigger, named Jim" (22). The word "nigger" appears over two hundred times in the novel, but raised few eyebrows in its time. In America today, of course, the inclusion of the "n-word" has gotten the book banned from many libraries and classrooms. In Twain's era, one could abuse African Americans in this way with impunity. The language created the reality: a black man like Jim was just a piece of property in a slave state before the Civil War. Huck and Tom don't think twice about using this word or playing cruel tricks on Jim. But Twain is neither Huck nor Tom. His novel becomes, finally, an eloquent defense of the humanity of Jim and (by implication) his race. (Many classrooms in America could do with frank conversation on the history of race.)

The shenanigans begin in chapter 2, when Tom and Huck trick poor Jim into thinking that witches have been at work around him. In the same chapter, they sneak away from the widow's house to the river, where they meet with other boys who belong to Tom's gang of supposed robbers. Even here, Huck remains an outsider, having no family he can swear to kill if he should reveal the secrets of the gang. This is all "boys will be boys" stuff, but Twain was a charming writer for boys, as *The Adventures of Tom Sawyer* proved; these chapters retain the charm of the earlier book without pausing to challenge anything that the boys say, even though it is often quite violent and based on fantasy.

Huck settles down to life with the Widow Douglas and Miss Watson, and all is well until he discovers a footprint in the freshly fallen snow. "There was a cross in the left boot-heel made with big nails, to keep off the devil," Huck says (35). Clearly Pap has returned. As Huck guesses, Pap wants his money.

In chapter 5, Pap turns up in town: "He was most fifty, and he looked it. His hair was long and tangled and greasy, and hung down, and you could see his eyes shining through like he was behind vines. It was all black, no gray; so was his long, mixed-up whiskers" (39). Pap is alcoholic and violent, and he wants to reclaim his son (or his son's fortune). The Widow Douglas gets help from Judge Thatcher, a benevolent figure, in order to keep Huck away from Pap; but there is a new judge in town who refuses to grant the widow custody of the boy. The judge naively thinks he can reform Pap, but this effort fails miserably, as nobody can keep Pap from his drink. The only way to reform Pap, the judge concludes, is "with a shot-gun, maybe."

The trouble really starts when Pap kidnaps Huck, taking him up-river to his cabin, some three miles away. It's a fearful place, almost mythic in the way Twain describes it as "an old log hut in a place where the timber was so thick you couldn't find it if you didn't know where it was" (45). Pap continues to pursue his legal options, trying to get custody of Huck and—more important—his money. Like a madman, he rails against the authorities. "Call this a govment!" he cries. "Oh, yes, this is a wonderful govment, wonderful. Why, looky here. There was a free nigger there, from Ohio; a mulatter, most as white as a white man."

This mulatto is, God forbid, a college professor. He's got the whitest shirt in town, and he boasts a gold watch and chain—items that do not befit his "real" station. "And that ain't the wust," says Pap. "They said he could *vote*." Twain relishes the ironies, and lets them resound. This undeserving and pretentious black man who struts about in his white shirt with a gold watch and chain is, in Pap's fantasy, an early version of the black welfare mother in her Cadillac. As ever, the reader can sense the dramatic irony, knowing more than Pap knows.

Escaping from a drunk like Pap should be no problem, especially for a clever boy like Huck, but Twain milks the situation for drama. Not until chapter 7 does Huck finally escape, and the setup is quite tense when he does, as Pap is sober at the time. Having faked his own murder, Huck slips away in a canoe, heading to Jackson's Island. Huck says: "It didn't take me long to get there" (60). The writing approaches a poetic height that Twain manages to sustain through much of the novel: "I went up and set down on a log at the head of the island and looked out on the big river and the black driftwood, and away over to the town, three mile away, where there was three or four lights twinkling." The language has an admirable concreteness and clarity, issuing from the depths of this writer's capacious memory.

On Jackson's Island, Huck meets Jim, who has run away, having overheard a conversation that led him to believe he might be sold down-river. (A similar plot twist, of course, propelled Eliza to escape from Kentucky with her son in *Uncle Tom's Cabin*.) Jim, alas, thinks he's seeing a ghost, and in a funny moment explains to Huck that he's always liked dead people and been good to them. Of course Twain falls into a comic stereotype of black people here. It played well in his day, alas, and still does.

Twain employs a variety of dialects and knows what he is doing, as he tells the reader in a coy prefatory note: "In this book a number of dialects are used, to wit: the Missouri negro dialect; the extremest form of the backwoods South-Western dialect; the ordinary 'Pike-County' dialect; and four modified varieties of this last. The shadings have not been done in a hap-hazard fashion, or by guess-work; but painstakingly, and with the trustworthy guidance and support of personal familiarity with these several forms of speech." He didn't want innocent readers to imagine that his various characters were all trying to talk alike and not succeeding.

In chapter 9, Huck and Jim form a bond, exploring the island, learning how to survive. There is evocative writing about a storm and the rising waters. One evening they lay hands on a raft that will convey them downriver in due course. Soon enough they find a whole house floating in the swollen stream. They climb aboard to salvage what they can for their own use, whereupon Jim observes a dead man on the floor. It's Pap, but he does not tell Huck. Exactly why he doesn't reveal this fact to Huck remains mysterious, although a likely explanation is that he does not want Huck to abandon him; without Pap to fear, the boy might well return to his comfortable life in town. There may also be some misguided inclination on Jim's part to protect Huck from a vision of his own father in such a terminal state.

Wanting to find out what is happening in town, Huck dresses like a girl to make his investigations. He drops in on a woman, calling himself Mary Williams, or Sarah . . . he forgets exactly. The woman quickly guesses that "she" is a "he." "What's your real name? Is it Bill, or Tom, or Bob?" she asks (88). Huck cringes, but he learns there is a good deal of gossip and misinformation about. Some assume that Pap killed Huck, then escaped. Some believe that Jim killed Huck. In any case, a bounty has been placed on Jim's head. The woman who questions Huck about his true identity thinks that Jim is hiding out on Jackson's Island. This is reason enough for Huck and Jim to escape downriver. "Git up and hump yourself, Jim!" Huck says. "There ain't a minute to lose. They're after us!" (92). And so the chase, or imagined chase, begins. This is good plotting. As E. M. Forster might have said: a man running is a story; a man running away from someone is a plot.

Huck and Jim take off on their raft, floating downriver to Cairo. The image remains among the most indelible in American literature and life. But it's not an entirely comfortable image, and never was. In a famous essay on *Huckleberry Finn* called "Come Back to the Raft Ag'in, Huck Honey!" (1948), Leslie Fiedler explored a covert homosexual undercurrent in the novel.[7] He referred to vaguely erotic relationships between men in many classic novels, such as *Moby-Dick,* with Ishmael's love for Queequeg as a telling example. Certainly a profound affection develops between Jim and young Huck, "the fugitive slave and the no-account boy lying side by side on a raft borne by the endless river toward an impossible escape." That a charged current of feeling exists between Huck and Jim cannot be denied. Yet I think Ralph Ellison hit the right note when he observed: "Jim's friendship for Huck comes across as that of a boy for another boy rather than as the friendship of an adult for a junior."[8] Jim only escapes the blackface minstrel stereotype on a few occasions; otherwise he is a "boy." And so the relationship between Huck and Jim operates in a realm that may even be called "normal," given the racial (and racist) transposition.

Life on the river turns toward the idyllic in chapter 12, as Jim and Huck improve their living conditions on the raft, creating a "snug wigwam." But the idyll breaks when a violent storm blows through. In its aftermath lies the eerily still wreckage of a steamboat. Huck persuades Jim to tie up alongside it, and Huck, ever curious, climbs aboard to inspect the scene. He happens upon three robbers, two of them having tied up a third, whom they threaten to kill by letting the boat sink with him aboard as they escape on a skiff tied up at the side of the steamer. Thinking quickly, Huck decides to get that skiff, and so maroon them on the boat, where the sheriff can nab them. He soon discovers, however, that the raft he shares with Jim has disappeared. As Jim frantically explains: "Dey ain' no raf' no mo', she done broke loose en gone!" (101). The skiff belonging to the robbers provides an escape route now. In a sense, the "robbers" are now robbed, and condemned to die on the steamboat or be captured by the authorities.

On and on, the twists and turns in the river offer fresh situations and dilemmas. Each presents opportunities for Twain to refine and develop Huck's character. In chapter 13, Huck and Jim find their raft again: its permanent disappearance would have been too great a loss for everyone, including the reader. And so the idyll resumes in chapter 14, with the odd couple discussing at length the biblical story of Solomon, among other things. The dialogue is pure *Amos 'n' Andy*:

> He [Jim] was the most down on Solomon of any nigger I ever see. So I went to talking about other kings, and let Solomon slide. I told about Louis Sixteenth that got his head cut off in France long time ago; and about his little boy the dolphin, that would a been a king, but they took and shut him up in jail, and some say he died there.
> "Po' little chap."
> "But some says he got out and got away, and come to America."
> "Dat's good! But he'll be pooty lonesome—dey ain' no kings here, is dey, Huck?"
> "No."
> "Den he cain't git no situation. What he gwyne to do?"
> "Well, I don't know. Some of them gets on the police, and some of them learns people how to talk French."

In such exchanges, Huck settles to Jim's level and pretty nearly speaks in black dialect himself—a point explored in interesting ways by Shelley Fisher Fishkin in *Was Huck Black?*[9] Fishkin argues that Twain modeled Huck on a black boy whose story he wrote about in an essay written soon before he began the composition of his novel. She also notes that Twain was entertained by the "signifying" of a particular African American child in Hannibal, where he grew up. To be sure, Huck adopts many aspects of black dialect, as Fishkin notes. He often seems as foolish—or uninformed—as Jim.

The goal of the journey is ostensibly Cairo, where the Mississippi joins the Ohio River. Huck and Jim plan to take a steamboat upriver to freedom in the North; but the course of their journey is badly diverted in chapter 15, when a "solid white fog" overwhelms the river. This is a literal but also a figurative fog, taken as a "dream" by Jim, who is fooled by Huck into thinking it was just that. It is also a moral fog for Huck, who once again plays a trick on Jim, repeating his earlier tendency to play tricks on him. Huck's allegiance to Jim, and the quality of his affection, are at stake here. At the end of this chapter, Huck feels sorry for deceiving his companion and apologizes, and one senses moral growth in the boy, who confesses to the reader: "I didn't do him no more mean tricks, and I wouldn't done that one if I'd a knowed it would make him feel that way" (121).

The issue of slavery comes front and center in chapter 16 as Jim contemplates his freedom, imagining he will save enough money to buy his wife's freedom as well, and then the freedom of their two children. If the master won't sell those children, he says he will simply "get an Ab'litionist to go and steal them" (124). The moral dilemma facing Huck presses in. Should he break the law and help Jim escape? As it happens, he cannot abide letting Jim fall back into the hands of slavery, and he makes the right decision. When he heads to shore to see how far he and Jim have drifted downriver, he meets two white men in search of runaway slaves. Using his wits, he dupes them into believing that Pap is on the raft and dangerously ill. The men conclude that Huck's father must have smallpox, and one of them puts a $20 gold piece on a board to float over to Huck—an act of generosity, and a bribe to get him away from them, as he might be contagious; his friend puts another one of equal value on the board. With wonderful irony, one of them advises Huck: "If you see any runaway niggers, you get help and nab them, and you can make some money by it" (127). The layers of irony accumulate.

Huck and Jim realize they have floated past Cairo and must head upriver again. Things appear to be finally on the right course when disaster arrives in the form of a steamboat, which plows into them: "We could hear her pounding along, but we didn't see her good till she was close. She aimed right for us" (130). As a former steamboat captain, Twain knew his stuff, and the ensuing description radiates authenticity: "She was a big one, and she was coming in a hurry, too, looking like a black cloud with rows of glow-worms around it; but all of a sudden she bulged out, big and scary, with a long row of wide-open furnace doors shining like red-hot teeth, and her monstrous bows and guards hanging right over us." Huck leaps off the raft, diving under the paddle wheel to escape death. When he comes up, Jim is gone and doesn't answer to his calls. Huck grabs a plank and drifts to shore.

Onshore again, Huck finds himself surrounded by yelping dogs. Confronted by a hostile man, Huck pretends to be one George Jackson, a Southern orphan who fell off a steamboat. The Grangerford family welcome him into their clan, as he is no relation to the Shepherdsons, their sworn enemies. Weirdly, given his recent history, Huck slips into the stream of life at the Grangerford plantation. Young Buck Grangerford becomes a good friend to Huck, who assumes many of the family's values. In this, Twain has something to say about the influence of environment. Huck seems quite untroubled by the fact that the Grangerfords own over a hundred slaves. Every member of the family has a slave-servant, and Huck gets one as well.

Huck's new slave, in fact, clues him into the fact that Jim is hiding out in a nearby swamp and that he has found the raft and repaired all damage. The question is: Will Huck resume his rafting life with Jim, or return to the bosom of his newfound family? He is an honorary Grangerford now. But when Huck sees Buck try to kill a Shepherdson who happens to ride by, he asks: "What did you want to kill him for?" Buck replies: "Why nothing—only it's on account of the feud." Huck asks: "What's a feud?" (147). It was at this point that Twain broke off writing for some time, having apparently lost confidence in where he was going to go with the novel, or how good it was.

By the end of the chapter, Huck has witnessed the dire human consequences of this nonsensical feud between families. Buck's father is shot dead, with two of his sons. Soon Buck himself and his cousin are murdered as well. Huck is undone. He has developed a deep affection for Buck, and he sees the sad results of hatred. "I cried a little when I was covering up Buck's face," he says, "for he was mighty good to me." And so he and Jim reunite, and the journey continues. "You feel mighty free and easy and comfortable on a raft," Huck concludes, relieved to resume life as before.

But Huck is allowed only a few days of easy freedom on the raft. In the next chapter he stops to paddle a freshly discovered canoe upstream for a bit of exploration—always a bad idea. He soon enough takes up with a couple of men on the run. One is seventy "or upwards" and balding, the other is about thirty; they pretend to be royalty, a Duke and a Dauphin (or King, as he is often called). Huck and Jim treat them accordingly, as royalty, though Huck shows increasing maturity as he takes a rather skeptical line: "It didn't take me long to make up my mind that these liars warn't no kings nor dukes, at all, but just low-down humbugs and frauds" (166). He keeps this opinion to himself, however, engaging in some white lies as he explains that he is a farmer's child who has lost his father and brother. Jim is the last slave owned by the family. He tells them he and Jim only travel by night because they don't want people to think Jim is a runaway slave.

Chapter 20 is full of amusing gags, as the Duke and King ("the wanderin', exiled, trampled-on and sufferin' rightful King of France") concoct a plan to swindle another town out of its money. They produce various moneymaking schemes, such as putting on scenes from Shakespeare. In one sequence they cleverly create a handbill that will make it appear they are taking Jim, a runaway slave, back to his rightful owners; this will allow them to run the river in broad daylight. The chapter includes a memorable portrait of a revival meeting: Twain could never resist any opportunity to make fun of piety or religious fervor. The King uses the revival as a stage for himself, explaining to the assembly that he was a pirate in the Indian Ocean before he found God. As he would, he takes up a collection to return himself as a missionary to his former partners in crime. The ploy works, and he returns to the raft with $87.75. He has acquired a three-gallon jug of whiskey as well.

The novel meanders into various subplots, one of them involving a murder and near lynching; these stories demonstrate yet again the depraved nature of the "civilized" world, an ever-present theme in *Huckleberry Finn*. There are further bogus schemes by the Duke and the King, as might be expected. Once Twain has hit upon such ludicrous characters, he doesn't easily let go of them, nor should he. In one scene, they recite bits and pieces from Shakespeare to a rather thin audience. But crowds do assemble when the Duke adds a fresh line to their handbills: "Ladies and Children Not Admitted." The production itself is ironically called the Royal Nonesuch, thus commenting on the "productions" of society, which are really quite empty. (In his way, Twain foreshadows Samuel Beckett, who would make an art of producing "nothing," in all its philosophical depth.) The audience soon realizes it has been "sold" but decides it would embarrass them in the eyes of their fellow citizens if everybody realized these scoundrels had deceived them so effectively. They agree to praise the show (much as reviewers have often done, praising "nothing" rather than pointing out that the emperor is naked). Eventually, chaos results, although the Duke and the King escape to the raft with their pile of loot. While such burlesque scenes provide raw entertainment for readers, they also work quite efficiently to test the moral fiber of young Huck. He colludes with the Duke here and proves much less innocent than readers might have imagined, thus making his future relations with Jim all the more tense, complicated, and interesting.

As he often does, Twain shifts gears ferociously, as Huck observes a sorrowful Jim. "When I waked up, just at day-break," says Huck, "he [Jim] was setting there with his head down betwixt his knees, moaning and mourning to himself. I didn't take notice, nor let on. I knowed what it was about. He was thinking about his wife and his children, away up yonder, and he was low and homesick" (201). Huck comes to the realization that "he cared just as much for his people as white folks does for their'n. It don't seem natural, but I reckon it's so." This is a stunning intuition for young Huck, and once again brings the novel back to the issue of race. Yet readers have long puzzled over the racial matter in this book.

One debate about *Huckleberry Finn* centers on the portrayal of Jim. To some, he seems a figure from black minstrelsy, innocently idiotic, and therefore a character white society can laugh at. No African American could find any of this amusing. The insistent use of the word "nigger" has—as noted—got the book banned from libraries and schools.[10] One can understand the argument behind this banning: young readers could miss the ironies of the book, failing to see through the racial epithet to understand that Twain is poking fun at white society as he underscores its racist tendencies. It takes an expert teacher to convey these complications to a classroom of teenagers, and teachers (or readers) at this level of expertise may be in short supply. And yet the novel succeeds brilliantly in its interrogations of race. In the above scene, for example, Jim's sorrow is palpable, and Huck's ignorant goodwill is clearly ironic. In these passages, the novel "teaches" itself. The narrative controls and persuades the reader. Twain was not a racist in any meaningful sense of that term. His narrative grows into a polemic *against* racism, however much the author cannot at times resist playing to the peanut gallery. Twain could at times vulgarize his material, and enjoyed doing so. But that's what makes him Mark Twain and not Henry James.

Huck's character evolves considerably in the later stretches of the journey, where he gradually (very gradually) acquires a moral sense and refuses to step aside and let bad things happen without comment or action. He is not content simply to roll along, disengaged, unwilling to commit himself—as in the earlier chapters. Evasion becomes less and less a comfortable position for him. In subtle fashion, Twain prepares us for the novel's conclusion, where Huck has to make a decision about his stance toward Jim, thus taking his moral life into his own hands.

In chapters 24 through 30, Huck is further tested by the shenanigans of the Duke and the King. For a start, they dress up Jim in Arab costume, painting him "all over a dead dull solid blue, like a man that's been drowned nine days" (203). He wears a sign that identifies him as a demented Arab. "Blamed if he warn't the horriblest looking outrage I ever see," Huck says. Soon the story shifts to scenes concerning the children of Peter Wilks, who has died and left his money to his three daughters and two brothers from Sheffield, England. The Duke and the King see an opportunity here and pretend to be these English brothers. Although Huck goes along with this ruse, his discomfort rises. He fibs without much shame, however, to the orphaned daughters, Mary Jane, Susan, and Joanna. In a fresh twist, he shows a genuine interest in these girls as female members of the species. He actually calls Mary Jane "beautiful" and seems attracted to her: a further sign of his advancement into maturity. Nevertheless, the immorality of a scheme to bilk orphans upsets Huck, and he wants badly to escape from the clutches of these two pranksters. In a wrenching scene in chapter 27, the King decides to sell some slaves he has "inherited." As it happens, a couple of slave traders conveniently appear. These were beloved slaves, and the girls are distraught as "away they went, the two sons up the river to Memphis, and their mother down the river to Orleans" (234). Huck remarks: "I thought them poor girls and them niggers would break their hearts for grief." It's only the knowledge that this "sale" will soon be exposed as false, and will result in these slaves being returned, that allows him not to intervene. This scene adds further to Huck's understanding of the cruelties of slavery and links him more intimately with Jim and his fate.

In chapter 31, Huck must finally own up to the consequences of conscience, having become aware of the miseries and injustices of slavery. He "knows" he should turn Jim over, as that is the law; but he refuses. In a memorable twist, he tries hard to pray, but he can't. The words just will not come. "Why wouldn't they?" he asks. "It warn't no use to try and hide it from Him. Nor from *me,* neither . . . It was because I warn't square; it was because I was playing double" (270). He doesn't want to "play double" anymore. He writes to Miss Watson to tell of Jim's whereabouts. But then he tears up the letter. He will certainly not bend to conventional morality, yet he will bow before a larger authority, the one that lies within his own conscience. And he will stick by Jim. "All right, then, I'll *go* to hell," he says, in a defining moment in the novel. "It was awful thoughts, and awful words, but they was said. And I let them stay said; and never thought no more about reforming" (272).

The novel shifts gears in the last ten chapters, when Tom Sawyer reappears on the scene. In a way, the novel returns to the mode of the opening chapters, where Twain summoned a world of boyhood fantasies, complete with scolding mother figures and a series of outlandish pranks or "adventures" designed by Tom. The overall narrative assumes an elegant shape, with the beginning and the end touching so neatly. But there is no question that something has changed, as Huck has experienced a journey, literal and figurative. He has almost become a man, and therefore seems less tolerant of Tom's immature pranks.

Huck slips away from the Duke and the King in chapter 31, planning to resume his journey on the raft with Jim, this exhilarating voyage to freedom, into adulthood. But the King has sold Jim to a local family by the name of Phelps, for $40. To rescue his friend, Huck sneaks up to the Phelps's farm, but is surrounded at once by dogs. The mother figure in the house is Aunt Sally, and she mistakes Huck for Tom Sawyer, who (as it happens) is coming by riverboat that very day. And so Tom arrives, a turn in the plot that allows Huck and Tom to resume their friendship. Jim is still captive, however. Although Tom knows that Jim was freed by Miss Watson (who has died) in her will, he conceals this knowledge in order to pursue another "adventure," concocting an elaborate plan to free Jim from the hut where he is held captive. Jim is freed, then recaptured. Were it not for a visit by Aunt Polly, another of Tom's aunts, the news that Jim is no longer a slave might not have been corroborated in such a way that the Phelps clan could accept it.

When Huck questions Tom about keeping the news of Jim's liberation a secret, Tom blithely explains that he had hoped to run down to New Orleans with Huck and Jim on the raft "and have adventures plumb to the mouth of the river" (364). At that point, he would tell Jim about the fact of his freedom and send him upriver "on a steamboat, in style." He would also compensate him financially for his "lost time," however anxiety ridden that time may have been. They would all return as heroes, with a brass band to welcome them. This is, of course, pure fantasy, and one can see from Huck's wry tone that he buys into none of it. He has grown beyond Tom Sawyer and his childish ways and has capitulated to the wild schemes only because he thinks they might really work. (He may continue to enjoy these pranks as well.)

At last, Huck learns that he does still have his fortune, and that Pap is dead. When pressed, Jim admits to Huck he has known all along that Pap was dead. He offers no explanation for why he didn't tell him, and so readers must try to figure this out for themselves. In any case, exactly what Jim had in mind remains a mystery. We do, however, know that Huck resolves to go his own way at last. He plans to "light out for the Territory ahead of the rest." He will not allow Aunt Sally to adopt and "sivilize" him. "I can't stand it," he says, in the last words of the novel. "I been there before."

The last four words explain a great deal about Twain's narrative strategy in *Huckleberry Finn*. The story, like the mythical world serpent, bites its own tale. That is, Twain circles back to the beginning to replay boyhood fantasies, calling up for readers a vision of boyhood adventures and scolding mother figures. But that is a racist world as well, a place where black people exist in a kind of limbo, hovering in the background, doing the hard work that sustained the boyhood environment of Tom Sawyer, with its clean houses, white picket fences, and square meals. Huck has sailed past that world. The raft has taken him on a journey to adulthood. He has witnessed the cruelties of life, observing the way men so happily torment, even kill, others. His conscience, as he confesses at the end of chapter 33, has been awakened, and its imperatives will not go away. He muses to himself in wonder: "Human beings *can* be awful cruel to one another" (291).

Critics have pondered the last chapters of this novel, from the point where Tom Sawyer reappears and the novel resumes the world of boyhood fantasy. In his praise for the book, Ernest Hemingway suggested tossing out the last ten or so chapters, and called them "cheating." Bernard De Voto, in a well-known book on Twain, described these final chapters as the most "abrupt and chilling" decline of a novel in the English language.[11] Perhaps Leo Marx lodged the fiercest attack on the ending when he suggested that the concluding ten chapters ruin the whole story. The elaborate plan to free Jim from his hut is just *"too* fanciful, *too* extravagant; and it is tedious," he says, suggesting that the "slapstick tone jars" with the underlying intent of the novel.[12] A whole range of critics have sided with Marx to some degree, noting that Jim is treated very badly in the "adventure" scene, and therefore Huck seems to have lost some of the racial sensitivity gained on the journey. One critic goes so far as to call the novel a "tragedy" because Huck cedes his moral authority to Tom.[13] In my view, this misses the point.

Tom is an artist figure, but a naive one. He represents the storytelling, fantastic imagination—an aspect of Twain, a man who loved telling a boy's story, as seen in *The Adventures of Tom Sawyer.* He perhaps thought he would be doing more of the same in *Huckleberry Finn.* However, once the journey on the raft began, he found himself in profound emotional and metaphysical waters. Twain can be seen to mature as a writer in the course of this novel, in the flight from the world of slavery and from the more naive aspects of boyhood. For Tom, of course, fantasy trumps reality. If people's feelings are hurt, so what? Boys will be boys.

Yet boys will be men, too. That is the real message of *Huckleberry Finn,* and when Tom returns at the end of the novel to replay the earlier chapters, taking up the role of artist-trickster, Huck stands in for Twain as his revised self. He has gone from the world of innocence to experience. In the final scenes, Huck capitulates to Tom, in part. He is still a boy. But he does so only because he does not know that Jim is already a free man. He wants to trust his old friend, although one senses a resistance to Tom's scheming that was never present before. "But looky here, Tom," Huck objects, when Tom wants to add yet a further twist to his plot (336). A skeptical note lurks beneath almost every comment he makes, and he seems out of sorts with Tom's fantasies. He goes along with the crazy plan, even its elaborations, because he has yet to arrive at the point of full maturity; that will come in future years. At this stage in his development, he merely turns a wry look on his boyhood friend and his pranks, acceding to them but without enthusiasm. He was, by contrast, only too willing to go along with Tom's pranks at the beginning of the novel, putting on fine clothes and acting like a bourgeois gentleman just for the privilege of Tom's sustained company. At the end, however, there is no sense in which he wants to rejoin Tom, under female authority, "sivilized." He will light out by himself, going where maturity will and must take him.

IV.

FED UP WITH PUBLISHERS and their methods, and always eager to market himself more effectively and sell more copies, Twain established his own publishing house, Webster and Company, in 1885. He put Charles Webster (his nephew by marriage) in charge of the fledgling company, which began auspiciously by bringing into print both *Adventures of Huckleberry Finn* and the *Personal Memoirs* of Ulysses S. Grant. Grant's book became a huge bestseller and established the firm on a sound financial basis, although nothing it produced in later years quite matched these initial publications. Webster himself was ultimately forced out of the company that bore his name, in 1888, and the house collapsed in 1894, having just brought out *Tom Sawyer Abroad,* one of Twain's later, much less interesting books.

Despite prolific advertising (which included the use of colorful handbills), *Huckleberry Finn* did not sell as briskly as some of Twain's earlier books, not at first; but it did well enough. After appearing in mid-February 1885, it had sold thirty-nine thousand copies by the end of March, despite being banned by the Concord Free Library, which condemned its "inelegant, rough, ignorant dialect expressions." The library board argued that the novel showed "a very low grade of morality" and was only "suitable for slums." It amounted to "the veriest trash."[14] Yet the novel continued to attract readers, and it remains one of the most widely respected American novels of all time.

Twain's "inelegant, rough" language opened a fresh vein in American literature, putting before the nation an example of lively vernacular equal to the more refined writing of the great English novelists, whom American novelists had previously tended to imitate. What Twain offered in *Huckleberry Finn* was the American language itself, plain and simple, and he showed that it could plumb the depths of human experience and rise to poetic heights. This plain-speaking language, with its ironic twang, sounded a major note, and one that American writers would sustain. Mark Twain taught his fellow citizens to appreciate the subtleties of their own native speech, even to value "uneducated" talk. Without Twain, one could never have had Hemingway or Faulkner or those who followed in their wake. Even a stream of American presidents has (sometimes weakly) tried to imitate Huck's wry plainspokenness, aware that the ordinary voter still identifies with this kind of talk. (Our towns and villages are full of Mark Twains to this day. Only recently I heard a local carpenter in Vermont say that somebody "fell out of the ugly tree and hit every branch on the way down." Twain would have chuckled, hearing the accents of his own voice.)

Twain was doubtless crude at times, and one sees elements of sexism and racism in his work that rankle, and should. Nonetheless, one must give him credit for putting muscle on what H. L. Mencken called "the American language." A pithy vernacular is our heritage, and we can trace this back to Twain. This is not to suggest that he "invented" a way of speaking: it already existed on the street and was used extensively by humorists of the day, especially those traveling from stage to stage in the Southwest—a lively crew that adored dialect and local color. One can also see the influence of black dialects on Twain: Huck shows an uncanny ear for these cadences and satirical modes.[15] Rather, Twain's achievement was to figure out how to use this kind of talk in literature, to make it sing.

With Huck Finn, the fourteen-year-old loner, America acquired one of its central character types: the outsider with a big heart, the kid who appreciates people from very different backgrounds but himself refuses to assimilate. He will, he *must,* "light out for the Territory." To some extent, this ending could be read as a prime example of the male flight from responsibility, even domesticity. Yet I suspect most Americans (male and female) can identify with Huck, appreciating his wry humor and taking kindly to his willingness to help a slave escape to freedom. It should also be noted that Twain put before us a model of racial integration in the friendship of Huck and Jim. The boy begins by seeing Jim as a piece of property, at least notionally. He ends up as Jim's friend, willing to stop at nothing to see that Jim escapes. He is even willing to step outside the law, if he must, to further this end.

Huckleberry Finn is a novel about American freedom, or about the American *idea* of freedom. This has been a governing idea in our nation from the time of the Revolution, or even before it. And yet perverted ideas of what freedom really means plague us to this day, as some believe that acting in self-interest is the exercise of "freedom." As Huck discovers, real freedom implies liberation from prejudicial behavior, from the most oppressive strictures of convention. The proposition that all men (and women) were created equal is fundamental to the operations of American democracy, yet the struggle for equality continues. For his part, Twain challenges us, asking us to rethink what freedom means at every turn in the river. He also invites us to believe in the powers of invention, and to celebrate the cockeyed world of boyhood. He presses us to erase the boundaries of class and color that keep us in our separate spheres, and he urges us to explore the depths of pleasure that nature, in the form of the river and its profuse environment, affords. Needless to say, he does all of this with a wry sense of humor that still seems peculiarly American and provides an antidote to the pompous, self-important rubbish that fills our newspapers and magazines and clogs our airwaves.

THE

SOULS OF BLACK FOLK

ESSAYS AND SKETCHES

BY

W. E. BURGHARDT DU BOIS

SECOND EDITION

CHICAGO
A. C. McCLURG & CO.
1903

EIGHT

The Souls of Black Folk

I.

"To BE A POOR MAN IS HARD," writes W. E. B. Du Bois in *The Souls of Black Folk* (1903), "but to be a poor race in a land of dollars is the very bottom of hardships" (49–50).[1] In a single sentence one hears the author's characteristic note of firmness and outrage combined with an almost biblical cadence, a sense of gravity and wisdom. More than a hundred years after its first appearance at the turn of the twentieth century, this book—a medley of essays and meditations on the meaning of race in America—has become a touchstone, offering a road map for those who wish to travel to freedom.

There is real indignation here, a note of anger amplified and modulated in the writing of future African American writers. For sure, the poets and novelists, playwrights and essayists of the Harlem Renaissance and the Black Arts Movement looked to Du Bois as a hero, someone who produced a voice of steely self-confidence in the face of virulent racism and its pale but no less deadly cousin, benign neglect. They saw him as a prophet, in that he declares repeatedly throughout his book that "the problem of the twentieth century is the problem of the color-line" (54). In this visionary declaration, so often quoted, he foresees that race will play a pivotal role in modern times. Other ideological rifts, of course, absorbed the twentieth century as a whole: the struggles of liberal democracy against Fascism and Communism being central to the twentieth-century story line. But the race issue has been a dominant concern in the world, from the long resistance to apartheid in South Africa to various campaigns to overthrow colonialism in Asia, India, and elsewhere. In the United States, the efforts to overcome segregation have been, and remain, absorbing—one thinks, of course, of the civil rights marches, the Freedom Riders, the Black Panthers, and so forth. African Americans continue to wrestle with the legacy of slavery and the violence of poverty and neglect that dogged them during the era of Reconstruction, those blighted years in the South after the Civil War. That was a time when newly liberated slaves worked, without much traction, to improve their status. In the twentieth century, racism continued to play a huge role in American life. Today, in the early years of the twenty-first century, the ideal of integration has yet to find its full realization on the ground, in schools, in the workplace, in the various corridors of power. And, of course, our prisons bulge with poor, angry, and bewildered black men who have been rejected by the society at large. As an editorialist in the *New York Times* recently noted with chagrin: "One in nine black men, ages 20 to 34, are serving time."[2] Such a statistic is unimaginable, and its implications both sad and terrifying.

Du Bois foresaw all of this, as though peering from a mountaintop at the future landscape. Writing from inside the race problem, he identified the issue of "double consciousness" in what is perhaps the most famous and influential passage he ever wrote: "It is a peculiar sensation, this double-consciousness, this sense of always looking at one's self through the eyes of others, of measuring one's soul by the tape of a world that looks on in amused contempt and pity. One ever feels his twoness,—an American, a Negro; two souls, two thoughts, two unreconciled strivings; two warring ideals in one dark body, whose dogged strength alone keeps it from being torn asunder" (45).

Has anything changed? The black man or woman still lives a double life, as a person of color as well as an American. There seem always to be these "two warring ideals in one dark body." And this "dogged strength" observed by Du Bois seems to persist as well, an antidote to the pain of racism, in which a person of color is not equal to a white person. This inequality is perpetuated by a system rigged to favor the wealthiest and whitest communities. For all his rage, Du Bois never lost faith in the ability of reason to stamp out prejudice. In this he stands beside the Founding Fathers as an Enlightenment figure. As Randall Kenan has wisely observed, Du Bois sought out "the intelligent white reader who was *ex facto* and de facto the cause of so much black strife."[3] But he also wrote for the intelligent black man, hoping to kindle a fiery resistance. In this, he works apparently in opposition to *Up from Slavery* by Booker T. Washington, which had been published two years earlier. In this acclaimed sequence of autobiographical essays, Washington argued that blacks should propel themselves forward by entrepreneurial energy; he didn't want even to think about the oppressive role of white people, preferring to focus on the idea that blacks should pull themselves up by the bootstraps, creating their own economy, showing their independence through transformative achievement. (He started the Tuskegee Institute in Alabama as a way of educating black men in the trades.)

Washington became a strong voice in the discourse of race and was someone whom Du Bois might well have seen as an ally. But Du Bois disliked the implicit note of accommodation in *Up from Slavery,* suggesting that "Mr. Washington represents in Negro thought the old attitude of adjustment and submission" (87). He argues that Washington's program for black advancement "practically accepts the alleged inferiority of the Negro races," and he says that Washington wished for black people to give up political power, the insistence on civil rights, and access to higher education while concentrating on "industrial education, and accumulation of wealth, and the conciliation of the South" (88). By following the program put forward by Washington, African Americans would experience a steady erosion of civil rights and educational opportunities—at least that is how Du Bois saw it. He poses a bold question: "Is it possible, and probable, that nine millions of men can make effective progress in economic lines if they are deprived of political rights, made a servile caste, and allowed only the most meagre chance for developing their exceptional men?" (88).

Du Bois took issue with Washington on many fronts, arguing that it was impossible for black men and women to rise as entrepreneurs and "defend their rights and exist without the right of suffrage." The cards were stacked against them. Yet Washington and Du Bois have for too long been put into simple opposition. Du Bois firmly recognized the considerable worth of his predecessor's efforts and calls them "noble." He refers to Washington as "a useful and earnest man" who gave "invaluable service." He notes that attacks on Washington come from various sides, including from the militant wing among the African American community, those "spiritually descended" from several symbolic figures of the past, including "Toussaint the Savior," as he refers to the Haitian rebel Toussaint-Louverture, and Nat Turner, the defiant slave whose failed rebellion in the antebellum South made him a heroic figure in some quarters (although his systematic slaughter of whites didn't much help his legacy). Du Bois calls this strain in African American thought the tradition of "revolt and revenge." This faction "hate[s] the white South blindly and distrust[s] the white race generally, and so far as they agree on definite action, think that the Negro's only hope lies in emigration beyond the borders of the United States" (89). As it turned out, this was the ultimate choice of Du Bois himself, who died in exile in Ghana, utterly discouraged by the fate of African Americans in the United States.

Some critics of Washington fall into the category of moderates, perhaps not unlike Du Bois in certain phases. They agree with Washington about the importance of fostering schools for trades in the black community, but they also support higher learning and insist that there is a "demand for a few such institutions throughout the South to train the best of the Negro youth as teachers, professional men, and leaders" (90). These moderate thinkers do not expect the shackles of oppression to fall at once; rather, they anticipate a slow, steady progress toward freedom. They, too, will often agree with Du Bois that "the way for a people to gain their reasonable rights is not by voluntarily throwing them away and insisting that they do not want them" (91). For himself, Du Bois could not abide the idea of sitting on the sidelines to watch the "industrial slavery and civic death" of black people.

The questions for readers of Du Bois today are these: Has much changed since the beginning of the twentieth century? Where does the responsibility for the "souls of black folk" really lie? Are we still to blame the legacy of slavery for the unstable situation of African Americans in the twenty-first century? Is racism what continues to keep black people in poverty in such large numbers, their career prospects so limited? To what degree does Washington's desire to keep the responsibility for freedom on black shoulders still seem useful? What does *The Souls of Black Folk* say to Americans generally about their system of government, its inherent strengths and weaknesses? How has this book helped to change, or shape, America's ideas about race?

II.

WILLIAM EDWARD BURGHARDT DU BOIS (1868–1963) was an unlikely figure, a black intellectual born and raised in Great Barrington, an idyllic town in the Berkshires of western Massachusetts: a community that belonged to the Dutch valley of the Hudson, rather than to the puritanical side of New England. His mixed heritage included African, French, and Dutch ancestors, making him a distinct anomaly in the Berkshires. (His mother's Dutch family had been in the Berkshires from the mid-eighteenth century; less is known about his father, who abandoned the family when his son was young. They lived in a cottage owned by a former slave who settled in Great Barrington after the Civil War.) Although light skinned, Du Bois identified with the African strain in his background—of course, he had no choice, given a racial bias that would disallow anything else. A brilliant child, he was considered a prodigy, and adults would consult him about what they should be reading. Young William himself seemed to have read everything, and he spoke and wrote eloquently, impressing his teachers and the community at large with his intelligence and learning. It would have been natural for him to matriculate at Harvard, as many clever, well-bred boys did in his time and place. But Du Bois was considered black, as he realized most concretely at the age of seventeen, when Harvard flatly rejected him.

Instead of making the shorter trip to Cambridge, he traveled southward, to Nashville, Tennessee, to enroll at Fisk, a pioneering black college. There, for the first time, Du Bois experienced the harsh realities of racism in the South. The legacy of slavery was manifested in lynchings and beatings, in discriminations large and small. Blacks stepped aside whenever white folk passed them on the street, not daring even to lift their eyes. They had little hope of participation in the legal system or civic government. They lived, for the most part, in poverty and ignorance. Du Bois noticed all of this with discontent, but the fact of the color line struck him even more painfully when he taught in rural schools in Tennessee. Nor did he forget the harsh lessons learned in the South when, in 1888, he was finally allowed to enroll at Harvard College (as a junior), eventually becoming the first black man to receive a Ph.D. from Harvard.

In a pivotal, characteristic moment, Du Bois gave a stunning baccalaureate speech at Harvard in 1890. His unlikely subject was Jefferson Davis, the president of the Confederacy, the man who symbolized Southern white power in the era of slavery. That a young black man exquisitely attuned to the problem of racism could give a balanced speech on Davis only twenty-five years after the Civil War seems unimaginable. Yet Du Bois loved the challenge, taking on this subject with a sense of glee. He began his talk, "Jefferson Davis as a Representative of Civilization," by calling Davis "a typical Teutonic hero," suggesting that "the history of civilization during the last millennium has been the development of the idea of the Strong Man of which he was the embodiment. The Anglo-Saxon loves a soldier—Jefferson Davis was a soldier."[4] One hears in this speech certain notes that reappear throughout the writings of Du Bois: the self-confident phrasing, the almost arrogant assumption of total understanding, the urge to put things into historical perspective, a sense of objectivity and detachment. By placing Davis within the confines of his historical moment and character type, Du Bois "places" him, or puts him in his place. It was a brilliant rhetorical strategy.

Du Bois left Harvard for Germany to further his studies. German universities had provided a model for the American graduate system, and so they attracted serious scholars. Du Bois stayed only for a brief while, however, having experienced difficulty in raising funds; nevertheless, his encounter with European life made a firm impression—he never ceased to admire the civilized way of life he witnessed firsthand in Germany. He returned to the United States to do research in social history, publishing a landmark study, *The Philadelphia Negro,* in 1899. This book established his reputation as a scholar, one of the first to treat African American life in such a detailed fashion. As Playthell Benjamin observes: "What excited Du Bois most about the study of African-American communities, north or south, was that these communities were virtual living laboratories that could provide a unique opportunity for social scientists to observe the process by which an illiterate, poor, peasant community made the jump from a rural folk society to a modern urban people capable of surviving and advancing in an industrial milieu."[5] Of course one could hardly hope to make a living as an independent scholar, then or now.

A career in teaching was the likeliest route to economic stability, and Du Bois aimed in that direction. He was soon hired by Atlanta University, in Georgia. He still held the idealistic belief that through the exercise of reason and good sense, blacks could help to overcome racism and its most obvious manifestation in society, segregation; but the intransigent nature of race relations in the South overwhelmed him, and he reacted against the methods of accommodation that Booker T. Washington appeared to advocate. The particular ideals of the Tuskegee Institute did not inspire his confidence. He flat out refused to accept discrimination, even temporarily, in the hope of winning future freedom, and he resisted the doggedly practical nature of the Tuskegee model. "Education must not simply teach work," he said, "it must teach life." And life meant liberty.

Du Bois founded the Niagara Movement in 1905, designed to foster civil rights for blacks. This organization morphed into the National Association for the Advancement of Colored People (NAACP) in 1909. He was a prominent figure in this association and edited its journal, the *Crisis,* an important organ of protest. Within a short while, Du Bois became a major voice for resistance, a public intellectual of unusual eloquence and force of character. He resisted the idea that black people should simply learn trades and accept prejudice for the time being, hoping for a better life in the future; his advocacy of higher education for the "Talented Tenth"—the top 10 percent of blacks—was a consistent theme in his writing (and one that often subjected him to the charge of elitism). His militancy grew in the 1920s and '30s, and he found himself at loggerheads with Walter White, the influential head of the NAACP in the early 1930s. One of the points of contention was whether black children would get a better education from black teachers. Du Bois thought so, believing that the educational system, especially in the South, was rigged to favor white students in such a way that black children could not acquire self-respect within it. He began to favor black separatism, and this shift of emphasis led to his resignation as editor of the *Crisis* in 1934.

Du Bois continued as a professor of sociology at Atlanta University until the early 1940s, publishing major studies of African American culture and history, including an important book on the role of blacks during Reconstruction. He was hounded by the U.S. government, however, as it regarded him as a dangerous fellow with Communist leanings. To a degree, this was true. His sympathies lay with the socialist movement, and he was formally prosecuted as a Communist in 1951. Du Bois was then eighty-three years old! A sympathetic judge threw out the case, yet Du Bois was by now thoroughly disillusioned with the prospects for civil rights in America. In 1961, he did in fact join the Communist Party officially and left the United States for good, taking up residence in Ghana at the age of ninety-three. A year later, he renounced his U.S. citizenship and died soon thereafter, in self-imposed exile from the country whose values he had worked so hard to shape.

That bare outline gives only a sense of the contours of this extraordinary and complex man. Du Bois lived such a long time that his life began (February 23, 1868) just five years after Lincoln issued the Emancipation Proclamation. He died shortly before the famous march on Washington where Martin Luther King delivered his luminous speech, repeating "I have a dream" and "free at last" with increasing urgency. King's dream was the same one that Du Bois had, so many years before, in *The Souls of Black Folk*. As Dolan Hubbard writes: "Du Bois challenges the prevailing orthodoxy that Africans were on the bottom rung of the great chain of being and that blackness was a badge of shame."[6] A man of ferocious courage, with a reflexive urge to defy those attempting to suppress him, Du Bois stands in opposition to the model of Booker T. Washington, whom he ultimately regarded as a wily fellow, a trickster who stepped with caution around the minefield of race in America. "Booker T. Washington was not an easy person to know," he later recalled in *Dusk of Dawn,* his autobiography. "He never expressed himself frankly or clearly until he knew exactly to whom he was talking and just what their wishes and desires were."[7]

Du Bois was himself no Br'er Rabbit, darting and weaving, trying to cause no offense. He was a fist raised in the air, a man who refused to sit at the back of the bus or be told what to do. Liberation was his goal, and he dedicated himself to this task, producing a vast body of work in his long lifetime. But most careers, even great ones, dwindle to a book or two in public memory. Du Bois is certainly best remembered for the book in which he gave "soul" back to his race, locating black identity within a spiritual realm, validating its music and traditions, and examining the history of black oppression in America in ways so intelligent and objective that nobody interested in this subject can ignore it.

His book should also be seen in context. In the racist ideology of the nineteenth century, especially in the South, it was often denied that black folk actually *had* souls, a point that Frederick Douglass makes in his *Narrative.*[8] That was why the white masters on plantations did not necessarily grant slaves the rights to receive baptism, take Communion, or get married. Burial ceremonies were actually frowned upon. Slaves were not full human beings with souls but creatures who moved on a lower plane, like animals. As Douglass says, these were not creatures in need of salvation but mere "hewers of wood and drawers of water," a phrase that Du Bois would repeat. It was against such nonsense that Du Bois took his position, positing a black soul and giving body to black realities, relocating the souls of black folk within bodies, in communities, in a heritage equal to any in the white world that nonetheless held them at arm's length, that "read" them as inferior beings.

Du Bois patiently searched for a black cultural heritage, in countless books and articles, but mainly in *The Souls of Black Folk.* The title of this collection of essays alone grants a certain dignity to a specific people, the black "folk," the word itself folksy in that it has a casual ring; but it has a dignity as well, with Germanic roots in a word that signifies a racial group with a long tradition. As Arnold Rampersad suggests, Du Bois used the term in a way that harked back to the German philosopher Johann Gottfried von Herder (1744–1803): "His definition of 'folk' is primarily a political one and should be understood as interchangeable with the more daring term 'nation.' "[9] Du Bois envisions a unified black culture, one that locates identity in a tradition of song and sermon, music and folklore. He argues that the cultural productions of black Americans have been consistently misunderstood and underestimated, and gives black folk their true value here. In doing so, he builds a foundation upon which later theorists of culture, artists, and political reformers could erect their temples of freedom.

Not surprisingly, the book caught on almost at once, with at least thirty-three editions published by A. C. McClurg, the Chicago publisher who first brought out the collection of essays, between 1903 and 1938, when the firm appears to have dwindled. In 1953, as the civil rights movement was beginning to find its modern voice, the book was brought out in a fresh paperback by Fawcett and translated into French and other languages, giving it a worldwide audience. In 1961, an edition introduced by the black historian Saunders Redding appeared from Dodd, Mead, a major New York publisher. A major British publisher, Longmans, issued a popular edition with an introduction by the Caribbean-born socialist C. L. R. James in 1965. A New American Library paperback edition that appeared in 1969 was immensely popular and helped to fuel the Black Power movement. And the editions have only kept coming, with cheap paperback reprints widely available at present. Among those who have written interesting and useful introductions to the book are Arnold Rampersad (1993, Knopf) and Henry Louis Gates Jr. (1999, Norton). For this chapter, I quote from the Signet Classic edition, which has an excellent introduction by Randall Kenan (1995).

III.

*T*HE SOULS OF BLACK FOLK consists of fourteen separate essays and sketches, most of which had a separate life before coming together in book form. There is even one piece of fiction, "Of the Coming of John." Not surprisingly, the texture of each is different, ranging from soulful memoir in the immensely rich tradition of black autobiography to straightforward sociology and cultural analysis to lyrical evocations of black "soul," as manifested in religious writings and poetry, music and speech. Nevertheless, the whole is oddly unified, as the distinct sensibility of Du Bois governs the work from first to last, and one always feels the pulse of resistance, hears a note of intelligent dissent.

The spiritual "strivings" of black folk are the subject of the first chapter, a general one in which Du Bois asks what it means to be both an American and a black person. "How does it feel to be a problem?" he wonders (43). That question hovers in the air around him. He posits a "vast veil" that separates black from white. "Why did God make me an outcast and a stranger in mine own house? The shades of the prison-house closed round about us all" (45). Here, as throughout, the language often echoes the King James translation of the Bible and the traditions of English poetry ("shades of the prison-house," for example, alludes to a poem by Wordsworth). This elaborate language may sound a strange note to contemporary ears not used to a rhetorical mode. It may seem excessively florid, even pompous. But Du Bois generally does not overdo any of this, and often falls back upon a simple syntax and diction, as when he frames his influential notion of "double consciousness."

Double consciousness, the sense of allegiance to two opposing camps, has permeated the discourse on race in the last century. And the problem of America is the problem of the color line: the division into black and white, and the agony this poses for the African American, who must negotiate these two worlds. The history of race in America is the history of this strife, Du Bois argues. The analysis is devastating, as he explains how the black man has been degraded, even when he is a professional—a minister or a doctor. As recent critics have pointed out, black *women* are rarely mentioned in this book, and when they are, they occupy the realms of domestic life. In this, Du Bois was a person of his place and time, writing well before the full awakening of a political consciousness in women. This said, Du Bois does single out (in the second chapter) the "crusade of the New England schoolma'am" in the Deep South, praising those countless white women who dedicated their lives to educating black children in the era of Reconstruction (64).

In the main, Du Bois sets up a framework for resistance by allowing his rage to speak in a controlled fashion, isolating prejudice as the core issue. "Men call the shadow prejudice," he says coolly, "and learnedly explain it as the natural defense of culture against barbarism" (50). Deftly pretending to go along with this, he suggests that black men as well would bow "humbly" before this effort. But he attacks a "nameless prejudice that leaps beyond all this," noting the "personal disrespect and mockery" that come along as well, "the ridicule and systematic humiliation" to which his race is commonly subjected. He finds such manifestations of prejudice utterly intolerable and offers a fierce polemic against them, showing white people what a black person might actually feel and think.

In the second chapter he reaches back to history, recounting the struggle for freedom, especially between 1861 and 1872—the first years of transition from slavery. In particular, he looks at the establishment of the Freedmen's Bureau, designed to help the former slaves in their transition to freedom. The argument is founded on the assumption, put forward in the first sentence of this chapter, that "the problem of the twentieth century is the problem of the color line" (56). One has often heard that the Civil War was not about slavery, of course, and Du Bois repeats this line to put it to rest, recalling that as soon as northern armies penetrated the South, fugitive slaves "appeared within their lines" (55). Lincoln is, without reverence, described as "the long-headed man with care-chiselled face who sat in the White House." Du Bois is not always quite in control of his irony, and his writing can seem heavy-handed, as when he talks about the Freedmen's Aid societies, "born of the touching appeals" of various benevolent people (57). But when he simply describes the historical dimensions of a problem, he does so vividly:

> Three characteristic things one might have seen in Sherman's raid through Georgia, which threw the new situation in shadowy relief: the Conqueror, the Conquered, and the Negro. Some see all significance in the grim front of the destroyer, and some in the bitter sufferers of the Lost Cause. But to me neither soldier nor fugitive speaks with so deep a meaning as that dark human cloud that clung like remorse on the rear of those swift columns, swelling at times to half their size, almost engulfing and choking them. In vain were they ordered back, in vain were bridges hewn from beneath their feet; on they trudged and writhed and surged, until they rolled into Savannah, a starved and naked horde of tens of thousands. (58–59)

The aftermath of the war was shocking in its brutality, as Du Bois says: "Guerrilla raiding, the ever-present flickering after-flame of war, was spending its forces against the Negroes, and all the Southern land was awakening as from some wild dream to poverty and social revolution" (67). The poetical use of alliteration ("flickering after-flame of war") may suggest overwriting; but the subject is well suited to such treatment, and Du Bois sweeps the reader with his prose. Exactly how the Freedmen's Bureau was established, and how its good intentions crashed upon the immovable rock of Southern prejudice, consumes much of this essay. The bureau certainly did succeed in planting free schools among the black population, as Du Bois acknowledges; but the fact of racism could not be overcome: "The opposition to Negro education in the South was at first bitter, and showed itself in ashes, insult, and blood; for the South believed an educated Negro to be a dangerous Negro" (71).

Du Bois mourns "the passing of a great human institution" before its work could be completed and states bluntly that "despite compromise, war, and struggle, the Negro is not free" (77). Literal slavery gave way to economic slavery, as black men and women were chained by necessity to their old plantations. The only escape for them was by "death or the penitentiary" (78). As it were, the prison system in America still functions in this way in too many cases.

The most controversial as well as the most influential essay in *Souls* is the third, "Of Mr. Booker T. Washington and Others," which holds the key to the author's political intent. In 1903, one simply did not attack Booker T. Washington. He was a remarkable man, born into poverty, rising to become a major cultural figure among blacks, and the founder of Alabama's Tuskegee Institute, which taught trades to hopeful black men. Perhaps more important, Washington had won the respect of whites as well, especially in the South. He sought, as Du Bois tells us, an "honorable alliance with the best of the Southerners" (80). But Du Bois cannot hide his scorn as he describes his "programme of industrial education, conciliation of the South, and submission and silence as to civil and political rights" (79). The Washington approach was called "the Atlanta compromise," and Du Bois considered it no gift to black folk. In return for their willingness to give up basic rights of citizens, including the right to vote, they were given access to a certain level of education.

As Du Bois observes, "There is among educated and thoughtful colored men in all parts of the land a feeling of deep regret, sorrow, and apprehension at the wide currency and ascendancy which some of Mr. Washington's theories have gained" (82). He regards the Atlanta compromise as a form of retreat and submission and says that Washington would have the black citizen trade political power, civil rights, and a foothold in the realms of higher education for meager benefits. In relinquishing these basic rights, the black man (women were not really factored into the equation) has been disenfranchised. What Du Bois wants for African American males is the right to vote, civic equality, and education according to their abilities.

According to Du Bois, Booker T. Washington "tended to make the whites, North and South, shift the burden of the Negro problem to the Negro's shoulders," whereas "the burden belongs to the nation" (94). Du Bois believes that black people should stand behind Washington as far as he preaches thrift, patience, and industrial training, as these are all good things. But he opposes any policies that imply retreat, or that seem to make excuses for injustice: "By every civilized and peaceful method we must strive for the rights which the world accords to men, clinging unwaveringly to those great words which the sons of the Fathers would fain forget: 'We hold these truths to be self-evident: That all men are created equal; that they are endowed by their Creator with certain unalienable rights; that among these are life, liberty, and the pursuit of happiness' " (94–95).

As Arnold Rampersad points out, Du Bois disliked the implicit pessimism of Washington, what he regarded as the older man's spiritual lassitude and Philistinism. He held strongly to a Platonic view of life, in which work becomes not just a means to material benefits, but a realm in which one could pursue "the ideals of truth, beauty, and love." In short, for Du Bois, "the purpose of life was aspiration to the ideal." This goes very much against the grain of Washington, who considered such highborn idealism "little more than vagrancy."[10]

Now Du Bois shifts effortlessly to autobiography in *The Souls of Black Folk*: a mode beloved of black writers, and one that emerged from the tradition of slave narratives, which typically described the progress from bondage to freedom, although Du Bois sees freedom as something far away and difficult to achieve. This excursion in autobiography ends on a bitter note: "Thus sadly musing, I rode to Nashville in the Jim Crow car" (108). The Jim Crow laws enforced segregation, keeping black and white citizens apart. Anyone who traveled in the South in the days before the era of modern civil rights will remember the way African Americans were forced to eat in separate restaurants, ride at the back of the bus, go to separate schools. (I still remember driving through the South to Florida with my parents in 1956. The motels along the way would brazenly advertise: "Whites Only." I recall a black boy watching me enviously as I drank from a public fountain reserved for white people in a town square in Georgia.)

This chapter, with characteristic irony, is called "Of the Meaning of Progress." Du Bois taught in poor black schools in Tennessee as a young man, and now he returns—fifteen years later—to see how things have "progressed." He begins in fairy-tale fashion: "Once upon a time I taught school in the hills of Tennessee, where the broad dark vale of the Mississippi begins to roll and crumple to greet the Alleghenies" (96). Then a student at Fisk, the legendary black college, he wanted badly to help the needy pupils in rural schools. His descriptions of black communities in these parts are admirably concrete, almost aromatic in detail: "Sprinkled over hill and dale lay cabins and farmhouses, shut out from the world by the forests and the rolling hills toward the east" (97). Description leads to revelation in such passages, as Du Bois recalls the "blue and yellow mountains stretching toward the Carolinas" (98). Even the classroom experience seems idyllic: "There they sat, nearly thirty of them, on the rough benches, their faces shading from a pale cream to a deep brown, the little feet bare and swinging, the eyes full of expectation, with here and there a twinkle of mischief, and the hands grasping Webster's blue-black spelling book" (100). Du Bois and the children "read and spelled together." They wrote a little, picked flowers, sang, and told stories to each other. The teacher would often go home with children to meet their parents. He was happily absorbed by the community, which—because of its isolation—became a world unto itself.

Upon his return, he finds that the lives of his former pupils have disintegrated. "My log schoolhouse was gone. In its place stood Progress; and Progress, I understand, is necessarily ugly" (105). One of his favorite students is now dead, and no sense of accomplishment or forward movement survives within the community. Everyone seems demoralized. There had been some trade-offs, but these proved ambiguous at best: "How many heartfuls of sorrow shall balance a bushel of wheat?" he wonders, as if writing a parable (108). And so, as he ponders such questions, he rides back to Nashville in the Jim Crow car: segregated, separate but very much an unequal citizen.

The odd fifth chapter is a meditation of the meaning of a university and the lack of adequate universities in the South. Du Bois idealized the academic village and yearned for an idyllic grove, a place where his notions of the learned life could occur. He thought this could only come about "by founding Right on righteousness and Truth on the unhampered search for Truth; by founding the common school on the university, and the industrial school on the common school; and weaving thus a system, not a distortion, and bringing a birth, not an abortion" (119). However lofty its intention, this vision has no real clarity; it shines dimly through a haze of abstraction.

In the following, related chapter, "Of the Training of Black Men," Du Bois contemplates education as "the one panacea" that "leaps to the lips of all" (123). Even at the turn of the twentieth century, education was regarded as the cure for racism. But Du Bois questions the notion that education can eradicate prejudice. In surveying the decades since the Civil War came to an end, he sees no redemptive pattern in the education of former slaves. "The Negro colleges," he says, "hurriedly founded, were inadequately equipped, illogically distributed, and of varying efficiency and grade" (125). The ordinary schools attended by black children were similarly ill equipped and badly formed. Meanwhile, racism in the South hardened, having been set into law. He suggests that the South has become "an armed camp for intimidating black folk" (136). Once again he puts forward his notion of the Talented Tenth, that elite crop of young black men who must be educated properly. These men will not "lightly lay aside their yearning and contentedly become hewers of wood and drawers of water," he says, alluding—as noted—to a phrase by Frederick Douglass (136). The function of the Negro college, he argues, remains clear, as "it must maintain the standards of popular education, it must seek the social regeneration of the Negro, and it must help in the solution of problems of race contact and cooperation" (138). It should also "develop men." These are men who seek to know themselves deeply, and their self-knowledge enhances their race generally. Using himself as an example, he ends the chapter beautifully, saying: "I sit with Shakespeare and he winces not. Across the color-line I move arm in arm with Balzac and Dumas, where smiling men and welcoming women glide in gilded halls." Is this, he wonders aloud, the promised land?

From this height of general eloquence he descends into the valley of concrete description, taking on a part of Georgia as a sociologist in chapter 7, "Of the Black Belt." This is a crucial chapter, but one that critics tend to overlook, concentrating instead on Du Bois as essayist or autobiographer. This work is nevertheless "grounded in his analysis of African American life in the South and an understanding of the relationship and importance of African labor leading to the slave trade and the perpetuation of southern planter interests," as James Daniel Steele has observed.[11] The chapter presents Du Bois as sociologist, working in a discipline as yet unformed. He looks at the world directly, taking one county in Georgia as an example of what has become of blacks in the South after the end of slavery. What troubles the South is not the prejudice of certain individuals but structural flaws, he argues. He chose Georgia because "the Negro problems have seemed to be centered in this State" (141). Reconstruction and its aftermath had led to a situation where the basic rights of black men and women had been denied to them. Laws had been put into place that codified racist feelings. The right to vote itself had been severely curtailed for black men (even white women could not vote, of course, until 1920). As it were, African Americans were pushed out of politics almost completely. In 1901, the last black member of the U.S. Congress, George Henry White of North Carolina, left office. Another black voice would not appear in the House of Representatives until 1928. Tellingly, the South—a major center of the African American population—had no black congressional representative until 1972, when Andrew Young of Georgia was elected to the House.

Du Bois surveys Dougherty County with a fierce eye, noting the multiple rows of old cabins filled with renters and laborers: "cheerless, bare, and dirty, for the most part, although here and there the very age and decay makes the scene picturesque" (155). He ruminates on the poverty everywhere on view, and its consequences, such as a lack of educational opportunities. By citing laws that have been used to enshrine a system of prejudice, thus guaranteeing failure for the black population, Du Bois sets the scene for social protest. "He sought to counter the racial status quo by asserting that the African American condition was not due to a natural order but to a social order," says Steele.[12] And one can protest a social order.

In essence, Dougherty was typical of other counties in the South as a kind of feudalism replaced the slave system. Majority rule was nonexistent in Southern counties, as black folk were in the majority in so many of them yet they had no political power. A handful of white landowners controlled local and state governments. Roaming the countryside, talking to the black folk who lived there, Du Bois offers a sympathetic portrait of an oppressed people. He contradicts the prevailing notion of African Americans as lazy but cheerful, in need of paternal guidance. This paternal guidance, as Du Bois notes in the final vignette, his portrait of a black preacher, is counterfeit. He asks the preacher and his wife if they own any land. " 'Own land?' said the wife; 'well, only this house.' Then she added quietly, 'We did buy seven hundred acres across up yonder, and paid for it; but they cheated us out of it' " (160–61).

Across the South the so-called Jim Crow laws shaped a system in which black folk could never prosper. ("Jim Crow" was a fictional black beggar in a popular vaudeville act by Thomas "Daddy" Rice. One song from the show was especially famous, "Jump Jim Crow.") One of the reasons for creating a legal system designed to "enslave" blacks was economic, as Du Bois argues in his eighth chapter, "Of the Quest of the Golden Fleece," where he continues to examine Dougherty County. "We seldom study the condition of the Negro today honestly and carefully," he writes. "It is so much easier to assume that we know it all" (163). He takes a hard look at life for black folk here, sketching an unpleasant picture, with hard, unrewarding labor in store for most. Even children are subjected to this dehumanizing labor, with no time for education or any of the refinements one associates with the good life. The agricultural round absorbs these people and crushes them.

Yet cotton was not an especially profitable crop, as Du Bois says: "The land on the whole is still fertile, despite long abuse. For nine or ten months in succession the crops will come if asked: garden vegetables in April, grain in May, melons in June and July, hay in August, sweet potatoes in September, and cotton from then to Christmas. And yet on two-thirds of the land there is but one crop, and that leaves the toilers in debt. Why is this?" (171).

Good question. Why abuse the land by failing to rotate crops? Why imprison so many laborers in this way? Du Bois answers these questions by arguing, and backing up his assertions with a blizzard of facts, that an "all-cotton scheme of agriculture" served white interests very well, reconstituting slavery in all but name in a marketplace in which cotton is the only currency: "The landlord therefore demands his rent in cotton, and the merchant will accept mortgages on no other crop" (174).

The "slavery of debt," as Du Bois calls it, kept the population under control. And so "Negro freedom," as he says, boiled down to "the ruined mansions, the worn-out soil and mortgaged acres" that confronted any visitor to the South in the latter half of the nineteenth century (180).

Despite his rage, Du Bois maintains a rational tone, eager to make fine distinctions and accurate statements. In his ninth chapter, he ponders the social conditions of the South after the Civil War and Reconstruction, seeing a shift: "The rod of empire that passed from the hands of Southern gentlemen in 1865, partly by force, partly by their own petulance, has never returned to them. Rather it has passed to those men who have come to take charge of the industrial exploitation of the New South,—the sons of poor whites fired with a new thirst for wealth and power, thrifty and avaricious Yankees, and unscrupulous immigrants. Into the hands of these men the Southern laborers, white and black, have fallen; and this to their sorrow" (192–93).

Only "dollars and dividends" matter to this new race of masters, Du Bois suggests. But he is no economic determinist. In fact, he reaches in many directions, engaging in a kind of soul-searching, acknowledging the complicated nature of the race problem in the South, arguing that "there has been going on for a generation as deep a storm and stress of human souls, as intense a ferment of feeling, as intricate a writhing of spirit, as ever a people experienced" (203). He sees vast social energies at work, for good and evil, within and without "the sombre veil of color." And he acknowledges that the solutions to the race problem do not lie in the direction of simple charity: "Human advancement is not a mere question of almsgiving" (207). Progress requires a complex meeting of minds: the empowerment of black folk, certainly, but a change of laws as well, a rebalancing of the system to promote justice. Du Bois suggests that sympathies must expand on both sides of the color line for good changes to occur.

In the tenth chapter, "Of the Faith of the Fathers," he contemplates the religion of the black South, putting forward a sharp, provocative study of the religious impulse in the black community, with its transformations from animistic African religions to Methodist and Baptist forms of Christianity. The slave encountered Christianity on the plantation, and the worship practices that evolved had one foot back in Africa, one foot in the New World. Black folk, according to Du Bois, possess a "deep emotional nature which turns instinctively toward the supernatural" (218). He discerns a "rich tropical imagination" at work, combined with "a keen, delicate appreciation of Nature." The world of the slave was "animate with gods and devils, elves and witches."

Eventually this world gave way to a certain fatalism. Du Bois quotes a preacher who cries, in poetry: "Children, we all shall be free / When the Lord shall appear!" This fatalism linked in the author's mind with Christian martyrdom of the kind associated with the figure of Uncle Tom in Harriet Beecher Stowe's novel. The downside here was a drift toward what Du Bois calls a "sensualist" approach, characterized by "a religion of resignation and submission" (219). In his view, the oppressions of slavery encouraged this drift, so harmful in its ultimate effects. But Du Bois celebrates the unique power of black religious practice, which he dissects with his usual frankness and sympathy.

"Three things characterized this religion of the slave," Du Bois informs us, describing them as "the Preacher, the Music, and the Frenzy" (211). To this day, the figure of the eloquent black preacher stands out. He is a leader of the community, a magnificent orator, someone who combines "a certain adroitness with deep-seated earnestness, of tact with consummate ability." The preacher himself shimmers at the white-hot center of the religious service, accompanied by the music, with its "plaintive rhythmic melody." This music, we are told, arose "from the African forests, where its counterpart can still be heard" (212). It was adapted, even intensified, by the "tragic soul-life of the slave." What Du Bois calls "the Frenzy" refers to the call-and-response of the black service, the "Shouting." This might be a low murmur from somewhere in the pews or a scream, entail clapping or stomping, even a "wild waving of arms." Always ready to historicize, Du Bois notes that this behavior was nothing new, reaching as far back as Delphi or Endor.

Du Bois recalls that the church became the social center of life among black folk—and has retained this centrality. But the church also seems to represent "the great world from which the Negro is cut off by color-prejudice and social condition" (214). The church becomes a large, all-powerful force, a world unto itself. Nearly all black people seem to belong to a church, he tells us, suggesting that "no such institution as the Negro church could rear itself without definite historical foundations," which he also traces back to African sources, including "the polygamous clan life under the headship of the chief and the potent influence of the priest." This religious life includes "nature-worship, with profound belief in invisible surrounding influences" (215–16).

Having identified the "deep religious feeling of the real Negro heart," Du Bois ends this essay on religion in high rhetorical mode: "Some day the Awakening will come, when the pent-up vigor of ten million souls shall sweep irresistibly toward the Goal, out of the Valley of the Shadow of Death, where all that makes life worth living— Liberty, Justice, and Right—is marked 'For White People Only' " (225). In a clever way, Du Bois diverts the rhetoric of religious revival toward a secular goal; indeed, "God" becomes "Goal," and the ends toward which this incantation leads become "Liberty, Justice, and Right"—the high but distinctly secular goals of the American Revolution, as embedded in the Constitution, then amplified by the Bill of Rights.

In the eleventh chapter, "Of the Passing of the First-Born," Du Bois mourns the death of a child, a little baby born into a world of prejudice: "And thus in the Land of the Color-line I saw, as it fell across my baby, the shadow of the Veil" (227). The Veil, which he invokes so often throughout *The Souls of Black Folk,* is that shroud of color that separates one race from another, black from white in America. The problem with this chapter is that, full of emotion, Du Bois overdoes it; the language expands, too floridly, and the biblical rhythms oppress: "Within the Veil was he born, said I; and there within shall he live,—a Negro and a Negro's son. Holding in that little head—ah, bitterly!—the unbowed pride of a hunted race, clinging with that tiny dimpled hand—ah, wearily— to a hope not hopeless but unhopeful, and seeing with those bright wondering eyes that peer into my soul a land whose freedom is to us a mockery and whose liberty a lie" (227–28). The point is well-taken, but the expression is so convoluted and self-consciously ornate that the reader must gnaw through the heavy flesh of language to get at the bone.

The same florid language occurs in "Of Alexander Crummell," his recollection of a black minister and his struggles with racist attitudes. Crummell had much in common with Du Bois; mainly, he believed, as Shanette M. Harris has observed, "that assimilation and acculturation into European American culture represented the only route for African Americans to acquire social equality and intellectual empowerment."[13]

There is poignancy here, in the idea that if one could only speak as well, and write as well, as white Europeans and Americans speak and write, one could overcome racial prejudice; that if one could only take on white culture fully, one would be admitted to its folds. This approach never worked for Crummell, who found himself rejected by the General Theological Seminary in New York and forced to reconsider his relations to the white people who rejected him. Nevertheless, he refocused his energies, devoting himself to the education and inspiration of his race. What he recovered, however, was never the "first fair vision of youth." It was a darker vision, transformed by harsh experience.

In due course, Du Bois despaired of finding justice for black folk in the United States and moved to Africa—in a sense, falling back into the cradle of African American civilization. Yet the fact remains that *The Souls of Black Folk* offered white Americans a glimpse of life and thought within the black community, making it more difficult for them to oppress those whom they previously considered devoid of an inner life, bereft of valuable traditions. Du Bois puts forward a series of concrete images of that inner life, and its traditions, in the shrewd essay "Of the Sorrow Songs," which maneuvers his sequence toward conclusion by looking at the hymns that slaves sang, their songs so full of hope and "a faith in the ultimate justice of things" (242).

Yet the book only achieves its emotional and intellectual conclusion in the riveting tour de force called "Of the Coming of John," the penultimate chapter.

This short story, a little myth, is the only piece of fiction within these covers. It has an archetypal quality, as Du Bois writes in the vein of an Old Testament prophet. He takes double consciousness, his leading idea, and plays with the notion of black and white, doubling the figure of John. There is the main character, John Jones, a young black man, who played as a child with the son of the local judge in his remote village in Georgia. The white boy is John as well, the son of Judge Henderson, a major figure in the village. White John goes to Princeton, while the other John goes to a black college up north, the Wells Institute. As black John discovers, the Veil persists in the North as well, as "black students have few dealings with the white city below" (246). The mythmaker keeps expanding the dualities: black and white, above and below, south and north. Like the ancient Hebrew storytellers, he wastes not a second in narration, moving swiftly from point to point, leaving a good deal to the imagination.

Black John doesn't take his studies seriously at first and gets tossed out of Wells, only to return as a more mature and responsible fellow, ready to complete his studies. Arriving home, he is broadly welcomed by the black community, although he feels estranged by his education. Knowledge has made him isolate. As we learn, he had a strange encounter in New York with his old playmate John Henderson, whom he met in a symbolic moment in a theater, where he was forced to relinquish his seat to accommodate a girlfriend of white John's. This sets the scene for the finale, when—in a fit of rage—black John attacks white John in the forest, when he happens upon a rape scene in which the white man (now returned from Princeton with scorn for his native village, which in his view is nothing but "mud and Negroes") is attacking his beloved sister, Jennie Jones. Du Bois writes with a ferocious economy of gesture as he narrates the murder: "He said not a word, but, seizing a fallen limb, struck him with all the pent-up hatred of his great black arm; and the body lay white and still beneath the pines, all bathed in sunshine and in blood. John looked at it dreamily, then walked back to the house briskly, and said in a soft voice, 'Mammy, I'm going away,— I'm going to be free' " (262).

Freedom is going north again, to a place "where the North Star glistened pale above the waters." In the murder scene, black John is reduced to the symbolic "great black arm," a primitive version of the powerful black man who turns the white man into a victim, "all bathed in sunshine and in blood." But of course John Jones has every right, even a duty, to rescue his sister from a rape. He does so after learning that white John's father will close his school because he heard from a villager that Jones was teaching the children about the French Revolution, referring to "equality, and such like." The villager says: "He's what I call a dangerous Nigger" (260).

John's world falls apart in a flash, although he has already been estranged from his own people by his education. He understands the reasons for his alienation but confesses to his sister that he has no regrets about what he has learned. The problem is, as Du Bois implies, that racial prejudice is woefully embedded in American society, north and south alike. Efforts to raise the black man—such as those encouraged by

Booker T. Washington—will go only so far. Major structural changes must occur if equality and freedom will triumph over prejudice and oppression. "Of the Coming of John," with its biblical title that echoes the story of John the Baptist (who comes before Christ and loses his head in the process), ends with the horses of the white avengers "thundering toward him." Our beleaguered John Jones will certainly lose his head, too, as one simply did not kill a white man in the Deep South—even to save one's sister from rape—and get away with it, not in those days. A lynching was inevitable.

The blues refrains or "sorrow songs" that flow through the various chapters of *The Souls of Black Folk* provide the appropriate sound track for a book about racial misery and a cultural divide. These songs "both frame and carry forward the most resonant arguments" of the book, as Eric J. Sundquist writes.[14] There is indeed a profound sadness in these fourteen essays; but there is hope as well, located in the anger of Du Bois, who refuses to let the racial Veil deter him. He identifies his rage precisely, gives it various local habitations. His evocations of black emotional and intellectual life position the subject in time and place. There is throughout this luminous work a vision of social transformation, however tentative and inchoate. Du Bois knew the sorts of changes that must occur if the United States were ever to embrace integration and equality, but he understood perfectly well what he was up against. The wonder is that he didn't shrink from the challenge, at least not while writing his book.

IV.

ONE GRATEFUL friend wrote to Du Bois about *The Souls of Black Folk*: "I am glad *glad* you wrote it—we have needed someone to voice the intricacies of the blind maze of thought and action along which the modern, educated colored man or woman struggles."[15] James Weldon Johnson, the poet who wrote *The Autobiography of an Ex-Colored Man* (1912)—a classic novel in the form of a memoir—said that this book by Du Bois "had a greater effect upon and within the Negro race in America than any other single book published in this country since *Uncle Tom's Cabin*."[16] Even among white readers, there was recognition of its importance in expressing, even shaping, the contours of race in America. Indeed, William James, the Harvard philosopher, sent a copy to his novelist brother, Henry, in England, who admired it deeply, calling it "the only 'Southern' book of any distinction published for many a year."[17]

This may seem condescending on the part of Henry James, but *The Souls of Black Folk* is mainly a Southern book, although the North hovers above it, literally and figuratively, as the industrial power dependent upon the labor of black folk in the cotton fields. The old colonial model replicates itself here, with the South as the captured and exploited land; within this model, black folk become peasants, tenant farmers, hired hands, slaves in all but name. With his usual perspicacity, Du Bois includes Africa in the larger model, aware that the black folk he writes about had actually been African villagers in their recent past and were still propelled by their pagan religions, rhythmic "sorrow songs," and tribal formations. Europe, too, figures in this equation, as a touchstone for the most cultured of Americans. Indeed, Du Bois had experienced European culture personally, and so few of his readers understood as well as he did the delicate bonds between Europe and the United States. For Du Bois, culture was a contest, a struggle between unequal groups; the mere fact that he thought in global terms in some ways elevates his discourse. As historian and sociologist, he had a range of reference that was wide and deep. By bringing Africa into the equation, he transforms and dignifies black experience as he interprets it.

One easily forgets that this book was published in 1903, when the Civil War and Reconstruction lay not so far in the past. Little in the way of historical perspective existed, and precious few efforts at genuine understanding had been made. By examining the history of the displaced black people, by looking at Northern efforts to help them, and by casting a cold eye on racial prejudice in the South, Du Bois uncovers a whole new way of thinking about the "double consciousness" and "the Veil." In effect, he sets in place the terms by which we still think about race in the United States. The framework may be traced back to this pivotal volume, with its call for black resistance to the various forms of injustice inherent in Southern white society, its awareness of the impact of racial prejudice and segregation.

One commentator of note, Shelby Steele, wrote a perceptive article on the hundredth anniversary of the publication of *The Souls of Black Folk.*[18] His take is typical of the response to this book throughout the century or more since it appeared. It was, says Steele, "the most prophetic book written on the subject of race" ever published within the United States. He considers the proposition that the problem of the color line would dominate the twentieth century, and he regards this as a fair prediction, suggesting that *Souls* "gave the 20th century its first encounter with unapologetic black protest." In this, it differed from Booker T. Washington's conciliatory *Up from Slavery,* even though Washington may well have entertained a perspective as important, if not more so, in that he urged black independence, with the implicit view that African Americans cannot depend on the white population to lift them out of poverty and subjugation.

Yet Du Bois opened a vein of fury that fed into later writers, such as Langston Hughes, Richard Wright, James Baldwin, Eldridge Cleaver, and Malcolm X. The idea of accommodation one associates with Uncle Tom, or Booker T. Washington, was swept away with a savage contempt. What Du Bois did was point to the immoral framework of Reconstruction, where the laws as well as the predominant cultural assumptions were such that no black man or woman could hope to erase the color line or move outside the Veil. White society, which pulled all the levers of political and economic power, had to take some responsibility for black misery; whites had produced it, after all. Black folk had to object to this treatment, and put their objections forward with boldness, refusing to take no for an answer.

Noting all of the above, Steele (himself black) prefers the way forward suggested by Booker T. Washington. (It should be noted that a handful of influential black conservatives in recent years have also found more to admire in Washington's arguments than in those of Du Bois.) Washington certainly had a strong point when he argued that blacks should take matters into their own hands, seeing to it that their children received a certain level of education, one that inspired entrepreneurial values that would ultimately lead to economic freedom. But Steele, in my view, goes too far when he asks: "Why is it that most any American commenting publicly on a racial issue in 2003 will drop right into the comfort zone of Du Boisian protest where whites are always responsible and blacks are always victims?" I don't believe "always" is the right word here, or that this characterization of the problem moves the argument forward in any useful way.

According to Steele, "We keep seeing oppression as the source of our racial problems when it no longer is." He regards the current problem as "the problem of emergence—the shock that formerly oppressed people experience when they first emerge into new freedom, and the struggle with responsibility that always follows." But is racism somehow "over," and has a "new freedom" emerged? Anyone looking at the racially segregated schools in the United States, where not a great deal has changed in half a century, must look with skepticism at such claims—despite the emergence of such a strong figure as Barack Obama. Young black men and women have not been given the same breaks as their white counterparts, and they consequently cannot find good jobs as easily. The legacy of slavery remains a heavy one, still carried on black shoulders. The mere fact that our prison populations are so overwhelmingly black suggests, to me, that something is seriously amiss. Yet the larger question cannot as easily be answered: Is white America responsible for black suffering? The answer must lie somewhere in the middle, and—at some point—responsibility must, and will, be shared.

It should once again be noted that Du Bois did not categorically oppose the arguments made by Booker T. Washington and praised his Herculean efforts to find a place for the education of black people in white society in the face of huge opposition. He admired Washington's "sincerity of purpose" and saluted his "honest endeavor which is doing something worth the doing" (82–83). He says "it is no ordinary tribute to this man's tact and power that, steering as he must between so many diverse interests and opinions, he so largely retains the respect of all." Nevertheless, he sees the limitations of accommodation. Washington seemed too willing to trade political power and civil rights for the freedom to cultivate a certain kind of education within the black community, accepting the notion of a separate but unequal black community. Du Bois would have none of this, refusing to allow for anything but equality in the fullness of that concept. He would erase the color line once and for all.

Steele attacks the idea of "double consciousness," the idea of regarding oneself through the eyes of others, as "not a truth as much as it is a protest, an idea fashioned for white consumption." Yet who can forget what Ralph Ellison made of this insight by Du Bois in the searing prologue to *Invisible Man*? "I am invisible," he writes, "simply because people refuse to see me. Like the bodiless heads you see sometimes in circus sideshows, it is as though I have been surrounded by mirrors of hard, distorting glass. When they approach me they see only my surroundings, themselves, or figments of their imagination—indeed, everything and anything except me."[19] Du Bois prefigures Ellison in *Dusk of Dawn,* his memoir, when he remembers that at Harvard he tried to "forget as far as was possible that outer, whiter world," although this proved impossible, as he (by sheer dint of color) "attracted attention and sometimes the shadow of insult."[20]

It is important to say boldly that things have changed for the better. They have. Yet the racial line in the United States has hardly disappeared, although it has faded. Black and white mix in public places where, in the time of Du Bois, such mingling could never happen. The civil rights movement—one of the many fruits of *The Souls of Black Folk*—has immeasurably enhanced the position of black Americans. It is now illegal to discriminate in the workplace, in schools, or anywhere in the public arena on the basis of race. But racism is hardly defunct, and Du Bois still calls to us, readers of all racial backgrounds, to understand the violence of prejudice and to seek equality for everyone. This is the American promise, and we shall never give up on its fullest realization.

THE
PROMISED LAND

BY MARY ANTIN

WITH ILLUSTRATIONS
FROM PHOTOGRAPHS

BOSTON AND NEW YORK
HOUGHTON MIFFLIN COMPANY
The Riverside Press Cambridge
1912

NINE

The Promised Land

I.

EXCEPT FOR NATIVE AMERICANS, everyone in the United States is an immigrant or the descendant of immigrants. A wide range of European colonists—English, Dutch, Irish, German, French, and Spanish—flourished or failed on North American soil over four centuries ago, but each of them made the long journey from the Old World to the scarcely imaginable new one. They came for a variety of reasons, though frequently in search of a better life than the one left behind. Not surprisingly, the immigrant memoir has always been a central feature of American literature. Indeed, *Of Plymouth Plantation* might well be considered a prototype of the genre, with the *Mayflower* as one of the earliest of countless hopeful crossings, with many of its passengers in search of religious freedom. Certainly Mary Antin's *Promised Land* (1912) ranks high among these memoirs.

Antin's book offers a paradigm of sorts, one that usually begins far away, in the Old Country, where living conditions are hard, even impossible. In the midst of poverty and oppression, the writer learns of a distant place across the sea, a promised land of milk and honey where the streets are paved with gold. Untold wealth lies within easy reach, and not only does freedom from oppression exist, but the class system itself has been seriously disrupted if not dismantled. The hopeful pilgrim crosses an ocean, in steerage. It's a difficult passage, and many die along the way. Making matters worse, the immigrant lands in the New World only to find out that the wonders and wealth have been exaggerated. A struggle ensues, and it takes many years before difficult odds (poverty, prejudice, ignorance) are overcome. In the end, the memoirist survives, even prospers. Assimilation occurs.

Antin's book "really established the genre of the immigrant autobiography," says Werner Sollors, who has recently edited *The Promised Land*.[1] As Sollors recalls, it was a national bestseller, "the most popular immigrant autobiography of its time," and a book that inspired a generation of newly minted Americans, who saw in Antin's story a version of their own.[2] It appeared during the so-called Great Migration, which runs from the last decades of the nineteenth century through the beginnings of World War I. As Roger Daniels frames it, "The new immigrants, persons from southern and eastern Europe who came after the 1880s, were of very different ethnicity (many late-nineteenth- and early-twentieth-century writers used the term *races*) who spoke strange languages and worshiped strange gods—that is, they were not Protestants."[3] These immigrants, often poor and unskilled, were mostly Jews and Catholics from Eastern Europe and Russia, from Italy, Greece, and Ireland.

The Promised Land reflects this tumultuous era of immigration, when the slums of cities teemed with fresh arrivals, many of whom spoke not a word of English. Antin's affecting memoir stands out as a major (and rare) consolidating document—a work of such rhetorical force that it helped to explain an era to itself and to those who came after. What it changed was American attitudes toward this frightening wave of newcomers. Her memoir also helped to confirm the United States as a land of promise, a place where people came (risking everything) with immense hope and where economic and educational opportunities could be found in ways previously unimaginable. That this vision of the promised land persists cannot be doubted, as millions continue to arrive at our borders each year, legally and illegally. They come with the same hopes and fears that enliven Antin's memoir.

II.

MARY ANTIN (1881–1949) was typical of the new wave of immigrants, coming from the Pale of Settlement, an area along the western boundary of Russia where Jews lived in tightly knit communities, perpetually under threat from the imperial powers of the tsar. (*Fiddler on the Roof,* adapted from a sequence of fetching Yiddish stories by Sholom Aleichem, offers a well-known portrait of this world.)

She arrived in Boston on the *Polynesia,* a three-hundred-foot vessel that carried over nine hundred immigrants in third-class cabins, in 1894. The family settled in an urban slum, where Antin encountered the characteristic abrasions of poverty. She quickly made the conversion, as it were, from Yiddish to English and was able to negotiate life in the New World remarkably well for a variety of reasons: mainly, she was very bright, and her parents pushed her forward. Antin believed in the virtues of assimilation, and she flew this flag proudly (though later she found her younger stance naive, even sentimental). Antin's eloquent book has remained at the center of debates on the so-called melting pot ideal of American society—a term deriving from a popular 1908 play by Israel Zangwill, one of Antin's mentors.

Her early years in Boston were not especially pleasant, as her family lived in cold tenements and dark alleys. But Mary herself did remarkably well under these circumstances, publishing poems and stories even as a young girl. Soon after her arrival, she wrote a long letter in Yiddish to her uncle, an account of her voyage from Polotsk to Boston. She later translated this document into English, and it was published (with a variant spelling of the Russian village in the title) as *From Plotzk to Boston,* in 1899, with a warm introduction by Israel Zangwill, already a well-known writer and Jewish figure. Antin attended the Boston Latin School for Girls, although she never quite finished her studies, and later took some college courses. In 1901 she married a well-known paleontologist, Amadeus William Grabau (1870–1946), whom she met in Boston, at gatherings of the Natural History Club, where she also encountered many of her earliest supporters. Grabau rose to considerable prominence in his field, taking a major position at Columbia University. The couple moved to the New York suburbs, where they had a daughter in 1907. Antin's career as a writer prospered.

The Promised Land grew from the letter that she wrote to her uncle and published when she was only eighteen. "I had no plan when I began," Antin recalled, some years later. "One day I found myself thinking of the time I went to school in Polotzk, and I wrote about that. Another day I kept seeing the little girls I used to play with, and I put them in. Then it was the market-place that haunted me, or the Dvina gurgled in my ears all night, or there came into my mind a tale the women used to tell while picking feathers of a Winter evening. I put these things down just as they came, and so grew the book. When it came to putting these fragments together, I found that they fitted wonderfully well, considering their haphazard origin. A little re-arrangement of the loosed sheets, an introductory sentence here, a connecting phrase there, and the story fell into chapters that named themselves. I never knew what I was going to do till it was done."[4]

If there is a faux-naïf aspect to this account, it nevertheless seems believable, especially when one realizes that Antin never wrote another book apart from *They Who Knock at Our Gates* (1914), a meditation on immigration that appeared shortly after *The Promised Land* and that the author referred to derisively in later years as "The Knockers," calling the book "an amazing mixture of naiveté and rhapsody."[5] After that sequel, there was hardly a word from her pen for the next three decades. Perhaps Antin had only one story to tell, her own; it was so utterly compelling that it consumed her. Once it hardened into print, the rest was silence.

The Promised Land generated a mass of publicity as well as royalties, yet life did not go well for Antin in later years. Her husband abandoned her and their daughter, moving to China, where he taught in a university for some decades. The marriage itself was never especially stable. Many reasons have been suggested for this instability, but certainly her husband's insistent pro-German attitudes toward World War I distressed her. Antin's life apparently fell apart in the 1920s as she struggled to raise her daughter alone and to make ends meet. She died in 1949, still living off royalties of *The Promised Land,* which had become a classic text by that time.

III.

I<small>T'S ALL THERE IN THE FIRST SENTENCE</small>: "I was born, I have
lived, and I have been made over" (1). Antin explains in her introduction that she has become a new person and barely recalls the figure
who lived in the Pale of Settlement among pious Jews. The religious aspect of this is evident from the second paragraph, where she considers
her rebirth: "My second birth was no less a birth because there was no
distinct incarnation." If anything, the language here is almost too obviously Christian: she is born again, but in a secular fashion. "All the
processes of uprooting, transportation, replanting, acclimatization, and
development took place in my own soul," she writes, pursuing an organic metaphor, that of the plant taken from one soil, put elsewhere,
nurtured, given new life in fresh circumstances (3). Antin is a natural
poet, working closely with metaphors; for example, metaphors of rebirth, even resurrection, recur throughout the text.

The first chapter is called "Within the Pale," and Antin seems to enjoy the linguistic roots of "pale," which is related to English words such
as "paling," "appalled," and "pallid." A pale is a stake, and a white fence
goes around a property, thus marking it off. The so-called Pale of Settlement was a place where the Jews lived, unblended, fully separated
from the Russians. "Russia was the place where one's father went on
business," Antin writes, inside the head of the little girl she was (5). She
charmingly describes one adventure in travel away from her village,
when she went to Vitebsk with her cousin: the first of many excursions
(and extensions) in her life. It is not a long journey by train; but it's an
entirely fresh place she encounters, the beginning of her uprooting. Yet
there is continuity as well, as the same river passes Vitebsk that flows
through Polotsk: the Dvina. "All my life I had seen the Dvina. How,
then, could the Dvina be in Vitebsk?" A river is a metaphor for the life
force itself, as T. S. Eliot writes in "The Dry Salvages"—"The river is
within us, the sea is all about us."

Antin seems isolated in this opening chapter. She is not, of course,
one of the Gentiles, who are another element within her childhood
world. A Gentile is simply a non-Jew: the Greek word is *ethnikos*. In this
sense, a Gentile is an ethnic person, not from the Jewish world, which is
the norm. The ironic reversals of meaning that eventually occurred as

the word evolved are hardly lost on Antin, who has a wonderful ear for dissonance, irony, and disjunction. "The Gentiles said that we had killed their God, which was absurd," she writes, "as they never had a God—nothing but images" (9). Biblical allusions flow through this chapter, as when the confinement of the Jews in the Pale is compared to the captivity of the Jews in Egypt. "Even in my father's house I did not feel safe," she tells us (12). And one of the chief elements of life in the Pale was uncertainty. Life was precarious. Pogroms occurred. There was inevitably the threat of being drafted into the Russian army, if you were a young man.

If you were wealthy enough, you could hire a substitute: someone who would do your military service for you. Antin recalls one such man, whom she dubs David the Substitute. In a single paragraph, she tells a story of biblical dimensions, with the concision and power of an Old Testament narrator. David took on this task of acting as a substitute in the army for the money alone and lived like a Gentile while in uniform. But he knew how wicked this was, "for he was a pious man at heart" (15). When he gets home, he trudges through the streets of the town in penitential fashion, calling the Jews to prayer on Sabbath:

> Now this was a hard thing to do, because David labored bitterly all the week, exposed to the weather, summer or winter; and on Sabbath morning there was nobody so tired and lame and sore as David. Yet he forced himself to leave his bed before it was yet daylight, and go from street to street, all over Polotzk, calling on the people to wake and go to prayer. Many a Sabbath morning I awoke when David called, and lay listening to his voice as it passed and died out; and it was so sad that it hurt, as beautiful music hurts. I was glad to feel my sister lying beside me, for it was lonely in the gray dawn, with only David and me awake, and God waiting for the people's prayers. (15)

Antin loves a story like this: one of devotion, persistence, passion, determination, and spiritual reward. The mini-tale of David the Substitute lodges in the narrative in isolation, although the clever Antin brings herself into the picture at the end, as she lies in bed and listens to the plaintive calling of David, saying that it "hurt" in the same way that beautiful music hurts. She clearly admires a man like David, who offers a kind of spiritual model, although her piety never really had a religious dimension. If anything, she becomes an Emersonian mystic in these pages: devoted to nature, and the spirit that resides in nature.

Antin nevertheless defends her Jewish community with vigor. "A favorite complaint against us was that we were greedy for gold. Why could not the Gentiles see the whole truth where they saw half?" she writes (23). Jews had to pay even for the right to breathe, she tells us. They had to buy permission to travel for business reasons, and to pay hundreds of rubles in fines to the government of the tsar if their sons were to avoid service in the army. And so forth. The price of being a Jew in Russia at this time was considerable. "The knowledge of such things as I am telling leaves marks upon the flesh and spirit," Antin writes.

In the second chapter, she develops her portrait of Jewish life in the Pale. There was, she explains, "a caste system with social levels sharply marked off, and families united by clannish ties" (32). She paints a generally dark picture of life in the Old World, where social classes have little flexibility. "A shoemaker's daughter could not hope to marry the son of a shopkeeper." The shoemaker was an artisan, of course, while the shopkeeper belonged somewhere in the middle class. The one thing that could lift a person was scholarship: "A boy born in the gutter need not despair of entering the houses of the rich, if he had a good mind and a great appetite for sacred learning" (32). Intelligent and scholarly girls were another matter, but Antin refuses to dwell on this point; in the New World, she simply assumed that her own good mind would redeem her. She would walk fearlessly into the homes of wealthy Bostonians, secure in her intellectual gifts, which provided her with a calling card.

The images of traditional Jewish life that Antin paints recall a number of Yiddish writers, including Aleichem. One cannot easily forget, for instance, her description of her father's wedding: "Merrily played the fiddlers at the wedding of my father, who was the grandson of Israel Kimanyer of sainted memory. The most pious men in Polotzk danced the night through, their earlocks dangling, the tails of their long coats flying in a pious ecstasy" (34). One also recalls the novelist Abraham Cahan (1860–1951), very much Antin's contemporary, who came from an Orthodox family in Lithuania and immigrated to the United States in

1881. His novel of Jewish ghetto life in New York, *Yekl,* appeared in 1896 and was widely admired. Antin would have had this book in mind as she wrote and certainly regarded herself—in the vein of Cahan—as mediating between the Jewish world and that of American Gentiles, who often regarded Jewish immigrants as mysterious, even unapproachable. "I was fed on dreams," Antin tells her readers, "instructed by means of prophecies, trained to hear and see mystical things that callous senses could not perceive" (35).

One often senses a rebellious aspect in Antin's recollections, as when she describes how her mother was forced to submit to the shadchan, or matchmaker. "My mother ran away every time the shadchan came," she writes (46). In the end, she submits "to being weighed, measured, and appraised before her face, and resigned herself to what was to come" (47). One knows implicitly that no such fate awaits Mary Antin. She is a defiant creature, respectful of Jewish traditions but certainly not the sort of person who likes being told what to do. She remains a self-creator, as implied in the proud (even self-important) final sentences of chapter 3: "Since I have stood on my own feet, I have never met my master. For every time I choose a friend I determine my fate anew. I can think of no cataclysm that could have the force to move me from my path. Fire or flood or the envy of men may tear the roof off my house, but my soul would still be at home under the lofty mountain pines that dip their heads in star dust. Even life, that was so difficult to attain, may serve me merely as a wayside inn, if I choose to go on eternally. However I came here, it is mine to be" (49).

As ever, Antin works in a poetic vein, building metaphors with meticulous care, letting them grow and govern the direction of her meaning. Note, for instance, the elaborate and extended nautical metaphors that conclude chapter 4: "Up to this point I have borrowed the recollections of my parents, to piece out my own fragmentary reminiscences. But from now on I propose to be my own pilot across the seas of memory; and if I lose myself in the mists of uncertainty, or run aground on the reefs of speculation, I still hope to make port at last, and I shall look for welcoming faces on the shore. For the ship I sail in is history, and facts will kindle my beacon fires."

Emersonian mysticism comes readily to hand, as in chapter 5, when she hears a peasant singing as he pushes his plow through the "long black furrows yet unsown" (71). "Only the melody reached me," she says, "but the meaning sprang up in my heart to fit it—a song of the earth and the hopes of the earth." A passage follows that Emerson himself might have written: "Something in me gasped for life, and lay still. I was but a little body, and Life Universal had suddenly burst upon me. For a moment I had my little hand on the Great Pulse."

A capacity to rise to a larger vision enlivens this work, makes it as much a book about spiritual awakening as about immigration and assimilation. One migrates, yet metaphysical migration is part of the journey. "This is a tale of immortal life," Antin says, without blushing. "Should I be sitting here, chattering of my infantile adventures, if I did not know that I was speaking for thousands?" she asks (72). One cannot help but think of Walt Whitman, who wrote in "Song of Myself" with a blithe defiance of conventional norms:

I celebrate myself, and sing myself,
And what I assume you shall assume,
For every atom belonging to me as good belongs to you.

One can imagine young Mary Antin reading this, nodding in agreement. She knew that, as Whitman would say, she contained multitudes.

It should be noted that Antin was lucky in her parents, who insisted that she become *wahl gelehrt,* or well educated. She and her sister, Fetchke, were taught Hebrew, as was her brother. "We were to study Russian and German and arithmetic," she recalls (90). Education would provide a key to unlock the adult world. Her first school was "a hovel on the edge of a swamp." But the windows of that school, she writes, "were not too small to afford me a view of a large new world" (94). As ever, she works metaphorically. This "large new world" is more than the swamp that lay within easy view.

Antin freely admits that she likes to exaggerate, adding details that make a story more palatable, interesting, even thrilling, than it might otherwise seem. "The truth is that everything that happened to me really loomed great and shone splendid in my eyes, and I could not, except by conscious effort, reduce my visions to their actual shapes and colors. If I saw a pair of geese leading about a lazy goose girl, they went through all sorts of antics before my eyes that fat geese are not known to

indulge in" (107–8). She forewarns us that the truth she offers is, perhaps, embroidered. Then again, memoirs represent a form of fiction,
subject to the "shaping" implied by the root of the word (*fictio*). This
memoir is, indeed, more like poetry than anything else, as in the last
lines of chapter 6, where Antin reaches for the sublime in a way remi-
niscent of William Blake, the English poet: "It seems to me I do not
know a single thing that I did not learn, more or less directly, through
the corporal senses. As long as I have my body, I need not despair of salvation" (109).

The idea of immigration dawned during Passover, with its yearning
for release from exile. Antin's parents began to think: "Not 'May we be
next year in Jerusalem,' but 'Next year—in America!' So there was our
promised land, and many faces were turned towards the West. And if
the waters of the Atlantic did not part for them, the wanderers rode its
bitter flood by a miracle as great as any the rod of Moses ever wrought"
(113). Such biblical overtones not only resound here, they nearly overwhelm the text. The journey to America becomes, for Antin and her
family, a journey to a land of dreams, to a place where the people of Israel may at last come to rest. "My father was inspired by a vision," the
writer declares. "He saw something—he promised us something. It was
this 'America.' And 'America' became my dream" (114).

Certainly life in Polotsk had become a nightmare: "How quickly we
came down from a large establishment, with servants and retainers, and
a place among the best in Polotzk, to a single room hired by the week,
and the humblest associations, and the averted heads of former friends!"
(114). And so, with hope in the family's hearts (and considerable sadness
as well, as so much of their life was being left behind), Antin's father (already in America, where he had gone to prepare the way) scraped together money for the passage of his wife and children to America. "So
at last I was going to America!" Antin writes, in ecstasy. "Really, really
going, at last!" (129).

Chapter 8 is called "The Exodus," in case any reader should have
missed the biblical overtones of the story so far. The crossing itself had
been fully documented by the young teenager in the letter to her uncle
in Yiddish that was translated and published, and she simply quotes
herself here, to good effect: "On a gray wet morning in early April we

set out for the frontier" (134). The "gray wet morning" seems fitting, and it may even be true. Were it a bright, sunny day, I suspect Antin would have made it a "gray wet morning," as all mythical journeys begin in a shroud of mist, a haze of expectation and anxieties. And it was indeed an anxious journey: "The plight of the bewildered emigrant on the way to foreign parts is always pitiful enough, but for us who came from plague-ridden Russia the terrors of the way were doubled" (138). The family made their way to Hamburg, in Germany, where they would embark on the long journey to America.

The crossing occupied sixteen days, and it frightened Mary as "the ship pitched and rolled so that people were thrown from their berths." She recalls "days and nights when we crawled through dense fogs, our foghorn drawing answering warnings from invisible ships." Nonetheless, the perils of the sea "were not minimized in the imaginations of us inexperienced voyagers" (141). There were good times as well, with "fugitive sunshine, birds atop the crested waves, band music and dancing and fun." As it should, the journey ends on a "glorious May morning" when, suddenly and in its full majesty, "our eyes beheld the Promised Land" (142). She fell happily into the waiting arms of her father.

Antin carefully shapes the myth, which will become a kind of template for all immigrants: the misery at home, which entails poverty and disease, the boot of the law. The anguish of migration mingles with hopefulness. The journey itself begins on a wet, cold day; it ends in glorious sunshine. These symbolic underpinnings illumine the tale, buoy it up. At last, the Antin family occupy their new home, in Boston. This chapter is called "The Promised Land," and the promise is largely fulfilled, though not without reversals of fortune, bouts of illness, missteps, and many turns in the financial road, all of which threaten to turn the American dream into a nightmare.

Antin is alert to the process of assimilation: "The most ignorant immigrant, on landing, proceeds to give and receive greetings, to eat, sleep, and rise, after the manner of his own country; wherein he is corrected, admonished, and laughed at, whether by interested friends or the most indifferent strangers; and his American experience is thus begun. The process is spontaneous on all sides, like the education of the child by the

family circle" (142). Judiciousness and common sense count for a lot as
Antin forges ahead. Part of her steadiness of vision comes from an un-
shakable sense of her own worth. She chides all who would admonish
the immigrant to think again about his or her attitude, and to remember that the "greasy alien on the street" has an ancient heritage, and
"was born thousands of years before the oldest native American; and he
may have something to communicate to you, when you two shall have
learned a common language" (144–45). Antin manages to keep a global
perspective, believing that anyone who crosses her may well regret it
one day. (One hears a defiant note in this, almost a threat.)

The Antin clan moved into the dreariest of Boston slums, where
poor immigrants gathered: "unkempt, half-washed, toiling." This
bedraggled group seemed "pitiful in the eyes of social missionaries, the
despair of boards of health, the hope of ward politicians, the touchstone
of American democracy" (145). This latter note made *The Promised
Land* a controversial book in its day, as not everyone agreed with Mary
Antin that the hordes of non–English speaking immigrants from Eastern and southern Europe who crowded the slums were "the touchstone
of American democracy." One snobby professor from Harvard, Barrett
Wendell, complained that Antin "has developed an irritating habit of
describing herself and her people as Americans, in distinction from such
folks as Edith [Wendell's wife] and me, who have been here for three
hundred years."[6] Criticism along these lines continued in the decade after Antin's book was published, much of it distasteful to read. "Real"
Americans—English speakers who came on the *Mayflower* or within
the next hundred or so years—could not believe that an upstart Russian
Jew dared to claim the Pilgrim fathers as her own ancestors.

Antin readily, even greedily, accepted the bounty of American
democracy, which included access to public libraries and public schools.
Her descriptions of what it felt like to attend American schools leap off
the page, and she writes with equal energy about shedding her foreign-
ness. Her name, for instance, and the names of her sister and brother
were transmogrified: "My Hebrew name being Maryashe in full,
Mashke for short, Russianized into Marya (*Mar-ya*), my friends said that
it would hold good in English as *Mary*" (149–50). Within the immigrant
population, first and last names shriveled or shrank, changing in ways
that shook loose as much ethnicity as possible, as when the Italian-

American singer Anthony Benedetto became Tony Bennett—a fairly typical transformation in the interests of Americanization.

Slowly, *very* slowly, the fortunes of the Antin family rose. Mary herself prospered in the public school system, winning good grades and the approbation of her teachers. She was invariably keen to further her own interests, too, and made friends with children of "better" families. At least in her persona, in *The Promised Land,* as "Mary Antin," she seems delighted by whatever befalls her. Most crucially, she falls in love with the English language. "It seems to me that in any other language happiness is not so sweet, logic is not so clear." She began to read English poetry, for one thing, and this had resonance for her. "I could almost say that my conviction of immortality is bound up with the English of its promise. And as I am attached to my prejudices, I must love the English language!" (164).

Such unabashed enthusiasm pleased contemporary readers, though it seems odd now, especially in a time when many in the multiculturalist camp would argue that English itself should *not* be a requirement for citizenship and that schools should offer classes in Spanish as well as English. So many questions swirl around this topic: To what degree should we force immigrants to learn English? Can we live, as a unified nation, with a diversity of tongues and different cultural habits or traditions? What about this business of hyphenation, which implies dual loyalties? Can one be fully Mexican or Cuban or Chinese or Vietnamese and American as well? Many people have, of course, been able to balance their allegiances. Solidly American families have retained an affiliation to Italy, Ireland, Poland, and so many other countries. They have enjoyed the right to worship (or not) as they saw fit. They have cooked their own ethnic foods. But this has never prevented them from fully engaging in the American system. In retrospect, Mary Antin's enthusiasm is touching but misplaced—something she later acknowledged, when she turned hostile toward her own patriotic notes.

Certainly Antin herself mastered the English language. Sentence by sentence, this memoir is nothing less than eloquent, even poetic. Like Joseph Conrad and Vladimir Nabokov, she somehow made the transition into English, writing brilliantly in a language that was not her native tongue. How exactly did she accomplish this? "Getting a language in this way, word by word," she recalls, "has a charm that may be set against the disadvantages. It is like gathering a posy blossom by blossom" (166). One can almost smell the bloom on her prose as she savors each word, each phrase.

The public schools worked their magic, introducing her (and millions of immigrants like her) to American myths and traditions. Never mind that George Washington never cut down a cherry tree, or that what gets written in history books for children too often avoids looking at the harder truths, such as the destruction of Native American civilization, the brutality of slavery, and the imperialist urge that has often beset our leaders. In any case young Mary did not want to hear this sort of thing. "The public school has done its best for us foreigners, and for the country, when it has made us into good Americans," she writes at the outset of "My Country," the eleventh chapter (175). The school system turned her into a patriot, however naive, and this was probably a good thing, too. For the raw immigrant, this was a necessary phase in the process of assimilation. And there was much to admire, even love: the free public schools and libraries, the general sense of forward movement and social fluidity. Back in Russia, her Jewish friends and family were isolated within the larger society; quite literally, they had been cordoned off, forced to live within a Pale of Settlement. In the United States, Antin belonged to the society as a whole.

George Washington became her hero, and she wrote a poem in his praise. She tells us at length about how she took this poem around to various newspapers in Boston, enjoying the attention of older male editors, who looked on her with sympathy. She actually got the *Herald* to publish the poem. "When the paper with my poem in it arrived, the whole house pounced upon it at once," she recalls (187). Her proud father went out to buy up all the copies he could find. In a real sense, this poem announced the arrival of his family in the New World. The publication itself prefigured the career of Mary Antin.

But not always did the finger of admiration point her way. At school, as she explains in the twelfth chapter, she brazenly admitted to the other girls that she did not believe in God. This aroused anger and shock among her pious classmates, a mix of Protestants and Roman Catholics. "You don't believe in God?" asks one of them. "Then who made you, Mary Antin?" With childlike simplicity, she answers: "Nature made me" (191). Never mind that such a response begs the question of who made nature: Antin was off and running in wild pursuit of free thought. And this included her allegiance to the feminist movement, such as it was in these days before women could even vote. Her father, she says, had done a lot of thinking about various matters, "but his line of thinking had not as yet brought him to include woman in the intellectual emancipation for which he himself had been so eager even in Russia." He had not, until recently, ever imagined a woman could write a book. Yet he had "always been a nonconformist in his heart" and a skeptic. He fell away from religious observance, though he tolerated his wife's desire to cling to the Jewish faith. Antin writes: "He certainly did not forbid her to honor God by loving her neighbor, which is perhaps not far from being the whole of Judaism" (194).

The author ends this chapter, in which her religious skepticism features prominently, with a further paean to the immortal self: "The heir of the ages am I, and all that has been is in me, and shall continue to be in my immortal self" (197). Here again, she echoes Ralph Waldo Emerson, who in *Nature* (1836) wrote: "In the woods, we return to reason and faith. There I feel that nothing can befall me in life,—no disgrace, no calamity." He added, with a breathless eloquence typical of him at his best: "Standing on the bare ground,—my head bathed by the blithe air and uplifted into infinite space,—all mean egotism vanishes. I become a transparent eyeball; I am nothing; I see all; the currents of the Universal Being circulate through me; I am part or parcel of God."[7]

Antin subscribes almost wholeheartedly to what Harold Bloom has called "the American religion," which is essentially an Emersonian faith in nature, in the natural cycles of birth, death, and renewal, and in the democratic self, which includes everyone as it intuitively senses within the undulating folds of consciousness a divine spark.[8] This faith is vaguely deistic, not unlike the faith that inspired many of the Founding Fathers. That Antin should have come to this faith intuitively, at such a young age, is impressive.

Antin's faith in the American system of justice grows from direct experience. As she tells it, "a great, hulky colored boy, who was the torment of the neighborhood," treated her roughly (203). Her father hauled the boy into court, where the judge scolded him. Antin watched a drama unfold that included "accused and accuser, witnesses, sympathizers, sight-seers, and all." "We were all free," she declares, "and all treated equally, just as it said in the Constitution!" (204). One cannot but admire such frankness of feeling, however idealistic it may sound. It may well be worth reminding ourselves at times that the American experience in republican self-government has its roots in idealism of the kind that Antin expresses.

Eager to relate her memories of life in the Old World to what she found in America, she often talks of freedom, as in chapter 14, where she writes: "In Polotzk we had been trained and watched, our days had been regulated, our conduct prescribed. In America, suddenly, we were let loose on the street. Why? Because my father having renounced his faith, and my mother being uncertain of hers, they had no particular creed to hold us to" (212–13). So Antin's parents turned her loose in the city, offering "boundless liberty." There is, she allows, a negative side to this freedom. "The result was that laxity of domestic organization, that inversion of normal relations which makes for friction, and which sometimes ends in breaking up a family that was formerly united and happy." In other words, there is a price for freedom: family disintegration. "This sad process of disintegration of home life may be observed in almost any immigrant family of our class and with our traditions and aspirations," she says. "It is part of the process of Americanization: an upheaval preceding the state of repose. It is the cross that the first and second generations must bear, an involuntary sacrifice for the sake of the future generations." Antin bluntly accepts "exile and homesickness and ridicule and loss and estrangement" as part of the immigrant cycle (213). While, after a generation or two, the estrangement may cease to be a factor, the original immigrants and their children pay for the liberation of those who come after them.

In 1897, when Antin was sixteen, she graduated from her grammar school in Boston. She was recognized as a gifted scholar and assigned two speeches at the ceremony. At one point, a member of the school board rose to praise her, although not by name. He claimed to see in this unspecified girl "an illustration of what the American system of free education" could offer the European immigrant (221). A burst of applause followed, and one or two classmates goaded Mary to rise and thank the speaker for his kind words. She stood and began to speak: "I want to thank you . . . ." The principal gestured for her to sit. As one might expect, she was utterly aghast. "I suffered agonies of shame," she writes

(222). It took many years for her to think about this incident without squirming. "I remember distinctly how the little scene would suddenly flash upon me at night, as I lay awake in bed, and I would turn over impatiently, as if to shake off a nightmare" (223). Most readers will have a similar embarrassment in their background, and so Antin's story has resonance. And the way she tells this tale on herself makes the flesh of her readers creep.

"A new life began for me when I entered the Latin School in September," Antin says in chapter 16 (230). Now she moved among "an aristocratic set" and felt painfully at odds with her family circumstances. Her father's health had been failing for some time, and he worked for low wages wherever he could find a job. The girls in the school, however, judged Antin by her academic talents, not her family's situation. "Poverty was a superficial, temporary matter," she writes. Not surprisingly, she still experienced moments when her "whole being protested against the life of the slum" (233). Such passages reek of unresolved conflicts.

One whole chapter is devoted to Mrs. Hutch, a landlady who made her family miserable by demanding rent when there was no money to give her. Young Mary determined to present herself to this woman and to make her understand she was no ordinary girl. She sought respect, showing Mrs. Hutch the Latin grammar she worked from at school; in passing, she mentioned that she hoped to attend college one day. This was meant to inspire Mrs. Hutch, to get her to see the Antin family in a fresh context. To her shock, Mrs. Hutch did not like any of this and regarded young Mary as an upstart. She went into a rage, cursing out her impudent visitor for her pretensions to middle-class gentility. Painfully, Mary Antin saw that not everyone in America thought well of immigrants who strove to better themselves. (Mary did attend college, a few years later.)

Needless to say, she persevered in her ways and met some distinguished people, including Dr. Edward Everett Hale, a well-known Boston preacher and man of letters. She also found a place within the Natural History Club, where she heard lectures by "eminent naturalists, travellers, and other notables" (254). Members of this club often went on excursions into the field, where "the marvellous story of orderly nature was revealed" to Antin (256). She does not mention this directly, but through the club she met her future husband: Amadeus Grabau, who was finishing his doctoral work in the natural sciences at Harvard. Antin writes: "I slowly gathered together the kaleidoscopic bits of the stupendous panorama which is painted in the literature of Darwinism" (258). Yet she takes pains to admit that she was not a naturalist of any sophistication. "If anything," she says, "I grew rather more girlish" in the midst of real scientists (262).

The great Dr. Hale would let her roam his house on Highland Street "and explore his library, and take away what books I pleased" (270). Friendship with this generous and influential man gave Antin a sense of her own agency in the world. On several occasions she posed for Hale's talented daughter, a portrait painter. Once or twice, she recalls somewhat breathlessly, she stayed for lunch with the Hales, and regarded Mrs. Hale as a figure on a par with Martha Washington. "Everything was wonderful in that wonderful old house" (273).

For the most part, she led a busy and studious life on Dover Street, in the slums. "When I was not reciting lessons, nor writing midnight poetry, nor selling papers, nor posing, nor studying sociology, nor pickling bugs, nor interviewing statesmen, nor running away from home, I made long entries in my journal, or wrote forty-page letters to my friends" (273–74). She always had faith that her financial troubles, and her residence in the slums, would end. With a self-confidence bordering on self-delusion, she writes: "Nothing could be quite common that touched my life, because I had a power for attracting uncommon things." She was almost magic. "To be alive in America, I found out long ago, is to ride on the central current of the river of modern life" (278). Life was here, in the United States, and Antin considered this a central tenet of her immigrant's faith.

How to end a book like this? Antin wavers in the final chapter, the twentieth, meditating on the genre itself. "One of the inherent disadvantages of premature biography is that it cannot go to the natural end of the story" (281). She admits, however, that anything she might add would be repetitious. Already she has described the journey of the immigrant, from Old World to ship to public schools, through the free libraries and lecture halls of the New World. She has accomplished the work of assimilation, and there is no more to say. By way of conclusion, she writes with special fondness for the Natural History Club and its members, who took her into their lives: "They opened their homes to me that I might learn how good Americans lived. In the least of their attentions to me, they cherished the citizen in the making" (283). The memoir's final sentences ring with an optimism that still warms the heart: "America is the youngest of the nations, and inherits all that went before in history. And I am the youngest of America's children, and into my hands is given all her priceless heritage, to the last white star espied through the telescope, to the last great thought of the philosopher. Mine is the whole majestic past, and mine is the shining future" (286).

IV.

*T*HE PROMISED LAND was published by Houghton Mifflin, one of the most prestigious of firms, giving it the imprimatur of an important work. Large sales and laudatory reviews confirmed its success, and yet its influence extended even beyond these facts. In the summer of 1912, the *New York Sun* reported on the books most called-for at the various libraries. Mary Antin's name led the list.[9] This is an important statistic, as so many immigrants—like Antin herself—could hardly afford to buy books; they borrowed them from public libraries. And the real interest in this book didn't fade; indeed, it appeared in countless editions in the decades after its publication, including educational formats that included manuals for instructors with student questions. It was used in high school civics classes as late as 1949, the year that Antin died. Although high school students rarely hear about it now, the memoir remains a popular text on college campuses and is taught in courses on immigration history and American autobiography.

With Abraham Cahan, Antin is regarded as one of the major early figures in American Jewish literature. Her book also inspired a long tradition of immigrant autobiographies. But the contemporary reviews often noted the "hard and ruthless egoism" of the author (the *Yale Review*), even "an orgy of egotism" (*American Hebrew*). A thoughtful and balanced review appeared in the *New York Times,* one that stressed that Antin's story was "typical" of the immigrant experience. The American sections were considered somewhat rosy and idealized, and the reviewer preferred the parts that take place in Russia; this same reviewer actually

felt that the Russian experience explained the idealized response to life
in America. In any case, *The Promised Land* was published around the
world, in many languages, and long excerpts appeared in newspapers
and magazines. In the scrapbook that Antin's husband kept for his wife,
over two hundred press clippings are found, and these date only from
1912 and 1913.[10]

For some years, critics dismissed Antin's memoir as being too rosy and
regarded her as unwilling to recognize the depths of her own struggle.
Steven J. Rubin notes that Antin's portrayal of the immigrant experience
has been regarded by many critics as "naive and unrealistic," that it puts
forward the story of a woman "who too eagerly surrendered her past, her
culture, and her religion for the promise of America."[11] Such criticism
can be traced to Ludwig Lewisohn (a well-known Jewish critic and novelist who taught at Brandeis University, which he helped to found) and
others, reaching back many decades.[12] Even a sense of betrayal surfaces,
as in Sarah Blacher Cohen's remark that Antin's Americanization constitutes a kind of "religio-cultural striptease" that ultimately prevented
her "from becoming a profound writer of Jewish-American literature, or
for that matter, any kind of literature."[13]

The Promised Land has always seemed an annoying book to some
readers, who bristle at Antin's self-confidence and bravado, as when she
writes: "In these discriminations I emerged, a new being, something
that had not been before" (1). In such passages, she certainly reveals a
fondness for herself, celebrating her uniqueness in the world, her power
to sway other people, her intellectual gifts, and her sense of herself as an
eternal being. Some of this is recycled Emersonian rhetoric, and we may
discount it. Yet there is arrogance here as well, even overreaching. Antin also seems rather masculine in her style and frequently suggests that
she prefers the company of men to women: "I did not care much for
playing house. I liked soldiers better" (86).

An underlying anxiety, a sense of the perils of ambition, will also be
found in Antin's pages. She writes about her sister, Frieda, for example,
with a good deal of confusion and regret. They were wonderfully close
in Polotsk, but this intimacy faded in America, when Mary was chosen
over her sister to be the one who kept going to school. Adding insult to
injury, Frieda was compelled to sew her sister's dress for school—a fact
that Antin recalls with a touch of shame. She opens chapter 13, which is

called "A Child's Paradise," with a particularly anguished passage. While she, Mary, was cavorting in the world, exploring "the borderland between the old life and the new," her sister was confined to the humdrum work of women, "never turning from the path of duty" (198). She confesses: "I did not, like my sister, earn my bread in those days" (200). Indeed, *The Promised Land* is a text full of worry, self-doubt, and the anxious seeking of approval by authority figures of one kind or another. Her overreaching causes her pain, even humiliation, as it did at her grammar school graduation, when she rose to speak without permission and was sternly motioned to sit down by her principal.

In all, Mary Antin was a creature of surprising uncertainty. She may boast of her self-made successes, but she cringes as well. Toward the end, when she attaches herself to the Natural History Club, she grows full of humility, aware of her lack of scientific prowess, eager to underplay herself. She never really mentions that she is under the spell of her future husband, but there is a shift of tone, a fresh sense of weakness, as the memoirist cultivates an apologetic tone. "I did not become a thorough naturalist," she confesses (258). Modestly, she explains that her life had changed since she began to think seriously about the natural world, which led her to reconsider spiritual matters. "Those who find their greatest intellectual and emotional satisfaction in the study of nature are apt to refer their spiritual problems also to science," she tells us (259). And she admits that old questions about the nature of the spiritual world, problems that had troubled her in Russia, now trouble her again. *The Promised Land* is, in fact, a spiritual autobiography as well as a tale of an immigrant's cycle of assimilation. And it remains a complex book, in tone and affect, by no means a simple declaration of independence, as in *Walden*.

After Antin, Jewish immigrant stories (often written in the form of novels) were more sober in their assessments of what was lost as well as gained. These include *The Rise of David Levinsky* (1917) by Abraham Cahan, *Out of the Shadow* (1918) by Rose Cohen, *Hungry Hearts* (1920) by Anzia Yezierska, and *Up Stream* (1922) by Ludwig Lewisohn. There were, of course, immigration tales from a range of refugees. One popular novel of immigration was O. E. Rølvaag's *Giants in the Earth* (1927), the story of Per Hansa and Beret, determined immigrants from Norway who settle in the wilderness of the Dakotas in the 1870s. There were a small number of Italian immigrant stories as well, some of them splendid, such as *Christ in Concrete* (1939) by Pietro Di Donato, an autobiographical novel about a bricklayer in the Lower East Side of New York City before the Great Depression. Yet the fact remains that Italian and Irish immigrants from Antin's era were less likely to produce memoirs, although exceptions will be found, such as *A Son of Italy* (1924) by Pascal D'Angelo, an eloquent recollection by a poet-immigrant who has largely been forgotten.[14]

Overall, the pickings among early immigrant memoirs are relatively thin. "With few exceptions, such as the Jews, many of these earlier ethnic groups produced little literature of note," writes Katherine B. Payant, who has studied patterns of ethnicity and immigration in the United States. "Even the Irish, from whose ranks later came great American writers such as Eugene O'Neill, produced little notable literature during the nineteenth century, the peak years of their immigration."[15] Irish and Italian immigrants, of course, were largely uneducated and came from oral cultures where the idea of writing itself was fairly remote.

In this country of immigrants, with legal and illegal knockers at our gates in profusion, the immigrant memoir (and autobiographical novel about immigration) has nonetheless enjoyed a steady audience, with recent additions by writers from various backgrounds, such as Amy Tan, Frank McCourt, Richard Rodriguez, Sandra Cisneros, Julia Alvarez, and Gish Jen. Each of these contemplates and embodies the immigrant experience, its cycles of arrival, optimism, confusion, and assimilation, from a particular ethnic viewpoint, often with aplomb. For the foreseeable future, the immigrant memoir—told as straight autobiography or fiction—is likely to remain a staple of our literature. And Mary Antin will remain a founding mother of the genre.

NOW OVER 4,717,500 COPIES SOLD

HOW TO WIN FRIENDS AND INFLUENCE PEOPLE
BY DALE CARNEGIE

1. What are the six ways of making people like you? See pages 57-102.
2. What are the twelve ways of winning people to your way of thinking? See pages 104-170.
3. What are the nine ways to change people without giving offense or arousing resentment? See pages 172-199.

TEN

How to Win Friends
and Influence People

I.

PEOPLE OFTEN FEEL HELPLESS, out of their depth, powerless. The boss frightens them. They have few real friends, or imagine this is so. The way forward in life looks impossible, a thicket through which no obvious path seems to lead. Failure looms. In the United States, where failure is shameful and success has become something of a religion, there has always been a need for advice about how to get ahead. In this realm, no book has been more successful at the business of success than *How to Win Friends and Influence People* (1936) by Dale Carnegie—an early prototype and iconic model of the self-help genre.[1]

It appeared in the dark of the Great Depression, when breadlines formed in the streets of cities and towns across the country. Never had failure been so palpable, so vividly on display. Men could no longer occupy the sacred pedestal of "breadwinner." Children were hungry. Women felt helpless to support their husbands, their families. Employment was scarce, and so the competition for the few precious jobs became cutthroat. In the midst of this dismal scene came Dale Carnegie, with a cheerful book that turned the heads of millions, giving them a specific way to reinvent themselves in a country where self-invention itself defines our culture. With its frank, confident tone, the book blazed like a grass fire in a windy drought, with seventeen printings in just a few months. By the time of Carnegie's death in 1955, over five million copies had been sold in the United States alone. The book had been translated into over thirty languages. Nearly half a million people had taken courses on public speaking and self-improvement at the Dale Carnegie Institute, with its many branches. More important, this book had changed lives.

Carnegie taught people how to get ahead by flattering those in power and by ingratiating themselves with those in a position to advance their interests. In any case, that is the negative way to see it. In a more positive light, he taught people to tap their hidden powers and use parts of themselves previously repressed. Carnegie's method opened them up to other people and their concerns. Indeed, at the core of Carnegie lies the notion of "honest appreciation." He taught his readers to find something valuable in others and to offer them reinforcement by noting their good points. If the side benefits of this activity happened to be highly beneficial to the noticing person, well, so much the better.

That Carnegie's book changed lives, and permanently influenced America, cannot be doubted. A nation of businessmen (and aspiring businessmen) found in Carnegie's book a pathway. The idea of the salesman has always been important in America, of course. As Timothy B. Spears says, "From advertising to public relations to politics, sales personnel and selling strategies pervade American life. Fuller Brush men, Avon ladies, retail merchants, door-to-door canvassers, telemarketers, even presidents constitute a partial list of people who have something to sell."[2] Not surprisingly, American writers have often focused (in less than flattering ways) on the figure of the salesman; he lies at the heart of such classic works of American literature as *Sister Carrie* by Theodore Dreiser, *Babbitt* by Sinclair Lewis, *The Iceman Cometh* by Eugene O'Neill, *Death of a Salesman* by Arthur Miller, and *Glengarry Glen Ross* by David Mamet—just to cite a few obvious examples.

Americans love their salesmen, however sleazy and manipulative. Our cable networks display a range of half-baked preachers or self-help gurus who sell themselves as well as their "product," which is self-invention. Joel Osteen strikes me as a classic example of this genre, preaching his own version of the Dale Carnegie method with a thin glaze of religion. God loves you, and He wants you to succeed. Believe in yourself. Go forward into the world. Trust the system, flatter it, and it will take care of you. This is, as the Reverend Dr. Norman Vincent Peale (a great fan of Dale Carnegie's method) said, "the power of positive thinking."

Carnegie's acknowledged forerunner was Benjamin Franklin, the man who said, "God helps them that help themselves," and put himself forward as an example of a young man from nowhere who got ahead by shrewd calculation as well as hard work. Franklin's aphorisms hinted at ways to get ahead in life, but Carnegie developed these glimmerings in a simple, apparently systematic fashion. And his book works, which is why after all these years it continues to succeed in the world, extravagantly. Indeed, one example will suggest the extent of this success. Between 1989, when Communism failed in Russia, and 1997, *How to Win Friends and Influence People* went through sixty-eight editions in Russian.[3] One might almost say that Carnegie represented (for aspiring Russian entrepreneurs) "the American way," and that way has been fiercely successful in the world. Its success sells itself.

II.

LIKE MANY OTHERS, I have a personal debt to this book. I was a shy boy in Scranton, Pennsylvania, in the 1950s and early '60s. The move from a small elementary school to the cavernous halls of the junior high in West Scranton terrified me. At fourteen, I thought I had no friends (many adolescents imagine such a thing). I rarely spoke in class, and did so only under duress. I felt lost until I found, in my local library, a battered edition of *How to Win Friends and Influence People*. How could I resist a book with that title? How could anyone?

Taking Carnegie's advice, I got myself a dime-store notebook and wrote out the steps for handling people, for making them like you. Carnegie tells us that to make friends you must become genuinely interested in other people. You must listen to them and say what you admire in them. I remember repeating to myself in my head a line from this book: "Be hearty in approbation and lavish in your praise." (The suggestion comes from Charles Schwab, who worked for Andrew Carnegie and made a million dollars a year because he could motivate the employees of Carnegie's steel company.) I drew up a list of all the kids in my class and beside their names noted the thing I most admired about each of them. It was difficult in certain cases, but there was always *something* I could find to admire.

I set about, quite shamelessly and systematically, to speak to each of them in turn. One by one, over a period of several weeks, I managed to buttonhole my classmates and to say something complimentary in their ears. With many, it was not so hard. Peter was incredibly good at math, and I told him so. Fred had the best arm of anyone on the ball field. I assumed that he knew this, but he loved to hear it put explicitly. (For months on end, he regaled me with pitching stories.) There was one girl, Edna, who nearly defeated me. She was massively overweight, slow, and wildly isolated by her idiosyncratic personality (she kept globs of already-chewed gum in her pencil box, in case she ran out of fresh slices). I could think of only one thing that I admired about her: her authentic accent in Spanish class. To my inexperienced ear, the way she rolled her *r*'s made her sound like a native of Madrid. "You have the most wonderful Spanish accent," I said to her one afternoon after class. "You sound almost . . . Spanish." I do believe she would have married me that day.

I spent much of a year working my way through the Carnegie system, trying to master it. In doing this, I learned a great deal about myself, about others, and about the ways of the world. I also developed a mild distaste for Carnegie, finding his method manipulative, even demeaning. As James Thurber once wrote: "Mr. Carnegie loudly protests that one can be sincere and at the same time versed in the tricks of influencing people. Unfortunately, the disingenuities [*sic*] in his set of rules and in his case histories stand out like ghosts at a banquet."[4] In due course, I was able to put this stuff in perspective, but I still think the Carnegie method had its benefits and that it worked wonders in my own life, making me much less self-conscious, more interested in the lives of others than I had previously been, and more likely to see good things in people. I've come to understand in a more complex way the fundamental idea of Carnegie's book: that people are interested mainly in themselves, their own lives, their families, their successes and failures. If you don't understand this, you will glide through life in something of a bubble, self-enclosed like most; it helps to be aware of this obvious fact, and to take it into account in dealing with those who come into your life.

Carnegie's presuppositions also point to depressing aspects of the American system, which values success over sincerity, individualism over community. (It's not for nothing that in Russia the book took off only after the fall of Communism.) Carnegie tells us over and over to be "genuine," but his system militates against genuineness. Rule 4 in part 2 of his book, for example, is: "Be a good listener. Encourage others to talk about themselves." There is a fine point between really listening to people, with sympathy, and encouraging them to live within their own narcissism. Carnegie just assumes (unconsciously) that he is dealing with a world of pathological narcissists, where people feed on those around them, salving their own wounds, inflating their egos, bolstering defenses. To put it bluntly: it is not always kind to encourage people in their compulsive egotism. There is ultimately something sad about the Carnegie way, which envisions a world of separate egos in necessary conflict as each struggles to get his or her piece of the limited pie. *How to Win Friends and Influence People* is ultimately a recipe for loneliness and spiritual lassitude, especially if it is read without perspective.

Dale Carnegie (1888–1955) was his own self-invention. Born in Missouri, he grew up in rural poverty, the son of an unsuccessful farmer. His mother, however, was ambitious for him and hoped he might become a minister. His real name was Dale Carnagey, but he changed the spelling of his name to improve his chances in the world. Andrew Carnegie had become a household name by now, associated with wealth and power. The great steelmaker was an American hero. And so Carnagey became Carnegie, adding luster to his name by the shift of a few letters. After attending a teachers college in Warrensburg, in his home state, Carnegie found his voice as a salesman and sold correspondence courses to ranchers and farmers in the sandy hills of western Nebraska and eastern Wyoming. Later, he made his way by freight train to Omaha, where he sold bacon and soap for Armour & Company. He apparently traveled around his large territory by freight train, stagecoach, and horseback, sleeping in fleabag hotels where the partitions between

rooms were nothing but sheets of opaque muslin. His energy was as-
tounding, and he turned a relative backwater into a productive territory
for the company he represented.

The United States was, in the first decade of the twentieth century,
experiencing a commercial boom. Henry Ford churned out his famous
motorcars by the thousands. Even modest homes were wired for electric
lights. Chain stores sprang up: J. C. Penney, A&P, Woolworth. George
Eastman was selling his new camera. R. W. Sears and A. C. Roebuck
had by now perfected the notion of a mail-order business, paving the
way for the endless retail catalogs that overflow our desks. John Wanamaker opened department stores that offered cheaper products, and lots
of them, to a mass audience. Millions of young men and women poured
into the cities of America to make their way, hoping to get ahead. And
Carnegie was among them. By 1910, he had become fed up with the life
of the rural traveling salesman and headed to New York.

He hoped for a stage career and auditioned successfully for a place at
the American Academy of Dramatic Arts. After completing the program, he tried to get roles without much success, although he toured
briefly in a play called *Polly of the Circus* by Margaret Mayo.[5] When this
came to an end, so did his acting career. He found an apartment in a
cheap tenement on Fifty-sixth Street, near Eighth Avenue, and took a
job selling Packard motorcars and trucks. He later recalled: "I came
home to my lonely room each night with a sick headache, a headache
bred and fed by disappointment, worry, and rebellion. I was rebelling
because the dreams I had nourished back in my college days had turned
into nightmares."[6]

It was at this time that Carnegie conceived of teaching people how
to speak in public—one of the great phobias, of course, and more terrifying to many than death itself. He talked the manager of the YMCA
on 125th Street into letting him teach a course on his methods, which
proved highly effective. He taught shy young men and women to conquer their fear of public speaking by doing it. "Do the thing that you
fear to do and the death of fear is absolutely certain," he often said, par-
aphrasing Emerson. By 1916, he had become so successful that he was
able to rent Carnegie Hall (the name itself drew him to the building) to
lecture to a full house about his techniques for public speaking. And he
was hardly alone. On July 10, 1916, for example, thousands of salesmen

met in Arcadia Auditorium in Detroit, attending the first World's Salesmanship Congress. President Woodrow Wilson gave the keynote address. "Lift your eyes to the horizon of business," he told these eager beavers. "Do not look too close at the little processes with which you are concerned, but let your thoughts and your imaginations run abroad throughout the whole world. And with the inspiration of the thought that you are Americans and are meant to carry liberty and justice and the principles of humanity wherever you go, go and sell goods that will make the world more comfortable and more happy, and convert them to the principles of America."[7] One hears much the same today from any number of American politicians and corporate leaders, who believe firmly in the free enterprise system as the key to spreading democracy around the world. (The Iraq War might be traced to this idea, as it was prevalent among the neoconservative thinkers who influenced George W. Bush in the wake of 9/11.)

Carnegie began to develop and extend his courses in public speaking, attracting wider audiences. His first major book was *Public Speaking: A Practical Course for Business Men* (1926). This was the basis for another book, *Public Speaking and Influencing Men in Business* (1932). Then, of course, came the blockbuster in 1936: *How to Win Friends and Influence People.* The days of selling anything but himself and his methods soon lay in the past. Indeed, he grew wealthy from his books and courses, marketing himself with astonishing skill, although relatively little is known about his private life. He ducked out of a bad early marriage in 1931, then remarried in 1944. He had one daughter, his only child, with his second wife.

The circumstances of his death remain somewhat obscure. *Time* reported that he died of uremia, but from what one can tell from later interviews with his widow, he probably had Alzheimer's or dementia of some kind as well. Although a doting older father in his last few years, he seemed frail and forgetful. Perhaps it makes sense that a man who wished for us to focus on others, who thought that the way to the top was through invisibility, was himself an invisible man, known mainly as a teacher of public speaking.

III.

*H*OW TO WIN FRIENDS AND INFLUENCE PEOPLE begins with
an arresting chapter called "If You Want to Gather Honey, Don't
Kick Over the Beehive." The notion has its origins in Benjamin
Franklin, who said: "I resolve to speak ill of no man whatever . . .
and . . . speak all the good I know of everybody." As Carnegie tells us:
"Any fool can criticize, condemn, and complain—and most fools do.
But it takes character and self-control to be understanding and forgiv-
ing" (28). He follows this concept with a vivid statement supposedly by
Thomas Carlyle, the British philosopher: "A great man shows his great-
ness by the way he treats little men."

A further line amplifies this idea: "To know all is to forgive all."
Carnegie understands that people act for reasons, most of which will be
unknown to the larger world. The worst murderer will have excuses for
what he does. This doesn't justify murder, of course, and it should be acknowledged that the real problem with Carnegie lies here: he asks us
never to criticize, never to upset the apple cart, as this sort of behavior
will often result in a retaliatory slap, a violent reaction from the person
criticized. But one has to draw a line somewhere. That said, there is a
good deal of truth in the general idea that one should attempt to understand the circumstances of those who behave in ways that confound or
annoy us. There is rarely anything to be gained by overt or harsh criticism.

Carnegie recalls that he has devoted a considerable amount of time
to Abraham Lincoln, even writing a book called *Lincoln, the Unknown*
(1932). He uses examples from Lincoln's life to teach his readers how to
deal with people. At the height of the Civil War, for instance, Lincoln
ordered General Meade to attack Lee and his troops on July 4, 1863,
only a day after the Battle of Gettysburg had concluded. Lee and his
army were trapped at the Potomac, and Meade could easily have swept
in, captured Lee, routed his army, and ended the war. But Meade dis-
obeyed Lincoln, did exactly what he was told not to do, and Lee escaped
with his army intact. Lincoln sat down at his desk and wrote a furious
letter to Meade, beginning it: "I do not believe you appreciate the magnitude of the misfortune involved in Lee's escape. He was within your
easy grasp, and to have closed upon him would, in connection with our

other late successes, have ended the war." It's a stinging rebuke, yet Lincoln never sent the letter, which was found among his papers after his death. Why did he not send it?

Carnegie imagines that Lincoln looked out the window and thought along these lines: "It is easy enough for me to sit here in the quiet of the White House and order Meade to attack; but if I had been up at Gettysburg, and if I had seen as much blood as Meade has seen during the last week, and if my ears had been pierced with the screams and shrieks of the wounded and dying, maybe I wouldn't be so anxious to attack either. If I had Meade's timid temperament, perhaps I would have done just what he had done. Anyhow, it is water under the bridge now" (26). One can only hope Lincoln, even within his own mind, had a touch more eloquence; nonetheless, Carnegie makes a good point as he cautions against attacking or criticizing people. It will only make them furious and eager to counterpunch. You will gain nothing. This doesn't mean, however, that you should not try to get people to do things your way. On the contrary, that is your goal. But you must set about the task of persuasion in ways that will actually work.

Chapter 2 is a meditation on how to get other people to act (in the ways you would like them to act). They will only do anything, Carnegie explains, because they want to do it. In his usual fashion, he cites many well-known authorities, including Lincoln, John Dewey, and William James, the latter two being well-known philosophers (in the school of American pragmatism) whom the author obviously admired and often quoted. "The deepest principle of Human Nature is the *craving to be appreciated*," James once declared. Carnegie bakes a large loaf of bread from this small grain of truth. He notes that even great men like Columbus and George Washington sought titles that recognized their greatness. (Washington wanted to be called "His Mightiness, the President of the United States," although—thank goodness—he declined a throne.)

Carnegie is fully conscious of the accusation that he preaches flattery. "No! No! No!" he writes. "I am not suggesting flattery! Far from it. I'm talking about a new way of life" (37). He quotes (or slightly misquotes) Emerson to good effect: "Every man I meet is my superior in some way. In that, I learn of him." Indeed. And if everyone that the eminent thinker Ralph Waldo Emerson met was superior to him, where does that leave the rest of us? "Let us cease thinking of our accomplishments, our wants," Carnegie urges, inviting us to figure out the good points of those around us and to let them know that we see these points.

There is, at the core of this, what I would call a religious impulse: a genuine wish to put aside your own wishes and to think about the needs of others. Depending how you look at it, the notion turns on self-erasure or self-transcendence: one must step outside oneself, in any case. Carnegie rightly understands that we "succeed" in life only by losing our lives, by dying to our old selves, and by living for the good of others. This insight lies at the core of Christianity—if not most of the world's religions. In the tradition of the Puritans, Carnegie harnesses the energy of this insight for practical purposes.

Carnegie continues with concrete advice about how to get people to do what you want them to do. The crucial point is that you, the reader, want something from other people. You want them to *do* something. But can you get them to do it by kicking and screaming? The odds are against it. As usual, Carnegie begins with a number of folksy examples, some of them personal. He cites Emerson again, recounting a story about Emerson and his son trying to get a calf into the barn. The great philosopher pushed, while his son pulled; the calf refused to budge. It took the peasant wisdom of an Irish housekeeper to get the calf into the barn. With magical ease, she led the calf easily into the barn by putting her finger in its mouth. It liked that feeling and followed her. As with all folk wisdom, the gist of this seems unassailable, and this little parable reinforces the point that people will do only what they really want to do. You have to "help them" to find the reasons for doing things. Translating this idea to sales, Carnegie notes that thousands of salesmen pound on doors without success because they want only to make sales. Carnegie shifts the emphasis: think what the person actually *wants*. Make the hypothetical customer see that it makes sense to own this product: a hairbrush, life insurance, or a better mousetrap.

The glitch is that the salesman might be selling a useless product. Many products *are* useless. Indeed, the United States is a nation afloat in pointless products that imitate other pointless products; but somebody somewhere has convinced the customer to buy this or that useless thing. Yet Carnegie is no social theorist, and he never entertains such a thought. So what if the salesman creates an artificial need in the customer? That's the American way. Again and again, we have seen "need" generated by the advertising industry. "First arouse in people an eager want," Carnegie tells us. You can't argue with that, if your goal is to make the sale.

Now Carnegie pauses, with a brief inter-chapter in which he explains to readers how to make use of his book. He urges them to acquire a profound desire to succeed, though he masks this as "a deep, driving desire to learn." You have to learn how to sell, how to influence people to behave in certain ways. He quotes George Bernard Shaw, one of the most quotable of playwrights and wits: "If you teach a man anything, he will never learn." I myself have come to understand this, having been a college professor for thirty-some years. Students usually forget what you tell them; but they remember what they take on personally. A good teacher leads them toward a body of knowledge, makes them understand how it will change their lives, for the better. They must actively use the knowledge they acquire, or it vanishes.

With his usual tendency to enumerate in a systematic fashion, Carnegie offers a list of nine things the reader must do, such as keep a journal of results. Progress must be externalized, cataloged, made apparent. As noted above, I followed this advice many decades ago, as a teenager, and it was exhilarating to see abstract principles put into action. I still recall my excitement as I saw the degree of progress I made: suddenly I had friends, lots of them. I became less interested in my own needs, more interested in the needs of those around me. There was, indeed, something vaguely religious about this project, and I still marvel at its mystery.

We all want people to like us, of course. This was probably true of Napoleon and Hitler, Stalin and Al Capone. It's certainly true of John Doe, the man on the street, or Susie Doe, the woman on the street. I don't think a person has ever lived who did not share this fundamental need to be appreciated, even liked. Only pathologically disturbed people don't care what others think about them. Quite brilliantly, Carnegie turns the tables on this and suggests that people will like you *only if you like them.* He urges us to focus on the lives of others, not ourselves. Again, a religious fervor enhances his argument. He pleads with the reader to understand this basic principle: forget about yourself, look around you, see what others care about. The brilliance of Carnegie's work, however, lies not only in his grasp of general principles. He is also a master of the anecdote, coming up with story after story of how successful people acted in ways that showed their genuine interest in other people.

Sometimes, however, I find the examples he chooses to put forward a little creepy, as when he tells us about a wily banker who desperately required some information from the president of a corporation. This president was reluctant to part with the information, which he considered confidential. The banker watched with interest as the president's secretary appeared with some interesting foreign stamps; these were for the president's son, an avid collector. The president lit up. On that visit he didn't give the banker the information he wished for, but the banker picked up on something personal about the corporate leader. A few days later, he realized that his bank received endless letters from abroad, all of them with foreign stamps on them. He gathered some of these, then called the president of the corporation to say he had access to a rich supply of foreign stamps for his son, and that he had already culled some of the good ones. Thrilled, the president invited the banker over and proudly showed him pictures of his son. A warm relationship began. Needless to say, the banker in due course got the information he required.

The morality of the above story is the issue. Is it right to manipulate people in this way? I suppose it often depends on the spirit of the transaction. There is no doubt that it pays to show interest in other people. But it certainly helps if this interest is genuine. In theory, there is no reason why one should not care about others and their children. Life is endlessly interesting, and one gets a good feeling when paying attention to others. However, to expect something in return is problematic. There is what Lewis Hyde has called "an economy of creative spirit." That is, one gives a gift without expecting something in return: the true gift is a gift to oneself, a benefit derived from the act of giving. "A man who owns a thing is naturally expected to share it," says Hyde, "to distribute it, to be its trustee and dispenser."[8] Or as Walt Whitman once put it: "The gift is to the giver, and comes back most to him."[9]

Sometimes the advice in Carnegie's book amounts to corny nonsense. Chapter 2, in the part called "How to Make People Like You," offers the simple, even simplistic, advice to go around smiling. Smile at everyone, the author commands us. Not a fake smile, Carnegie warns, but a genuine smile. As often before, he quotes William James, the philosopher and Harvard professor. (It's his favorite technique in argument: the appeal to authority. Do this because so-and-so, a well-known authority, says so.) James said: "Action seems to follow feeling, but really action and feeling go together." In Carnegie's terms, this means: smile and you will feel like smiling. I remember being deeply puzzled over this chapter as an adolescent. I hated smiling at people. Sucking it up, I went around smiling like an idiot for about a week, but abandoned the practice when a girl in my class asked if something was wrong. She said my smiling had unnerved her. To this day, I hesitate when someone smiles aggressively in my direction, and I try to ration my own smiles. Being open to people, eager to see them, makes life a lot more pleasant than the opposite. Nobody likes a person who glowers or sulks. But neither is anyone terribly charmed by a person who grins all the time. It can seem downright weird.

Remembering people's names comes next. Successful politicians all know this strategy. Carnegie tells us about Napoleon III, emperor of France, who boasted that he could remember the name of every person he met. He did this by getting it right the first time, asking the person to spell the name if it was complex. He took the trouble to repeat the name during this first encounter, several times, making sure he identified the name with the features, the expressions, or the general appearance of the person. As with any of Carnegie's techniques, this one can be overdone, even made ridiculous. Haven't we all encountered sleazy salesmen who bandied about our names in too obvious a fashion? Once I took a dear friend, the poet and novelist Robert Penn Warren, to the hospital for a minor procedure. As we checked in, the woman at the desk smiled condescendingly and said, "Why, Bob, it's nice to see you. How are we feeling today, Bob?" Robert Penn Warren was not Bob, and he was feeling distinctly worse with every moment spent in this woman's company. The point is, good sense must enter into the calculation when using the name of another person. It should not be overdone, and overfamiliarity will often breed contempt.

Now Carnegie approaches the subject of being a good conversationalist. As you would expect, the key to being a good talker is not talking but listening. He advises us to get people to talk about what interests them. To be sure, this works. I've rarely met a person who didn't like to talk about what interested him or her. But this means being *really* interested in other people. I remember meeting President Bill Clinton when he was in office, at a reception at Oxford University. He held my hand when he shook it, looked me straight in the eye, and asked me where I came from and what my subject was. When I told him I taught literature, he asked me what books he should be reading. He seemed eager to learn what I thought were good books to read, and said he would try to find those books. I certainly believed he was sincere. When we parted, he said, "Jay, I hope you get back to Vermont soon. It's a lovely state." He had remembered my name, and that I had said in passing that I came from Vermont. This was an exhilarating experience for me—one of countless people whom this man encountered every week in passing.

Was I manipulated? Yes, perhaps. Clinton had mastered the art of conversation, and he knew instinctively to focus on the other person, to listen, and to figure out who this stranger was who stood before him, and what interested him. I also suspect that Clinton is a natural learner, that he is deeply interested in the world, and that he genuinely likes people. He probably likes different sorts of people, too. He certainly likes to talk: the whole world knows that. But he let me do much of the talking when we met. Dale Carnegie would have been clapping for Clinton in heaven.

The truth is, we know so little about the world and its manifold operations. It's well worth listening to most people. Some are narcissistic bores and want only to talk about their own lives and accomplishments, and such people are impervious to conversation anyway: they just talk, and you cannot influence them. But there is much to be gained, personally, even spiritually, from learning how to listen and pay attention to the other person. One must work to acquire the skill of asking the right questions and waiting for the replies. Yet Carnegie extends this insight a little too far in the next chapter, "How to Interest People." You interest people, he suggests, by figuring out what makes them tick, what rings their bell, and focusing there. He tells us to talk in terms of "the other man's interest." (It's always a man in Carnegie, as he wrote in the days before women had moved fully into the business world, even though plenty of women took his courses on public speaking.) Sometimes he pushes this technique to the point of exhaustion.

Chapter 6 follows, called "How to Make People Like You Instantly." You do this by making them feel important. In crude terms: you flatter them. Carnegie recalls going into a post office in New York and telling the clerk how much he admired his head of hair. The clerk beamed: "Well, it isn't as good as it used to be." A pleasant conversation followed. Good human feeling abounded. "What did you want to get out of him?" asked a listener, when Carnegie told this anecdote to an audience. Carnegie was outraged by the mere suggestion that he was trying to get anything out of this clerk at the post office. A discount on a stamp? He just wanted to promote good feeling. Now Carnegie falls back upon his usual argument from authority (one of the classic types of illogical argument). He supports his assertions with references to Zoroaster, Confucius, Lao-tzu, the Buddha, and Christ. It's all a question of doing unto others as you would have them do unto you.

On a simple level, there is nothing wrong with this advice. It makes perfect sense to attune yourself to others, and to treat them as you would wish to be treated yourself. If you want people to recognize your strengths, recognize theirs. As ever, the fine line between genuine appreciation and flattery—false praise—must not be crossed, and yet it's easily crossed. The cringe-making part of this chapter comes when Carnegie tells us how three businessmen used compliments to their advantage. This seems calculating and makes the reader's skin crawl. And yet indisputable wisdom resides in Benjamin Disraeli's famous remark, quoted by Carnegie to summarize his chapter: "Talk to a man about himself and he will listen for hours" (102).

Part 3 centers on getting people to come over to your side, and it begins with a simple truth: "You Can't Win an Argument." And you can't. You might score points and make a statement that cannot be refuted; but you don't really "win" somebody over to your side by argument. "Nine times out of ten, an argument ends with each of the contestants being more firmly convinced than ever that he is absolutely right" (105). Again, Carnegie draws from the religious traditions of the world, quoting the Buddha: "Hatred is never ended by hatred but by love." (I once took a course in one of the martial arts and learned that it never paid to confront anybody; the essence of self-defense is stepping aside. Flight is always better than fight—especially in a back alley!) But the avoidance of conflict can also be taken to extremes. Sometimes, in fact, conflict is necessary and leads to a better situation—a point Carnegie would never allow.

One could also argue that Dale Carnegie teaches passive aggression in this chapter and elsewhere. His approach involves—or often seems to involve—working in underhanded ways, even secretively, to convince another person of something. In my view, it is usually better to state a difference of opinion openly, yet with compassion and humility—aware that your argument may not be the best one. Getting exactly what you want should not always be the ultimate goal.

The next chapter deals with the problem of enemies and how to avoid making them. Benjamin Franklin occupies the center of this chapter, in a long anecdote about how he learned from bitter experience not to assert himself too boldly, too combatively. "I made it a rule to forbear all direct contradiction to the sentiments of others," Franklin once said (115). He never stated things categorically, but preferred to say "I imagine" or "I conceive that . . ." This is certainly one way to go when putting forward a possibly contentious idea. Say "I think that" and the person knows that you know it's just your opinion, and only an opinion. (I remember a student in Britain who began every argument with the word "Surely." Surely nothing, I thought. I disliked this fellow intensely, and so did most of those who had to suffer him.)

Yet there is something a little mind-boggling about the lengths to which Carnegie takes this commonsense advice. "Never tell a man he is wrong," he warns. I wish to God more people, earlier in my life, had told me directly that I was wrong about certain things. Again, success is all in the approach and the degree of sensitivity that can be summoned. You can tell people anything if you tell them sincerely, in a loving way. Perhaps this is Carnegie's real point—although he seems incapable of making it. A tendency to trivialize his material remains a problem from first to last. He is absolutely on the mark, however, where he says that if you are wrong, you must admit it readily. It is always disarming to tell someone that you have made a mistake and you are sorry. Admit your errors, and start over. That is simple, good advice, yet a hard bit of advice to swallow.

Practical suggestions follow in the next chapter, which is called "The High Road to a Man's Reason." It's more of the same, however: be nice to people, and make them believe that you are sincere in appreciating what they have to say. He begins with John D. Rockefeller meeting a gang of strikers' representatives. Rockefeller soothed them, made them feel they were important, and claimed it was a red-letter day in his life that he had the privilege of meeting them. The men retreated, we are told, and never said another word about an increase in pay for the miners they represented. A couple of things strike me as problematic about this odd story. For a start, Carnegie appeals to powerful authorities once again, especially millionaires like Andrew Carnegie and John D. Rockefeller. He cannot resist a wealthy man, nor (apparently) could his vast audience. If a man is wealthy, he must know something that poor people don't. He must be right, in fact. This seems an ill-conceived, even dangerous, assumption. In the case of Rockefeller and his strikers, the strikers were probably right. Rockefeller was ripping them off. Yet somehow his smooth-talking approach got him off the hook.

Carnegie gives a lot of advice here about how to deal with people, and some of it seems useful. Who can argue with the suggestion that one should begin every meeting (especially where conflict potentially looms) in a friendly way? It can almost never be a good idea to telegraph hostility at the outset. The deeper point, however, is that Carnegie thinks one should do whatever it takes to "win," and this may involve pretending to be friendly to an adversary in the hopes of beating him or her down. This approach to "solving" problems has an unpleasant, manipulative side.

For a salesman, there is obviously good advice in "The Secret of Socrates." Don't let the potential customer ever say no under any circumstances, he explains. Carnegie calls this—for reasons that elude me—the Socratic method and describes Socrates as "a brilliant old boy." He praises Socrates for being able, as a bald-headed and barefoot man of forty, to win the hand in marriage of a nineteen-year-old girl, suggesting that the Greek philosopher, when arguing, got his listeners to agree with his points over and over. With an armload of yeses in hand, he marched to argumentative victory. But the Socratic method (as portrayed by his pupil and friend Plato) was not so simple. It involved asking questions and drawing forth the knowledge already buried in his students, getting them to see and truly understand what in theory they already knew. There is a naive and plainly ignorant quality to Carnegie's writing here that is off-putting.

The core of the next chapter lies buried in this line: "We ought to be modest, for neither you nor I amount to much" (144). This seems wonderfully acute. Most of us do not matter a great deal, except to those in our immediate circle of family and friends. One only wishes Carnegie could have taken this insight further, recognizing community values as well as individual ones. He pointedly fails to do this. Every insight is put at the service of "getting ahead," making the sale, getting the promotion. This becomes distasteful in the end, although one can see how millions of "unsuccessful" men and women in business have looked to Carnegie for guidance. Humble salesmen who pay attention to the customer certainly will sell more widgets than loud, self-centered, and arrogant ones who pay no attention to their audience.

The seventh chapter argues, quite effectively, that the best way to get people to go along with an idea is to let them think it's their idea. Here is the Depression mentality boldly on display. You're a poor schmuck, and you want something. So you get those in power to think it's their idea, and they let you implement it. This is manipulative, but its effectiveness cannot be denied. All of us come into situations where we want someone else to do something that will benefit us in some way. It may well benefit the larger community. So how does one get others to do this thing, especially if it's not something they especially want to do? Carnegie tells us to "make suggestions," then to let the other person think out the consequences. He ends this chapter with a shocking, even bizarre, line from Lao-tzu, the founder of Taoism: "The reason why rivers and seas receive the homage of a hundred mountain streams is that they keep below them" (150). Let's translate the aphorism: You're a lowly fellow in the company. But you want something. A raise? People to follow your lead? A corner office? Then get the people in power to continue to look down on you; they will like the feeling of having power over you. Indeed, they won't mind giving you what you want, as they will enjoy the position of height above you.

This is off-putting, but the technique apparently has worked for millions.

In the next chapter, Carnegie urges readers to put themselves in the place of those who oppose them and try to understand the other side of the argument as best they can. This is the path of the "wise, tolerant, and exceptional" person. It means that one must sympathize with the wishes of others and attempt to understand the origins of their wishes, to dig into their motivation. When you want to try to change them, appeal to their "nobler" side. Assume the best about them. While this advice lacks psychological sophistication, it seems fairly straightforward and sound.

You must also learn to dramatize your ideas, Carnegie argues next. The theatrical training that he received as a young man appears to have come in handy as he argues for real showmanship. By way of example, he notes that a store trying to sell a new rat poison created a display in its windows that included a number of live rats. This display certainly caught the attention of the public. The rat poison did well, apparently— except for the rats. Interestingly, this is one of the least effective of Carnegie's chapters. He doesn't really tell anyone how to dramatize anything, or suggest what is dramatic and what isn't. He simply states, over and over: Be dramatic! Of course trillions and trillions of dollars have been spent in advertising, and everyone wants to sell products in a dramatic fashion. The devil is in the details, and Carnegie lacks the time or inclination to provide them. (Then again, how could he? This book operates on a general level, leaving implementation to the individual reader.)

Inspire excellence in your workers, your salesmen, Carnegie suggests in the final chapter of part 3. Create a challenge, stimulate competition. This was doubtless good advice for managers who needed to get those under them to perform better. But once again, this is a chapter without a great deal of substance. I suspect that most of his readers skipped ahead to the next part of the book, as they were rarely in a position to need to know how to inspire others to produce or sell more widgets. Most of them just wondered how to get off the factory floor into an office. They hoped to exchange their blue collar for a white one.

The nitty-gritty of this book comes in the fourth part, "Nine Ways to Change People Without Giving Offense or Arousing Resentment." The first way is to compliment someone before you offer real criticism.

He begins with President Calvin Coolidge, who once complimented his secretary on her lovely dress, then asked her to be more careful with her punctuation when typing his letters. On a more serious level, he quotes another letter from Abraham Lincoln (Carnegie's ultimate authority) to one of his generals. The letter begins with considerable and genuine praise, then proceeds to necessary criticisms and suggestions. A good deal of common sense underlies this approach. It's something anyone in a position of power will learn—or fail to learn with dire consequences. If you are going to criticize someone, and sometimes you must, it's important to present this criticism in an atmosphere of support. It won't do, for example, to say to a young teenager: "You talk too loud, and embarrass us at dinner parties." A parent must think of something positive, such as: "It's good that you like to participate in dinner conversations when we have guests. But it might be sensible to speak more softly and to acquire the habit of listening. You will often learn something valuable, and everyone will be happier with your behavior."

In an extension of this idea, Carnegie suggests that we call attention to people's faults indirectly, if possible. John Wanamaker, the famous owner of department stores, becomes a focal point. He was walking through one of his large stores and found a customer waiting for service at a counter. A group of salespeople stood in the background, gossiping and laughing, ignoring the customer. Wanamaker himself got behind the counter, helped the person to purchase an item, then handed it to the salespeople to wrap. Not a word was said in criticism, but the point was made. One can hardly quarrel with this advice. It does indeed make sense, as a manager, as a parent, as a friend or spouse, to point to someone's faults indirectly—as long as this doesn't turn into passive aggression, which is always a danger when indirection is involved. As ever, a good example is worth a thousand suggestions.

Carnegie advises in the next chapter, rather wisely, that one should talk about one's own faults first. It pays, in human terms, to put oneself on the same plane as the other person. I myself learned, when talking to my three sons, to make sure I included myself in the equation when I could. If I wanted to suggest to one of them that he was not putting enough time into his homework, I would try to follow the Carnegie notion and say something like: "I was very lazy in junior high school. I hated doing homework. I wasn't used to it. And I did badly in school as a result of this negligence. It took me a long time to understand in a real way that there is no substitute for hard work." Such a line has the virtue of being true as well as, perhaps, useful. And yet Carnegie goes way too far here, as he often does.

He tells a story about Prince von Bülow of Germany, an adviser to the arrogant kaiser Wilhelm II. The kaiser had said some terribly dangerous and stupid things to the press, and this created an international stir. He called in von Bülow and asked him to take the blame for advising him to say such a ridiculous thing. The loyal adviser balked, saying he would never have advised him to talk such nonsense. The kaiser exploded. Then von Bülow took another tack, saying that the kaiser was his superior in almost every way. He knew more about science and military affairs, more about almost everything in the whole wide world. Von Bülow claimed to possess only this one little gift, a talent for diplomacy. The kaiser was thrilled by the talk about his immense knowledge of so many things, and he swore to stick by von Bülow through thick and thin. The crisis passed. The moral here is this: Abase yourself in front of the boss. Tell him he is marvelous, that the sun shines from his ears and out of every other orifice in his wonderful body. And all shall be well.

Carnegie certainly understands that saving face is important. Nobody likes to be called onto the carpet or blamed directly for things he or she has done, however stupid or thoughtless. So Carnegie argues in the next chapters for working indirectly—once again. When trying to "handle" people, especially those under your control, you should ask questions, not give orders. According to Carnegie, the questions you should ask are leading and manipulative ones, such as "Don't you think you should do this or that?" That is a gentler way of saying: "Do this or that." I wonder if the technique really works. (My own children would see right through it.)

Carnegie's advice about managing people often seems obvious or naive. In the chapter called "How to Spur Men on to Success" he preaches the art of encouragement, saying that it pays to give little compliments along the way. This is true enough. Certainly if I were running a business, I would make a point of noticing the good things that people did, hoping it would encourage them to do more good things. It certainly works this way as a parent. But this method will go only so far and does not account for either Caruso or Charles Dickens, although Carnegie claims otherwise. He tells us, for example, that Dickens grew up in extremely poor circumstances, having had to work in a factory plastering labels on bottles as a boy because his father was put in prison for bankruptcy. This is all true. Then, he explains to us, Dickens mailed in his first piece of writing, and a kindly editor accepted it, with compliments that pleased the young author. This one success changed Dickens's life, we are told, and he became a great novelist as a result. This is nonsense, of course. The drive that powered Charles Dickens through a massive career in writing, and led to the production of many of the finest novels ever written, was hardly spurred by one editor accepting his first piece with a few nice words. Dickens was a complex man, and the furies that drove him to write could not be counted on one hand. His talents were beyond easy comprehension as well. His imagination was a unique thing in this world, and eventually he would have gotten his wonderful, sad, ferocious, and hugely entertaining books into print. Sooner or later he would have become what he was: Charles Dickens. Carnegie's pontificating about Dickens is, in this instance, reductive and ridiculous.

Carnegie often puts the cart before the horse, saying something *is* the case that he hopes *will become* the case. So he recommends giving people a "good reputation" in the belief that they will then live up to it. He says: "Always make the other man happy about doing the thing you suggest." This is better than the opposite, to be sure, but there is something distinctly misplaced about the sentiment. One would like people to do one's bidding cheerfully. The question is how to achieve this, and Carnegie shrinks from the practical side here, leaving the reader in a cloud of abstraction.

The book ends on a strange, slightly hilarious note. Carnegie turns into a marriage counselor, and he advises (as would any good marriage counselor) that it's important not to nag your spouse. He says that you should never attempt to "make over" your partner. They are what they are. Accept it, and move on. Work with it, perhaps. Once again, he suggests that criticism is a bad idea. You should only make suggestions and criticize indirectly. You should give honest appreciation whenever possible, in the spirit of saving your pennies for a rainy day. Put your feelings into words, and tell your partner that he or she is good at this or that. You should pay little compliments. He quotes a famous judge who presided over forty thousand marital disputes as saying that many of these difficulties would have been avoided if the man's wife had only waved goodbye when he went to work. Carnegie preaches the virtues of courtesy. Treat your spouse as you would be treated yourself: with respect. Then comes the mother of all marital advice: get a good book about sexual practices and read it. Carnegie, with blissful indirection, hints that there are intimate aspects to married life that must not be neglected. These intimate things demand a certain degree of proficiency and knowledge, like anything else. He recommends several books and discreetly avoids saying anything more about how to be a good sexual partner. This was, indeed, the year 1936—decades before *The Joy of Sex* hit the bestseller lists or John Lennon posed nude with Yoko Ono.

While there is something obviously dated about Carnegie's book, there is much to think about in these pages, and millions have carefully followed his advice on a broad range of matters. The ideal reader imagined by Carnegie is perhaps a businessman. He is a "little man" in the company. He wants to make the sale and to rise in the world of difficult bosses and bossy wives. To do so, he must use every ounce of wile he can muster. He must use his wits, be cleverer than his boss or his wife. He must outwit the customer time and again. But he must, above all, be sincere. Sincerity is the key. Otherwise, the Carnegie method lapses into a recipe for falseness, flattery, deceit, and passive aggression. To a stunning degree, Dale Carnegie shaped a generation of young men in America, helping them to learn to help themselves.

His message of self-improvement had long and deep roots in American culture, going back to Benjamin Franklin, of course, but also to Horatio Alger, the author of endless stories about getting ahead in life, rising from rags to riches through the magic of self-belief and perseverance. What Carnegie did, quite brilliantly, was to give self-improvement a systematic face. His method worked, and it works. The book continues to have a worldwide appeal, although it may have lost some of its original shimmer. Many of his best ideas, needless to say, are drawn from the pages of the world's sacred scriptures. Do unto others as you would have them do unto you. That is the essential message of this book, and there is enough truth (and complexity) there for the ages to contemplate without ceasing.

IV.

THE REAL INFLUENCE of such a book is hard to calculate, but one can test its effectiveness on one's own pulse. *How to Win Friends and Influence People* changed my own life as a teenager, and it has probably affected me in subtle ways since then. Before writing this chapter, I had not reread the book in four decades, but I was startled to see that I recalled it so concretely. I could almost complete the sentences as I read them. For better or worse, I have probably internalized much of what Carnegie preaches. If this is true of me, it's probably true of many others—millions of others.

The edition I have, which dates from 1964, notes on the cover that over 9,783,000 copies had been sold by the time of this printing. That figure has probably doubled by now, in the United States alone. The book has been translated into dozens and dozens of languages, and—as noted above—sold extremely well in Russia after the fall of Communism, a fact that says something about its connection to an entrepreneurial culture. Only in a world where "getting ahead" by sales—or selling oneself—matters profoundly can such a book attract a wide, devoted audience. In such a context, however, Carnegie proves a welcome source of advice. Book sales on this scale depend heavily on word of mouth; and readers do not voluntarily recommend a book that did not mean something to them.

Yet a book of this magnitude is, as I've said, more than a book; it's a climate of opinion. It draws on books already written—such as those by Franklin and Alger—and generates books in a similar vein. The ideas in the writing circulate and enlarge, and often the book may well be influential even when those influenced have never heard of it. This is certainly the case with *How to Win Friends and Influence People*. Manuals to help salesmen were extremely common in the first decades of the twentieth century, and Carnegie readily absorbed this advice. One can walk into any bookstore in America today and find a long shelf of self-help books that owe a huge debt to Carnegie.

For instance, there is *The One Minute Manager* (1981) by Kenneth Blanchard and Spencer Johnson, which has sold over twelve million copies in twenty-seven languages. The book is pure Carnegie, and adopts his technique of offering summary checklists of important points to remember. It is full of small anecdotes, which serve to illustrate the central point of each chapter. One of the chief ideas of the book is that one should catch people in the act of doing something right, then praise them for it. When you are being critical of people, you should let them know you are on their side. Shake their hands. Smile at them. Remind them again and again that you think well of them generally, even though you may be pointing out something that is wrong about their behavior. The authors continually remind readers that employees who feel good about themselves will behave in productive ways. Carnegie would have liked this book, I suspect. It comes straight from him.

Among the most visible of recent self-help books is *The 7 Habits of Highly Effective People* by Stephen R. Covey, which has sold well over fifteen million copies since it first appeared in 1989. In a fascinating introductory chapter, Covey talks about the long tradition of books about success, which he traces back to Benjamin Franklin. He suggests that prior to World War I, such books focused on the character ethic, and he regards Franklin as the source here. Success would follow if one were humble, sincere, faithful, temperate, and so forth. (There is a quietly spiritual undertone in Covey's writing, although he mentions God only in passing.) Without mentioning Dale Carnegie by name, he seems critical of him, suggesting that after World War I writers on how to succeed in life focused on personality issues. "Success became more a function of personality," he writes, "of public image, of attitudes and behaviors, skills and techniques, that lubricate the processes of human interaction." Indeed, Covey rails against books that are "clearly manipulative, even deceptive, encouraging people to use techniques to get other people to like them." He indirectly quotes Carnegie when deriding the idea that "smiling wins more friends than frowning."[10]

Covey has a good point. Carnegie and others in his vein, such as Norman Vincent Peale, author of *The Power of Positive Thinking* (1952), emphasized specific techniques for handling people over taking a more holistic approach, seeing "personality" as part of some larger thing called "character." One of the clear developments in self-help books of the past few decades has been an emphasis on understanding what might vaguely be called the spiritual dimensions of human interaction. After the 1960s, the whole notion of "success" has shifted; there has been a growing awareness that success cannot easily be marked in promotions, financial benefits, material goods, and public recognition. I recently saw an interview with a man who knew a very famous person extremely well; he was asked in the interview: "Was this man happy?" The fellow answered: "Oh, yes. He was very happy. Except in his personal life."

There is only one's personal life, of course; and yet we live this life among others. A proper understanding of human experience entails a complex sense of community, of interconnectedness. The major religions of the world almost universally teach us that service is the key to happiness and "success." We succeed to the extent that we can help each other. To a degree, Dale Carnegie understood this, and his emphasis on listening to others gave a certain moral weight to the program he espoused. He asks the person who craves success and influence to forget about himself or herself, to look to the *other* person. This is a beginning, however limited.

To his credit, Covey grounds his plan for "happiness" and "success" in ethics, in spiritual values. So does Rick Warren, another popular author of self-help books—including *The Purpose-Driven Life,* which has sold over thirty million copies around the world since it first appeared in 2002. Warren is a Protestant minister, the founding pastor of the Saddleback Church in Lake Forest, California; not surprisingly, his work moves in explicitly theological directions. He is also programmatic, like all writers of these books since Dale Carnegie; he offers readers a forty-day spiritual journey, a way to transform their lives. God has a plan for us, he argues, saying we are here on earth to serve God and our fellow creatures. His basic idea follows Saint Matthew 10:42: "If you give even a cup of cold water to one of the least of my followers, you will surely be rewarded." Warren urges us to behave like servants, noting that "servants think more about others than about themselves."[11] One can see Dale Carnegie's book hovering in the background here, however distantly; yet Warren's approach unfolds within a specific religious context that would have seemed excessive to Carnegie.

Carnegie had no overt religious message, as it were; but he was once invited by Norman Vincent Peale to preach at his church, and this was, for him, a special moment in his life. Warren, as a Christian preacher, offers a straightforward philosophy of life based in the principles of his faith. What he gets from Benjamin Franklin and Carnegie, and the countless self-help authors before him, is the notion that one can put into a book a plan for the reader's life, a plan that will be transformative. It must be based on practical ideas, although the main assumption is that *it's not about you, the reader.* Life is not about self-aggrandizement, ma-terial goods, honors, and accolades. It's about putting others first (or, in the case of Warren, putting God first by putting others first).

As publishers all know, a huge thirst for self-help books exists. Americans in particular love these books, and there is no end to them. I recently read one called *Maximum Achievement: Strategies and Skills That Will Unlock Your Hidden Powers to Succeed* by Brian Tracy. Tracy is yet another of the many children of Carnegie, and he urges the reader to set goals and to act in deliberate and rational ways. "If you see yourself now as you wish to be, and you walk, talk, and behave as the very best per-son you can imagine yourself being, your dominant thoughts and goals will materialize as your reality. You *will* become what you think about most of the time."[12] This might be called applied, *secular* Christianity, as the New Testament repeatedly offers versions of this advice.

Often enough, writers in the tradition of Dale Carnegie are preach-ers of one kind or another, and today they sometimes project their ideas on television, where they can reach massive audiences. Americans seem to fall for hucksters, and it's the rare huckster who does not operate without some grain of truth in his message (they are almost always males, and so I didn't trouble to write "his or her message"). As noted earlier, one of the shallowest of current hucksters is Joel Osteen, author of *Your Best Life Now* and *Become a Better You: 7 Keys to Improving Your Life Every Day.* As it says on the dust jacket of the latter: "Joel Osteen reaches a huge audience in the United States and across the globe. Tens of millions of people in more than a hundred nations worldwide are in-spired through his weekly television broadcasts, his *New York Times* bestselling books, his sold-out international speaking tours, and his weekly top-ten podcasts."[13] I have myself watched him many times on television, and see the appeal of his message. It's the power of positive thinking, via Dale Carnegie, via the Bible-lite. My own problem with

Osteen is the emphasis on getting rich and aggrandizing oneself. He believes that you deserve a bigger house, a nicer car, a better salary. He thinks God wants you to have these things. All you have to do is wish upon a star—that is, pray to God to give you what you deserve.

This approach reflects one of the worst aspects of the Puritan strain: the idea that God rewards his favorites with material goods. On the other side of this is the idea that if you are poor, it's your fault. You must have done something wrong, behaved badly in some way, and so God has chosen to punish you. Therefore, part of this Puritan ethic is the tendency to admire, even fawn over, those who are wealthy. They must have done something right. Why else would they own such a big house, wear such nice clothes, and have so many people in their thrall?

Like Carnegie, Osteen relies heavily on homey anecdotes about famous people. He begins *Become a Better You* with a story about Frank Lloyd Wright, who was once asked which of his many beautiful designs was his favorite. "My next one," he answered. And so readers are told to press forward, never look back. Osteen tells us: "Neurologists have discovered that the average person uses less than 10 percent of his or her mind."[14] This comes straight from Carnegie (whether or not Osteen knows it), who repeatedly said the same thing, often citing William James on the exact point. Also like Carnegie, Osteen frequently summarizes his main ideas, offering bullet points, encapsulations. He puts his main ideas in boldface, as did Carnegie. Sometimes he simply rewrites Carnegie with a very slight twist, as when he says: "Complimenting each other is the glue that holds relationships together." In general, Osteen reworks the Carnegie formula somewhat crassly.

Yet many who came after Dale Carnegie added value to what they found. Writers such as Covey and Warren, for example, have added a spiritual dimension that was somewhat buried in Carnegie, who quoted the scriptures but didn't seem to understand them deeply. Covey and Warren are less embarrassingly practical, too, and less dedicated to self-promotion. They put forward plans for living that are less manipulative. Carnegie's book, of course, is firmly rooted in the Depression, aimed at readers who felt disempowered. It seems (unconsciously) to promote what psychologists call passive aggression.

Nevertheless, there is something immensely valuable in *How to Win Friends and Influence People*. Carnegie, like Benjamin Franklin before him, understood the essential American idea of self-creation. We can, and must, create ourselves. Unlike our European counterparts, who derive their sense of self from family connections, Americans are by nature entrepreneurs of selfhood. They may not begin with a blank slate, but they think they do, and that is a powerful idea, one that gestures hopefully in the direction of self-invention and agency.

WINNER OF THE 20th ANNUAL
PARENTS' MAGAZINE AWARD

A POCKET BOOK
SPECIAL
35c

377

THE POCKET BOOK OF
BABY AND CHILD CARE

by BENJAMIN SPOCK, M. D.

An authoritative, illustrated, common-sense
guide for parents on the care of children
from birth to adolescence.

COMPLETE & UNABRIDGED

ELEVEN

The Common Sense Book of
Baby and Child Care

I.

ORIGINALLY PUBLISHED IN 1946, *The Common Sense Book of Baby and Child Care* by Dr. Benjamin Spock changed the way Americans raised their children, probably forever. It became the sourcebook of choice for parents in the postwar years; as such, it helped to shape the baby-boom generation, and its effects still reverberate. Its commercial success remains the stuff of legend. According to one source, it ranks as the seventh-bestselling book of all time, with over fifty million copies in print in thirty-nine languages.[1]

The advice that Spock offered young mothers in particular was straightforward, in some ways conventional, but revolutionary in tone. He explained to them in a reassuring, gentle voice that they knew more than they realized, urging them to trust their instincts. If they felt like picking up their baby when it cried, they should just do it, and no harm would come to the infant. He encouraged a warm connection between parent and child. Whereas parents of previous generations obsessed over setting strict guidelines and establishing certain patterns of behavior, Spock showed little interest in such things. He was not worried about "spoiling" kids. He wanted children to grow in ways that suited their individual personalities, and to make the most of their innate abilities.

Before Spock, most advice on the raising of children came from the pulpit, with variations on a theme from Proverbs 13:24: "He who spareth the rod, hateth his son; but he who lovest him, correcteth him betimes." In common parlance: spare the rod and spoil the child. A few experts had arisen in the late nineteenth century, including Dr. L. Emmett Holt, author of *The Care and Feeding of Children* (1894), a popular handbook for many decades. Dr. Holt warned that mothers could *not* trust their guts, as "instinct and maternal love are too often assumed to be a sufficient guide."[2] His book, like most parenting books, magazine articles, and pamphlets prior to Dr. Spock, stressed an "objective" or no-nonsense approach. That is, you got toilet training over as quickly as possible. You didn't pick up a child when it cried, as that would only reinforce crying. Promptness mattered in weaning a child from the breast or bottle. You didn't tolerate thumb sucking—a sure sign of regression, even neurosis. You established firm schedules for sleeping and eating.

Benjamin Spock assumed a very different approach, advocating a relaxed but clear-eyed posture on the part of the parent. He took into account the individual needs of the child but addressed the parent's feelings and needs, too. He seemed to hover in the room with the parent, encouraging a more natural and humane approach—although a close reading of Spock will reveal a fairly conservative bias as well, one that puts authority in the hands of mothers and fathers. Yet the seismic shift was mainly tonal: Spock gave parents a way of moving ahead with the task at hand, unhampered by the lore of parents and grandparents, by the stern admonitions of the church.

Critics have long regarded Dr. Spock's approach as too permissive, suggesting that his methods laid the ground for all sorts of personal problems that, expanded into a large population, became social problems as well. Among those to attack Spock during his lifetime were the Reverend Dr. Norman Vincent Peale and Vice President Spiro T. Agnew, both of whom argued that a lack of parental discipline had ruined a generation of young people, turning them into selfish ogres. This is complete nonsense, as Spock himself noted, but something of this attitude persists in the public imagination to this day.[3]

Perhaps the main thing to be said about Dr. Spock is that he used the insights of Freudian psychology as a key to parenting. He understood that each child was an individual on a growth trajectory, with needs and desires, and that part of a parent's responsibility was to meet the child's needs and, if possible, answer those desires (although never at the expense of the parent's mental health). He also thought about family dynamics and saw the family itself as a system, meaning that each member of the family tugs on every other member in influential ways. Spock urged parents, directly and indirectly, to pay attention to the dynamics of the family as a whole and to remain flexible when it came to responding to children. His natural warmth and distinct personal voice (as captured in the soothing rhythms of his book) offered parents a model they could adopt; they were urged (directly and indirectly) to show their affection, to express their feelings, and to allow children to develop naturally. If there is one implicit rule in Spock, it would seem to be this: never force the issue.

All sorts of little things shifted with Spock, whose basic principle was always: trust yourself. Indeed, the famous opening lines of *Baby and Child Care* (as the book is usually known) are these: "You know more than you think you do" (3).[4] This reassuring tone continues as the book proceeds, taking parents through the successive stages of raising a child, addressing the most obvious problems from breast-feeding and toilet training through adolescence and its myriad pitfalls. Without fail, Spock remains confident and resolutely modest, never insisting on the absolute rightness of his methods: "The book is meant to be a source of helpful general suggestions," he says, "not the final word" (2). A genial modesty and sense of balance shimmer through his writing, as when he writes: "Our ideas about how to treat a child have changed a lot in the past and will certainly change in the future."

Spock's own ideas would certainly develop, even shift, in subsequent decades, and he revised his book again and again, always taking into account new research in medicine and fresh ideas. The most recent edition, in fact, appeared after his death, revised by Robert Needlman, M.D., who addresses ideas that no parent in 1946 could have imagined, such as how to deal with the Internet or international adoption agencies or how to talk to children about terrorism.[5] (Needlman often isolates the wisdom of Spock in separate boxes called "Classic Spock," so that readers can both hear the original voice and see how things have shifted.)

Nobody, least of all Dr. Spock, could have predicted the large, enthusiastic response to this book from parents over many decades, or the societal tremors it produced—or seemed to produce. *Baby and Child Care* may not have shaken the world in any literal sense; but it rocked the cradle and affected a generation of parents in their attitudes toward the ancient art of parenting. It set a tone for the postwar era, shaping a generation that has yet to make its full and final impact on the United States.

II.

Benjamin mclane spock (1903–98) was born into the upper-middle, professional class, in New Haven, Connecticut, where his father worked as a lawyer for the New York and New Haven Railroad Company. The Spocks lived in a spacious house on Cold Spring Street, with broad porches and balconies, on a street lined with elms. He was the oldest of six children and learned something about dealing with young children from firsthand experience as a teenager with younger siblings. By all accounts he held the attention of his doting mother, Mildred Spock, who repeatedly told him: "You must have lots of fresh air."[6] Not surprisingly, getting plenty of fresh air was something he continued to recommend to parents to the end.

Spock's father was somewhat remote, spending much of his time at the office, where he climbed the corporate ladder with relentless energy, but his mother dedicated herself (almost obsessively) to her children. "She wanted to be the perfect mother," her daughter Hiddy later recalled, "and to have the perfect children."[7] Relying heavily on Dr. Holt's popular handbook, she stressed exercise and simple, healthy food as well as lots of fresh air. Like Holt, she believed that tropical fruit was bad for children, as it upset their digestive systems. She adopted a firm hand, teaching her children about right and wrong, encouraging them to think broadly about the world, in moral terms, taking their responsibilities seriously.

In some ways, Spock had the ideal American boyhood, buoyed by the resources that money and social position could provide. The Roaring Twenties found him exactly where any young man would hope to find himself at this time: at Yale. Spock had read and loved Owen Johnson's *Stover at Yale* (1912), one of the most popular novels of the era, featuring Dink Stover, the ideal Yale man. He took the novel to heart, and proved himself a scholar-athlete worthy of this legacy, becoming a member of Scroll and Key, a prestigious secret society, and succeeding beyond his wildest dreams at rowing. Indeed, he was a member of the crew that won an Olympic gold medal in Paris in 1924: a victory so amazing that the national columnist Damon Runyon wrote ecstatically that Yale itself had "never had athletic representation in any field to compare with its Olympic crew."[8] To the end of his days, Spock enjoyed both rowing and sailing, and often recalled to friends and family his adventures as a member of the Yale crew.

Spock strode the world as a young man, full of pride and honor, beloved by his family and (despite his big ears, which embarrassed him) loved by a beautiful young woman, Jane Cheney, who became his first wife. He proceeded to medical school at Yale, where he apparently planned from the outset to become a pediatrician, in part because of his mother's interest in babies, which she had obviously communicated to her eldest son. Somewhat to the surprise of his family, he married Jane halfway through his medical studies at Yale, and they decided to move to New York, where Benny (as he was called) would finish his studies at Columbia. To his amazement, and that of many friends, he graduated from medical school at the head of his class. As one classmate exclaimed, teasing him: "Spock, of all people! Why, I thought you were stupid!"[9]

He was far from stupid, and began to specialize in pediatrics, although this field was difficult at the onset of the Depression. Not many families could afford a specialist, or even a doctor, except in dire emergencies. Yet Spock found work in a poor hospital in New York's Hell's Kitchen and developed a reputation for his willingness to spend time with anxious mothers, answering their questions patiently for hours on end. He felt at odds with the profession because he thought about each child as an individual; for him, it was difficult to accept the old ideas about (for instance) putting a stop to thumb sucking as soon as it appeared. He was much less fierce about toilet training, too. To him, it seemed foolish to attempt to train children who were just too young for it. His kinder, gentler approach appealed to new mothers.

Needless to say, a long history of beliefs and prejudices lay behind the attitudes that confronted Spock in his efforts to think freshly about child rearing. The early Puritans had considered children utterly depraved by nature and encouraged parents to "correct" their children in severe ways, forcing them to submit to the will of God. It was their only hope of salvation. Things shifted somewhat in the seventeenth century, when John Locke, the English philosopher, produced a handbook for raising children that American colonialists admired. Like many in his day, he believed that the child's mind was a blank slate (tabula rasa); in other words, he didn't simply assume that a child was born into sin. This meant, in effect, that a parent could make an impression on a child; indeed, the very idea of childhood as a separate phase of growth began to gain a foothold. Nevertheless, Locke strongly recommended cold baths, strict codes of dress, and a simple diet—there was nothing "permissive" about him. In the eighteenth century, John Wesley (founder of the Methodist movement) urged parents to root out the sin in their children, warning against indulgence, urging strictness and parental inflexibility. In the nineteenth century, the concept of a good Christian education arose, with an emphasis on shaping the moral development of the child; it was stern, yet a far cry from Puritan ferocity. This was, after all, the century of Charles Dickens, who did so much to focus attention on the development of children, doing so with a profound sympathy for this period in a person's life. Of course most Victorian-era writers on child rearing cautioned against leniency and indulgence, thinking it was important to nip any dangerous tendencies in the early stages of a child's life.

By the time Spock came onto the scene as a young pediatrician, a more scientific approach had gained currency as the field of child psychology flourished. John Dewey's ideas about progressive education had begun to take hold early in the century, and one saw many writers advocating for an approach to child raising and education that seems not so different from what Spock himself would later advocate. For example, there was Ellen Key's popular *The Century of the Child* (1909), which breathed fresh air into the old discourse on the proper way to raise a child. In her chapter called "Education," she writes: "To suppress the real personality of the child, and to supplant it with another personality continues to be a pedagogical crime common to those who announce loudly that education should only develop the real individual nature of the child." She added, with conviction: "Education must be based on the certainty that faults cannot be atoned for, or blotted out, but must always have their consequences."[10] That sounds awfully close to Spock in tone and content.

Among the many books on child raising that Spock read closely was John B. Watson's *Psychological Care of Infant and Child* (1928), which brought thinking on this subject up-to-date with a chapter called "Too Much Mother Love," wherein he wrote: "When you are tempted to pet your child remember that mother love is a dangerous instrument. An instrument which may inflict a never-healing wound, a wound which may make infancy unhappy, adolescence a nightmare, an instrument which may wreck your adult son or daughter's vocational future and their chances for marital happiness."[11] This surely offered no hint of comfort to the anxious mother.

Increasingly, Spock wanted to think about, and study, the psychological foundations of childhood. This interest led him to take a residency in psychiatry and to study Freud and his followers closely. He underwent analysis himself with a well-known Freudian practitioner, Dr. Bertram Lewin, who had trained with one of Freud's own students. This work proved revelatory, and Spock soon did further training with the Psychoanalytic Institute in New York. As Thomas Maier, his biographer, explains: "Spock resolved to bring Freud's insights to his work as a pediatrician."[12] In the late 1930s, he entered into a second round of analysis with Dr. Sandor Rado, a brilliant post-Freudian who had written a famous article, "An Anxious Mother," in 1927. The idea here was that a mother can, indeed, do lasting harm to a child by being overprotective. Rado was a pioneer in thinking about the harmful effects of narcissism in relation to mothering. Certainly from Rado the young Dr. Spock learned that a mother's interactions with her child are hugely important and that a good deal of thought and preparation should go into this delicate interaction.

Word got around New York that a young pediatrician called Benjamin Spock was very interested in Freudian psychology and had used this training quite effectively in his work with parents. An editor from Doubleday approached him in 1938, suggesting that he write a book about raising children. Spock refused the offer, but a fuse was lit that would, eight years later, explode in *The Common Sense Book of Baby and Child Care*. Yet first Dr. Spock had to reconcile his understanding of Freud's view of childhood and its crucial impact on adult life with his own approach to the subject. Should one adopt a stern approach with parents, warning them that they could mess up a child for life? Or was there another, gentler way?

The army rejected Spock at the start of the war because he had recently suffered from a bout of pneumonia, which had a lingering effect on his lungs, but in 1944 he was taken on by the U.S. Naval Reserve, drawn into the war effort to serve as a psychiatrist at naval hospitals in New York and California. Yet there were a couple of quiet years at the beginning of the war when he had a little more time than usual on his hands, and he turned this period to good use, making notes that would lead to his book. It so happened that another editor, Charles Duell (of Duell, Sloan, and Pearce), approached him about writing a baby book, as Spock was his own child's pediatrician and he had witnessed first-hand the freshness of Spock's approach. The shape of the book had by this time grown clearer in Spock's head. He accepted the proposal.

In outline, Spock's book would look not terribly unlike Dr. Holt's, the book his mother had admired; that is, it would proceed from infancy through childhood and adolescence, with lots of practical advice; but the tone, even the specific advice, would be sharply different. Spock would urge parents to adopt a loving approach that nevertheless showed firmness and resolve. He did not want a parent to act as a law enforcement officer; instead, a parent should talk to the child, play with the child, encourage and guide the child. In direct opposition to the advice of John B. Watson, he suggested that a parent must not worry about feeding and sleeping schedules, as these would take care of themselves. He dismissed the traditional obsession with bowel movements as so much nonsense. In short, he told parents to relax and to let their good instincts guide their behavior. If they did so, all would be well.

The condescending, often bossy tone of previous manuals on child rearing disappeared, and the kinder, softer approach of Spock emerged. As someone trained in psychology, he understood that it was not a smart idea to frighten the parent of a newborn child. He knew that when parents consulted his book, they often did so in distress. There was no point in frightening them off or making them feel more anxious than they already were. Spock reassured them, speaking as a wise friend with experience of the matters at hand. He did so in clear, concrete language, adopting an avuncular tone.

Spock was careful *not* to use language that would summon the ghost of Dr. Freud, as an American audience could never swallow too much of that. Indeed, he never mentioned Freud at all, and offered a benign version of his theories. The originality of Spock's work lay in using Freud to govern his own thinking about child development and sexuality. He knew well enough that most Americans in the 1940s would not tolerate open talk about sexual matters, and he downplays this side of things. For instance, he never talks explicitly about the Oedipus complex; on the subject of breast-feeding, he simply tells the mother that babies like to eat, and they particularly like to suck. He sounds much like any country doctor here, homey and reassuring. There is barely a hint of the man who has recently been through two rounds of Freudian analysis, the doctor trained in the most advanced modern theories of child development.

The arbitrary rules of previous manuals on child rearing were replaced by this lighter approach. A mother could decide for herself when it was time to stop breast-feeding. She didn't have to worry about the child's bowel movements, or lack of them. As for eating, it seemed obvious that children tended not to starve themselves. They ate when they were hungry and because they were hungry. Freud suggested that people were driven by natural impulses or drives, and Spock accepted this understanding. He applied it to children gently and carefully, and to parenting as well. It all made a good deal of sense. On the subject of discipline and morality, Spock fell back on Freud's basic idea of the superego, the notion that an individual conscience develops in due course and that this itself becomes a force that holds in check the wild libido, that tames and shapes the ego itself. It was Freud's notion that children gradually adopt their parents' superegos, and so parenting becomes a process of alignment between parent and child.

Exactly how this alignment should take place was up for grabs, and here Spock confidently added his two cents, suggesting that parents should model discipline and good manners in their own lives. He knew it was impossible to force a child to comprehend these things abstractly and that such a theoretical approach was never effective in any case. Sensible parents simply offered a behavioral example and quietly encouraged their children to align themselves with the models before them. Rather than advising the use of punishment and terror as parental tools, Spock recommended common sense combined with the expression of warm feeling.

This change of approach was radical in its day, when children in schools were still subjected to corporal punishment and when spanking children was ordinary behavior in the American household. Spock unobtrusively noted that children who were slapped because they stole toys from other children usually continued to steal toys. Slapping and spanking just did not work, he explained to his readers. This was no reasonable way to control children or influence their behavior in a positive way. It only modeled a violent approach to solving problems. Yet Spock also suggested that a short burst of anger from the parent was no bad thing. He discouraged systematic "nagging" or regular spankings, but a brief display of anger was natural, and expected. Again, it was this balanced approach that governed his method and made his book so appealing. (It is the rare parent who has not had to deal with an impulse to smack a child, and Spock has been enormously helpful in easing the parental conscience on this count.)

Spock spoke mainly to the mother, as one might expect. This was simply the way of the world in 1946, as well as throughout the 1950s and '60s. Yet Spock took fatherhood seriously and emphasized the importance of getting a father closely involved in the raising of children from the outset. He explained in no uncertain terms that a father's influence could last a lifetime and argued that it was crucial for boys in particular to experience intimacy with their father. All of this seemed refreshing and new. Casually and quietly, Spock drew on Freudian insights, combining his own Yankee common sense with his analytical training to create a voice that comforted and informed generations of anxious parents. He sifted out the harsher aspects of Freud, and downplayed sexuality, tending to favor nurture over nature, thus enhancing the role of parents in the moral development of the child. And, most important for the common reader, he gave plenty of good advice on medical questions.

The Common Sense Book of Baby and Child Care sold by word of mouth, and it sold well. Within seven years, over five million copies had been bought. Spock's royalty payments were never what they should have been, unfortunately, as he had signed a weak contract (from his standpoint). According to his records, he had accumulated only $37,000 in royalty payments on the paperback by 1953, whereas with a more standard contract he might have earned over $200,000 by this time. Nevertheless, the continued success of the book meant that Benjamin Spock eventually became a wealthy man. More than this, he became a household word, his name synonymous with good parenting, his book (now in its eighth edition) still relevant a decade after his death.

III.

SPOCK BEGINS with "A Letter to the Mother and Father" (I use the 1946 edition throughout). Already he slipped ahead of previous books by including the father; moreover, he apologizes for using the word "he" when discussing the child—a remarkable advance in itself. He explains that girls are wonderful creatures but that he did not want to have to say "he or she" repeatedly. There is an extraordinary candidness to this letter, as he explains that *The Common Sense Book of Baby and Child Care* need not be read from cover to cover and that it unfolds as the child grows. He also lets readers know he is not the last word on the subject, and parents should not imagine they have made some horrible mistake because he, Dr. Spock, suggests something that is contrary to their practice. Mother knows best, and so does Father.

He proceeds quickly to the opening line about trusting yourself in "Preparing for the Baby." As he realized, every new parent is panicky, not quite sure what to expect when the screaming little bundle arrives. Spock reassures: "You know more than you think you do." He cautions against listening to everyone with a bit of advice to offer. "Don't take too seriously all that the neighbors say," he says, explaining that "natural loving care" is the only thing that really matters, not how you pin a diaper or make a formula. Then he provides a sensible checklist for what all new parents require: a place for the child to sleep, waterproof mattress covers, warm blankets, and so forth. He describes the ideal sort of nursing bottles and talks about sterilization and proper handling. He advises on medical care for the child, taking into account the fact that many parents will live too far from a city to see a specialist.

In talking about the role of parents in the subsequent section, he dwells on the importance of the father, noting that he is apt to get the mistaken impression he is unimportant. "The poor father is a complete outsider" at the hospital, he observes, having noticed as much in his years as a pediatrician (14). He argues in no uncertain terms that a father's "closeness and friendliness" will play a role in the child's life forever. This was new information for many readers, who had somehow forgotten about fathers.

Never afraid of controversial topics, Spock plunges into the arguments for and against circumcision, coming down (softly) on the side of those who oppose the practice. In later editions, he grew more definite on the subject, arguing that one should not perform this medically useless operation. He even notes a "danger of psychological harm" that can be produced by the procedure. Again, Spock was ahead of the curve on this one. In the eighth edition, we get his summary view of this matter: that it's a safe operation but a pointless one. It should only be undertaken for religious reasons, not health reasons. (If there are religious reasons, he suggests, that is fine: the child will suffer no harm.)

Now Spock moves into full gear, telling his readers that a baby should never be considered "a schemer" trying to get attention. "Your baby is born to be a reasonable, friendly human being," Spock writes (19). In case you don't believe him on this point, he refers to a fairly recent book, *Babies Are Human Beings,* by C. Anderson Aldrich and Mary M. Aldrich. This argument by appeal to authority is a bit unlike Spock, who usually rests on his own experience and common sense. The main gist of his argument here is that parents should enjoy their baby, not fret about parenthood and its pitfalls.

Odd as it may now seem, this marked a seismic shift in the literature of parenting. In the old days, parenthood was regarded as stern, perilous work. If you got it wrong, you ruined the child. Spock says repeatedly that a parent cannot harm a child by making a mistake. He notes, for example, that babies are strong, so one need not panic about handling them. In the chapter on feeding, he rubs against the prevailing wisdom that a parent reinforced a bad habit by excessive night feedings, making the baby want to continue with these feedings. "The 2 a.m. feeding doesn't start a habit," he says firmly (27). Babies want to sleep, he explains, and so they naturally stretch the time between feedings as they grow. Above all, Spock urges the mother to remain flexible in everything, adjusting to the baby's individual needs, letting nature work its magic. This will produce "happiness," he suggests (31).

The trend had turned away from breast-feeding when *Baby and Child Care* first appeared. Spock disliked this trend, though he remained cautious in his advice, not wishing to upset anyone. "Breast feeding is natural," he writes (33). For Spock, natural is good. The psychological benefits of breast-feeding, for mother and child, appealed to him, and he pointed out these benefits in no uncertain terms. Breast-feeding was cheaper, he pointed out, as one did not have to buy expensive formulas. Yet Spock made sure to allow for mothers who, for various reasons, preferred to use bottles, providing a good deal of up-to-date information on making formulas. Much of this now sounds quaint, of course. He tells mothers to add vitamin D to the baby's diet to prevent rickets—a disease no longer mentioned in the latest edition of Spock. And he celebrates the use of cod liver oil, a noxious substance rarely heard of these days (although the use of fish oils has been recently in the ascendance, in large part because of the omega-3 benefits).

As for sleeping arrangements, Spock recommends getting a child out of the parents' bedroom by six months. There has been considerable disagreement among pediatricians over the years about babies and children sleeping with their parents. The practice is widespread, however, and always has been; in part, this relates to a lack of space in many countries. In the United States in the twenty-first century, it is common practice to give a child a separate room from the start, if possible. Spock, as ever, takes a moderate stance here. The Freudian note enters in a subtle way, when Spock notes that babies may be "upset" by the sexual activity of their parents, which they will "misunderstand" (101). For Sigmund Freud, this was a *very big deal indeed,* especially within the parameters of the Oedipus complex.

On the matter of crying, Spock did his best to sound reasonable, but he was indisposed to let a baby cry and cry. "I don't think it's good to let a baby cry miserably for long periods," he says, unable to disguise a certain testiness (117). He does not, however, advocate rushing to pick up a child every time it whimpers. He tells mothers to be patient, and if they have the bad luck of a baby who cries too often, they should make sure to get out of the house twice a week or so, to give themselves a break. He also advocates rotating infant care between parents: "The baby doesn't need two worried parents at a time to listen to him" (118). As ever, his tone is both reassuring and firm—an odd combination, but it obviously worked wonders. Parents could listen to Spock. They could learn from him as well.

In a systematic fashion, Spock runs through the usual parental concerns, taking parents from care of baby to care of toddler and child. He discusses toilet training, diet, and behavioral matters. On this last subject, he takes what now seems a fresh approach, one that would get him in deep trouble with those who accused him of being "permissive." On page 211, for example, there is an interesting illustration: A toddler is about to pull a lamp off a table. The frantic mother, who has just entered the room, is pointing and shouting, "No, no!" Spock comments: "Better to remove and distract him than to say, 'No, no!' " This flew in the face of centuries of parental scolding. Saying no in a loud voice has been a staple of parenting since the cave dwellers began to grunt in words. But Spock said no to no. Spare the rod and spare the child, he seems to argue. When confronted with a child in a dangerous situation, a parent, according to Spock, should pick up the child and remove him from the scene, distracting him if possible. It was important to avoid conflict and remember that children were born to try different things, some of them dangerous. If parents squashed experimentation, they risked stifling creativity. This was not a good trade-off.

Spock also cautions parents against yelling at kids who put their hands into their food. "Feeding is learning," he writes (222). Let the child play around with the stuff. How else will he learn the textures of reality? This kind of thing must have puzzled and angered some parents, especially those with squeamish feelings about food. It is not easy to change centuries of habit. But in this, as in everything, Spock advises parents to keep a balanced attitude, urging them not to react too strongly when "bad" behavior occurs, as this might have a withering effect on a sensitive child. On the topic of swearing, for instance, he notes that all children swear. They learn "dirty words" from other kids, and it's natural for this to happen.

In particular, he urges fathers to get involved, especially with sons, who need a good example before them. "A boy doesn't grow spiritually to be a man just because he's born with a male body," Spock opines (254). Nurture is more important than nature, and so fathering involves nurturing. He adds (wisely) that a girl needs a father, too, and talks sensibly about this. The girl is also getting ready for her adult life, Spock explains. She will have to deal with men throughout her life, and her father is obviously the first man in her life. He must understand her developmental needs and respond to them properly. This was heady stuff in 1946.

Spock suggests that, in general, a parent should behave in a firm yet friendly fashion. It is this balance that succeeds. As for punishment, he takes a controversial stand (that has become commonplace). In general, he recommends that parents insist on good behavior and model it themselves. Punishment should, if possible, be avoided. In a well-known passage, he writes: "I don't think an agreeable parent should feel ashamed or a failure because he gets cross and uses punishment occasionally. But I disagree with the grim or irritable parent who seriously believes that punishment is a good regular method of controlling a child" (270). This comment flew in the face of old-fashioned parenting, raising the specter of the "spoiled" child and opening Spock to the accusation that he advocated "permissiveness." Yet quite a gap exists between permissiveness and refusing to condone punishment as a reasonable or effective means of controlling a child's behavior.

Spock argues that logical consequences should follow bad behavior, a point that later authors would develop and extend in useful ways (as in *1-2-3 Magic* by Thomas W. Phelan or *Setting Limits with Your Strong-Willed Child* by Robert J. MacKenzie—just to note a couple of recent and highly popular books on the discipline of children). Spock suggests, for example, that if a child breaks a plate on purpose, it might be wise to make the child pay for a replacement with his or her allowance. "A child beyond the age of 6 is developing a sense of justice and sees the fairness of reasonable penalties," he tells his readers (271). This sense of justice was crucial to the moral development of the child.

Moving through the stages of a child's growth, Spock addresses various crises that parents must commonly confront. When a child lies to a parent, for example, as all children do, he urges a calm response. "A little imagination is a good thing," he says. "You don't need to jump on him for making up stories occasionally, or make him feel guilty, or even be concerned yourself, as long as he is outgoing in general and happy with other children" (295). Centuries of American clergymen must have turned in their graves when these lines were written. As ever, Spock adopts a philosophical pose, wondering why a child would lie in the first place. The old answer was that children were born in sin and could never hope to shed their evil natures without fierce discipline from above. Spock prefers a more secular stance, suggesting that children, especially older ones, lie because they are under psychological pressure. "If he is failing in his schoolwork and lying about it, it isn't because he doesn't care. His lying shows that he cares" (296). This was revolutionary stuff, and still seems breathtaking in its simplicity and grace.

On the matter of sex education, Spock popularized the frank approach now common fare. It is highly unlikely that any parent today would tell a child that the stork brought him or her into the world. Even young children quickly pick up the facts of life, as Spock observes. When a child of three notices that his or her mother is pregnant, suspicions normally arise, however unspoken. Spock urges parents to move slowly, giving the child only as much information as he or she requires. Good parenting, according to him, means that parents search for appropriate moments to convey information about the facts of life in a natural, unthreatening way, in age-appropriate language. His approach intrigued teachers as well as parents, and the contours of contemporary sex education in schools owe a good deal to Spock's interest and method.

Spock was especially good when it came to dealing with adolescence—a phase in child raising that confounds many parents. All sorts of delicate issues arise during puberty, and Spock summons more than the usual quantity of common sense as he runs against the received wisdom. For instance, it was common for mothers to tell their daughters at the age of ten or eleven that they might soon find themselves in a "delicate" condition. Spock argues that this only frightens girls and provides no useful information. Tell them the truth, he says. He urges parents not to focus on the "dangerous" sides of sex, but to keep a matter-of-fact attitude. "A nervous mother," he says, "may make her daughter so scared of becoming pregnant that the poor girl has a terror of boys under all circumstances" (310). An adolescent should learn to think about sex as something "wholesome and natural and beautiful." (Welcome to the Age of Aquarius.)

Children often develop tics and exhibit unease among their peers. Spock counsels parents to ease up on their afflicted child, as such problems often follow from parental anxiety. The message is clear: let the child alone. Here we see Spock as a descendant of Jean-Jacques Rousseau (1712–78), the French philosopher who believed that if one followed one's inclinations, all would be well. The human being was naturally good, and the function of education was to enhance this goodness, not interfere with its progress.[13] Spock writes: "Tics, like compulsions, are more common in tense children, with fairly strict parents. There may be too much pressure at home" (318). This advice chimes with everything Spock has argued thus far: a child is by nature good, sensible, joyous, and healthy. Parents should not interrupt the normal growth of the child. While this advice may sound like pie in the sky to many readers, even now, it has roots in the Enlightenment era, which influenced key American educational thinkers such as John Dewey (who often quoted Rousseau as the source of his theories).[14] Spock flows naturally from Dewey.

At the center of most homes in the 1940s sat the radio (a function now performed by the TV set). The question arose: How much radio time should children be allowed? Spock suggests, tentatively, that children should be allowed to listen to their favorite programs if they have done their homework and otherwise accomplished their daily tasks. With the introduction of television into homes, Spock grew increasingly wary of its influence. In the eighth edition of *Baby and Child Care* the advice is clear: Get rid of the TV if you can. If you can't, limit the time a child can watch the tube. Acquisition of the V-chip, which blocks certain programs, is seen as a godsend for parents who cannot always be home. Watching television with your child is recommended as an antidote to the unhealthy messages that programs so often send.

The chapter on schooling is straight from Dewey, who advocated a hands-on, active approach to learning. This method was called "progressive" because Dewey believed that forcing children "into line" was wasteful and counterproductive. "Education is life itself," Dewey famously wrote, and Spock agreed. He urged teachers to link education to the outside world, associating the work pursued in the classroom with real life. As with Dewey, the political dimensions of education were not lost on Spock. In a seminal passage, he writes: "Another thing that a good school wants to teach is democracy, not just as a patriotic motto but as a way of living and getting things done. A good teacher knows that she can't teach democracy out of a book if she's acting like a dictator in person" (329). This notion still presents a challenge to teachers as well as parents. One cannot act like a dictator and imagine that children (or high school or college students) will understand how democracies function. A good example is all.

Spock had much to say about how parents should function in relation to the school system, advising them to speak with teachers in a friendly and cooperative way. He reminds them that their fear of talking to a teacher is natural and points out that the teacher may also experience some trepidation in the face of a parent whose child is having trouble. As usual, Spock cautions against immoderate behavior. Be calm and reasonable, he urges. This will make it possible for communication to occur between parent and teacher, and it will be useful in getting to the bottom of a child's problems in school. This remains utterly sensible advice, if rather obvious. (Spock was himself an excellent teacher, so had a talent for being enthusiastic about the obvious.)

The book concludes with several chapters on common medical problems, such as colds and fevers, stomach ailments, sinusitis, tonsillitis, allergies, scarlet fever, and diphtheria. As it should, the advice on how to deal with these problems shifted from edition to edition as new information became available and the medical establishment changed its collective mind about the best treatment for various problems. Some of these diseases, such as scarlet fever, have fallen from the roster of major issues. But when it comes to first aid—treating cuts, burns, and common injuries—the old advice still seems fresh as new paint. "The best treatment for scratches and small cuts is to wash them with soap and pure water on a piece of sterile absorbent cotton," Spock tells us (448). In the book's eighth edition, half a century later, the advice has not changed. Wash a cut with soap and warm water. Put on a bandage. Bingo.

The Common Sense Book of Baby and Child Care concludes with "Special Problems." Some of these still have relevance, such as "Traveling with a Baby" or "The Handicapped Child." The advice is always humane and balanced; but time has shifted us away from many of these issues, such as "the problem" of a working mother. Spock wrote his book during the period when "the feminine mystique" (as Betty Friedan described it) had recently taken hold with a vengeance. Men had come home from a catastrophic war, eager to get back to work and settle down. Women shifted back into the home, where they soon got pregnant. Like most people, Spock bought into the mystique wholesale, arguing that the government should pay mothers to stay home, as a stay-at-home mom was the best way to ensure "useful, well-adjusted citizens" (484). Professional women who believed they could not be happy without working were tolerated, *barely*. "After all," says Spock, "an unhappy mother can't bring up very happy children." His assumption was that children needed a mother whose attention was focused on them, much as Spock's own mother had focused on him.

Spock derided the idea of day care. "The average day nursery or 'baby farm' is no good" for a child, he says categorically (485). In declaring this, he reflects a common prejudice of the day, just as now we reflect the common prejudices of ours. What surprises a careful reader, however, is the extent to which Benjamin Spock lifted himself over so many ordinary assumptions, creating a fresh aura around the project of parenthood. He encouraged tolerance, restraint, warmth, and common sense and argued against coercion and stubbornness. It was his firm conviction that the greatest security a child can possess is the knowledge of "being loved, wholeheartedly and naturally" (507). This belief illumines every page of *Baby and Child Care*.

IV.

THE PUBLIC encountered two versions of Benjamin Spock during his lifetime. There was the benevolent pediatrician who wrote the bestselling book on child care, which moved through edition after edition, selling a million copies every year.[15] This was the same man who served on the staff of several famous institutions, including the Mayo Clinic and the Rochester Child Health Institute. He was endlessly in demand as a speaker in the related fields of pediatrics and child psychiatry and often wrote articles on parenthood for national magazines. Yet another Spock emerged, as if from nowhere, in the early 1960s.

He became an antiwar activist, drawing on his enormous prestige to advocate for nuclear disarmament. As he told one interviewer: "I suddenly realized the whole *world* was in peril. We've got to keep testing more, keep accumulating more nuclear arms—and of course Congress is always enthusiastic for more arms . . . It suddenly struck me—it was a *terrible* moment. After that, I was hooked for the peace movement."[16] He joined the board of a national organization devoted to the reduction of nuclear arms, signing his name to various petitions. He subsequently found himself the object of a great deal of criticism, even scorn.

When the 1964 election came, Spock saw a clear choice between the man who would escalate the war in Vietnam (Barry Goldwater) and the man who would not (LBJ). He hurled himself into political activity, appearing on television as a member of a group called Scientists and Engineers for Johnson and Humphrey. But how wrong it all went. Soon after the election, President Johnson escalated the war, sending tens of thousands of troops to Southeast Asia, basing everything he did on the Gulf of Tonkin Resolution, which even at the time seemed bogus. Spock regarded Johnson's activity as a threat to world peace, a criminal example of warmongering. He began to engage in antiwar activities and stood wholeheartedly behind the movement for draft resistance. He sponsored a declaration titled "A Call to Resist Illegitimate Authority" and supported the public burning of draft cards as a form of free speech. To his amazement, he was indicted by a federal grand jury in Boston on January 5, 1968, along with four others, charged with conspiring "to sponsor and support a nation-wide program of resistance" to the draft.

Spock and his co-defendants went on trial before Judge Francis J. W. Ford, and these proceedings riveted the public. They were, much to their astonishment, convicted. At the press conference after the trial, Spock put the matter succinctly: "Judge Ford said that the law must be obeyed. We agreed. I am not convinced that I broke the law; there was no evidence of conspiracy. Millions of Americans are opposed to the war. There is no shred of legality or constitutionality to this war; it violates the United Nations Charter, the Geneva Conventions, and the United States promise to obey the laws of international conduct. It is *totally, abom-*

inably, illegal."[17] Fortunately for Spock and his co-defendants, an appeals court overturned their convictions on technical grounds, and the government never pursued the case.

Benjamin Spock was a noble creature, utterly himself as both pediatrician and peace activist. And yet the connection between these very different sides of Spock remains confusing. Was Vice President Agnew correct to draw a connect between the "permissiveness" advocated by Spock and the apparent lawlessness of the young, who dared to resist the draft and protested a war that had been directed by the president and paid for by the U.S. Congress? Had Spock and his approach to parenting created a generation of self-absorbed narcissists, as some believed?

In *The Culture of Narcissism* (1979), a brilliant analysis of the American character in the postwar era, Christopher Lasch makes the obvious but somehow unnoticed point about Spock that he had actually encouraged parental authority. "Often blamed for the excesses of permissive child-rearing," Lasch writes, "Spock should be seen instead as one of its critics, seeking to restore the rights of the parent in the face of an exaggerated concern for the rights of the child."[18] *Baby and Child Care* is, indeed, a book that encourages parents to trust their feelings and take independent action. The old-fashioned idea of a "maternal instinct" made a comeback with Spock. He handed parents the authority to make decisions for themselves, not forcing them to rely on the dictates of preachers, folk wisdom, or memories of how their own parents behaved. "Trust yourself" was a powerful message, and one that could hardly be blamed for "permissiveness."

That charge has much to do with Spock's advice to let children enjoy themselves, digging their fingers into the food on their plate, as needed, or playing in the fresh air without worrying about the mud on their clothes. He cautioned against harsh or unreasonable punishment and discouraged physical abuse. He asked parents to relate to their children in loving ways. Was it really possible to trace mass antiwar protests and the excesses of the hippie movement back to the pages of *The Common Sense Book of Baby and Child Care*? I hardly think so. Indeed, if Spock had never lifted a voice against the spread of nuclear weapons and the Vietnam War, he would probably not have been charged with being the father of permissiveness, with helping to create a generation of self-indulgent boomers. Yet the legacy of his book is inextricably linked with his political activities in the 1960s and early '70s. These associations have been hard to disentangle.

No book single-handedly shifts public attitudes, but Spock's handbook played a significant role on many fronts. For a start, it handed parents a wonderful gift: they could operate with a sense of optimism, believing it was indeed possible to behave in ways that enhanced the lives of their children. They could deal with ordinary problems like bed-wetting and stuttering without excessive anxiety. They could teach their children about sex without resorting to ridiculous fantasies about storks. They could enforce rules about listening to the radio or, later, watching television. They could control what their children ate, providing healthy food without resorting to coercion. They could deal with things like fevers, stomach upsets, cuts and scratches, or allergic responses without panic, even without immediate help from a doctor. Spock's handbook inspired confidence and gave parents a tone of voice they could model. He gave them permission to be themselves, assuring them that no expert could really tell them what was best for their child. It was *their* child, after all.

A flood of handbooks on child raising arose in the wake of *Baby and Child Care,* and many of these followed Spock's lead. One could not, for example, imagine the popular (and excellent) books by T. Berry Brazelton or Mary Sheedy Kurcinka—just to pick two obvious names among parenting gurus—without Spock. Everything from the tone to the commonsensical approach in these writers is Spock with a twist. The long shelf of parenting books in any American bookstore will attest to Spock's enduring influence on the field. One cannot imagine the world of parenting handbooks without his genial, encouraging presence.

Spock's handbook engendered a revolution of sorts in 1946, and its effects reverberate still. Perhaps the final word on Benjamin Spock himself belongs to Garry Wills, the writer who spent time in jail with the elderly pediatrician in the late 1960s, having been arrested beside him for protesting the Vietnam War. Twenty years later, Wills remembered the good doctor fondly: "Spock was the father not of a permissive age, but of an imaginative one. He had a respect for individuality, in babies as in grown citizens. Like most respect, it comes from a sense of his own dignity. He was the most patrician of radicals, always polite in every picket line, solicitous for the well-being of the police as well as of the demonstrators. He had come to protest war, not to wage it, and he soothed hot heads even while appealing to bold hearts."[19]

As such, Dr. Spock remains a figure of heroic proportions, a great American if one ever lived. His *Common Sense Book of Baby and Child Care* has lodged itself permanently in the psyche of a nation, which it helped to shape.

a novel
by Jack Kerouac

ON THE ROAD

TWELVE

On the Road

I.

ON THE ROAD (1957) identified, and helped to define, the notion of an American counterculture. The book also established Jack Kerouac as a primary figure in the so-called Beat Generation, which he gave its name. In the course of its sprawling travelogue, the novel recapitulates and transforms many of the key ideas described in this study so far. As a road novel, it presents a major example of this important American genre. Yet it's also an immigrant novel, as its hero, Sal Paradise, has Italian ethnic roots (in the same way that Kerouac had strong connections to his French-Canadian heritage). Huck Finn's theme of lighting out for the territory permeates Kerouac's narrative, which features Dean Moriarty as a latter-day Huck—a wild boy and son of an outlaw, a born outsider keen to escape by hook or by crook the conformity of postwar American life. Finally, the zigzag journeys of Sal and Dean distantly recall the travels of countless pioneers, including Lewis and Clark, who sought gold or glory in the promised land of the West.

The phrase "promised land" recurs almost obsessively throughout Kerouac's novel. Even the name of his hero, Sal Paradise, has biblical (even allegorical) overtones. Religious feeling runs deep in Kerouac, as we shall see, linking him with earlier writers (such as William Bradford) who sought the kingdom of God on earth. Kerouac was himself a lifelong Roman Catholic who grew more devout as he aged, even though his interest in Buddhism deepened as well (especially in later years, after he learned more about Buddhist teachings from the poet Gary Snyder, whom he portrays in *The Dharma Bums*). *On the Road* might easily be described as a quest for redemption, as well as an affirmation of God's hand in the world. As Dean puts it bluntly: "God exists without qualms. As we roll along this way I am positive beyond doubt that everything will be taken care of for us" (121).[1] Elsewhere, Sal recalls, "Dean and I had the whole of Mexico before us," thus echoing the famous lines of Milton's *Paradise Lost* (Book 12), where Adam and Eve, having been cast out of Eden, become aware that "the world was all before them" and remain confident they had "Providence their guide."

In its wildness, its struggle to separate from the puritanical confines of American middle-class life, this novel recalls the seventeenth-century residents of Merry Mount, where Thomas Morton gathered his free-thinking, hard-drinking band of revelers, who cavorted freely with Native American women and tormented the nearby Plymouth Colony. William Bradford and his militia put an end to the wicked ways of their neighbors at Merry Mount, this "wild throng that stood hand in hand about the Maypole," as Hawthorne put it in a famous story; yet Morton and his throng (perhaps even more so than Thoreau or Whitman) may be considered our Founding Hippies.[2] Kerouac and his Beat friends represent a late flowering of this impulse, which came to full bloom in the late 1960s.

Mainly, *On the Road* represents a fresh and shining American example of the road novel, a narrative tradition that begins in the modern era with *Don Quixote* (1605) and runs through such crucial American works as *Huckleberry Finn* (1885), Jack London's *Valley of the Moon* (1913), Nelson Algren's *Somebody in Boots* (1935), John Steinbeck's *Grapes of Wrath* (1939), and Vladimir Nabokov's *Lolita* (1955). It's a robust tradition celebrated in Walt Whitman's effusive "Song of the Open Road" (1856), a poem that opens:

> *Afoot and light-hearted, I take to the open road,*
> *Healthy, free, the world before me,*
> *The long brown path before me, leading wherever I choose.*

The tradition of the road novel culminates, most recently, in Cormac McCarthy's masterpiece, *The Road* (2006), in which a father and son travel through a bleached, broken landscape in postapocalyptic America, searching for food and shelter, for a safe haven of any kind, an inverted search for the once-promised land.

Readers flocked to Kerouac's novel, making it a bestseller in its day and fixing in the public mind the notion of a countercultural movement. As Gilbert Millstein observed in his landmark review in the *New York Times,* Kerouac's book was instantly regarded as a testament of the Beat Generation.[3] In the half century since its publication in 1957, it has established itself as a classic text, one both taught in college courses in American literature and read by voluntary readers—the ultimate test of a book's power. Generations of American youth have, in imitation of Kerouac (knowingly or not), taken to the road with a backpack, hitching across the continent, often adopting the novel's antic (if not frantic) mood. In general, the rolling vision of America that Kerouac summoned offers a map of sorts, not only to a promised land of prairies, small towns, swamps, jagged mountains, and throbbing cities, but to what Milton in *Paradise Lost* described as "a paradise within thee, happier far." I would argue that *On the Road* altered, and expanded, the consciousness of countless Americans, even when they didn't know it.

II.

J ACK KEROUAC (1922–69) was born in Lowell, Massachusetts, a dreary mill town in serious decline from its heyday in the nineteenth century. He was baptized as Jean-Louis Lebris de Kerouac. This immigrant family spoke a French-Canadian dialect called joual, and Kerouac didn't actually begin to speak English until he was six. He lost his brother, Gerard, in childhood and became an only child, with a devoted mother who remained the only woman in his life, although he married (briefly) several times. His father, who lost his job as a printer during the Great Depression, was a distant, inaccessible figure in young Jack's life. The social world of Kerouac's childhood was working-class, ethnic, and largely anti-intellectual. Although he liked to read, Kerouac never embraced school and refused to conform to classroom disciplines. It was his excellence on the football field that won him scholarships first to Horace Mann, a private school in New York City, and then to Columbia, where he played football until a broken leg sidelined him. He studied for a little over two years before joining the navy, from which he was discharged in 1942 because of his brooding, rebellious nature. He joined the merchant marines for a while, and moved in with his parents after the war.

He adored his mother and continued to live with her after his father's death in 1946, although he often stayed with friends in Greenwich Village, including the poet Allen Ginsberg, and traveled (as described in *On the Road*) with Neal Cassady and others in the summer, roaming from New York to Denver to San Francisco to Texas to Mexico. During the late 1940s, he worked sporadically on a first novel, *The Town and the City,* which he published in 1950. But he remained an obscure writer until the immense success of *On the Road,* which changed his life forever. It might well be argued that the success of this novel ruined him, as he tried desperately to live up to an image that included hard drinking, and it was alcohol that ultimately destroyed him.

One legendary draft of *On the Road* was written on a huge scroll, three inches thick and 120 feet long. Kerouac worked feverishly, completing this version of the novel in three weeks. It was accomplished during the spring of 1951, and that document was auctioned by Christie's on May 22, 2001, when it sold to Jim Irsay, a wealthy businessman and owner of the Indianapolis Colts football team, for $2.2 million. Kerouac made the scroll himself from a series of twelve-foot-long rolls that he taped together then fed continuously into his typewriter to enable a process that he called "spontaneous writing." He ignored the conventions of paragraphing, refusing indentations of any kind, in a visionary blast of composition. Dashes were often used instead of periods or semicolons, with the dash representing a long breath between effusions of prose. To commemorate the fifty-year anniversary of the novel, Viking published the scroll version in *On the Road: The Original Scroll* (2007).[4]

In his introduction to the published scroll, Howard Cunnell provides a detailed examination of the many false starts, drafts, outtakes, and revisions that went into the making of *On the Road*. Its sketchiest origins may be traced back to an early story of four pages, written in

1940; but the novel itself began to form in Kerouac's journals, kept during travels in the United States and Mexico between 1947 and 1950. On August 23, 1948, he mentions the novel explicitly, saying that *On the Road* is "about two guys hitch-hiking to California in search of something they don't *really* find, and losing themselves on the road, and coming all the way back hopeful of something *else*."[5] This pretty much describes the novel that would emerge, although it did so in fits and starts.

In some ways, it arose from his autobiographical first novel, *The Town and the City,* a story about the decline of a family not unlike Kerouac's own working-class, immigrant family. This rather sentimental novel (which owes a great deal to Thomas Wolfe, an early influence on Kerouac) offers an early portrait of Beat culture and reveals some resistance to the loose living it portrays: a stance that implicitly favors the conservative values of "the town" over those of "the city." Kerouac's attitude in that novel may surprise readers of *On the Road,* who perhaps too easily assume that the author despised conservative values because his characters appear so "wild," engaging in free sex and drugs, flouting authority, living on the edge of the law. In fact, Kerouac struggles with his values in *On the Road* as well and never quite fell into line with the wild boy Dean Moriarty, who is simply called by his real name, Neal Cassady, in the scroll version, which is more of a memoir than a novel.

Cassady, as Dean Moriarty, is among the most unforgettable figures in American fiction. He fascinated Sal (Kerouac), challenged him, and eventually undermined him. *On the Road* is Kerouac's attempt to get Cassady down on paper, to sketch him, to understand him. Yet no book could hope to contain the Dionysian energies of Cassady, who seemed to embody what Freud once called the realm of "polymorphous perversity." This terrifying wild boy has no boundaries, sexual or social. He is gay and straight, outlaw and Boy Scout, friend and foe. He is what D. H. Lawrence might have called a Priest of Love, a young man devoted to the pure spirit that moves him, twists him around, sets him down in one taxing situation after another. "With the coming of Neal there really began for me that part of my life that you could call my life on the road," Kerouac writes in the scroll version, at the outset.[6] This is a religious moment for Sal Paradise, the author's stand-in, and recalls the "coming" of all prophets.

The scroll notwithstanding, the novel really emerged in hundreds of pages of rough-draft fiction, letters, journal entries, and many conversations with Allen Ginsberg, Neal Cassady, William S. Burroughs, and many others. Kerouac wrote to a friend in 1948 that plans for this work just flowed out of him, "even in bars with perfect strangers."[7] Howard Cunnell identifies several major proto-versions of the novel, including a fifty-four-page draft called the "Ray Smith Novel of Fall 1948," the Red Moultrie/Vern (later Dean) Pomeray version of 1949 (he sometimes spelled the name Pomery or Pomeroy), the 1950 "Gone on the Road" manuscript of thirty pages, which features Cook Smith and Dean Pomeray, and the scroll version itself, which was strenuously revised to create the final 1957 novel, with Sal Paradise and Dean Moriarty as protagonists.

It is worth reading the scroll version carefully, as the writing is more spontaneous, sometimes more lyrical, certainly sexier, wilder, and funnier. In chapter 5 of book 3, for example, Sal and Dean hitch a ride back east in what they call a "fag Plymouth" as it belongs to "a tall, thin fag who was on his way home to Kansas." This car "had no pickup and no real power" and was called an "effeminate car" by Dean, who often makes rude remarks about homosexuals, although he himself is unabashedly bisexual and had worked in his youth as a gay hustler—as he admits, even in the 1957 version (207).

In Sacramento, the older gay fellow gets a hotel room, inviting Dean and Sal up for a drink. "The fag . . . liked young men like us," Sal recalls, "and would we believe it, but he really didn't like girls and had recently concluded an affair with a man in Frisco in which he had taken the male role and the man the female role" (210). With barely controlled scorn, he notes: "The fag said he would like nothing better than to know what Dean thought about all this." In the 1957 novel, Dean merely frightens the "fag" into thinking he's a hustler, and so the man keeps checking his wallet to make sure Dean hasn't stolen anything. Dean remarks of gay men: "Offer them what they secretly want and they of course immediately become panic-stricken." This may be true for some homosexuals, but it's obviously not a general truth. We find out what really happened in the scroll, which makes a good deal more sense and reveals the bisexual aspect of Dean (as Neal in this draft) that, without such details, remains elusive, even confusing at times. In the scroll, Kerouac writes: "Warning him first that he had once been a hustler in his youth, Neal proceeded to handle the fag like a woman, tipping him over legs in the air and all and gave him a monstrous huge banging."[8]

This is what the man wants, and Neal gives it to him—most explicitly in the scroll. He "tames" the older man, who had just bragged to the boys about playing the male role in homosexual acts. He is sodomized (and therefore "feminized") in the missionary position. In a real sense, this is a power play by Dean (and more so by Neal), not a sex act. We are left to believe that Dean doesn't "really" want the sex. He wants to drive the car, and to have a feeling of control. To be sure, Sal explains that Dean had "sufficiently conquered the owner of the Plymouth to take over the wheel without remonstrance, and now we really traveled" (210). Without the explicit sodomy scene, as it appears in the scroll, I doubt that readers have sufficient access to what Sal (in the 1957 novel) is talking about.

Kerouac worked with Malcolm Cowley, the distinguished editor at Viking and gifted poet who had chronicled the so-called Lost Generation of Hemingway, Fitzgerald, and others in *Exile's Return* (1934), his superb memoir of Paris in the 1920s. In a memo written to his colleagues at Viking, Cowley suggested that obscenity and libel threats were the two roadblocks to the publication of *On the Road.* Eager to see the book into print, Kerouac (with advice from lawyers at Viking) took a hatchet to the scroll version, disguising various figures who might sue, cutting the most explicit sex, and generally tightening the story to make the whole thing fit together in a more conventional way. Paragraphs made a big difference for the general reader. The final version was submitted to Cowley on January 8, 1957, and the author received an advance of $1,000 against future earnings. It was hardly a fat contract, but it was standard, and the royalties certainly followed.

The obscenity laws in America in the 1950s made it dangerous to write freely, especially in a "lewd" manner. Allen Ginsberg (along with his publisher at City Lights, Lawrence Ferlinghetti) found himself on trial in March 1957 for *Howl,* an effusive and coruscating long poem that had been deemed obscene because of one line, about men "who let themselves be fucked in the ass by saintly motorcyclists, and screamed with joy." To the amazement of many, the judge in the case, Clayton Horn, decided that the poem had "redeeming social importance." The way opened for *On the Road,* which appeared on September 5, 1957.

As noted above, the first important review was Millstein's in the *New York Times,* where he called *On the Road* "a major novel" and characterized its publication as "an historic occasion." Not all critics agreed. Robert C. Ruark in the *New York World-Telegram & Sun* insisted the book was nothing more than a "candid admission" that the author had "been on the bum for six years."[9] William Murray, in the *New Leader,* recognized the importance of the novel as a social document but concluded that the author was "certainly not an artist, for that would imply a discipline and unity of purpose which his writing does not reflect."

Readers paid scant attention to these negative remarks, and the novel sold well, churning through three printings within its first year. The publicity director at Viking at the time, Patricia McManus, noted in a memo to colleagues (in January 1958) that "at least two colleges have adopted it for modern literature courses (how the schools are using it hasn't yet been ascertained . . . perhaps for after-curfew reading)."[10] The novel has never been out of print since its day of publication. According to Paul Slovak, a vice president at Viking, it still sells about a hundred thousand copies every year and has been translated into thirty-two languages.[11] The novel has, indeed, achieved more than mere cult status; it has achieved classic status, regarded as one of the most influential books ever written by an American.

Kerouac never wrote another book equal to *On the Road,* although glimmers of brilliance occur in everything he produced. His alcoholism got in the way of steady writing, and he died from this disease in 1969, although not before seeing many of his earlier manuscripts and later books into print. Among the best of these are *The Dharma Bums* (1958), *Visions of Cody* (1960), *Big Sur* (1962), and *Desolation Angels* (1965). These, including *On the Road,* form part of a fourteen-novel sequence of road novels that fall under the general rubric of "The Duluoz Legend," although anyone seeking much in the way of unity here will be disappointed. Narrative unity was not Jack Kerouac's ideal. He preferred a kind of spontaneous, associated writing—a style not unlike a prose version of jazz, which features importantly in *On the Road.*

III.

THE NOVEL is divided into five parts and centers on four major road trips (five in the scroll version), as it also focuses on Dean Moriarty. It's a book of evasions, as seen in the second sentence of the book: "I had just gotten over a serious illness that I won't bother to talk about, except that it had something to do with the miserably weary split-up and my feeling that everything was dead" (1). The death of Sal's father hides beneath the surface of the text, as does the breakup of his first marriage. One senses other obscured things: Sal Paradise cannot get his life together, and his search for happiness gives the novel its frenetic quality. The road represents life itself. And the hero is himself a writer—putting *On the Road* in the tradition of novels about young writers trying to discover their vision, such as *A Portrait of the Artist as a Young Man* (1916) by James Joyce, a book that Kerouac admired.[12] (He modeled his autobiographical Duluoz character on Stephen Dedalus, Joyce's fictional counter-self.)

Dean Moriarty catches and holds the narrator's attention from the outset. This "young jailkid shrouded in mystery" comes east, supposedly to learn the writer's craft, which is why he approaches Sal in the first place. Dean is married to Marylou, "his beautiful little sharp chick." Already the word "chick" will have signaled to readers in 1957 that a jazzy, slang-filled novel opens before them. Dean seeks out Sal in Paterson, New Jersey, where he lives with his aunt. In the scroll version, Sal is Jack Kerouac himself and lives with his mother, as he did. Dean has no such family ties; indeed, he is utterly, almost innocently, devoted to sex, which he considers "the one and only holy and important thing in life" (2).

Dean and Sal strike up an immediate bond, and agree to go "out West sometime" (4). This is Huck Finn's legacy, embodied in the wish to "light out for the Territory." The West represents freedom from the jacket-and-tie values of the East; it is big skies, cowboys, mountains, and the right to do whatever you damn well please. Mother (or Aunt Sally) is not there, making sure you come home at night, turning off the lights when you go to bed. Other Beat friends appear: we soon, for example, meet Carlo Marx (Allen Ginsberg), "the holy con-man with the shining mind" (5). In the scroll version, Neal and Allen have sex; but not in the 1957 revision. One also hears rumors of Old Bull Lee (William S. Burroughs in the scroll). Sal rolls out a long catalog of characters and places, alluding to sex and drugs in a way that had never quite been seen before in American fiction.

Sal justifies his urge to travel with Dean because he hopes to get to know Dean better, but also because his "life hanging around the campus had reached the completion of its cycle and was stultified" (7). (In the same way, Tom Sawyer looked at Huck and his freewheeling way of life, and he envied that freedom.) The homoerotic currents are never terribly explicit, but the charge that Sal feels in the presence of Dean Moriarty is nothing if not sexual. He glows whenever Dean enters the room. He hangs on his words and considers his intelligence "shining and complete, without the tedious intellectualness" that others have (7). What he most loves about Dean is his "wild yea-saying overburst of American joy" (7–8). He is "a western kinsman of the sun" and a god of sorts. Sal believes that if he follows Dean, "somewhere along the line the pearl would be handed" to him (8).

This is the pearl of wisdom, a gleam that includes "girls, visions, everything." And so the first journey begins, in July 1947. These are the years immediately after World War II. The cool youth of the 1950s were different, not nearly as energized, hopeful, and daring as the young men and women pictured by Kerouac. Sal has been reading books about the pioneers, such as *The Journals of Lewis and Clark,* and poring over maps of the United States. And so the journey begins, like all mythic journeys, in the symbolic mist: "All I could see were smoky trees and dismal wilderness rising to the skies" (10).

The travel writing here is gorgeous, as it remains throughout *On the Road.* In the manner of Whitman, Kerouac offers a vast catalog of sights and sounds, names and places. He hitches a ride into Colorado, and writes with prophetic clarity: "Now I could see Denver looming ahead of me like the Promised Land" (14). Repeatedly, the promised land looms, then fades. It is difficult to find, to occupy its center. As W. H. Auden once wrote:

> As in previous years we have seen the actual Vision and failed
> To do more than entertain it as an agreeable
> Possibility.[13]

As a picaresque novel, *On the Road* features a rogue-hero, or picaro, who roams the countryside, leaping from bed to bed, from adventure to adventure. Kerouac works within the old form, reinventing it. In his hand, it's a jazzy form, too, with endless riffs, long passages that might be considered solos. There are abrupt changes of mood and pace. The language itself is used in a musical way, with the words as notes. There is never much of a plot, nothing but story. (The difference is that in a story, one thing follows another, a serial explosion of unrelated events. In a plot-driven narrative, consequences obtain, and everything is linked in some inevitable fashion.) Sal is our picaro, and we follow him wherever he goes, meeting whomever he should meet, such as Eddie, described as "a typical New Yorker, an Irishman who'd been driving a truck for the post office most of his work years and was now headed for a girl in Denver and a new life" (16). Many of these characters just fall by the wayside as the novel proceeds.

In Denver, Sal discovers that Dean has fallen out with his old crowd, which includes such characters as Chad King, Tim Gray, and Roland Major. He has to make a choice; but it's no choice at all. He will and must take off with Dean, heading west, as planned. Sal is quite excited about connecting again with Dean, who has been "making love to two girls at the same time" in Denver. These girls are Marylou, his first wife, and Camille, a new girl. Carlo Marx explains all of this: "Between the two of them he rushes to me for our own unfinished business." That this "business" may be sexual is never stated. Doubtless Marx and Moriarty try to connect on a spiritual level, too, as they sit "on the bed, cross-legged, facing each other." They make an effort to "communicate with absolute honesty and absolute completeness" (41). This style of conversation, so utterly naked and personal, appealed strongly to readers in the late 1960s and '70s, the hippies and hippie wannabes, who sat on their beds in college dormitories and smoke-filled apartments, baring their souls to each other as they traded joints.

Sal himself begins a series of sexual adventures, as with Rita Bettencourt, "a fine chick, slightly hung-up on a few sexual difficulties" (43). The phrase "hung up," used in this way, infiltrated the language via Kerouac (who had picked it up from his Beat friends), and it has never lost its usefulness for a certain kind of anxiety or hesitancy (often sexual). Some of the slang in *On the Road,* however, seems wildly dated, even quaint, as when Old Bull Lee is described as "that gone cat" (48).

This part of the novel includes a trek into the mountains and various wild parties, as well as the introduction of a puzzling figure, Denver D. Doll, who is fleshed out with greater clarity in the scroll version, where he almost makes sense. Apparently libel reasons prevented Kerouac from doing anything with this strange middle-aged fellow, who concentrates rather obsessively on wayward young men or juveniles, whom he "reforms" and helps to get into college. Dean was among his protégés, but he seriously fails to live up to Doll's vision of him. He will not suffer reformation, any more than Huck would.

Whitman continues to haunt this novel, as when Sal and his friends go into the mountains: "We were on the roof of America and all we could do was yell," he says. (In "Song of Myself," Whitman writes: "I sound my barbaric yawp over the roofs of the world.") In a crucial passage, Sal talks about "the sordid hipsters of America, a new beat generation" that he "was slowly joining" (54). One senses his purposeful identification with a particular group, a postwar band of rebellious youth. These were not exactly the beatniks of the 1950s, but they foreshadowed them, constituting a countercultural fringe who loved jazz and sex and drugs. They gave birth to a new consciousness, one that would flower in the 1960s as a fresh generation defined itself against the conformity of their parents' generation.

Sal and Dean often (and sometimes pretentiously) drop allusions to literary works. Hemingway is mentioned several times, and often parodied. There are references to Céline and Goethe, to Hart Crane and others, yet some of the most important allusions here, to Whitman, Twain, and Joyce, to F. Scott Fitzgerald and Melville, are never explicit. The echoes of these writers are just that: echoes. With these persistent reverberations, however, Kerouac consciously placed his novel in a literary tradition, and his novel reads like a covert anthology of great American writing. It's a jazz novel, one that takes many well-known themes and passages and plays with them, offering riffs. It's a tissue of allusions, overt and covert.

San Francisco plays a huge role in the narrative, as many of the Beat Generation migrated there after the war at some point, including Gary Snyder, Ginsberg, and Lawrence Ferlinghetti. Once in San Francisco,

Sal moves in with an old friend from prep school, Remi Boncoeur, who goes around saying, "You can't teach the old maestro a new tune" (63). This becomes a kind of refrain for him. He lives in Mill City, outside of San Francisco, and "had fallen on the beat and evil days that come to young guys in their middle twenties" (62). In one of the most amusing scenes in the novel, Sal joins Remi as a security guard in a local barracks, where they are charged with keeping the peace among a crowd of sketchy characters ready to ship out for Okinawa. "The job of the special guards was to see that they didn't tear the barracks down," Sal tells us. They take on a badge and uniform and wear guns (doing so with mock authority). As they must, they associate (awkwardly) with other guards, "a horrible crew of men, men with cop-souls" (65). At one point, Sal gets into trouble for putting an American flag on the pole upside down. He is told by one "fat cop" that he can go to jail for that offense, and he is shocked. "I was horrified; of course I hadn't realized it." Needless to say, one does not entirely believe Sal. He probably did not set out to put the flag upside down. "I did it every morning mechanically," he says (66). But his very lack of respect for the flag belies a current of resistance, a streak of passive aggression. Sal and Dean have not theorized their attitudes to the U.S. government and its culture of death—represented by the "fat cops." Nevertheless, an underlying rebelliousness breaks out willy-nilly. Sal, after all, is a veteran, as was Kerouac. They know what the United States stood for, and what it didn't. In short, they didn't buy into the myths, not fully.

In postwar America, there was a strong urge toward conformity—perhaps a natural reaction to the chaos of the war. Kerouac saw himself in the years when he was writing *On the Road* as someone in the tradition of Thoreau, a man who separates from the crowd and waits on his own for Judgment Day. In a feverish, exuberant letter of 1949, for example, he wrote: "I decided someday to become a Thoreau of the Mountains. To live like Jesus and Thoreau." He would simply "wander the wild, wild mountains and wait for Judgment Day, but not for men . . . for society." As for his judgment on American society, he could not have been more explicit or damning: "It is evil. It will fall."[14]

Sal describes one security guard, a dreadful young man called Sledge, as "a walking torture chamber," with his low-hanging jacket and cocky hat, his revolver and ammunition belt. He wants nothing better than to punish those who won't listen to him. "I never gave a man more than two chances," he boasts repeatedly. Sal watches in smoldering contempt as Sledge goes after some of these poor souls, to punish them for refusing his orders. "This is the story of America," Sal says. "Everybody's doing what they think they're supposed to do" (68). But Sal Paradise belongs to a different order, seeking a visionary gleam. He will march to the beat of his own drummer. The period of working as a guard comes to an abrupt close.

"I was on the road again," Sal says (74). "Here I was at the end of America—no more land—and now there was nowhere to go but back" (77). He pauses at the end of chapter 11, part 1, to think about "the great raw bulge and bulk of my American continent" that lies before him, stretching eastward, culminating in New York City. "There is something brown and holy about the East," he suggests, in a mode more poetical than sociological.

The trip home takes a circuitous route, as Sal pauses for an affair with a Mexican girl called Teresa (or Terry) in one of the memorable stretches of the novel. He picks her up on a bus, and their affair begins in wonderful innocence: "Without coming to any particular agreement we began holding holds" on the bus (82). They sleep together as soon as they can. This sort of impulsive behavior, although common enough, was rarely written about with such freshness and candor. Sal finds nothing sordid or "dirty" about this sex; it was decided "beautifully and purely" that he and Teresa would sleep together in the hotel room in Los Angeles. "For the next fifteen days we were together for better or for worse," Sal writes, in parody of traditional matrimonial vows (86). Kerouac finds nothing, and everything, sacred.

Of course Southern California was (and is) full of countercultural types. "The beatest characters in the country swarmed on the sidewalks," Sal recalls, noting that in the air you could smell the "tea, weed, I mean marijuana" (87). He picks up work with a farmer, and the writing here echoes Steinbeck as Kerouac describes "the great plague of the thirties" and refers to the entire family driving "in a jalopy truck." *The Grapes of Wrath* often seems only slightly out of view at many turns in *On the Road*. Other American masterworks also linger in the margins, as when Sal refers to "ragged poverty in Simon Legree fields," summoning the ghost of Stowe's evil slave driver from *Uncle Tom's Cabin*

(96). Yet the chief note sounded here, utterly Kerouac's, is joy itself. "I was adventuring in the crazy American night," Sal says, almost sings (100).

Sal is a writer, but like all good writers, he is mostly a reader. The allusions to other writers and books are endless, as when he begins chapter 14 with a comment on Alain-Fournier's *Le grand Meaulnes*—a wistful novel about a rebellious young man in love, written by a French novelist killed in battle in 1914. In fact Kerouac himself read a good deal in French, and often wrote in French, this being his first language. Mainly, however, Sal "reads" the American landscape, which he often filters through texts, as when he describes the Mississippi and dwells on the old steamboats "with their scrollwork more scrolled and withered by weathers," thus recalling Twain (103). Only a few pages later he alludes to Benjamin Franklin, who "plodded in the oxcart days when he was postmaster" through the "wilderness in the East" (105). This self-consciously literary young man eagerly makes connections and associations; he reads the landscape for its cultural and intellectual content. Always in Kerouac, as in Emerson, "Nature is the symbol of spirit." Natural facts in the landscape are signs of spiritual facts, and one grazes the surface of the world, always aware that one's foot can sink through the crust at any moment into the realm of pure spirit.

Part 2 begins, as did part 1, with Dean. Sal and his aunt have gone to Testament, Virginia, to visit Sal's brother (in the scroll version, the aunt is really his mother, and the person visited is the writer's sister). At his family's home in the South, a Hudson appears, a wonderful car, bearing Dean and Marylou and Ed Dunkel, "a tall, calm, unthinking fellow" (111). (Dunkel was based on Al Hinkle, another of Kerouac's Beat friends.) Sal has got the Christmas spirit and savors the smell of the roasting turkey, but he cannot stay put when his friend Dean wants him on the road again, beside him; indeed, "the bug was on me again, and the bug's name was Dean Moriarty" (115).

Dean has been turning into a mystic of sorts, although these were "the first days of his mysticism, which would lead to the strange, ragged W. C. Fields saintliness of his later days" (121). Dean goes on his first big riff about God here, pronouncing: "God exists without qualms." The free sex angle of the book expands along with the mysticism, a necessary parallel shifting between the erotic and the spiritual aspects of life.

"Marylou began making love to me," Sal confesses, "she said Dean was going to stay with Camille" (125). But the real subject of this part is the search for God through jazz, especially in the form of George Shearing, the legendary jazz pianist. Dean and Sal go to see him in the midst of a "long, mad weekend," and they go into ecstasies over his playing. His chords "rolled out of the piano in great rich showers," Sal recalls (128). Shearing is a man who has what Dean calls "IT," meaning a deep mystical access to truth, an almost occult relationship with the universe.

We soon learn a little more about Dean's mysterious father, "old bum Dean Moriarty the Tinsmith," who is perhaps "riding freights, working as a scullion in the railroad cookshacks, stumbling, downcrashing in wino alley nights, expiring on coal piles, dropping his yellowed teeth one by one in the gutters of the West" (132). He becomes a version of Huck Finn's Pap, though less ominously present. He is the missing father, not unlike Sal's own lost father, or Kerouac's. Sal and Dean are both waifs, Tom and Huck on the road, having to father themselves. (And Dean becomes a brother to Sal, perhaps in reaction to Kerouac's early loss of his only brother in childhood.)

Sal and Dean head west again, loving the "purity of the road" (135). Once again, Sal becomes a latter-day embodiment of the spirit of Walt Whitman, offering beautiful and detailed catalogs of American life. One hears Whitman, for instance, in passages like this, when Sal and Dean view the Mississippi: "On rails we leaned and looked at the great brown father of waters rolling down from mid-America like the torrent of broken souls—bearing Montana logs and Dakota muds and Iowa vales and things that had drowned in Three Forks, where the secret began in ice" (141). A clear echo of T. S. Eliot may be heard in this passage as well, as in "The Dry Salvages," where Eliot calls the Mississippi (the river of his boyhood in St. Louis) "a strong brown god." Twain's *Life on the Mississippi* also lies beneath such writing. Kerouac is a magpie, catching echoes and voices, refracting them, doing his own jazzy riffs on American literature.

In part 2 we finally meet Old Bull Lee, a thinly fictionalized version of William S. Burroughs (1914–97), author of *Naked Lunch* (1959), an impossibly jumbled, eloquent, influential novel that made Burroughs a primary figure in the Beat movement. Lee lives with his wife and two young children. (Young Ray is poetically described as "a little blond child of the rainbow.") Sal's portrait of Lee's family offers an early version of the countercultural families who populated hippie communes in the late 1960s and the '70s (one such community, which thrived well into the 1990s, was called the Rainbow Children of Light, echoing Kerouac). "Their food bill was the lowest in the country," Sal recalls of Lee's family, "they hardly ever ate" (143). This might not have been as pleasant for the children as Sal thought, but he remains enamored of prophetic Old Bull Lee, who delivers memorable zingers, as when he meditates on an economic system in which products self-destruct after a brief while, thus ensuring the need for replacement: "Why, Sal, do you realize the shelves they build these days crack under the weight of knickknacks after six months or generally collapse? Same with houses, same with clothes. These bastards have invented plastics by which they could make houses that last *forever.* And tires. Americans are killing themselves by the millions every year with defective rubber tires that get hot on the road and blow up. They could make tires that never blow up" (149).

Kerouac uses Old Bull to voice his skepticism about American waste and extravagance and the culture of built-in obsolescence. But soon the time comes to get back on the road; "zoom went the car," Sal says, and almost reflexively they were "off again for California" (155).

Some of the most evocative passages in the novel follow, when the drivers move through a southern swamp: "We were surrounded by a great forest of viny trees in which we could almost hear the slither of a million copperheads" (157). Dean and Marylou often make love, leaving Sal by himself. But the charge between Sal and Marylou has not extinguished; in fact, one senses (as Sal later notes) that she is using Sal to try to get closer to Dean, who tends to spiral into madness, pulling away from her. "I'm sad about everything," Marylou tells Sal at last. "Oh damn, I wish Dean wasn't so crazy now" (163). But crazy he is, whirling in his ecstasy of movement, a dervish spinning out of control in ways bound to alienate Sal, despite his patience and adoration.

The trio pushes on, eventually returning to San Francisco "the fabulous white city of San Francisco on her eleven mystic hills with the blue Pacific and its advancing wall of potato-patch fog beyond, and smoke and goldenness in the late afternoon of time" (169). Note the elevation of the rhetoric here, the reaching for significance, for general truth. This isn't just an afternoon that Kerouac talks about, it is "the late afternoon of time." Time itself seems close to running out, giving the novel its apocalyptic aura. Certainly this visit to San Francisco will be short-lived for Sal Paradise, although he comes into close contact with the Beat scene, which features Slim Gaillard, "a tall, thin Negro with big sad eyes" (176). Eager crowds gather in nightclubs to sit at his feet and listen to him on the piano, guitar, and bongo drums. The descriptions of Slim's jazzy improvisations are splendid, here as everywhere in *On the Road*. Nevertheless, before leaving, Sal admits: "What I accomplished by coming to Frisco I don't know" (178).

In the spring of 1949, the third major trip begins. This is part 3 of the novel, and Sal heads west again. "I ran immediately to Dean," he tells us. "I was burning to know what was on his mind and what would happen now, for there was nothing behind me any more, all my bridges were gone and I didn't give a damn about anything at all" (182). Exactly why Sal should feel so lost and fed up isn't made clear. That is simply how he judges his situation. Having cut loose again from home and hearth in New Jersey, he will link his fate with Dean's, at least for a while. In the meantime, Dean has been bouncing between Marylou and Camille, and his level of maturity remains less than wonderful. Nevertheless, he talks to Sal, who is actually a few years older, in the confident tones of a man of considerable wisdom, although what he says is nonsense: "We know life, Sal, we're growing older, each of us, little by little, and are coming to know things." He plays into Sal's need for a connection: "I've always dug your feelings." In a kindly turn, he encourages Sal to "hook up with a real great girl," if he can only find one. He regrets the problems he has had with Marylou and Camille, "these damned women of mine" (187).

Dean is a mess, with an injured thumb, a ragged appearance. "He was wearing a T-shirt, torn pants hanging down his belly, tattered shoes; he had not shaved, his hair was wild and busy, his eyes bloodshot, and that tremendous bandaged thumb stood supported in midair at heart-level" (188). He adopts a goofy grin and seems quite unfocused and unsteady. Dean becomes, in Sal's caps, "the HOLY GOOF" (194).

The best episodes of this visit to San Francisco occur in the jazz clubs, and Kerouac excels in description. At one performance, for example, "the tenorman jumped down from the platform and stood in the crowd, blowing around; his hat was over his eyes; somebody pushed it back for him. He just hauled back and stamped his foot and blew down a hoarse, baughing blast, and drew breath, and raised the horn and blew high, wide, and screaming in the air" (198). Almost breathlessly, the writer competes with the music itself, his syntax looping around the melodies. Jazz—which in its West Coast flowering was largely in the tradition of rhythm and blues, as opposed to the bebop style that flourished in the East—operates in this novel on many levels, but mainly it sets the tone, announcing a fresh generation, one devoted to the primitive blasts of the music, the sense of a soul soaring in free flight. The music is physical, and everyone sweats—musicians as well as listeners. The dance of the beat consumes everyone.

The gang's all here, including Carlo Marx, with his "beady, glittering eyes" and "spindly legs" (201). Sal and his friends inhabit the city almost viscerally, occupying "the great buzzing and vibrating hum of what is really America's most excited city" (205–6). But one cannot survive long at this pitch of frenzy, searching for IT, whatever IT is (mystic union with God, satori or enlightenment, a heightened consciousness). Sal tries repeatedly to understand "the IT of our final excited joy in talking and living to the blank tranced end of all innumerable riotous angelic particulars that had been lurking in our souls all our lives" (209). But, clearly, every time he approaches a verbal equivalent, IT dissolves in a haze of syntax that never quite adds up.

The drive in the old "fag Plymouth" occurs at this stretch of the narrative, taking Sal and Dean back east. They sweet-talk the people at a travel bureau into letting them deliver a 1947 Cadillac limousine to its owner in Chicago, marking another miraculous turn in their luck. A couple of innocent students from a Jesuit school in the East tag along as passengers, but these poor fellows are in for the ride of their life. "Not two miles out of Denver," Sal explains, "the speedometer broke because Dean was pushing well over 100 miles an hour" (226). By the time they get the limo home to its rightful owner, very little will be left unbroken.

Driving eastward, Sal absorbs the landscape. "The kind of utter darkness that falls on a prairie like that is inconceivable to an Easterner," he says. "There were no stars, no moon, no light whatever" (228–29). The writing soars, coasting on a high level, as when they move through Nebraska and the entire state unrolls before Sal: "A hundred and ten miles an hour straight through, an arrow road, sleeping towns, no traffic, and the Union Pacific streamliner falling behind us in the moonlight" (231). With a dreamlike quickness, the towns slip by: Ogallala, Gothenburg, Kearney, Grand Island, Columbus. Sal appears to savor each name as his catalog of towns and vistas unfolds. But it's worth recalling that the war, and whatever experiences Sal may have had, remain just under the surface, breaking through occasionally, as when he recalls: "As a seaman I used to think of the waves rushing beneath the shell of the ship and the bottomless deeps thereunder" (235). A giddy feeling permeates this writing, as if Sal feels lucky to be alive, though he feels guilty as well because he did not die like so many of his cohorts in the war. Survivor's guilt smolders here, agitating these "beat" young men, who risk their lives now by driving at ridiculous speeds, by living at the speed of light. They arrive in Chicago after seventeen frenzied hours, which is "a kind of crazy record" (238).

Now Chicago shimmers before their eyes, bathed in the strange glow of Kerouac's heightened visionary language. Sal grows excited, speaking in ecstatic gulps of prose, especially when he and Dean go "to see the hootchy-kootchy joints and hear the bop" (240). He goes down into these dives to experience amazing jazz performances and reflects on some of the greats, such as Thelonious Monk and Charlie Parker. "Here were the children of the American bop night," he tells us, in one especially lovely phrase (241). At one show, George Shearing reappears and plays "innumerable choruses with amazing chords that mounted higher and higher till the sweat splashed all over the piano and everybody listened in awe and fright" (242–43).

Soon it is time to move on, back to New York, where Dean meets "a big, sexy brunette." Now he wants to get divorced from Camille, who stays behind in San Francisco, pregnant with Dean's second child. There is, of course, no sense of responsibility in Dean. This moral-free environment remains, in its way, quite shocking. The dark side of the counterculture emerges, and Kerouac portrays it honestly. He was, at heart, a good Catholic boy, and he never quite countenanced such irresponsibility, however much it excited him. Nor could he ever come to terms with this contradiction, which is perhaps why he slid into complete disarray in his later years, killing himself with booze.

Part 4 opens with Sal having sold a book. With a little money in his pocket, the itch to travel once again overcomes him: "Whenever spring comes to New York I can't stand the suggestions of the land that come blowing over the river from New Jersey and I've got to go" (249). Sal absolves himself of moral responsibility, as if he has no control over what happens to him. The road beckons, unfolds, becomes an "endless poem" to Sal, who rushes to Denver, where inevitably he hooks up with Dean Moriarty. Who else? "Officially, Sal, this trip is to get a Mexican divorce," Dean explains to Sal, who will accompany him south of the border (262). They head off into the night in a 1937 Ford sedan "with the right-side door unhinged and tied on the frame." Dean has high hopes for this journey. "Man, this will finally take us to IT!" he proclaims (265).

They drive through Texas, at last arriving in Mexico, where you could "almost smell the billion tortillas frying and smoking in the night" (273). Everything seems to change when they cross the river into foreign territory. Even the cops in Mexico seem different, "lazy and tender." Giddily, the travelers trade dollars for pesos, thus magnifying their possibilities, as the exchange rate tilts wildly in their favor. They stuff the big rolls of foreign money into their pockets. "We had finally found the magic land at the end of the road," Sal claims (276). The promised land looms; but it will certainly not be found in Mexico.

At first glance, however, the place looks wonderful. "Everybody's cool," Dean says. And everywhere are "gurls, gurls" (278). There is plenty of marijuana, too. Indeed, they smoke "the biggest bomber anybody ever saw" (282). Soon the girls appear, almost magically, in a dilapidated brothel. Sal paints a wild, nightmarish portrait of a rural whorehouse, where the girls often seem too young for this kind of work. The final bill comes to three hundred pesos, or thirty-six American dollars, "which is a lot of money in any whorehouse," Sal exclaims, showing off his worldliness. "Still we couldn't sober up and didn't want to leave, and though we were all run out we still wanted to hang around with our lovely girls in this strange Arabian paradise we had finally found at the end of the hard, hard road." Dean wants to move on, of course: "So much ahead of us, man, it won't make any difference." Suddenly Sal hears a baby wail and remembers that he is in Mexico, and not "in a pornographic hasheesh daydream in heaven" (289). Reality keeps breaking in.

Everything gets worse for Sal, who gets horribly ill with dysentery.

After becoming delirious, he falls unconscious. When he comes to, Dean is saying goodbye, leaving him alone in Mexico. "I got my divorce from Camille down here and I'm driving back to Inez in New York tonight if the car holds out," he says, as if that explains his selfish behavior. "Gotta get back to my life," he tells his friend (301). Sal merely shrugs, although one senses that he has learned something about Dean. "When I got better I realized what a rat he was, but then I had to understand the impossible complexity of his life, how he had to leave me there, sick, to get on with his wives and woes" (302).

Part 5 takes up less than five pages, being more of a coda than a fresh extension of Sal's journeying. Back in New York City, he and Dean briefly cross paths again; but the Mexican trip, even time itself, has changed everything. Sal still loves Dean, but he cannot trust him. In the last pages of the novel, Sal agrees to attend a Duke Ellington concert on a double date with his old friend Remi Boncoeur. Dean asks for a lift to Fortieth Street, in the Cadillac driven by Remi's bookie; but Remi won't have it. "Absolutely out of the question, Sal!" he says (306). So Sal turns from Dean, waving to him from the back of the Cadillac: a wistful, symbolic parting.

The novel ends on a lyrical note, not unlike the one heard at the end of Fitzgerald's *Great Gatsby*—that sad, forlorn, beautiful note where Fitzgerald's narrator broods on "the old, unknown world" and thinks of Gatsby's yearning for his ideal love, Daisy Buchanan, as he "picked out the green light at the end of Daisy's dock." Gatsby had come close to realizing his dream, and yet "it was already behind him, somewhere back in that vast obscurity beyond the city, where the dark fields of the republic rolled on under the night." But the green light for Sal is Dean Moriarty. He reflects on the coming of old age and death, "the final shore," and says with some ambivalence in the nostalgic last sentence of the novel: "I think of Dean Moriarty, I even think of old Dean Moriarty the father we never found, I think of Dean Moriarty" (307).

Exactly what he thinks of Dean we shall never know. But the fun has gone out of the game for him. The road no longer beckons with quite the same urgency. Perhaps Peter Pan has to grow up now? Who knows? It might be argued that Kerouac never really draws a conclusion. Wisely, I think, he leaves that to the reader.

IV.

MORE THAN ONE GENERATION of readers has found in *On the Road* an appealing mood, an attitude, a way of being in the world. The exuberance of youth shines on every page. Kerouac's hipsters live at breakneck speed, on the edge, in opposition to the mainstream culture of their parents' generation. They become a tribe of sorts, frequenting the jazz clubs, living in ecstasy, through perpetual movement. They refuse to abide by the usual sexual mores. They search for God, even find Him; but they do so not in conventional churches; more like Emerson and Thoreau, they find God in the mountains, in the deserts, on prairies. They also (*unlike* Emerson and Thoreau) appreciate the vitality of city life, especially as lived in New York and San Francisco.

James Dean and Bob Dylan (among other American rebels) are kinsmen of Sal Paradise, with touches of Dean Moriarty in each of them. The Beat Generation gave way, in due course, to the counterculture of the late 1960s and the '70s, and a version of that beat still drums in the ears of young people. The Grateful Dead will never die, as their songs play on, or the impulse in their music finds new voices and rhythms. The road beckons, and so does *On the Road*. This is a novel for seekers, and the world will never lack for these.

Like many Americans of my generation, I came to *On the Road* in the late 1960s, when opposition to mainstream culture peaked, briefly, in reaction to the Vietnam War. The flower children in San Francisco, the free speech movement at Berkeley, the antiwar protests at Columbia, Yale, and around the world, seemed to follow naturally from the Beats, although Kerouac himself, in his last years, refused to acknowledge that the hippies and war protesters had anything to do with him. By this time, he had become a pitiful alcoholic, still living under the sad gaze of his mother. (One of the ironies of Kerouac's life is that he really never managed to cut the apron strings, and that he failed to find anything like spiritual peace or artistic satisfaction. He certainly never found that "paradise within" mentioned above. Sal Paradise was, in so many ways, a fantasy for him.)

On the Road inspired a movement—the countercultural movement—that already had deep roots in American society, going back to Thomas Morton and his Dionysian revelers at Merry Mount. The note of rebellion takes many forms, often orphic, in seekers of religious ecstasy. It inhabits those, like Thoreau and Emerson, who sought a still, small voice in the woods. It was there in Whitman, who sounded his "barbaric yawp" over the rooftops of young America and who embraced everyone he met on the streets of the New World, male and female. It ran through the jazz clubs of the Harlem Renaissance, through the tradition of rhythm and blues, into the bop heroes—Charlie Parker, for example—who inspired Kerouac. The movement continued through many writers of the postwar era, from the Beats and Norman O. Brown (author of *Love's Body,* a philosophical meditation that draws on the mysticism of William Blake and the "polymorphous perversity" of Freud) to Dylan, and to any number of writers, including Thomas Pynchon, Robert Stone, and Denis Johnson.

One can hardly deny the aggressively male quality of Kerouac's imagination, which has sometimes offended or excluded female readers. Tom and Huck are boys, of course, and so are Sal and Dean. This is a "buddy" book, a road novel in the classic mold. There is a direct line from *On the Road* to films such as *Easy Rider.* And yet one can't deny that the women in this novel have an energy of their own. Terry, the young Mexican girl who links up with Sal for a wild, brief fling, willingly and eagerly plays her role in the sexual dance, as do Dean's women, who seem as possessed by the road as Dean and Sal and who swing to the beat. Nevertheless, there remains a defiantly male swagger in Kerouac's prose, and one hears its echoes in writers from Norman Mailer to Robert Stone, even as 1950s "hipster" gave way to 1960s "hippie." The feminist movement didn't really find its true voice until the early 1970s, in such books as *Fear of Flying* (1973) by Erica Jong and in feminist writers such as Kate Millett, Robin Morgan, and Gloria Steinem.

Mainly, *On the Road* is about the search for IT. This search never ends, as it must not. It's the search for enlightenment, for heightened consciousness, for God, for whatever (as the theologian Paul Tillich put it) is one's "ultimate concern." The Beat movement was about the discovery of self, and Kerouac's novel is a form of spiritual reportage, an account of "front[ing] only the essential facts of life," as Thoreau put it. It's about encounters with the sacred, in music and the arts, and about con-

frontation with the American landscape. It's about the quest for a promised land, that far, impossible shore where liberty and equality flourish
and where every vote counts. But like the mythical land of Canaan, it
remains an elusive goal, always just beyond one's grasp, never fully occupied. It's the goal, perhaps, but—as we learn from *On the Road*—the
going may well be more important than actually getting there.

THE FEMININE MYSTIQUE

BETTY FRIEDAN

"I found *The Feminine Mystique* absorbingly interesting, pertinent, relevant to my own problems and those of every woman I know, and far and away more real, truer and more moving than Simone de Beauvoir's *The Second Sex*. Betty Friedan has both grasp and passion—and has put her finger on the inner wound we all carry around. But to name the suffering is relatively easy. What Mrs. Friedan has done is to show both cause and cure. The book should be read by every anxious woman in the country, and all of us are troubled about ourselves and where we belong. She has done a great service in underlining the fact that *before* we are women, we are human beings."

—*Virgilia Peterson*

THIRTEEN

The Feminine Mystique

I.

MANY BOOKS have played a role in the women's movement, but few had the shock effect of Betty Friedan's *The Feminine Mystique* (1963), which almost single-handedly ignited a revolutionary phase that has deeply affected the lives of countless American women and men. Acknowledged by many as a book that "paved the way for the contemporary feminist movement," as one critic writes, it changed our culture in ways difficult to overstate.[1] It prompted a wave of new thinking about sexual politics that led, ultimately, to the advances of feminism that have become so much a part of modern lives. As Alvin Toffler observed, with perhaps a touch of overstatement, this was a book "that pulled the trigger on history."[2]

Social revolutions come in waves, and the movement that Friedan helped to start is usually known as second-wave feminism, referring to a shift that occurred in the 1960s, when women (such as those surveyed by Friedan, who were largely middle-class housewives) began to feel frustration with being relegated to the kitchen and the bedroom. The original American feminists (the first wave) were the suffragettes, including Elizabeth Cady Stanton (1815–1902) and Susan B. Anthony (1820–1906)—women who took up the cause for the rights of women in

the United States. The Seneca Falls Convention (1848) marks the starting point for the women's movement on these shores, and was also attended by Frederick Douglass, who hoped to join the abolitionist cause
to women's rights. This movement culminated, in effect, with the ratification of the Nineteenth Amendment to the U.S. Constitution, which
gave women the right to vote. (Interestingly, women were excluded
from the Fourteenth and Fifteenth amendments, the post–Civil War revisions of the Constitution that enfranchised male ex-slaves.)

Women acquired voting rights in 1920, but that was about it. Their
place was still in the home, with few exceptions; the only professional
roles for women were in the schools and hospitals, as teachers and
nurses, and these jobs were usually given to unmarried women, who
had to support themselves. Not until World War II did women burst
into the workforce en masse, as they were desperately needed in the
weapons industry. Rosie the Riveter was the new model, the can-do
woman who could help to build warships and tanks, bombers and ar-
tillery. When the men came home from the front, they required jobs
and a place in society; women were simply pushed back into the home.
It was this situation that grabbed the attention of Betty Friedan and her
cohorts from Smith College, whom she surveyed in the 1950s. In an introduction to her book written ten years after its first publication, she recalls: "In 1957, getting strangely bored with writing articles about breast
feeding and the like for *Redbook* and the *Ladies' Home Journal,* I put an
unconscionable amount of time into a questionnaire for my fellow
Smith graduates of the class of 1942, thinking I was going to disprove
the current notion that education had fitted us ill for our role as
women."[3] The results shocked her, as a huge percentage of respondents
regretted getting married soon after graduation and most believed their
high-powered education had been largely wasted. The results of this
survey set in motion the thinking that led to *The Feminine Mystique.*

A tidal wave—the so-called second wave of feminism—had been
slowly building since the war, and its first crest came in 1961, when John
F. Kennedy issued an executive order to create the Presidential Commission on the Status of Women, headed by Eleanor Roosevelt. The
Civil Rights Act of 1964 gave women a further boost as Title VII of that
measure made it illegal to discriminate against people on the basis of
race, religion, ethnic origin, or sex. (The part about sex was added as a

late measure, and almost sank the boat.) The Equal Employment Opportunity Commission was created to bolster this act, but there was reluctance on the part of many on the commission to enforce the part that dealt with women. In 1966, NOW (National Organization for Women) was founded, with Betty Friedan as its outspoken and controversial president. In the early 1970s, Title IX was passed, forbidding schools to favor boys over girls in sports: a huge step forward for women, and one that has had far-reaching effects. The Supreme Court delivered its landmark decision *Roe v. Wade* in 1973, thereby legalizing abortion in all fifty states, bringing the second wave to a crest of sorts.

The question remains: Did Betty Friedan ride a wave already building, or did she provide the earthquake that set the wave in motion? In the end it hardly matters. What seems true beyond doubt is that Friedan's book shifted the minds of countless women, drawing attention to the uncomfortable circumstances of their lives, forcing them to consider alternatives. This is one of those extremely rare books that helped to launch a social movement, one that harked back to the campaigns for women's suffrage in the nineteenth and early twentieth centuries while anticipating the sweeping changes that would be brought on by feminism in the 1980s and '90s, a revolution still in motion. No historian of the American feminist movement, in its various phases, can step around *The Feminine Mystique*. It is one of those books that somehow "break through the thought barriers of time and reverberate for decades," as one of Friedan's biographers, Judith Hennessee, has observed.[4]

II.

BETTY FRIEDAN (1921–2006) was a feisty iconoclast, born in Peoria, Illinois, less than six months after the ratification of the Nineteenth Amendment. She was the daughter of a Jewish immigrant from Russia (Harry Goldstein) who owned a successful jewelry store, which he opened in 1908. Her mother, Miriam (Horwitz) Goldstein, was a doctor's daughter; well educated, she edited the woman's page at a local newspaper, although she abandoned this work to become a mother and housewife. In later life, Friedan believed that her mother's imperious nature masked a certain bitterness that came from her self-sacrifice in the decision to abandon her professional career.

Smart and sassy, Friedan did not go down well in Peoria, Illinois, at least among her schoolmates. (Anti-Semitism played a role in this, almost certainly.) Hennessee describes her childhood as hampered by certain physical disadvantages as well: "Life was a struggle at first. Betty was a sickly child. She had bow legs and had to wear iron braces for three years. Bronchitis afflicted her every winter, as did various lung problems that later developed into asthma. She could hardly see out of one eye and had to wear glasses."[5] And so forth. Young Bettye (her parents spelled the name in this odd, affected way) suffered a good deal.

But she spread her wings at Smith, an elite women's college in Massachusetts, where she changed the spelling of her name to Betty: an act of normalization on her part. She loved college and shone there brightly, graduating summa cum laude. Graduate school followed at the University of California in Berkeley, where she had a fellowship in psychology and studied with Erik Erikson, the famous developmental psychologist, among others. She dated a young physicist and turned down a prestigious second fellowship at his urging, much to her later regret. She often mentioned this fact in interviews, although she rarely talked about her connections to various progressive movements while in graduate school—a point that would later stir some passion among her critics, who accused her of being a fellow traveler among socialists and labor activists.

Friedan broke up with the physicist and soon moved (after a spell in Peoria) to Greenwich Village, where she worked as an editor for a news service connected to labor activism. To be sure, she associated with a range of people who worked for social justice, and many of them would have called themselves socialists if not Communists. Her world was largely the world of labor activists, and this contributed to her self-image as a person who could change things by persistent effort. The activist side of her life continued until the end, as she was always ready to begin or join another committee, sign a petition, support a cause, or attend a protest march.

At twenty-six, she married Carl Friedan, a war veteran who became a theater director and later shifted to a career in advertising when he got married. As Hennessee writes: "Even after they decided to marry, the omens were not encouraging. There was always fighting going on, like a persistent, low-grade infection."[6] The marriage would end in 1969; nevertheless, Betty and Carl persevered in the marriage and had three children in relatively quick succession. They moved to a house in the suburbs of New York, where Friedan settled, somewhat unhappily, into the role of a housewife. With considerable skill and care, she raised her children and did the housework and cooking without a great deal of help. She also worked as a journalist, writing for popular women's magazines, as a way of picking up extra money and having a place for herself outside the home. It was in the mid-1950s that she began to think about the role of educated women and what had happened to them after the war. The results of her questionnaire surprised her, and she tried several times to get one of the women's magazines to publish them. But editors were blinded by "the feminine mystique," as Friedan described the postwar vision of women as homemakers, mothers, and housewives. They believed that readers of magazines like *Redbook* and *Ladies' Home Journal* would never accept her disruptive ideas.

Betty Friedan was hardly the first person after the war to think about women in a fresh way. *The Second Sex* by Simone de Beauvoir represents the foundational work of second-wave feminism. (It was published in 1949 in French, in 1953 in English.) This wide-ranging study looks at women in a radical way, examining how they have been treated as "other" for centuries, distinguishing between "sex" and "gender," asking many of the same questions that Friedan asked. *The Feminine Mystique,* on the other hand, spoke to the middle-class American housewife in ways that would have seemed remote to Simone de Beauvoir, who lived with but never married Jean-Paul Sartre and associated with Parisian intellectuals. Some of Friedan's critics wished she had referred specifically to *The Second Sex* as an influence, but she only mentions it in passing. In a sense, her book was more polemic than scholarly study. It was meant to change the minds of her readers.

When she finally got a contract for the book from Norton, with a modest advance of $3,000, she was already thirty-seven years old; her editor, George Brockway, gave her a year to finish the book.[7] This tight schedule meant focusing intensely on the project—not an easy task with children to raise and a husband to look after. Three or four days a week she went into the city, working at the New York Public Library, often staying up late at night to write, when the house grew quiet. The book came slowly, and it was five years before it was actually published. But the rest is history. It flew off the shelves, selling 300,000 copies within the first year. Translations into thirteen languages followed, and it sold well abroad, too, making Friedan a widely known figure among feminists. "Friedan had touched women like no other author before," says Lisa Frederiksen Bohannon.[8] By 1966, the book had sold over 3 million copies.

Having published *The Feminine Mystique*, Friedan stepped forward to take a leading role in the women's movement, as founder of NOW, which called for an end to discrimination against women in the workplace, an end to caps on the number of women who could be admitted to graduate schools, a curtailment of distorted images of women in the media, and the expansion of opportunities for women everywhere. In 1969, the year of her divorce from Carl, she played a part in the founding of NARAL (National Association for the Repeal of Abortion Laws). In 1970, although at odds with some of the younger activists in the women's movement (who found her abrasive and controlling), she led a widely publicized march down Fifth Avenue in New York, an action called the Women's Strike for Equality. Behind the New York Public Library, in Bryant Park, she gave a passionate speech, joining hands with other feminist icons, including Bella Abzug, Gloria Steinem, and Kate Millett, author of *Sexual Politics* (1970), a critical study of patriarcy in Western society and literature.

Second-wave feminism came into its own in the 1970s; reaching an intellectual peak with *Of Woman Born: Motherhood as Experience and Institution* (1976) by Adrienne Rich.[9] This was groundbreaking work, by one of America's finest poets, and it explored the huge gap between the actual experience of mothering and the theories and descriptions of motherhood imposed by the patriarchal culture. As Rich suggests, men seized on the Madonna myth, converting this energy into a force that reinforced male power. That is, if you place a woman on a pedestal and idealize her as mother or virgin bride, she remains beyond criticism but also beyond reach. Certainly she does not go to work, join the army, make love, swear at the kids, or expect to run the board of directors, let alone sit in the White House. This myth continues to exert a subtle force. Even as women attempt to break the glass ceiling in the boardroom and within the corridors of political power, doubts linger (in the minds of some) about women in positions of authority. It is not easy to negotiate the role of mother and CEO or mother and senator. Sexist stereotypes persist and are difficult to break down. The feminist movement pushes against the various forms of patriarchy, as one historian writes; using a geological metaphor, she suggests that feminism itself is a "fluid form of discontent that repeatedly presses against . . . weak spots in the sedimented layers of a patriarchal crust."[10]

In the 1980s the so-called third wave of feminism began, with writers and thinkers such as Bell Hooks, Gloria Anzaldúa, Chela Sandoval, and Maxine Hong Kingston, who share a certain irreverent approach, viewing the feminist cause from various ethnic or sexual (perhaps lesbian or bisexual) viewpoints.[11] To a degree, the pop musician Madonna signaled the arrival of this wave, with her insistence on both female sexuality and cultural power. The third wave is complex, comprising a swirl of often contradictory ideas that challenge the essentialist ideas of the second wave, in which writers like Friedan simply assumed they understood what a woman was, and wasn't. In effect, the third wave reconsiders feminism from the standpoints of class and gender as well as ethnic identities. To them, Betty Friedan seems naive in her ideas about gender, focusing too obsessively on the upper-middle classes without a full understanding of the impact of class on her arguments. In truth, Friedan never found it easy to accept lesbian activism. As Hennessee puts it: "If Betty saw the parallel between the position of women in society and the position of lesbians in the movement (and of Jews in Peoria), she gave no indication. The issue would worry her for years, until the first American convocation of women—in Houston in 1977—when she would make her separate peace with them."[12]

The third wave has taken feminism in unexpected directions. An important early anthology of essays by younger feminists was *To Be Real: Telling the Truth and Changing the Face of Feminism,* edited by Rebecca Walker (not coincidentally, perhaps, the daughter of Alice Walker, who wrote *The Color Purple*).[13] Another was *Manifesta: Young Women, Feminism, and the Future,* edited by Jennifer Baumgardner and Amy Richards.[14] What both of these anthologies, and others like them, suggest is that feminist concerns have evolved in unexpected but interesting ways from the time of Friedan, who would never have understood or approved of so-called girlie culture, or films like *Buffy the Vam-pire Slayer* (1992) (the TV series ran from 1997 to 2003). It may, in fact, be true that the "girlie" turn, with its ironic use of lipstick and reclaim-ing of words like "slut" and "bitch," signals a weird retrenchment, an inadvertent embracing of the feminine mystique. Yet, as June Hannam says in *Feminism* (2007), "the many differences between women are bound to lead a variety of feminisms, but this does not have to prevent women from working collectively."[15]

Friedan and her cohorts in the second wave shuddered when they saw women stuck at home, with young children, alone at PTA meet-ings, or wandering the aisles of supermarkets or malls with a blank stare on their faces. They felt the waste of such expensive educations, and of-ten longed for the empowerment of the workplace, for the responsibili-ties of leadership, for creative activity. The third wavers, so to speak, hope to continue to fight for the rights of women, but they want to do so without relinquishing aspects of their sexuality, including the repro-ductive function. They want it all, as they should: children, sex, a house, a career, and respect.

In the early twenty-first century, the feminist movement is alive and well, riding any number of waves, and this has something to do with pi-oneers such as Betty Friedan, a massive figure in her day and someone whose legacy as a writer we must continue to honor as well as decon-struct.

III.

FRIEDAN BEGINS WITH "The Problem That Has No Name," sub-versively echoing Lord Alfred Douglas on his homoerotic love for Oscar Wilde. The problem that she isolates is the yearning of women for something more than the pleasures of being a housewife and stay-at-home mother. "As she made the beds, shopped for groceries, matched slipcover material, ate peanut butter sandwiches with her children, chauffeured Cub Scouts and Brownies, lay beside her husband at night," these bored middle-class women in the 1950s wondered: "Is this all?" (15).

The average age of marriage had dropped to twenty by the end of the 1950s, says Friedan, whose statistics throughout *The Feminine Mystique* have been challenged by scholars in recent years, although her points generally hold true, even when the numbers are not exact.[16] She argues that after World War II, the "mystique of feminine fulfillment became the cherished and self-perpetuating core of contemporary American culture" (18). In the media, an image of the benevolent housewife who kissed her husband goodbye in the morning and saw her children off to school had become iconic. One can easily call to mind a vision of Betty Crocker: the white middle-class mother, at home at the stove, apron clad, smiling.

But housewives had lost their smiles. "I feel empty," said many women to Friedan. These were the original Desperate Housewives, and their problem grew to a point where, by 1960, the women's magazines themselves had begun to report that something was amiss. Children were being ferried to schools over long distances, absorbing many hours in a mother's day. The men who came to repair the washing machine or dryer or toaster or television were incompetent. The PTA meetings lasted too long. Dissatisfaction was recognized at the time, with major articles in the periodicals of record, including a substantial piece in *Newsweek* (March 7, 1960) that considered the problem in a comprehensive and sympathetic way. "A good education," says the writer in *Newsweek*, "has given this paragon among women an understanding of the value of everything except for her own worth."

Friedan contemplates the image of "the happy housewife," reporting on the table of contents for *McCall's* (July 1960), one of the most popular magazines for women. One shudders to see what was put forward as a "solution" to the unhappiness of women. There was, for example, a short story about an uneducated young woman who won the hand of a college boy, stealing him from a college girl. (The underlying message was: Don't think those fancy girls have it over *you*!) There were six pages of photographs showing women in sexy maternity clothes. The ubiquitous article on how to lose weight appeared. As a sign of the times, there was even an article about how to find a second husband. For the most part, the image of the housewife was that of the frivolous woman, besotted with clothes and children, eager to please her husband in bed as well as in the kitchen. "Fulfillment as a woman had only one definition for American women after 1949," says Friedan, "the housewife-mother" (44).

Friedan surveys the fiction in these glossy women's magazines—romantic stories by writers we have blessedly forgotten—and finds the work as ridiculous as it surely was. She concludes: "The feminine mystique is so powerful that women grow up no longer knowing that they have desires and capacities the mystique forbids" (68). So what gave the mystique its astonishing power to repress millions? In the powerful third chapter, Friedan opens with a recollection of how she gave up her graduate school fellowship for the sake of love, unable to look beyond the dream of romance.

Having made this confession—and thus putting herself on an equal footing with her readership—Friedan goes on to interview a number of students currently in college. She finds them troubled by their situation, afraid to look at their own circumstances too closely. "I don't want to be interested in a career I'll have to give up," says one girl, a college junior from South Carolina (74). Friedan recalls that her own generation of college women hoped for interesting careers, being aware that their mothers had been unhappy during the years of the Great Depression. Yet they were unable to capitalize on this knowledge. More young women than ever before had access to higher education by the 1950s, so why didn't this lead to fulfillment? How had the horizons of these women been narrowed to such an extent? Why could they not look beyond their twentieth birthday, as she found they could not? "The search for identity of the young man who can't go home again has always been a major theme of American writers," Friedan notes (78). Why, then, couldn't young women acknowledge a similar crisis of identity?

In her fourth chapter, Friedan returns to the suffragettes, who (in the wake of Seneca Falls) were able to summon the strength and will to accomplish what they did. For them, the right to vote provided a clear goal. And yet, after 1920, what was left? Movements tend to coalesce around specific goals, and these grew harder to nail down. Some women felt the work had already been done. Almost inadvertently, they slipped back into the home, out of sight. Not surprisingly, the image of the early suffragettes suffered, as these "dead feminists" became caricatures of "man-eating" women who threatened male identity.

Perhaps too easily, Friedan points to Sigmund Freud as one of the originators of the problem of the feminine mystique. "It is a Freudian idea, hardened into apparent fact, that has trapped so many American women today," she asserts (103). She refers to the notion of "penis envy," a tendency that Freud observed in women in Vienna in the late nineteenth century. However fragile this theory may be, there can be no doubt that men feared the envy of women, and so wished to keep them out of the workplace. Although trained in psychology, Friedan writes without special insight about Freud and his theories, reducing many of his key ideas to biographical quirks, as when she compares him to "the puritanical old maid who sees sex everywhere," regarding him as a man whose own "mental bisexuality" confused him (111). To her credit, she quotes at length from Ernest Jones, Freud's translator and biographer, who rightly portrayed Freud as a creature of his era, locked into the patriarchal system. "There is little doubt that Freud found the psychology of women more enigmatic than that of men," Jones had said.

To be sure, Freud wrote before the modern developments of ego psychology and related fields. Sex is only one aspect of life, and the need to grow and change is multifaceted and powerful—it surely does not cease with the end of adolescence. Yet Friedan's book was written at a time when Freud still held massive sway in psychological circles, well before other schools of thought had fully begun to revise (and even contradict) his theories. (Psychologists now consider Freud a literary figure more than a scientific one, although his ideas have had immeasurable influence in the field. He remains a touchstone of incomparable value.)

Friedan's intelligence beams through chapter 6, where she contemplates the fact that the social sciences, which should have liberated women from old ideas and functions, actually worked to freeze women in place in the twentieth century. She took dead aim at the "functionalist" heresy that had swept the social sciences. In particular, she examines the thinking of Margaret Mead, the anthropologist who had studied primitive societies in *Coming of Age in Samoa* (1928) and other books. What Friedan found in Mead was a sense of "the infinite variety of sexual patterns and the enormous plasticity of human nature" (136). Yet what readers and other social scientists derived from Mead's work was a "glorification of women in the female role—as defined by their sexual biological function" (137). Once again, anatomy became destiny—

exactly what had landed women in their uncomfortable position in the first place. Friedan interrogates the reductive Freudianism of Mead's approach, noting that Mead associated the penis with assertive and creative aspects of civilization as she linked the uterus with passive forms of creativity (139). In the primitive societies Mead studied, women earned respect just for playing the role of reproductive mother; in the United States of the twentieth century, no such esteem attached to women simply because of their reproductive powers. The biological argument could no longer obtain, as women became educated and lived well beyond the moment of their sexual roles as child bearers and mothers of children. Friedan points out that Mead herself worried about this, yet her work implicitly reinforced the functionalist approach.

Friedan now turns to the educational system, which in the postwar era was decidedly male. (My own students often gaze in disbelief when I tell them that, in the 1960s and early '70s, I went through nine years of college and graduate school without encountering even *one* female professor.) She says that female scholars who persevered in graduate school, acquiring graduate degrees, were deeply suspect. Boys were expected "to achieve personal autonomy," but girls were not (165). Girls were supposed to find a husband as early as possible; indeed, education itself was often seen as a bar to getting a husband. Friedan could find relatively few exceptions to this sad state of affairs, even within elite women's colleges.

Conformity ruled everywhere, as Friedan observes with distaste. Like Thoreau, she scorns regimentation, especially as it worked so harshly against the cause of women, undermining their sense of agency. She does not condemn the social sciences as the direct cause of conformity, but she does take aim, as before, at functionalism, which in her view has twisted thinking in fields such as psychology, anthropology, and sociology. Friedan was, of course, not the only one to deride the conformist pressures of the American educational system. Paul Goodman's *Growing Up Absurd* (1960), a shrewd, innovative book on the problems inherent in American schools, had already unearthed many of the issues that Friedan discusses. Yet Friedan puts the choices before young women succinctly. They must choose between "adjustment, conformity, avoidance of conflict," on the one hand, and "individuality, human identity, education in the truest sense," on the other (175).

What caused this crisis of identity among American women?

Friedan adopts a wider perspective in chapter 8, noting effects of the Depression, the war, the dropping of atom bombs, and the deep loneliness and dislocation caused by these catastrophic events. Against the "cold immensity" of history, men and women sought "the comforting reality of home and children." "We were all vulnerable, homesick, lonely, frightened," she recalls, wisely including herself (182). A relentless urge to find stability by whatever means had overcome men and women alike after the war. The baby boom was itself a response to this crisis, an uncontrolled explosion of the nesting instinct.

But Friedan's survey of the culture often seems cursory and reductive. She hurls contempt at the various arts of the day, for example, and sees Abstract Expressionism in painting as an attempt to step around meaning itself. She attacks the theater of the absurd for its apparent meaninglessness and takes swipes at Norman Mailer, the Beats, Tennessee Williams, and others, detecting in their work an evasion of sexual politics (*The Feminine Mystique* is very much about the politics of sex). She concludes this phase of her argument by suggesting "the American woman made her mistaken choice. She ran back home again to live by sex alone, trading in her individuality for security" (204). Her husband, as it were, followed her into the house, and together they shut the door to the outside world, living in the myth of the feminine mystique.

In "The Sexual Sell," Friedan reveals her progressive bias, although she may be right in saying that the forces of industry joined to "sell" the idea of the feminine mystique. If fulfillment for a woman occurred within the home, there must be material acquisitions to assist in this process. Sterling silver, for example, became a coveted item, as did fine bone china and other luxury goods. The fur industry went so far as to explain to its salesmen that they must somehow "begin to create the feeling that fur is a necessity" (222). Admen tried to "put the libido back into advertising" (227). With disgust, Friedan concludes that only a sick society would reduce human beings to "housewives" who make a "thing-ridden house" an end in itself (232). This was a form of spiritual bankruptcy. (One has to recall here that Friedan's husband, Carl, was now working for an advertisement agency, and this may account for the negative feeling that animates this part of the book.)

In the caustic tenth chapter, Friedan examines the daily work of the

housewife, finding much of it meaningless. With a caustic edge she
notes that millions of women each day passed the bulk of their time "at
work an eight-year-old could do" (256). This was indeed a dismal state
of affairs, although nowadays some overworked and exhausted women
look back with a certain misplaced nostalgia on housework of the kind
Friedan describes. She says that many men also found themselves doing
work that did not satisfy their emotional or spiritual needs, and that it
left them feeling "vacant" and desperate to escape through such avenues
as "television, tranquilizers, alcohol, sex" (252). Friedan, as it were, had
mostly interviewed women among the upper fringes of middle-class society, which necessarily skewed her conclusions. "To do the work that
you are capable of doing is the mark of maturity," she states, axiomati-
cally (253). But it was not easy to find fulfilling jobs if you were not from
a certain class and educated. This was true in Friedan's day and remains so.

In "The Sex-Seekers," Friedan suggests that "sex in the America of
the feminine mystique is becoming a strangely joyless national compul-
sion, if not a contemptuous mockery" (261). Her bored housewives
looked around for erotic kicks, and found little to excite them. Their
husbands were lousy in bed, so they sought lovers elsewhere; yet even
these illicit lovers gave no lasting satisfaction. Friedan writes: "From
1950 to 1960 the interest of men in the details of intercourse paled before
the avidity of women" (263). How can she know this? Perhaps she had
never met a man like Dean Moriarty in *On the Road*. She derides the two
Kinsey reports, of 1948 and 1953, which reduced sexual activity to its
most basic level, that of physiology. "What the Kinsey investigators reported and the way they reported it," she says, "no less than the sex-
glutted novels, magazines, plays and novels, were all symptoms of the
increasing depersonalization, immaturity, joylessness and spurious
senselessness of our sexual overpreoccupation" (263). A certain puritanical streak shows through such pronouncements, but a good deal of
truth underlies the statement. Sex is more than mere hydraulics.

Friedan reveals little understanding of male homosexuals, whom she
describes as "Peter Pans, forever childlike, afraid of age, grasping at
youth in their continual search for reassurance in some sexual magic"
(275). She quickly turns to Freud for explanations of homosexual behavior, and this goes nowhere. Freud wrote: "In all the cases examined

we have ascertained that the later inverts go through in their childhood a phase of very intense but short-lived fixation on the woman (usually the mother) and after overcoming it, they identify themselves with the woman and take themselves as the sexual object; that is, proceeding on a narcissistic basis, they look for young men resembling themselves in persons whom they wish to love as their mother loved them."[17]

Such thinking has long since been dismissed as reductive. Overall, it seems odd that Friedan castigates Freud when it reinforces her argument but uses him uncritically when it suits her needs. In this case, she felt able to blame homosexuality on the fact that mothers, being frustrated in their own careers, took to living vicariously through their sons.

Friedan subsequently addresses the "progressive dehumanization" of women that follows from their reduced role in the world. Without a sense of agency, they flounder, walk through life as if in a daydream, seek thrills where and when they can. They develop a "symbiotic" relationship with their children, living through them. Needless to say, "the child is virtually destroyed in the process" (290). Neglecting their own growth, these suburban housewives caught in the feminine mystique pay a huge emotional price. From the moment they assume their duties as housewives, they no longer live with "the zest, the enjoyment, the sense of purpose that is characteristic of true human health" (293). Any number of ailments follow as the night the day from their state of heightened anxiety, including heart attacks, ulcers, and fatigue.

But illness is only part of it. A sense of forfeited selfhood afflicts the despondent housewife. In the early 1960s, psychologists talked increasingly about emotional or spiritual growth as a human need that must be satisfied. Abraham Maslow, Rollo May, and others wrote about the need for self-realization, and Friedan—trained in psychology at Berkeley— was keenly aware of this thinking. For years, psychologists believed that well-adjusted people managed to fit themselves to their environment. Now that idea seemed less plausible. If the environment itself was skewed in ways that retarded development and fulfillment, how could one possibly expect a "cure" by adjusting individuals to fit their surroundings? This was, after all, the Age of Anxiety, as W. H. Auden described it in a postwar volume of poems by that title. Anxiety, as Friedan notes, comes from the gap between yearning and fulfillment.

Friedan's thirteenth chapter reads like a primer of contemporary psychology, and it remains a useful synthesis. Maslow, in particular, gets a good deal of attention. A fresh and fine thinker, he began to study women during the Depression, looking at a group of well-educated women in their twenties, most of whom were Protestant, white, and married. He discovered that the more "dominant" the woman, the greater her satisfaction in sexual activity. Being secure in herself, fulfilled by her work, she was able to "submit" to the sexual act more freely. It struck Friedan that this study was conducted before the onset of the feminine mystique, as she describes it. For these strong women—educated, well-adjusted—no conflict existed between self-realization and love. They had it all, so to speak. Friedan wonders: "Would a new Kinsey study find the young wives who are products of the feminine mystique enjoying even less sexual fulfillment than their more emancipated, more independent, more educated, more grownup-when-married forebears?" (331).

Erik Erikson had famously described an "identity crisis" in men, tracing this problem to the lack of creative work. As Friedan says, for most of human history, men had to work in order to live, producing food and shelter for themselves and their families. But the situation had grown more complex in the industrial age, for instance, when men were reduced to machines; they saw only a part of the process, as products were formed on the assembly line. They became integers in a larger formula of production. In the postindustrial age, the connection between "work" and "product" has become even less calculable, and so alienation arises. Friedan has an intuitive grasp of this situation, describing the anxieties that follow from unsatisfying work. She says that women without creative outlets could never feel satisfied with their lives, or fulfilled in a wider sense.

Friedan alludes to Olive Schreiner, the South African writer and activist, who warned at the turn of the twentieth century that the lives of women would deteriorate as the quality of their work diminished. If women did not win their full share of "honored and useful work," they would become parasitical, even pathetic. The children of these women, male and female, would lose their purchase on reality. Schreiner and the early feminists understood that women needed to participate fully in society; but their granddaughters, says Friedan, chose to waste their educations and to neglect their social responsibilities (335). She puts it bluntly: "The feminine mystique has succeeded in burying millions of American women alive" (336). Her book now becomes a rallying cry, a summons to action.

In her final chapter, she admits that merely facing a problem does not solve it. The first step is to see that housework is not a career but something that must simply be done, gotten out of the way. The next thing was to understand the sexual mystique and the "marriage trap." Friedan wants to put women in a position "requiring initiative, leadership and responsibility" (347). She dismisses the idea of doing creative work at home—painting, sculpting, writing. This is "one of the semi-delusions of the feminine mystique" (350). According to Friedan, a married woman cannot do genuinely creative work at home, given the demands of children and housework. A "no-nonsense nine-to-five job" is easier for a woman to arrange, she says. The job creates a hard line between work and home. "A woman must say 'no' to the feminine mystique very clearly indeed to sustain the discipline and effort that any professional commitment requires," she insists (351).

As might be expected, many other roadblocks to liberation exist. Friedan contemplates the difficulties that arise from religious traditions, for instance, citing notions that have hardened into prejudice. She also considers the resistance that husbands often present. Sometimes they want "an ever-present mother," and their wife takes on this role. There is the added problem of hostility from other housewives. A woman who lives vicariously through her husband and children may resent the spectacle of someone with a life of her own. This hostility can mask envy, Friedan says, and seems to speak from experience. Nevertheless, as she argues, a woman has no choice; she must move on, embracing her freedom. Yet a woman "moving on" should also prepare for, and accept, a "sense of loss" (355). Old routines and habits will fall away. A fresh relationship with her husband must be forged. The children may feel abandoned. Friedan is quite good in the way she summons most objections, roadblocks, and potential problems that face the woman who wants to change her life. This is, after all, a book designed to get women to create change, to make it happen.

Stepping beyond this, Friedan confronts educators, exhorting them to "see to it that women make a lifetime commitment" to some field of knowledge, to serious work that will make an impact on society at large, beyond the family circle. She asks them to reject the feminine mystique and everything that it forces people to assume about what a woman will do after college. In keeping with her activist past, she even calls for a national plan for women along the lines of the GI Bill, which educated so many returning veterans after the war; this bill would exist "for women who seriously want to continue or resume their education" (370).

Toward the end of her provocative book, Friedan steps back, taking a deep breath, offering a summary judgment, a gem of wisdom: "In the light of woman's long battle for emancipation, the recent sexual counterrevolution in America has been perhaps a final crisis, a strange breath-holding interval before the larva breaks out of the shell into maturity" (377). That is, women had effectively put themselves on ice for a decade or more. They would soon understand this and break free. With hindsight, this idea seems prophetic, as the sexual liberation of the late 1960s led (in zigzag ways) to the women's liberation movement, then to the continuing feminist revolution. The second wave gave way to the third, with its many sides. Friedan did not, of course, know what direction history would take; but she argues persuasively that "the time is at hand" for women to realize their intrinsic power, to grow to their full human potential. These were invigorating words, and her audience responded, in little and large ways.

IV.

THE LANDSCAPE of sexual politics shifted dramatically in the years after *The Feminine Mystique*. Friedan certainly did not create the feminist revolution by herself, as some of her more enthusiastic boosters have suggested. Rather, her work boosted a revolution already in progress—a movement in its initial stages when her book appeared. One can easily guess that many of her readers felt a sincere gratitude for the ways she framed the picture of their lives and gave words to feelings. The idea of a feminine mystique was catchy, and it worked well to explain what had happened in the immediate postwar era, as women who had been in the workplace found themselves confined to the home. Indeed, a subtle publicity campaign had been mounted to make them feel good about their confinement. But they were often not happy with their lives.

As might be expected, there was resistance to Friedan's ideas, and this took many forms. In some religious quarters, especially on the Christian right, her ideas were dismissed out of hand. This rejection took on a consolidated shape in Mary Kassian's *Feminist Mistake*—a revision of an earlier book of hers that appeared in 1992. Kassian argued on largely biblical grounds that Christianity and feminism were incompatible and that gender equality went against God's plan. Kassian takes dead aim at *The Feminine Mystique* and the identification of what Friedan famously referred to as "the problem that has no name," suggesting that she, like Simone de Beauvoir, falsely identified patriarchy as the source of this problem: "According to feminists, patriarchy was the power of men that oppressed women and was responsible for their unhappiness. Feminists reasoned that the demise of patriarchy would bring about women's fulfillment and allow them to become whole."[18] She argues that "God's plan for male and female" could not be altered, and reflects on the history of feminism: "Looking back over the past fifty years is a sobering exercise. Feminism was the dream that promised women happiness and fulfillment. But I suspect if we were to administer Betty Friedan's questionnaire today, we would find that women are unhappier and less fulfilled than ever."[19] As evidence of the misery inflicted on women by feminism, she points to the rise in the divorce rate, the fact that marriage rates have decreased, and the increase in sexual activity "prior to marriage." She claims, with horror, that "79 percent of single women aged twenty to twenty-four were sexually active." It also upsets her that, by 1997, "61.6 percent of all married women were in the workforce."[20] Clearly the society had moved in directions that Friedan approved and that Kassian found distasteful.

The change in values heralded by Friedan and put into action over the past half century was bound to trouble many, especially those wedded to what feminists called a patriarchal perspective. *The Feminine Mistake* appeared in 2007, written by Leslie Bennetts, a well-known journalist, and it takes the opposite line from Kassian. "I was thirteen when *The Feminine Mystique* was published," writes Bennetts, "and it helped to guide my views and choices from then on."[21] She argues *against* what she sees as the continuing pressures for women to stay at home and raise the children. "The stay-at-home idea now exerts such a potent lure that many more women would apparently quit their jobs were it not for financial considerations," she suggests.[22] Modeling her approach to the subject on Friedan's, she mixes riveting stories with statistics and suggests that women who abandon their careers take a risk. She notes that recent psychological research has shown that having options and making choices are necessary for happiness. The sense of being in charge of one's life enhances life itself. As for what happens to the children when mothers are working as well as raising them, Bennetts quotes a pediatrician who says: "I have taken care of thousands of children from all sorts of backgrounds, and the one consistent thing in raising well-adjusted children was parents who were happy with their choices."[23] She insists that people who do a lot of things inside and outside the home are actually better off, and she always addresses her reader eye to eye, adopting a tone heard throughout Friedan's book: "Yes, you can have a full work life and a full family life, too."[24]

Another turn came with *Betty Friedan and the Making of "The Feminine Mystique": The American Left, the Cold War, and Modern Feminism* (1998) by Daniel Horowitz.[25] Horowitz is largely supportive of Friedan and her politics, but he rejects her self-presentation as a suburban housewife not unlike her imagined readers. Digging up her personal history, he recalls that she had been a labor activist in the 1940s, associating with many socialist and Communist-leaning thinkers who had developed a theoretical framework for social criticism. Friedan was able to popularize and build on these insights, Horowitz argues. He also suggests that the anti-Semitism she experienced as a child in the Midwest may have fueled her passion for social justice. All of this is true enough. She certainly developed an interest in Marxist and socialist analysis, and in psychology, at Smith, where she also learned a good deal from her teachers about the labor struggles of the Great Depression. At Berkeley, needless to say, she found herself in the midst of left-leaning activists. It was hardly surprising, as Horowitz says, that Friedan should develop in the ways she did; but he criticizes her efforts to erase her past, to present herself as an average middle-class and suburban wife in *The Feminine Mystique*.

To me, it seems obvious enough that Friedan knew *exactly* what she was doing in creating this narrative voice for herself. Her book radiates expertise in the art of rhetoric, which is after all the art of persuasion. A good journalist, and a canny writer, she understood that the middle-class women who formed her audience would hardly respond to a self-described lefty, a social activist who bragged about consorting with the sorts of people targeted by McCarthyism. She knew her audience, in other words. And by the time she wrote *The Feminine Mystique,* she had indeed become a suburban housewife, tied to her children, supported mostly by her husband. Her book was never meant as a form of autobiography. It was designed to effect a change in society, and it succeeded beyond the author's dreams.

A few critics seized on the Horowitz book, using some of its findings to deride Betty Friedan. The conservative critic David Horowitz (no relation of the author whose book he reviewed) wrote a scathing piece in *Salon* (January 18, 1999) in which he "exposed" her for what, in his view, she really was: a socialist troublemaker. "With *The Feminine Mystique,* Friedan began a long tradition among American feminists of seeing compulsory domesticity as the main consequence of 1950s McCarthyism," Daniel Horowitz had written, in a rather neutral tone. David Horowitz comments: "Well, perhaps it's not American feminists Friedan has sold this bizarre version of reality to, so much as American Communists posing as feminists and unsuspecting young women whose only understanding of this past will come from their tenured leftist professors." It goes without saying that this sort of criticism had very little effect on Friedan's reputation. Her book was the right book at the right time. It has its place in feminist history, and in American intellectual history, and *The Feminine Mystique* cannot be dislodged from that place of honor.

American women had, indeed, found themselves in constrained circumstances after the war. Unhappiness was rampant, although the degree of unhappiness suggested by Friedan may have been exaggerated for rhetorical purposes. She grabbed whatever statistics lay at hand and used them to bolster her arguments in the most effective ways possible. Her book is a work in the tradition of political tracts, meant to force changes in attitude and behavior among American women, not a work of academic sociology. But this is not to suggest that the book has not deserved some of the thoughtful criticism it has received.

Bell Hooks, for instance, in an important recent study, notes that *The Feminine Mystique* continues "to shape the tenor and direction" of the feminist movement. She cites Friedan's famous phrase "the problem that has no name," suggesting that it "actually referred to the plight of a select group of college-educated, middle- and upper-class, married white women—housewives bored with leisure, with the home, with children, with buying products, who wanted more out of life."[26] Yet Hooks wonders who would be asked to look after the home, and the children, when these privileged women went off to work. Friedan, she says, "ignored the existence of all non-white women and poor white women. She did not tell readers whether it was more fulfilling to be a maid, a babysitter, a factory worker, a clerk, or a prostitute than to be a leisure-class housewife." According to Hooks, Friedan made her own plight, and the plight of women like herself, synonymous with the situation of all women in America, thus deflecting attention from "her classism, her racism, her sexist attitudes towards the masses of American women."[27] Hooks believes that *The Feminine Mystique* "remains a useful discussion of the impact of sexist discrimination on a select group of women." But she is scathing about many aspects of the work, including its "narcissism, insensitivity, sentimentality, and self-indulgence."[28]

Whatever the truth in these various critiques, it seems important *not* to make claims for the feminist revolution that outstrip what actually happened, and what is happening today. The second-wave feminists urged middle-class women to enter the workplace and established the idea that women needed fulfilling work. Everyone does. The education of women has undergone a transformation in the years since *The Feminine Mystique* appeared, as anyone can see who spends any time on an American campus. Almost every faculty now boasts a fair number of women among its ranks, although this seems truer of the humanities than the sciences. Certainly the student body of most colleges is evenly divided between men and women (except on the diminishing number of single-sex campuses), and the fact is that girls outperform boys in most high schools, making them attractive to college admissions offices. But what happens to women after graduation remains troubling.

The boardrooms of American corporations, and the corridors of power in Washington, remain bastions of male privilege, even when exceptions (such as Hillary Clinton) appear. How many women CEOs will be found among the Fortune 500 companies? The answer is not comforting. When the Supreme Court is evenly balanced between men and women, perhaps then the "glass ceiling" will have been broken, and women can assume that the movement toward equality has succeeded fully. I suspect the problems that Bell Hooks points out will remain especially difficult to solve, as women of color and poor white women remain in the margins of American society, for the most part. (Having had an African American woman as secretary of state during the second Bush administration has certainly been good for everyone, but we still have a long way to go before such examples are not exceptional and eye-catching.)

The Feminine Mystique helped to change America in dramatic and subtle ways, and the revolution it fanned continues to improve the lives of women at many different levels. It should also be noted that the feminist project has dramatically altered the lives of men as well, as they have gradually acquired more (and deeper) access to their children, learning how to live their lives in balance, making full use of their emotional intelligence as well as their analytical skills. Yet the complications of social transformation are real, and make the going rough at times. Change, as always, requires skill as well as fortitude, even chutzpah— all characteristics modeled so effectively by Betty Friedan, who dared to imagine a society where equality between the sexes could simply be assumed.

CONCLUSION

Let the slave grinding at the mill run out into the field,
Let him look up into the heavens & laugh in the bright air;
Let the enchained soul, shut up in darkness and in sighing,
Whose face has never seen a smile in thirty weary years,
Rise and look out; his chains are loose, his dungeon doors are open.
　　　　　　　　　　　—William Blake, "America" (1793)

THE UNITED STATES OF AMERICA represents an adventure in self-government. As a political experiment, it had the distinct advantage of having been created in the modern era. Its founders were, for the most part, men of the Enlightenment, a band of sensible and well-educated people who valued rational thought and weighed carefully the elements that constitute a successful nation. By "successful nation"—a perilous phrase—I mean one that does not obtrude on the liberty of its citizens and allows for diversity of opinion without crushing those who disagree with the majority in power. Part of its success, of course, involves the manner in which authority is distributed among its three branches of government, for a limited time. It is the people who pick their leaders and who get rid of them. In theory, heredity plays no real

part in the succession, unlike in the Old Country left behind by countless immigrants.

We sometimes forget that the American idea was fresh and remarkable in the eighteenth century and that it startled the world—as in
Blake's poem "America," quoted above. That a nation could form itself
in such a self-willed fashion was both inspiring and terrifying, and the
creative throes of the people who pulled off such a trick are registered
in the striking books that so many of them left behind, beginning with
the early settlers, who came to these shores for a variety of reasons—
commercial, religious, and personal.

In *Promised Land,* I examined a baker's dozen of the books that
changed America in some discernible way, reaching back to the myth of
origins as embodied by William Bradford in his memoir of the Plymouth Colony, that tiny group of Pilgrims who forged an enviable relationship with the indigenous population of Massachusetts—a model of
cooperation as well as perseverance in the face of steep odds. I then
moved through the various stages of American self-invention, stopping
at a dozen more texts that attracted me for one reason or another. In doing so, I tried to touch on representative strains, or signal aspects, of
American thought, exploring a range of American myths. Myths, in
short, are the stories we tell ourselves about ourselves, however "true."
Much to my own surprise, many of these books deal, in some way, with
the biblical idea of a promised land, often visualized as a dream of independence: not so much a physical place but, as John Milton wrote in
Paradise Lost, "a paradise within thee, happier far." By its very nature,
this land lies just out of reach, and the note of yearning can be heard
again and again in these works.

One learns a lot about America by looking at these texts closely—
and the texts that swirl around them. As I said at the outset, each of
these books represents a climate of opinion, consolidating a tradition or
marking a fresh turn in a long and winding road. I could easily have
chosen another thirteen books, with fairly similar results. Only a few of
these works—*The Federalist Papers,* for instance, and *The Autobiography
of Benjamin Franklin*—seem undeniably central to the American project, while others—*The Promised Land* and *On the Road*—stand in for a
particular line of thought or feeling. That is, one might have chosen

other works in a similar vein: another immigrant memoir or book about the emergence of the counterculture in the postwar era. The theme of westward expansion is important, yet I might have focused on something other than *The Journals of Lewis and Clark*, although this still feels like the best choice. The same may be said for *The Souls of Black Folk*, which can hardly be read except in tandem with *Up from Slavery* by Booker T. Washington. I might well have preferred the *Narrative of the Life of Frederick Douglass*, a work of equal value in the troubled history of race relations in the United States, or any number of other works by African Americans. But this steely-edged work by Du Bois has cut deep, and it repays close attention.

A few of my choices are classic works of literature, such as *Walden* and *Huckleberry Finn;* they have meant so much to me (and Americans generally) that I could not avoid them, and would not have wished to do so. Others, such as *Uncle Tom's Cabin* and *The Feminine Mystique,* shifted public opinion in crucial ways. That was reason enough to include them. Perhaps a couple of the books on my list—*How to Win Friends and Influence People* and *The Common Sense Book of Baby and Child Care*—will strike some readers as whimsical choices. I don't deny the whimsicality here, but I believe each of these books had a crucial impact on the formation of this intangible thing, the American character—if, indeed, one can use such a lofty, abstract term.

Gore Vidal once referred to this country as the United States of Amnesia, and he was right to call attention to our general ignorance of our own history. We sometimes forget we are a nation made of words. And these words have shaped our sense of ourselves and governed our behavior. It is worth saying that these were remarkable words, assembled in texts that have modified (even created) our thinking. Certainly a picture emerges from the sum of this language. Having just finished writing about these books, I look back over them and see a nation eager to cut its ties with the Old World, eager to feel its own powers of self-invention. Our practical side remains undeniably present, embodied by Benjamin Franklin, the person most responsible for our self-image as hardworking, ordinary, wise, and often bemused folk who go about our business with considerable skill and ingenuity. This can-do, practical spirit enlivens the journals that Lewis and Clark kept as they journeyed into the unknown. Mark Twain, too, had an immensely practical side, selling himself to the world at large, publishing his own books. He is the bastard child of Franklin, or his reincarnation as wit, gambler, and scourge of empire. Even Dale Carnegie seems, in a more low-key way, a dutiful grandchild of Franklin, offering homey wisdom to his readers, urging us to pull ourselves up by the bootstraps, inch by inch if necessary.

Reading these books, I have also felt our intense connection to the traditions of spirituality. The Puritans were indeed committed Christians, although they bowed to no external authorities, such as those established in Canterbury or Rome. This strain of spirituality had its mystical (although churchless) wing, too, represented in the writings of Emerson and Thoreau, who rank high among the world's unorthodox spiritual guides. Their visionary gleam has never faded and informs many of our finest works of literature. Their independent, even rebellious, spirit ripples through so many later writers, including Du Bois, Mary Antin, Benjamin Spock, and Jack Kerouac. Their defiant note will be heard as well in Betty Friedan, who urged American women toward what was a defiant act of civil disobedience—to discard the patriarchal system itself.

The American character exists, however idealized or complex, even contradictory and, at times, unpalatable. It has its own tenor and flexibilities, its peculiar hopefulness, its oddities and affectations. Our novelists, perhaps, have been our best biographers, and the sum of their work presents a character mingling aspects of Natty Bumppo, Eliza Harris, Captain Ahab, Jay Gatsby, Sula, and so many others. This composite figure shimmers in the atmosphere of our libraries, calling us back to ourselves, informing us (quite literally), making us whole.

We often lose sight of what Abraham Lincoln called "the better angels of our nature," and this is sad. We have pursued dreams of empire and behaved badly in the world, sucking up its resources, forgetting that we must participate in the larger community of human beings. The laundry list of our faults is long, and it's easy to fall into despair about the American project, to lose sight of its idealistic origins, forgetting that we do, in fact, have a collective destiny, which our forebears have consciously shaped and which we continue to forge as citizens and readers.

But readers we are, or should be, and the texts that underlie our republic, that have created its contours and textures, must be reread, even rethought, at regular intervals. Studying the past is important because, as Thomas Jefferson once suggested, this activity teaches citizens "how to judge for themselves what will secure or endanger their freedom." This is information we cannot do without.

ONE HUNDRED MORE BOOKS
THAT CHANGED AMERICA

Below you will find my choice of a hundred more books that changed America in some way. I could have supplied yet another hundred, without much trouble. In choosing these, as with the thirteen discussed in the body of this book, I have focused on works that actually shifted something or solidified a change already in place. In only a very few cases do I refer to masterpieces of fiction, such as *Moby-Dick* or *The Catcher in the Rye,* as novels have rarely had a discernible effect on the public. (This is, of course, a slippery slope, and I have restrained myself, not including many of my favorite novels, such as *The Scarlet Letter* and *The Great Gatsby,* each of which reflected an era with accuracy and force, as have countless other novels.)

Once again: the hundred books that follow are not the "greatest" books in American history, although some of them would fall into such a category. They are works that either defined a period or produced a notable shift or expansion of consciousness. Some of them helped to transform a field of inquiry, such as Noam Chomsky's *Syntactic Structures* (1957), which influenced a wide range of disciplines. Others simply brought the revelations of new developments to wide public notice, as in *The Double Helix.*

I did not, in fact, allow for influential short works, such as Lincoln's

Gettysburg Address or Martin Luther King's "Letter from Birmingham Jail," both major documents with a broad influence. Nor did I deal with plays, as they are not really "books." One might, for example, have included Israel Zangwill's *Melting-Pot,* which has provided a useful metaphor to those thinking about immigration and ethnicity ever since it first appeared on the stage in 1908. Thornton Wilder's *Our Town* has rarely been off the stage since it first appeared at the Wilbur Theater in Boston in the winter of 1938, and it has forever defined a certain kind of small-town world that one imagines is especially American. *Death of a Salesman* by Arthur Miller appeared in 1948, and it has certainly defined certain attitudes toward class and yearning in America. But these are not books per se.

Some of the books that follow are "reports" by commissions, catalogs, and studies (such as the Kinsey reports). I tried to include some of these, as a few have been widely influential. I did not usually include major bestsellers, such as *Peyton Place* (1956), in large part because they merely reinforced ideas (even prejudices) already in place: this is the function of most bestsellers. *Gone With the Wind,* for various cultural reasons, struck me as an exception to this rule and therefore worth adding to the list. For the most part, I shied away from poetry as well, even though I personally view poetry as the most important form of writing. The few poets I could *not* avoid in the context of this list were Walt Whitman, Robert Frost, and Sylvia Plath. A larger list would certainly include Emily Dickinson, T. S. Eliot, and Wallace Stevens, among others.

The list proceeds chronologically:

Bartolomé de Las Casas, *A Brief Relation of the Destruction of the Indies* (1552)

This is a searing account of the atrocities committed by the original conquistadors in the Americas, especially in the Caribbean, written by a priest who was literally on the scene. It has profoundly influenced the way the conquest of the New World has been viewed over the centuries. Las Casas wrote: "What we committed in the Indies stands out against the most unpardonable offenses ever committed against God and mankind." He also edited the diaries of Christopher Columbus, another major source of information on this era.

John Smith, *The General History of Virginia* (1624)

This account of the establishment of Virginia includes the story of Pocahontas and her aid to Smith and the early colonists. Smith extolled the resources of the New World and lured a fresh generation of settlers, who found his vision immensely appealing.

Thomas Morton, *New English Canaan* (1637)

A stirring defense of Morton's activities at Merry Mount, this book offers an influential view of life among the Native Americans and a detailed account of the flora and fauna of New England. It was also influential as an early work in ethnography.

Roger Williams, *A Key into the Language of America* (1643)

This account of relations between early settlers and Native Americans was written by the founder of Rhode Island, a theologian who notably supported the idea of the separation of church and state. He also argued for fairness in dealing with Native Americans. This is a hugely important linguistic treatise as well.

Cotton Mather, *Magnalia Christi Americana* (1702)

This fundamental text consists of seven smaller "books" that provided invaluable source material on New England life in the colonial era. Later writers, including Hawthorne and Harriet Beecher Stowe, drew on it. Mather sought to understand the colonial adventure in terms of biblical ideas and recognized the importance of place itself in shaping human aspirations.

Jonathan Edwards, *Discourses on Various Important Subjects* (1738)

These five sermons riveted early American colonists and contributed dramatically to the so-called Great Awakening, a major religious revival that swept the United States and changed the lives of large numbers of early Americans.

Thomas Paine, *Common Sense* (1776)

This was the first text to openly challenge British rule in North America. The author's plain language appealed widely to the colonists and strongly fanned the flames of rebellion.

J. Hector St. John de Crèvecoeur, *Letters from an American Farmer* (1782)

This author put the American dream before the wider world, portraying the United States as a land of self-determination where equal opportunities could be found, especially on the frontier.

Thomas Jefferson, *Notes on the State of Virginia* (1784–85)

Jefferson's only published book, this volume contains many of his important and influential ideas on republican government, the environment, education, and race relations.

Judith Sargent Murray, *On the Equality of the Sexes* (1790)

One of the first feminist texts written in the United States, it was both controversial and influential in its day. Murray was a journalist, essayist, poet, and novelist. This founding work in feminist thinking was daring and revolutionary.

William Bartram, *Travels Through North and South Carolina, Georgia, East and West Florida* (1791)

This is an early account of the American Southeast by an influential naturalist and travel writer. The book was popular throughout the English-speaking world and noted by English poets such as Wordsworth and Coleridge. It drew attention to the region, and it attracted settlers as well.

Parson Mason Locke Weems, *Life of Washington* (1800)

This early biography of George Washington shaped the myth of the man and was popular for a century. It put forward the story of the cherry tree, which the father of our country supposedly chopped down. "I cannot tell a lie," he said. This story is apocryphal, yet it remains a part of America's mythology.

Washington Irving, *The Sketch Book of Geoffrey Crayon* (1820)

This volume contained both "Rip Van Winkle" and "The Legend of Sleepy Hollow." These tales formed part of America's early mythology. Irving was among the first American voices to gain a European audience.

James Fenimore Cooper, Leatherstocking Tales (1823–41)

This series of five novels features Nathaniel "Natty" Bumppo, an intrepid frontiersman who moves westward in each of these well-told adventures. Bumppo shifts between the two worlds of European settlers and Native American tribes. These popular novels shaped America's idea of frontier life and Native American culture.

Noah Webster, *An American Dictionary of the English Language* (1828)

Webster was a pioneering lexicographer, spelling reformer, and author of textbooks. His influential dictionary took twenty-seven years to complete. His blue-backed spelling books taught five generations of American children how to spell.

Joseph Smith Jr., *The Book of Mormon* (1830)

This sacred book about Israelites who traveled to the New World in ancient times is believed by Mormons to represent a translation of the golden plates discovered by Smith, the founder of their religion. This is an important document in American religious history, and one that continues to shape the lives of millions of believers.

Lydia Maria Child, *The American Frugal Housewife* (1832)

A must-read for every new bride in the mid-nineteenth century, this handbook offers cooking tips and advice on raising children and addresses many other domestic concerns. Child was herself an abolitionist, an advocate for women's rights, and a critic of American expansionism. She wrote the poem "Over the River and Through the Woods."

Alexis de Tocqueville, *Democracy in America* (1835, 1840)

This brilliant study by a French political philosopher and early sociologist was written after his extensive travels in the United States. He studied the workings of democracy carefully and discerned a fine balance between liberty and equality. Putting forward a critique of individualism, he suggested that the association of people for a common good would unite the nation. Tocqueville worried, however, about the rise of materialism in the fledgling country and drew attention to the negative aspects of market capitalism.

Ralph Waldo Emerson, *Nature* (1836)

This remains among the most influential works by this indispensable American philosopher, poet, and essayist. It offered a transcendentalist view of the natural world, in which "Nature is the symbol of spirit." Generations of poets and nature writers have considered this volume a major source of inspiration and ideas.

W. H. McGuffey, *The Eclectic First Reader for Young Children* (1836)

Often called *The McGuffey Reader,* this anthology of reading for beginners was a standard textbook throughout the country during the years of westward expansion. Every one-room schoolhouse had this book at the center of its curriculum for nearly a century.

Caroline Kirkland, *A New Home—Who'll Follow?* (1839)

This popular account of establishing a frontier home in Michigan offered a mildly satirical look at westward expansion and the trials of living on the frontier. It inspired thousands to get up and go west.

John James Audubon, *The Birds of America* (1840)

This landmark book was the "first octavo edition" of the naturalist's seven volumes, which present his important descriptions and drawings of birds. His 435 life-size drawings had no rivals in their day. Audubon inspired a reverence for American wildlife, and he energized the conservation movement at a crucial, early moment in its evolution.

George Catlin, *The Manners, Customs, and Condition of the North American Indians* (1841)

This important early study of Native American tribes included three hundred of Catlin's engravings. In describing the "buffalo country" of the Great Plains, he recognized that these herds would be destroyed by "profligate waste" that he attributed to the coming of the white man.

Frederick Douglass, *Narrative of the Life of Frederick Douglass* (1845)

A massively resonant work by a former slave who became a leading abolitionist, editor, and writer, this memoir was followed by two further autobiographies. Douglass attended the Seneca Falls Convention, where women and blacks came together in the attempt to gain the vote in 1848.

Margaret Fuller, *Woman in the Nineteenth Century* (1845)

This work helped to generate the movement for women's rights, which had its formal beginnings at the feminist conference at Seneca Falls. Fuller was a versatile thinker.

Edgar Allan Poe, *Tales* (1845)

This late selection of Poe's major stories established him as an innovative writer in the Gothic tradition. His work has continued to influence American writers from H. P. Lovecraft to Joyce Carol Oates and Stephen King. His detective stories, such as "The Murders in the Rue Morgue," made him a founding father of the genre itself.

Francis Parkman, *The Oregon Trail: Sketches of Prairie and Rocky-Mountain Life* (1847)

This popular volume has influenced the writing of narrative history, and Parkman's views on the relations between white settlers and Native Americans marked an era in studies of the American West. Parkman believed that the white man represented a coming of civilization over savagery. His view of the Native American as "man, wolf, and devil, all in one" has been much discussed, although often criticized as well.

Herman Melville, *Moby-Dick* (1851)

In many ways the most important American novel ever written, it's the story of Ishmael, the sailor, and his whale-hunting aboard the *Pequod* with the mad Captain Ahab. This is the ultimate American quest narrative, with universal implications. Although not popular in its day, it eventually achieved the status of an American classic.

Walt Whitman, *Leaves of Grass* (1855)

This was the first of many editions of the poet's deeply influential work, which inspired generations of poets and writers. Here was the original voice in American poetry. In the twentieth century, writers from William Carlos Williams and Ezra Pound through Theodore Roethke, Allen Ginsberg, and Jack Kerouac drew on his poetry for inspiration.

Horatio Alger Jr., *Ragged Dick; or, Street Life in New York with the Bootblacks* (1868)

This was the first of an immensely popular series of novels about the rise of young men from rags to riches through hard work and perseverance. Alger wrote well over a hundred novels in this vein.

Mary Baker Eddy, *Science and Health with Key to the Scriptures* (1875)

This was the founding text in the religious sect known as Christian Science. With *The Book of Mormon,* it represents one of the major religious offsprings of the New World. This work contained Eddy's revelation of the "divine laws of Life, Truth, and Love."

Joel Chandler Harris, *Uncle Remus* (1880)

The first of seven books featuring Uncle Remus, a black narrator of folktales in the tradition of African American trickster stories. Br'er Rabbit is the main character, and he outwits those who oppose him. Although considered offensive by many in later years for its patronizing attitudes toward blacks and the author's acceptance of slavery, these stories were widely read in their day and captured a version of black dialect in the South.

William James, *The Principles of Psychology* (1890)

This foundational study has influenced the field since its two hefty volumes first appeared. James believed that consciousness functioned in a purposeful way to organize thoughts; thus, his approach was called functionalism, in contrast to the traditional associationism prevalent at the time. James was also a founder in the philosophical school of American pragmatism (also associated with John Dewey and, more recently, Richard Rorty). His work was so far-reaching that one might have put several of his books on this list, including *The Varieties of Religious Experience* (1902), a seminal study of religious feeling and experience.

Alfred Thayer Mahan, *The Influence of Sea Power upon History* (1890)

This meticulous study shaped the thinking of Theodore Roosevelt, whose notions of global expansion crystallized as he read Mahan. It remains a key work in American military history. The idea of American empire may be traced, in part, to this seminal work.

Booker T. Washington, *Up from Slavery* (1901)

This riveting autobiography was criticized by W. E. B. Du Bois in *The Souls of Black Folk*, yet it remains a classic account of Washington's astonishing rise from slavery to his founding of the Tuskegee Institute. Washington supports the idea that African Americans must make their own way, by themselves, not asking for help from white society.

The Sears, Roebuck Catalog (1902)

This was the first edition of this important catalog, which equipped Americans from New York and Boston to the Wild West with an incalculable ray of goods. This catalog prefigures the range of mail-order catalogs that clog the mailboxes of America today, although some of these have gone online. But it all started with Sears and Roebuck, the original wizards of merchandising.

Upton Sinclair, *The Jungle* (1906)

A muckraking investigation of conditions among the poor in America, this novel details the horrors of the meatpacking industry and led to the passage of the Food and Drugs Act as well as the Meat Inspection Act of 1906.

Charles Alexander Eastman, *Old Indian Days* (1907)

A member of the Sioux tribe, a physician, and a reformer, Eastman wrote several influential books that brought the details of Native American life to the broad American public. This is a book of legends, important as a work of ethnography, a mythmaking work.

Jane Addams, *Twenty Years at Hull-House* (1910)

A classic of American sociology and intellectual history, this is also a moving autobiographical account of Addams's work in the field, offering a guide to practical action. It helped to shape the idea of social work as a discipline and practice.

John Muir, *My First Summer in the Sierra* (1911)

This book so impressed President Teddy Roosevelt that he went camping in the Sierras with Muir and began talks about establishing the National Park Service. Muir's beautiful book—a prime text in American nature writing—set in motion the conservation movement.

James Weldon Johnson, *The Autobiography of an Ex-Colored Man* (1912)

Johnson, a fine poet, published this novel (in the form of an autobiography) anonymously at a time when African American consciousness was just beginning to deal with the complications of race in complex ways. It was republished in 1927, under the author's name, when writers of the Harlem Renaissance began to change the course of American literature. It offers an ironic meditation on prejudice in the South in the wake of Reconstruction and an early evocation of the problem of "passing" as a white.

Charles A. Beard, *An Economic Interpretation of the Constitution of the United States* (1913)

This radical look at the U.S. Constitution posited economic motives on the part of the original framers. Beard discerned a conflict of interests between landed and mercantile classes among the Founding Fathers. He was a leader in the Progressive school, which included later historians such as C. Vann Woodward. Beard's *Rise of American Civilization* (1927–42) was influential as well.

Robert Frost, *North of Boston* (1914)

Frost showed that poetry could be found, in abundance, in the everyday speech of uneducated farmers from northern New England. He summoned a vision of nature, and farming life, that permanently affected our understanding of this region, and the idea of "regionality" itself.

John Dewey, *Democracy and Education* (1916)

Only William James has been more influential as an American philosopher. Dewey transformed ideas on American education, too, when he argued that students should not be taught "dead fact" but that these materials should be part of their lives. He was a progressive thinker in many fields, including psychology and social anthropology. He was crucial in the development of American pragmatism.

H. L. Mencken, *The American Language* (1919)

This is a groundbreaking study of what became of the English language in the mouths of American speakers. Mencken argues that Americans transformed the language, giving it fresh life. Like Noah Webster, he defended "Americanisms," which were often derided by English critics. Mark Twain was among his heroes.

Frederick Jackson Turner, *The Frontier in American History* (1920)

This pivotal volume in American history incorporates Turner's famous lecture "The Significance of the Frontier in American History" (1893), which put forward the influential "frontier thesis": that the American frontier was the source of all energy and innovation. The consequences of coming to the "end" of frontier were unsettling and motivated some of Turner's admirers, such as Teddy Roosevelt, to think in terms of imperial expansion as a way of maintaining a frontier.

Sinclair Lewis, *Babbitt* (1922)

This satire by the popular author of *Main Street* (1920) offers a withering portrait of an American real estate salesman whose aura of success belies an inward vacancy and sadness. Mercantile values have rarely been more vividly etched or analyzed. Lewis was among the most influential portraitists of American life in the early decades of the twentieth century.

Emily Post, *Etiquette in Society, in Business, in Politics, and at Home* (1922)

This book remained a bestseller for decades, ushering millions of upwardly striving Americans into the middle classes by teaching them how to behave "properly." The Emily Post Institute continues to offer advice on manners on a wide range of topics.

Bruce Barton, *The Man Nobody Knows* (1925)

Founder of a major advertising agency, Barton in this bestselling book portrayed Jesus Christ as the ultimate salesman, a role model for the successful businessman. Here lies a foundational text in the American religion of self-improvement and material progress. He was perhaps the most influential adman of the century.

Alain Locke, *The New Negro* (1925)

This groundbreaking anthology presented to readers the writers of the Harlem Renaissance, a movement among African American writers that included Langston Hughes, Countee Cullen, and Claude McKay. "In the last decade something beyond the watch and guard of statistics has happened in the life of the American Negro," Locke wrote in his introductory essay.

Ernest Hemingway, *The Sun Also Rises* (1926)

Hemingway's first and (perhaps) greatest novel, featuring an expatriate group of Americans abroad, members of the so-called Lost Generation. Hemingway revolutionized English prose, taking it down to the bare essentials. A modern masterpiece that has continued to influence writers, including Raymond Carver and Ann Beattie.

Margaret Sanger, *Happiness in Marriage* (1926)

Sanger was an early advocate of sex education and birth control. This was perhaps the most widely read of her books. She remains an iconic figure in the movement for reproductive rights, and her ideas lead straight to *Roe v. Wade* (1973). Her early work in family planning led to the establishment of Planned Parenthood.

Charles A. Lindbergh, "We" (1927)

Subtitled *The Daring Flyer's Remarkable Life Story and His Account of the Transatlantic Flight That Shook the World,* this is the famous aviator's own story, and it inspired a generation of readers. Lindbergh predicts the future of aviation here and establishes himself as a role model for can-do Americans.

Robert and Helen Lynd, *Middletown* (1929)

This landmark work of American sociology pioneered the use of social surveys and provided a model for later writers in the field. The Lynds "discovered" the scandal of class in the United States, suggesting that the business class worked with ideas, the working class with things. This book looked at mass production in ways that continue to influence thinking in a variety of social sciences. *Middletown in Transition* followed in 1937.

Irma and Marion Rombauer, *The Joy of Cooking* (1931)

A widow in St. Louis, Irma Rombauer self-published this book, with illustrations by her daughter. Nine major editions have followed, making this one of the most successful cookbooks of all time. Tens of millions of Americans learned how to cook from Mrs. Rombauer.

Reinhold Niebuhr, *Moral Man and Immoral Society* (1932)

A major theologian and social critic, Niebuhr made a distinct impact on American identity during the 1930s, '40s, and '50s. Martin Luther King Jr. identified him as a key influence. His political realism struck an important note as he adopted a rather deflationary attitude toward progressive thought, asking readers to keep in mind the difficulties brought on by humanity's own natural inclinations. Niebuhr had a major effect on American planners in the postwar era, and his work has continued to interest a wide array of figures, including Barack Obama, who has cited Niebuhr as one of his favorite thinkers.

Margaret Mitchell, *Gone With the Wind* (1936)

One of the bestselling American novels of all time, this book about the Old South and the Civil War (and its aftermath) had the power of myth to transform readers. Scarlett O'Hara inspired a generation of women. The film of the novel (1939) ranks among the most watched and admired films in Hollywood history. The sequels have been endless, culminating most recently in *Rhett Butler's People* by Donald McCaig (2007). Will it never end?

Zora Neale Hurston, *Their Eyes Were Watching God* (1937)

A leading figure associated with the Harlem Renaissance, Hurston was a social anthropologist and folklorist who brought all her talents to bear in this novel, which has become a centerpiece of African American literature and continues to direct thinking about black culture in the United States, where it has been a popular novel in schools and universities for decades.

John Steinbeck, *The Grapes of Wrath* (1939)

Steinbeck's road novel remains among the key works of the Great Depression, a book that galvanized Americans, drawing attention to the plight of the so-called Okies—migrants from Oklahoma who made their way over the Rockies to California. The novel led to legislation in Congress that benefited migrant workers.

James Agee, *Let Us Now Praise Famous Men* (1941)

A powerful look at white sharecroppers in the South during the Depression, this book includes remarkable photographs by Walker Evans and text by Agee. Agee stepped outside the usual boundaries of journalism, writing a deeply textured prose that mixes ethnography with poetry. It offered a prototype for the so-called New Journalists.

Friedrich von Hayek, *The Road to Serfdom* (1944)

This Austrian economist taught for many years at the University of Chicago. He set in motion a revolution that inspired several generations of conservative and libertarian thinkers, including Milton Friedman and Ronald Reagan. His main idea is that collectivism leads inevitably to tyranny, as in the Soviet Union and Nazi Germany. It represents a passionate defense of market economics.

Richard Wright, *Black Boy* (1945)

This compelling memoir of boyhood and youth describes the writer's progress from innocence to experience in the South. A classic work of American autobiography, it is also a book that inspired protest and played a role in the transformations of the South, including the civil rights movement.

John Hersey, *Hiroshima* (1946)

In August 1946, the *New Yorker* devoted a whole issue to Hersey's detailed account of the effects of the atom bomb on the city of Hiroshima in Japan. The article soon became a book, detailing the lives of six individuals affected by the bomb. The public was deeply shocked, and the beginnings of the movement for nuclear disarmament were sown. The book is still often cited by anti-nuclear-weapons activists.

The Kinsey Reports (1948, 1953)

Two reports, on male and female sexual behavior, written by Dr. Alfred Kinsey, Wardell Pomeroy, and others. These reports shocked the general public, who had never before looked so closely into the bedroom windows of their neighbors. Extremely controversial in their day, these reports represent a first glimmering of what became the sexual revolution.

Thomas Merton, *The Seven Storey Mountain* (1948)

This deeply poetic autobiography tracks the conversion of a young man to Roman Catholicism and his commitment to monastic life. A surprising bestseller, it drew countless readers back to some form of spiritual practice, and it continues to influence those in search of spiritual direction.

Gore Vidal, *The City and the Pillar* (1948)

This bestseller by the young Vidal created a scandal as one of the first major novels to deal openly with homosexuality. It should be read in tandem with Vidal's important essay on the subject of homosexuality, "Pink Triangle and Yellow Star." This novel helped to introduce the subject of gay life in America to a broad public.

Norbert Wiener, *Cybernetics; or, Control and Communication in the Animal and the Machine* (1948)

An American mathematician, Wiener created the field of cybernetics, which systematized the idea of feedback. The implications of this work were profound in a number of areas, including engineering, systems control, computer science, and biology.

Joseph Campbell, *The Hero with a Thousand Faces* (1949)

This seminal book offered a paradigm for plots, from ancient myths and sagas to the modern novel, tracing the cycle of the hero's journey. It has been influential in literary studies and has had broad influence in the arts, including on filmmakers such as George Lucas and his *Star Wars* sequence.

J. D. Salinger, *The Catcher in the Rye* (1951)

This perennial favorite of teenage readers fixed a certain kind of rebellious attitude forever in the American psyche. Holden Caulfield rejects the "phoniness" of adult life. The novel anticipated attitudes that matured in the Beat writers and found later expression in Bob Dylan and other countercultural heroes.

Ralph Ellison, *Invisible Man* (1952)

An influential novel by one of the finest black writers of the twentieth century, it addresses issues of black identity, telling the story of an "invisible" but extremely well-educated and thoughtful black man who remains nameless in the face of hostility and prejudice. The novel added a great deal of nuance to the complex debate on African American identity. Ellison suggests that education has not helped his invisible hero to overcome prejudice; he later claimed that he did not write this book for its insights into social problems, but wrote it simply as a work of art.

Norman Vincent Peale, *The Power of Positive Thinking* (1952)

Peale was pastor of the Marble Collegiate Church in Manhattan for over half a century, and his book was almost in a league with Dale Carnegie's *How to Win Friends and Influence People*. It rode the bestseller list for years and inspired a generation of Americans to look on the bright side.

B. F. Skinner, *Science and Human Behavior* (1953)

A crucial figure in modern psychology, Skinner redirected the field of psychology, creating the famous Skinner box, where he studied the behavior of animals. In this book, he looks at human institutions, such as government and religion, as "controlling agencies." The Skinnerian approach sought to place psychology on a scientific footing. It may have failed, but this remains an influential book.

Noam Chomsky, *Syntactic Structures* (1957)

This single book by one of America's leading intellectuals changed linguistics forever, but its impact went far beyond one narrow academic field. Chomsky introduced a new approach to the study of language itself and how the human mind actually acquires knowledge. His work had far-reaching effects, transforming research in philosophy and psychology, extending into the social sciences as well. Chomsky has also been widely influential as a critic of American foreign policy, beginning with *American Power and the New Mandarins* (1969).

Alan Watts, *The Way of Zen* (1957)

Although it was D. T. Suzuki who brought the teaching of Zen Buddhism to America, it was Watts who popularized this spiritual tradition. His accessible books influenced a generation or more of spiritual seekers.

John Kenneth Galbraith, *The Affluent Society* (1958)

Galbraith made his ideas on economics accessible to a wide public in this influential book, which offers a critique of modern capitalism, noting how advertising artificially creates an audience for mass-produced goods and services. The phrase "conventional wisdom" started with Galbraith, in this book. The author contemplates the abiding problem of wealth and poverty, advocating government spending in education and health care.

William Strunk Jr. and E. B. White, *The Elements of Style* (1959)

This little book was self-published by Strunk, a professor at Cornell, in 1918. It made little impact, but when White agreed to revise it, in the late 1950s, the book became a bestseller. With its stripped-down approach to grammar and style, this introductory volume has profoundly influenced generations of high school and college students as they attempted to master the basics of writing.

Joseph Heller, *Catch-22* (1961)

Set during the early stages of World War II, the novel tracks the career of Yossarian, the hapless bombardier and antihero at the center of this compulsively readable novel. As much as *On the Road,* it shifted attitudes, noting the absurdity of war and large organizations, attacking the system itself as absurd.

Helen Gurley Brown, *Sex and the Single Girl* (1962)

Welcome to the sexual revolution. Brown suggested that "the rich, full life of dating" did not require beauty or wealth. She advised young women to work with what they had and never give up. The pursuit of sexual pleasure, success, and good fun had never been so neatly packaged. It only took a decade for *The Joy of Sex* (1972) by Alex Comfort to provide all the details, in case anyone was in doubt about how the parts all fit together.

Rachel Carson, *Silent Spring* (1962)

This book launched the modern environmental movement in the United States. It inspired national concern about the use of pesticides and prompted legislation that would attempt to control pollution. Carson accused the chemical industry of spreading lies about the effects of pesticides on the environment.

Milton Friedman, *Capitalism and Freedom* (1962)

Friedman represents the opposite end of the pole from Galbraith. In this influential work of economics, Friedman (who won a Nobel Prize in Economics) considers the operations of capitalism within a democratic society. For him, the free market is essential to the success of a society. This book helped to shape conservative thought in the United States and was the basis for Reaganomics and its aftermath.

Michael Harrington, *The Other America: Poverty in the United States* (1962)

A pivotal study of poverty in the United States, it was read by Lyndon B. Johnson and contributed to his creation of a "war on poverty." This book has been widely influential in progressive circles for many decades. Medicare, Medicaid, food stamps, and expanded governmental benefits can be traced back to Harrington's wake-up call.

Thomas S. Kuhn, *The Structure of Scientific Revolutions* (1962)

This strenuously thoughtful account of how science actually proceeds argues for what the author calls "paradigm shifts." That is, scientific progress is not linear and inexorable. The impact of this book can be measured by the shifts in diction within the scientific community that can be traced to it. Philosophers and social scientists often refer to Kuhn's work.

Sylvia Plath, *Ariel* (1965)

The stark originality of these poems, their naked self-exposure and harrowing chronicle of a life at the edge, shocked and moved a generation, and Plath continues to inspire and terrify readers. Her mode of confessional poetry has been widely imitated.

James D. Watson, *The Double Helix* (1968)

Written by a groundbreaking molecular biologist who helped to discover the structure of DNA, this book explained to the world what was at stake and how this discovery was made. The implications of this discovery can hardly be fathomed as medicine begins to make use of genetic therapy.

Whole Earth Catalog (1968)

Edited by Stewart Brand, among others, this expansive catalog was published twice a year from 1968 to 1972, and periodically thereafter. It crystallized the counterculture movement in the United States, promoting early versions of back-to-the-earth ideas and environmentalism. It was meant to provide education and "access to tools." Steve Jobs, who founded Apple Inc., has described this catalog as a forerunner of Web search engines.

The Pentagon Papers (1971)

Leaked to the *New York Times* by Daniel Ellsberg and published by the Beacon Press, these top-secret papers commissioned by the Department of Defense revealed a great deal about the way the Vietnam War was prosecuted. For example, they showed that while President Lyndon B. Johnson pretended not to escalate the war, he was secretly expanding air strikes against Laos and conducting raids off the coast of North Vietnam. These papers fueled the antiwar movement during the Nixon years and permanently widened the so-called credibility gap between government and the American public.

Robert C. Atkins, *Dr. Atkins' Diet Revolution* (1972)

One of several major diet books that changed the eating habits of Americans. Atkins famously stressed the low-carbohydrate diet, influencing later diet books, which offered versions of his diet. *Jane Brody's Good Food Book* (1985) took a different approach, stressing high-carb, high-fiber foods. Either way, it's all about the calories.

Our Bodies, Ourselves (1973)

This book about women's health and sexuality was compiled by the Boston Women's Health Book Collective. Its approach to such issues as birth control and gender was revolutionary at the time, and the book remains a useful handbook for women. It is a feminist classic.

Carl Bernstein and Bob Woodward, All the President's Men (1974)

These were the feisty young reporters from the *Washington Post* who brought down President Nixon in the Watergate scandal. Their account of how they managed to do this has inspired a generation of investigative journalists.

Annie Dillard, Pilgrim at Tinker Creek (1974)

This is one of the most recent works in the tradition of Thoreau's *Walden,* describing a remarkable journey back to the land itself, with spiritual dimensions unfolding as the narrative proceeds. The book helped to kindle a fresh interest in what is loosely called nature writing. It has deservedly become a modern classic.

Alex Haley, Roots: The Saga of an American Family (1976)

Haley traced his familial roots back to an African villager known as Kunta Kinte, who was captured by slave traders in the late eighteenth century and brought to the New World. This wonderful story about slavery and its legacy awakened many to their painful but also noble history in a way no other work had done. The impact of the book was enhanced by a subsequent miniseries on television. Its overall effect on a generation of African Americans cannot be overstated.

Adrienne Rich, Of Woman Born: Motherhood as Experience and Institution (1976)

This major poet's study of motherhood looks at her own experience and the institution of motherhood itself. Her research, and the way she employs her materials, made this a landmark study, a key text in the feminist movement.

Smoking and Health: A Report of the Surgeon General (1979)

This momentous health report from the Office of the Surgeon General led directly to the reduction in smoking that has had a major impact on health in the United States. It linked smoking with cancer, heart disease, and other health problems.

Jane Fonda, *Jane Fonda's Workout Book* (1981)

Americans suddenly found themselves working out in large numbers, losing weight, gaining self-respect. Jane Fonda's book, and the videos that followed, began a revolution in exercise that continues to this day with an array of workout programs. Fonda followed in the footsteps of Jack LaLanne, the fitness guru, whose television show in the 1950s and '60s attracted a considerable audience.

Thomas J. Peters and Robert H. Waterman Jr., *In Search of Excellence: Lessons from America's Best-Run Companies* (1982)

This bestselling work explores the art of management, looking closely at forty-three leading American companies, each of which had a proven track record of profitability over the long term. The ideas in this study have been influential within major corporate headquarters for over two decades.

Stephen R. Covey, *The 7 Habits of Highly Effective People* (1989)

Not since Dale Carnegie has a book so captivated people who read self-help books. The universal character traits of ethical behavior provide the "true north" of experience for Covey and his followers. Over fifteen million copies have sold, and the book has been translated into over thirty-eight languages.

Bill McKibben, *The End of Nature* (1989)

This was the first major book written for a general audience on the subject of global climate change and what it means. Serialized in *The New Yorker,* it set in motion a movement that has gathered momentum with each passing year. McKibben remains an important voice in the environmental movement.

Samuel P. Huntington, *The Clash of Civilizations and the Remaking of World Order* (1996)

Stemming from an article originally published in *Foreign Affairs* (1993), this book expanded on Huntington's insights. He perceived fault lines growing between Islam and Christianity and foresaw a period of intense conflict. Although he believed the West must be confrontational at times, he argued finally for tolerance and cooperation. Many architects of the Iraq War looked to this work for inspiration.

Rick Warren, *The Purpose-Driven Life* (2002)

Over thirty million in print, and still going: this devotional book added a fresh twist to evangelical Christianity, attacking what Warren calls the five "Global Goliaths"—spiritual vacancy, egotistical leaders, poverty, disease, and illiteracy.

Al Gore, *An Inconvenient Truth* (2006)

Gore's bestselling book (which became a popular documentary film) assembled research from top scientists, with plenty of charts and diagrams, to warn the world about the reality of global warming. Gore regards global warming as a moral problem as well as a scientific and political one. His book and film focused the attention of the world on this topic, offering a major boost to the campaign to save the planet. He won a Nobel Prize for his efforts, as well as an Academy Award.

NOTES

Chapter 1: *Of Plymouth Plantation*

1. This remark was made in a lecture by Senator George Frisbie Hoar on the occasion of the manuscript being returned to Massachusetts in 1897. See William Bradford, *Of Plimouth Plantation* (Boston: Wright & Potter, 1898), p. xli.

2. William Bradford, *Of Plymouth Plantation, 1620–1647*, ed. Francis Murphy (New York: Modern Library, 1981). Text references are to page numbers of this edition.

3. See "Scandal in Brownists Alley," in George F. Willison, *Saints and Strangers* (New York: Reynal & Hitchcock, 1945), pp. 58–80. This is a readable, thorough study of the Pilgrims, from their origins in Scrooby and elsewhere to their adventures in the New World.

4. Quoted by Murphy in a note to *Of Plymouth Plantation,* p. 133.

5. See Alan B. Howard, "Art and History in Bradford's *Of Plymouth Plantation,*" *William and Mary Quarterly* (April 1971), pp. 237–66.

6. From the original charter for the settlement and possession of Virginia of James I, dated April 10, 1606.

7. Perry Miller, *The New England Mind: The Seventeenth Century* (New York: Macmillan, 1939), p. 365.

8. Thomas Morton, *New English Canaan,* ed. Jack Dempsey (Scituate, Mass.: Digital Scanning, 2000), p. xxxi.

9. See Edmund S. Morgan, "The Labor Problem at Jamestown, 1607–18," *The*

American Historical Review, vol. 76, no. 3 (June 1971), pp. 595–611. See also Jill Lepore, "Our Town," *The New Yorker,* April 2, 2007, pp. 40–45.

Chapter 2: The Federalist Papers

1. *The Federalist Papers,* ed. Clinton Rossiter, with introduction and notes by Charles R. Kessler (New York: Signet, 2003), p. ix. Text references are to page numbers of this edition. The quotation from Lord Acton was taken from Garry Wills, *Explaining America: The Federalist* (New York: Doubleday, 1981), p. xi.
2. This is quoted by James Madison in his notes for September 17, 1787. See *The Records of the Federal Convention of 1787,* ed. Max Farrand (New Haven, Conn.: Yale University Press, 1937), vol. 4, doc. 3.
3. *Writings of George Washington, vol. II, 1785–1795* (New York: G. P. Putnam's Sons, 1891), p. 31.
4. *The Anti-Federalist: Writings by the Opponents of the Constitution,* ed. Herbert J. Storing (Chicago: University of Chicago Press, 1985), p. 39.
5. See W. B. Allen, with Kevin A. Cloonan, *The Federalist Papers: A Commentary* (New York: Peter Lang, 2000).
6. See Robert Dahl, *A Preface to Democratic Theory* (Chicago: University of Chicago Press, 1956).
7. Edward Millican, *One United People: "The Federalist Papers" and the National Idea* (Lexington: University Press of Kentucky, 1990), p. 229.
8. Wills, *Explaining America,* p. 76.
9. Bernard Bailyn, *To Begin the World Anew* (New York: Random House, 2003), p. 120.
10. Ibid., pp. 112–13.
11. Morton White, *Philosophy, "The Federalist," and the Constitution* (New York: Oxford University Press, 1987).
12. Ibid., p. 57.
13. Gore Vidal, *Inventing a Nation: Washington, Adams, Jefferson* (New Haven, Conn.: Yale University Press, 2003), p. 145.

Chapter 3: The Autobiography of Benjamin Franklin

1. John Adams to James Level, Feb. 20, 1779. Quoted by Walter Isaacson, *Benjamin Franklin: An American Life* (New York: Simon & Schuster, 2003), p. 352.
2. All quotations from *The Autobiography of Benjamin Franklin,* 2nd ed., eds. Leonard W. Labaree, Ralph L. Ketcham, Helen C. Boatfield, and Helene H. Fineman (New Haven, Conn.: Yale University Press, 1964). I quote from the paperback Yale Nota Bene edition of 2003.

3. *The Works of Thomas Jefferson,* ed. Paul L. Ford (New York: G. P. Putnam's Sons, 1904), vol. 1, p. 90. Quoted in the Yale Nota Bene edition of *The Autobiography of Benjamin Franklin,* p. 160.

4. Isaacson, *Benjamin Franklin,* p. 144. Isaacson also quotes J. J. Thomson.

Chapter 4: The Journals of Lewis and Clark

1. Although I have myself used a reprint of the multivolume edition by Reuben Gold Thwaites (1904), I have quoted throughout this chapter from the more widely available selection by Bernard De Voto (Boston: Houghton Mifflin, 1953). Page numbers from this edition appear after the quotations in parentheses.

2. See the work of Peter J. Castor and Conevery Bolton Valencius on this subject. These historians point out that people often spoke euphemistically about their health in these days, especially when referring to women's reproductive health.

3. John L. O'Sullivan wrote in defense of the annexation of the Republic of Texas, supporting "the right of our manifest destiny to over spread and to possess the whole of the continent which Providence has given us for the development of the great experiment of liberty." The column appeared in the *New York Morning News* on December 27, 1845. He had begun to develop the term as early as 1839.

Chapter 5: Walden

1. Robert D. Richardson, *Henry Thoreau: A Life of the Mind* (Berkeley: University of California Press, 1986), p. 193.

2. I quote from the Penguin Classics edition of *Walden* (New York: Penguin, 1986).

3. Henry David Thoreau, *A Week on the Concord and Merrimack Rivers,* ed. Carl J. Hovde (Princeton, N.J.: Princeton University Press, 1980), p. 140.

4. *Selections from Ralph Waldo Emerson,* ed. Stephen E. Whicher (Boston: Houghton Mifflin, 1957), pp. 23–24.

5. Ibid., p. 31.

6. Richardson, *Henry Thoreau,* p. 50.

7. See Lawrence Thompson, *Robert Frost: The Years of Triumph, 1915–1938* (New York: Holt, Rinehart, and Winston, 1970), p. 693.

8. See George Hendrick, "The Influence of Thoreau's 'Civil Disobedience' on Gandhi's Satyagraha," *New England Quarterly* 29, no. 4 (Dec. 1956), pp. 462–71.

9. Lawrence Buell, *The Environmental Imagination: Thoreau, Nature Writing, and the Formation of American Culture* (Cambridge, Mass.: Harvard University

Press, 1995). See chapter 11 for a detailed examination of critical reactions to Thoreau from the mid-nineteenth through the late twentieth centuries.

10. Ibid., p. 422.

11. Edward Abbey, *Desert Solitaire: A Season in the Wilderness* (New York: Ballantine, 1968), p. 7.

Chapter 6: *Uncle Tom's Cabin*

1. This comment was reported by Mrs. Stowe's son.

2. George Orwell, "Good Bad Books," in *The Collected Essays, Journalism, and Letters of George Orwell,* eds. Sonia Orwell and Ian Angus (New York: Harcourt, Brace & World, 1968), vol. 4, p. 21.

3. Joan D. Hedrick, *Harriet Beecher Stowe: A Life* (New York: Oxford University Press, 1994).

4. Ibid., pp. 180, 181.

5. Harriet Beecher Stowe, *The Annotated "Uncle Tom's Cabin,"* edited with an introduction and notes by Henry Louis Gates Jr. and Hollis Robbins (New York: Norton, 2006), p. xxxiii. I will quote from this popular edition.

6. Hedrick, *Harriet Beecher Stowe,* p. ix.

7. See Jane P. Tompkins, "Sentimental Power: *Uncle Tom's Cabin* and the Politics of Literary History," in *Sensational Designs: The Cultural Work of American Fiction, 1790–1860* (New York: Oxford University Press, 1985).

8. *The Letters of Charles Dickens,* ed. Walter Dexter (London: Bloomsbury, 1938), vol. 2, p. 406.

9. Quoted by Gates and Robbins, *Annotated "Uncle Tom's Cabin,"* p. 361.

10. Gates, introduction to ibid., pp. xxiii–xxiv.

11. James Baldwin, *Notes of a Native Son* (Boston: Beacon Press, 1955).

12. Ann Douglas, *The Feminization of American Culture* (London: Papermac, 1977), p. 245. See Gates and Robbins, who discuss recent responses to the novel in their excellent introductory essays in *The Annotated "Uncle Tom's Cabin."*

13. See Jane Smiley, "Say It Ain't So, Huck," *Harper's,* Jan. 1996, pp. 61–70.

14. Bill Goldstein, "Every Time You're Free, You're Lonely," *New York Times,* April 4, 1998.

Chapter 7: *Adventures of Huckleberry Finn*

1. Ernest Hemingway, *Green Hills of Africa* (New York: Charles Scribner's Sons, 1935), p. 22.

2. Ron Powers, *Mark Twain: A Life* (New York: Free Press, 2005), p. 398.

3. See the afterword by Victor A. Doyno in *Adventures of Huckleberry Finn,* ed.

Shelley Fisher Fishkin (New York: Oxford University Press, 1996). I will quote from this authoritative edition, which is part of the massive twenty-nine-volume Oxford Mark Twain series.

4. *The Autobiography of Mark Twain,* ed. Charles Neider (New York: Harper & Row, 1959), p. 10.

5. Powers, *Mark Twain,* p. 471.

6. This comparison of passages is made by Victor Fischer and Lin Salamo in their definitive edition of *Huckleberry Finn* (Berkeley: University of California Press, 2003).

7. Leslie Fiedler, "Come Back to the Raft Ag'in, Huck Honey!" *Partisan Review* (June 1948). For a review of this essay and its legacy, see Christopher Looby, " 'Innocent Sexuality': The Fiedler Thesis in Retrospect," in *Mark Twain: Adventures of Huckleberry Finn: A Case Study in Critical Controversy,* ed. Gerald Graff and James Phelan (Boston: Bedford Books, 1995), pp. 535–50.

8. Ralph Ellison, "Change the Joke and Slip the Yoke," *Shadow and Act* (New York: Random House, 1964), p. 51.

9. See Shelley Fisher Fishkin, *Was Huck Black? Mark Twain and African-American Voices* (New York: Oxford University Press, 1993).

10. For a thorough discussion of the novel from an African American perspective, see James S. Leonard et al., eds., *Satire or Evasion? Black Perspectives on "Huckleberry Finn"* (Durham, N.C.: Duke University Press, 1992). The essay by Peaches Henry called "The Struggle for Tolerance: Race and Censorship in *Huckleberry Finn*" is especially worth reading for a balanced look at this complicated subject.

11. Bernard De Voto, *Mark Twain at Work* (Cambridge, Mass.: Harvard University Press, 1942), p. 92.

12. Leo Marx, "Mr. Eliot, Mr. Trilling, and Huckleberry Finn," *American Scholar* 22 (Autumn 1953), p. 117.

13. See Harold P. Simonson, "*Huckleberry Finn* as Tragedy," *Yale Review* 59 (Summer 1970), pp. 532–48.

14. Quoted by Doyno in his afterword to the Oxford edition of *Huckleberry Finn.*

15. See the writing on Twain's use of southwestern dialects and African American traditions in such critics as M. Thomas Inge, David E. Sloane, David Sewell, and—especially—Shelley Fisher Fishkin.

Chapter 8: *The Souls of Black Folk*

1. W. E. B. Du Bois, *The Souls of Black Folk,* with an introduction by Randall Kenan (New York: Signet, 1995). Text references are to page numbers of this edition.

2. "Prison Nation," editorial, *New York Times,* March 10, 2008, p. A10.

3. Du Bois, *The Souls of Black Folk,* p. xxxi.

4. Quotation in Stanley Crouch and Playthell Benjamin, eds., *Reconsidering "The Souls of Black Folk"* (Philadelphia: Running Press, 2002), p. 55.

5. Ibid., p. 35.

6. Dolan Hubbard, ed., *The Souls of Black Folk: One Hundred Years Later* (Columbia: University of Missouri Press, 2003), p. 9.

7. W. E. B. Du Bois, *Dusk of Dawn: An Essay Toward an Autobiography of a Race Concept* (1940; reprint, New Brunswick, N.J.: Transaction, 1984), pp. 78–79.

8. Hubbard, *Souls of Black Folk,* p. 318.

9. Arnold Rampersad, *The Art and Imagination of W. E. B. Du Bois* (Cambridge, Mass.: Harvard University Press, 1976), p. 74.

10. Ibid., pp. 85–86.

11. James Daniel Steele, "The Souls of the 'Black Belt' Revisited," in Hubbard, *Souls of Black Folk,* p. 42.

12. Ibid., p. 45.

13. Shanette M. Harris, "Constructing a Psychological Perspective: The Observer and the Observed in *The Souls of Black Folk,*" in Hubbard, *Souls of Black Folk,* p. 243.

14. Eric J. Sundquist, *To Wake the Nations: Race in the Making of American Literature* (Cambridge, Mass.: Harvard University Press, 1993), p. 458.

15. Jessie Fauset to Du Bois, 1903, as quoted by Rampersad, *Art and Imagination,* p. 68.

16. James Weldon Johnson, *Along the Way* (New York: Viking, 1968), p. 203.

17. Henry James, *The American Scene* (Bloomington: Indiana University Press, 1968), p. 418.

18. Shelby Steele, "The Souls of Black Folk: Why Are We Still Caught Up in Century-Old Protest Politics?" *Wall Street Journal,* April 29, 2003.

19. Ralph Ellison, *Invisible Man* (New York: Modern Library, 1952), p. 7.

20. Du Bois, *Dusk of Dawn,* p. 35.

Chapter 9: The Promised Land

1. Mary Antin, *The Promised Land,* ed. Werner Sollors (New York: Penguin, 1997). Text references are to page numbers of this edition. Sollors's remark is from an article by Ken Gewertz, "Revisiting *The Promised Land,*" *Harvard University Gazette,* March 6, 1997.

2. Keren R. McGinity, "The Real Mary Antin: Woman on a Mission in the Promised Land," *American Jewish History* 86, no. 3 (Sept. 1998), p. 285.

3. Roger Daniels, *Coming to America: A History of Immigration and Ethnicity in America,* 2nd ed. (New York: HarperCollins, 2002), p. 121.

4. Mary Antin, "How I Wrote *The Promised Land,*" republished as an appendix in the Sollors edition, pp. 295–96.

5. Antin, *Promised Land,* p. xlv.

6. Quoted by Sollors in his introduction to ibid., p. xxxvii.

7. *Selections from Ralph Waldo Emerson,* ed. Stephen E. Whicher (Boston: Houghton Mifflin, 1957), p. 24.

8. See Harold Bloom, *The American Religion: The Emergence of the Post-Christian Nation* (New York: Simon & Schuster, 1992).

9. Sollors, introduction to *Promised Land,* p. xxxii.

10. Ibid., pp. xxxii–xxxiii.

11. Steven J. Rubin, "American Jewish Autobiography," in *Handbook of American-Jewish Literature,* ed. Lewis Fried (Westport, Conn.: Greenwood Press, 1988), pp. 289–90.

12. See, for example, Lewisohn's article "A Panorama of a Half-Century of American Jewish Literature," in *Jewish Book Annual* (1950–51), pp. 3–10.

13. Sarah Blacher Cohen, "Mary Antin's *The Promised Land*: A Breach of Promise," *Studies in American Jewish Literature* 3, no. 2 (1977–78), p. 32.

14. For an excerpt, see *The Norton Book of American Autobiography,* ed. Jay Parini (New York: Norton, 1999).

15. Katherine B. Payant and Toby Rose, eds., *The Immigrant Experience in North American Literature: Carving Out a Niche* (Westport, Conn.: Greenwood Press, 1999), p. xix.

Chapter 10: *How to Win Friends and Influence People*

1. I quote from the standard edition, published by Simon & Schuster in 1937 and endlessly reprinted. My edition dates to 1964, its 122nd printing.

2. Timothy B. Spears, *100 Years on the Road: The Traveling Salesman in American Culture* (New Haven, Conn.: Yale University Press, 1995), p. vii.

3. Sheila Fitzpatrick, *Tear Off the Mask!* (Princeton, N.J.: Princeton University Press, 2005), p. 309.

4. Review of the book in the *Saturday Review* (Jan. 1937) by James Thurber, quoted in Giles Kemp and Edward Claflin, *Dale Carnegie: The Man Who Influenced Millions* (New York: St. Martin's Press, 1989), p. 151.

5. See Kemp and Claflin, *Dale Carnegie,* pp. 46–49, for the full story of Carnegie's show business career.

6. Ibid., p. 58.

7. Quoted in Walter A. Friedman, *Birth of a Salesman: The Transformation of Selling in America* (Cambridge, Mass.: Harvard University Press, 2004), p. 1.

8. Lewis Hyde, *The Gift: How the Creative Spirit Transforms the World* (London: Canongate, 2007), p. 15.

9. Ibid., p. 11.

10. Stephen R. Covey, *The 7 Habits of Highly Effective People* (New York: Free Press, 1989), p. 19.

11. Rick Warren, *The Purpose-Driven Life* (Grand Rapids, Mich.: Zondervan, 2002), p. 265.

12. Brian Tracy, *Maximum Achievement: Strategies and Skills That Will Unlock Your Hidden Powers to Succeed* (New York: Simon & Schuster, 1993), p. 107.

13. See the dust jackets of Joel Osteen, *Your Best Life Now* (New York: Warner Books, 2004) and *Become a Better You: 7 Keys to Improving Your Life Every Day* (New York: Free Press, 2007). For more information, visit the Web site www.joelosteen.com.

14. Osteen, *Become a Better You,* p. 5.

Chapter 11: The Common Sense Book of Baby and Child Care

1. See Russell Ash, *The Top 10 of Everything, 1997* (New York: Dorling Kindersley Press, 1996), pp. 112–13.

2. Dr. Holt is quoted in Thomas Maier, *Dr. Spock: An American Life* (New York: Harcourt, Brace, 1998), p. 87.

3. See the transcript of *The NewsHour with Jim Lehrer* (March 16, 1998) for an interesting discussion of the public reaction to *Baby and Child Care* with Dr. Spock, Dr. Steven Parker, and Elizabeth Farnsworth. Go to www.pbs.org/newshour/bb/health/jan-june98/spock_3-16.html.

4. Benjamin Spock, M.D., *The Common Sense Book of Baby and Child Care* (New York: Duell, Sloan, and Pearce, 1946). For this chapter, I will quote mainly from this first edition. The book is currently in its eighth edition.

5. See Benjamin Spock, M.D., and Robert Needlman, M.D., *Dr. Spock's Baby and Child Care,* 8th ed. (New York: Pocket Books, 2004).

6. Maier, *Dr. Spock,* p. 3.

7. Ibid., p. 4.

8. Ibid., p. 57.

9. Ibid., p. 76.

10. Ellen Key, *The Century of the Child* (New York: G. P. Putnam's Sons, 1909), p. 108.

11. Maier, *Dr. Spock,* p. 90.

12. Ibid., p. 96.

13. Rousseau put forward his main ideas on education in a semi-fictional novel called *Émile* (1762). John Darling, in *Child-Centered Education and Its Critics* (1993), argues that Rousseau is the dominant figure in thinking about education along the lines that Dr. Spock advocated.

14. See, for example, Dewey's *Schools of Tomorrow* (1915), which opens with a long

quotation from Rousseau, followed by comments on *Émile* as a source that had a huge influence on his thinking.

15. Jessica Mitford, *The Trial of Dr. Spock* (New York: Knopf, 1969), p. 10.

16. Ibid., p. 11.

17. Ibid., p. 247.

18. Christopher Lasch, *The Culture of Narcissism* (New York: Norton, 1978), p. 163.

19. See Garry Wills, "Dr. Spock's Gracious Consciousness-Raising," Universal Press Syndicate, May 1988, quoted by Maier, *Dr. Spock,* p. 458.

Chapter 12: On the Road

1. Jack Kerouac, *On the Road* (New York: Viking, 2007). This is the fiftieth-anniversary edition. Text references are to page numbers of this edition.

2. See Nathanial Hawthorne, "The May-Pole of Merry Mount." A more factually based, although self-serving, account of the Merry Mount community appears in Thomas Morton, *New English Canaan,* ed. Jack Dempsey (Scituate, Mass.: Digital Scanning, 2000).

3. This important review, published on September 5, 1957, is included as a prologue to the Viking anniversary edition of *On the Road.*

4. Jack Kerouac, *On the Road: The Original Scroll,* ed. Howard Cunnell, with introductions by Howard Cunnell, Penny Vlagopoulos, George Mouratidis, and Joshua Kupetz (New York: Viking, 2007).

5. Ibid., p. 3.

6. Ibid., p. 109.

7. Ibid., p. 4.

8. Ibid., p. 307.

9. Quoted by Cunnell in his introduction to ibid. The other reviews quoted are also from Cunnell's introduction.

10. Quoted by Cunnell in ibid., p. 51.

11. Quoted by Hillel Italie. See *"On the Road,* and Jack Kerouac, Still Inspire," Associated Press, Sept. 2, 2007.

12. Kerouac makes numerous allusions to Joyce throughout his novel, and refers to his admiration in his letters. The extent of this influence is documented by Michael H. Begnal in " 'I Dig Joyce': Jack Kerouac and *Finnegans Wake," Philological Quarterly* 77 (March 1998), pp. 209–19.

13. W. H. Auden, "For the Time Being: A Christmas Oratorio" (1944).

14. Quoted in John Lardas, *The Bop Apocalypse: The Religious Vision of Kerouac, Ginsberg, and Burroughs* (Urbana: University of Illinois Press, 2001), p. 99.

Chapter 13: *The Feminine Mystique*

1. Bell Hooks, *Feminist Theory: From Margin to Center* (Cambridge, Mass.: South End Press, 2000), p. 1. Hooks is, however, sharply critical of Friedan, as I suggest toward the end of this chapter.

2. Betty Friedan, *The Feminine Mystique* (New York: Dell, 1983). Toffler's quotation is from the cover of the twentieth-anniversary edition. I quote from this paperback edition throughout.

3. This introduction appears in ibid., p. 6.

4. Judith Hennessee, *Betty Friedan: Her Life* (New York: Random House, 1999), p. 79.

5. Ibid., p. 5.

6. Ibid., p. 47.

7. These details, and many others about the writing and publishing of this book, are taken from Lisa Frederiksen Bohannon, *Woman's Work: The Story of Betty Friedan* (Greensboro, N.C.: Morgan Reynolds, 2004). See chapters 5 and 6.

8. Ibid., p. 84.

9. See Adrienne Rich, *Of Woman Born: Motherhood as Experience and Institution* (New York: Norton, 1976).

10. Karen Offen, *European Feminisms, 1700–1950* (Stanford, Calif.: Stanford University Press, 2000), p. 25.

11. See Stacy Gillis, Gillian Howie, and Rebecca Munford, eds., *Third Wave Feminism,* 2nd ed. (Houndmills, U.K.: Palgrave Macmillan, 2007).

12. Hennessee, *Betty Friedan,* p. 144.

13. Rebecca Walker, ed., *To Be Real: Telling the Truth and Changing the Face of Feminism* (New York: Doubleday, 1995).

14. Jennifer Baumgardner and Amy Richards, eds., *Manifesta: Young Women, Feminism, and the Future* (New York: Farrar, Straus & Giroux, 2000).

15. June Hannam, *Feminism* (Harlow, U.K.: Pearson, 2007), p. 168.

16. There is an entire Web site devoted to Friedan's factual mistakes in *The Feminine Mystique.* See "Cheerless Fantasies: A Corrective Catalogue of Errors in Betty Friedan's *The Feminine Mystique,*" cf.en.cl.

17. Friedan quotes from Sigmund Freud's *Three Contributions to the Theory of Sex* (1910). She cites a 1948 reprint of this work.

18. Mary Kassian, *The Feminist Mistake* (Wheaton, Ill.: Crossway, 2005), p. 27.

19. Ibid., p. 298.

20. Ibid., pp. 8, 9.

21. Leslie Bennetts, *The Feminine Mistake: Are We Giving Up Too Much?* (New York: Hyperion, 2007), p. xix.

22. Ibid., p. 5.

23. Ibid., p. 284.

24. Ibid., p. 321.

25. Daniel Horowitz, *Betty Friedan and the Making of "The Feminine Mystique": The American Left, the Cold War, and Modern Feminism* (Amherst: University of Massachusetts Press, 1998).

26. Hooks, *Feminist Theory,* p. 1.

27. Ibid., p. 2.

28. Ibid., p. 3.

PHOTO CREDITS